THEY PLAYED FOR
JOHN LYALL

THE WEST HAM YEARS

By Tim Crane
Foreword by Sir Alex Ferguson

First published in England in November 2017 by:

Tim Crane
Tel: 07798 934 824
tcrane183@gmail.com
©Copyright Tim Crane

Photographic credits:
Players and families
EX Hammers Magazine (www.ex-hammers.com)
Dave Alexander (www.footballwanted.com)
Steve Marsh (www.theyflysohigh.co.uk)
John Helliar (programme master)
Steve Bacon (photographer)

Designed by David Barclay
Resporta
david@resporta.com
Tel: 07907 302 802

Printed by Henry Ling Ltd
The Dorset Press, Dorchester, Dorset, DT1 1HD
Tel: 01305 251066

Distributed by Tim Crane
183 Westcombe Hill, Blackheath, London, SE3 7DR, England
Distribution email: tcrane183@gmail.com

ISBN: 978-0-9930286-1-8

To Helen, Emily, Hannah and Gracie
My girls

CONTENTS

FOREWORD
BY SIR ALEX FERGUSON

I first met John in 1982, at the World Cup in Spain. During our time there we got to know each other and became friends. He was someone who I felt I could talk to. John was West Ham's long serving manager, and knew the game inside out. Quite often, when I was managing in Scotland, John would call me when he was on a scouting mission. I would meet him and his assistant, Eddie Baily, and drive them to a game. I looked forward to those nights. He knew so much about the game, and I was always eager to learn.

So, in 1986, when I took over at Old Trafford, John was the person I turned to, for information on players and teams, and he would always provide me with team reports, which was so helpful in my early days at Manchester United. I had inherited an ageing group of players, whose discipline was very different to mine at Aberdeen. I remember John saying to me: *"I don't see an Alex Ferguson in your team."* I knew it was going to be a struggle, there was a great deal of work to do, but that was what I had been brought in to do, and that's what I set about doing.

In 1989, after a long conversation with our Chief Scout, Les Kershaw, who was raving about Paul Ince of West Ham, I too liked what I saw of the boy, and decided to pay John a visit at his home in Essex.

I soon realised that it was going to be a short conversation when I mentioned to John that I wanted to take Ince to Manchester United: *"No chance,"* was the reply: *"He's like a son to me."* Just then, John's wife Yvonne arrived with tea and sandwiches, whilst I carried on trying to talk him around, but he was having none of it. As I left, I resolved, that regardless of my great respect for John Lyall, I was going to make a formal bid for the player.

It was only a few days later that the shock announcement came through that John had been sacked from West Ham. I was stunned when I heard, and rang John to commiserate with him. I could sense the injustice he was feeling, after the years of service he had given to the club. But the removal of John from West Ham, relieved me of any trace of guilt I had about pursuing a deal for Ince. Once again, I turned to John for information about Paul, his background, and how to deal with him. This information was to prove invaluable in the years ahead and I will always be grateful to John for his friendship and advice he gave me.

John had an incredible career from Youth player to Manager. In 1963, his own football career was cut short by a serious knee injury, after only 36 first-team appearances. He went on to serve his apprenticeship as a coach under Ron Greenwood, his mentor, and finally took over as Manager in 1974, when Ron took on the role of Director of Football.

John Lyall gave 34 years of his life to West Ham, including two FA Cup successes. He rose from ground staff boy, to Manager - an amazing career from an incredible man.

Sir Alex Ferguson
November, 2017

They Played For John Lyall – The West Ham Years

The author with Sir Alex Ferguson and Sir Trevor Brooking

A NOTE
FROM YVONNE LYALL

John and I went to the same Ilford Primary School and only lived three turnings away from each other. We really got together in 1957 after meeting every day at our local bus stop on the way to work. One morning, he told me he was playing for England Youth that evening. I just said: "Yes," not really knowing the importance of such an honour and carried on talking about all and sundry. He must have forgiven me though as we soon started courting, got engaged in 1959 and married in 1961.

In 1963 he had to cease playing due to his long term knee injury. He joined Eddie Chapman's office staff and did clerical work and wages for West Ham. He gained his full Football Association coaching badge and started coaching in East End schools. He was brilliant in accepting he could no longer play. On becoming Youth Manager for West Ham and scouting for Ron Greenwood it became a different way of life for us in as much as he worked longer hours and was away from home much more than as a player.

John was very much a home person, but despite the long hours he always had time for me and our son Murray. I never went to matches when John was manager and preferred to watch him and his teams from the outside. He never brought football home with him even after losing a game or a bad run of results.

He always said he would retire by the age of 55, which he did, one year earlier thank goodness. We had 12 precious years together on our Suffolk Farm with Murray and his family, gardening and fishing, until his early and sudden death in 2006, at the age of 66. There is, and always will be, such a void in my life and that of my family.

I feel so proud of all his achievements in football and it means so much that many of his ex-players regularly ring me to see how we all are. To this day, wherever I go, nobody has a bad word to say about John.

Finally, sincere thanks to Tim for writing this book, to all John's players from way back for all their touching tributes over the years and to Sir Alex Ferguson for penning the foreword.

Yvonne Lyall
Summer, 2017

A love of Christmas and family

With John's 1957 England Youth cap

A West Ham wedding - L-R Walker, Musgrove, Greenwood, Malcolm, Brown, Rhodes, Bond (stealing a kiss), Dick, Jenkins, Kirkup, Gregory, 1961

A favourite pastime

A comforting presence

ACKNOWLEDGEMENTS
HELP PROVIDES THE INSIDE LANE TO ACHIEVEMENT

This book would certainly not exist without the efforts of so many people.

Top of the list is **my dear mum, Pauline.** Her encouragement and top class company have ensured a much needed boost to my efforts. A healthy dose of comedian Tim Vine kept our humour levels high and ensured fun and laughter were never too far away – essential to a 200,000 word slog!

The lovely Helen for her kind words of support – "Not another damn book!" and her expertise at mothering our three children – Emily, Hannah and Gracie – with a cunning blend of fruit smoothies and an 'Ask dad' approach to parenting…

The players for their time, stories, support, photos and for just being great.

Very special appreciation to **Steve Marsh** and **John Northcutt** for their patience and provision of programme scans, photos and statistical excellence. Dedicated West Ham minds with willing hearts to match.

David Barclay for his skill and no fuss approach to book design. His creative agency, Resporta, embodies his innovative, efficient and reliable work ethic.

Steve Blowers for his exceptional guidance around the rules of the English language. Any errors – and there will be a few – have been made solely on account of my lack of attention to his wise instruction.

Our boys at the **Professional Footballers Association - Bobby Barnes** and **Paul Allen.** They were super-helpful with contact information on **David Kelly, Dave Swindlehurst** and **Gary Strodder.**

Murray Lyall for his help in ensuring **Sir Alex Ferguson** wrote the Foreword. No better man for the job.

Sir Alex Ferguson for never forgetting and penning a first class Foreword. Another layer of excellence from the great man.

Paul Goddard for opening a door to **Steve Whitton** in Marbella. **Iain Cook,** club historian at Arsenal, for connecting me with **John Radford. Terry Creasy** for arranging an interview with **Frank Lampard.**

Rob Jenkins for his friendship and first class company, plus his trusty companions **Bert Wilson, Peter Gurr** and **Alan Olsen.** His wife **Ros** for her kindness and their son **Billy** for his excellent vegan friendly cuisine!

The genealogy skills of **Barbara Shrimpton** for unearthing the whereabouts of the elusive **Nicky Morgan.** Nicky's wife, **Liz,** for being super helpful.

John Helliar for access to 15 years of West Ham press cuttings. A cup of coffee with him in his print works is always a delight. His family name will forever stand as a colossus in the printed history of the club.

They Played For John Lyall – The West Ham Years

Much appreciated moral and practical support from dyed-in-the-wool Hammers: **Hilary Tunbridge, Brian Dear, Eddie Presland, Trevor Dawkins, Mick McGiven, Alan Stephenson, Joe Durrell, John Ayris, Alan Dickens, Everald La Ronde, Mark Smith, George Parris, Chris Ampofo, Michael Hart, Tony Hogg, Jeff Garner, Tony Hoskins** and **Vic Lindsell**, respectively.

Both **Gary Firmager,** at the much lamented Over Land and Sea, and **Tony McDonald**, at the much lamented EX Hammers magazine. Both provided me with an opportunity to write about all things claret and blue.

Stuart Liddell, for breathing, and filling my mind with 40 years of brilliant humour.

My much loved Uncle Sid. Continue to rest in peace you absolute gentleman! One pair of eyes I would give anything to read this book.

Last, for reasons only to provide special attention, is **Yvonne Lyall.** The journey started with this remarkable lady and her touching letter about John was the final resting place for a few of my own tears. I hope I haven't let you down and that, at some stage over the Christmas period, you will find laughter and happiness when leafing through this book.

John Lyall took us all on an emotional rollercoaster. I hope this book has captured its essence.

Back row: Bonds, McGiven, K Robson, T Taylor, Ferguson, Day, Best, Brooking, Lock, McDowell.

Front row: A Taylor, Coleman, Holland, Gould, Lampard, Paddon, Jennings.

They Played For John Lyall – The West Ham Years

CHAPTER ONE
1974-75

"It is now my team and I'm going to stamp my personality on the side." John Lyall

All change at West Ham United. 34-year-old John Lyall is appointed first team manager ahead of the league visit of Everton, on August 24, 1974. It would be a landmark first season, culminating in FA Cup final success over a Bobby Moore led Fulham at Wembley.

In an interview by The Observer's pioneering female sports journalist, Julie Welch, West Ham fans gain an insight into the reasons behind Ron Greenwood's handing over of first team affairs to John Lyall: *"I think there was getting to be an age barrier. I wasn't as close to this present team as I was with the boys who won the Cups in 1964-65. I felt the lads wouldn't open up to me in quite the same way."*

In a statement of intent, West Ham sign three strikers by Christmas – 22-year-old Billy Jennings from Watford for £110,000, 21-year-old Keith Robson from Newcastle United for £70,000 and 21-year-old Alan Taylor from Rochdale for £40,000.

Lyall is made Bell's Football Manager of the Month for September 1974 – his first full month in charge. After 20 goals in four matches the press roll out the first references to: 'Lyall Style.'

Lyall's former teammate at West Ham, Noel Cantwell, offered an assessment of his first few months in charge: "John is a strong character, with personality. He will have learned a lot from Ron Greenwood. John was a hard player and although he was brought up in the purist traditions taught by Ron, I am sure he is the man who has put the steel into West Ham's game. Ron would have nothing to do with the ruthlessness or hard tackling side of football."

During his first season in charge, John Lyall selected 18 players for his West Ham team. They were: Mervyn Day, Keith Coleman, Frank Lampard, Billy Bonds, Tommy Taylor, Kevin Lock, Pat Holland, Graham Paddon, Bobby Gould, John McDowell, Clyde Best, John Ayris, Billy Jennings, Trevor Brooking, Keith Robson, Alan Taylor, Alan Curbishley and Alan Wooler.

Here is their story...

March 16, 1974. End of an era. Bobby Moore's final farewell to the Hammers' faithful. Ron Greenwood would soon relinquish first team affairs

John Lyall is appointed first team manager, August 1974. L-R Reg Pratt, Roland Brandon, Will Cearns, Eddie Chapman, John, Brian Cearns, Ron Greenwood and Len Cearns

1 - Mervyn Day

"John was a man I totally respected and working the West Ham United way is ingrained in me. That is down to both Ron Greenwood and John Lyall."

Born: Chelmsford, June 26, 1955 • **Position:** Goalkeeper • **Games played for John Lyall:** 95 194 (1974-1979)

Games played for West Ham United: 232 (1973-79) • **Honours under John Lyall:** 1975 FA Cup winner, 1975 FA Charity Shield runner-up, 1975 PFA Young Player of the Year, 1976 European Cup Winners Cup Runner-up

First game under John Lyall: August 24, 1974 v Everton (h) L 2-3 (Bonds, McDowell – Royle, Latchford, Harvey) Att: 22,486

West Ham United: Day, Coleman, Lampard, Bonds, Taylor T, Lock, Holland, Paddon, Gould, McDowell, Best.

Everton: Lawson, Darracott, Seargeant, Clements, Lyons, Hurst, Buckley, Harvey, Royle, Latchford, Connolly.* Sub: Pearson.

Mervyn Richard Day was John Lyall's first West Ham United goalkeeper. He was born to parents, Albert and Peggy and grew up on the Meadgate Estate in Chelmsford. His father was a head clerk in the surveyors department in Essex County Council and his mother worked for Britvic Soft Drinks.

Day joined the club in July 1971. He'd already pulled on the green jersey on 39 occasions by the time John Lyall took over first team affairs in August, 1974.

Day would go on to register a total of 232 appearances for West Ham United and remains one of only three goalkeepers to have won an FA Cup winners medal, the other two being Jim Standen in 1964 and Phil Parkes in 1980. He is one of only 12 Hammers to have kept goal behind the immortal Bobby Moore. Quirkily, Mervyn began his West Ham United career with a 3-3 draw – at home to Ipswich Town in August 1973 – and ended it, some six years later, with a 3-3 draw – at home to Sunderland in February 1979.

Day had excelled at cricket, hockey and athletics as a schoolboy, before pursuing a career in football which continues, in a scouting capacity, to this day: *"I am head of scouting at Bristol City and usually take in four or five games each week. I often see Patsy Holland, Billy Jennings and another ex-Hammer, Johnny Cartwright, on the scouting circuit. They are*

all good men with fantastic knowledge and experience."

After leaving West Ham United in 1979, Mervyn went on to have spells at Leyton Orient, Aston Villa, Leeds United, Luton Town, Sheffield United and Carlisle United, clocking up over 700 appearances along the way.

He returned to Upton Park as second-in-command to fellow Hammer, Alan Curbishley, during 2006-2008.

In September 2017, Mervyn attended a reunion of John Lyall's 1975 FA Cup winning team at the London Bridge Hilton Hotel, where he was reunited with John McDowell, Kevin Lock, Billy Bonds, Trevor Brooking, Alan Taylor, Billy Jennings, Pat Holland, Bobby Gould and Keith Robson.

"At 62, I'm still enjoying life. My wife, Moira, and I celebrated our 42nd wedding anniversary in October, 2017. We've also got five grandchildren so when I'm not working I'm working! Long may it continue!"

Mervyn had the following recollections of John Lyall and his time at West Ham United:

I had a decent relationship with John, but I probably had a better one with Ron Greenwood. There is a specific reason for this. My dad died when I was a 17-year-old apprentice at West Ham United. Ron made me a professional straight away which meant some extra money. I was a council house kid at the time so that made a big difference. At the end of the season,

Ron gave me another pay rise and took me on a first team tour. At the start of the 1973-74 season - Ron's last in charge - he gave me my debut against Ipswich Town. I was 18-years-old. My dad was only 50 when he died. Ron's handling of that whole situation is the reason West Ham are my club. It means something more to me than just a football club.

John was as steeped in West Ham as Ron. It's hard to separate the two. They both gave me the technical know-how to enter the world of football, which I am still involved in today. I can't remember a great deal about what John said in the dressing room on matchday because he had a cigarette in his mouth most of the time!

Obviously, the 1975 FA Cup final is a special memory for me. I broke down in tears at the final whistle. I had a wave of emotion which just forced me to cry. I gave my medal and gloves to Ernie Gregory to look after while I did the lap of honour.

I really enjoyed the European campaign after the FA Cup victory. It felt like we were behind in every round and came back with some stunning performances. There is an interesting story relating to the Den Haag match. We were 0-4 down at half-time in the first leg but managed to go through on away goals, after drawing 5-5 on aggregate. In my current job as a scout, I have been to Den Haag quite a bit. On one occasion I was with a Dutch agent who introduced me to a chap called Lex Schoenmaker: He scored two of the goals for Den Haag in that quarter final. They had no idea that I was in goal for those games and I had no idea who had scored their goals. "Look!" they said, pointing at a huge blown-up photo in the foyer of Den Haag scoring one of their goals, with me stranded on the floor beaten all ends up! "That's me!" I replied. They were completely shocked and must have thought I was mad. It really was a strange coincidence.

The best defence I played with at West Ham was the FA Cup final line-up - John McDowell, Frank Lampard, Tommy Taylor and Kevin Lock. Tommy Taylor should have played for England. He had absolutely everything. Kevin Lock was a very clever player. He read the game well and had a lovely left foot. Frank Lampard was one of the best volleyers of a ball that I've ever seen, with both his right-foot and left-foot. John McDowell was a much underrated player who would be worth an absolute fortune in today's game.

I kept goal against some really tough strike partnerships: Allan Clarke and Mick Jones at Leeds United, John Toshack and Kevin Keegan at Liverpool and Francis Lee and Rodney Marsh at Manchester City. The toughest strike force were Bob Hatton and Kenny Burns at Birmingham City. Whenever I came out to claim a cross from those guys, I knew I was going to get clattered.

I always enjoyed playing on Merseyside. One of my best performances came very early on in John's time as

An emotional hug with John Lyall after the 1975 FA Cup final win over Fulham

manager - against Everton at Goodison Park. We drew 1-1 and I displayed my best form that day. I had a good record in games against Liverpool at Anfield. Under John, I played in four matches up there and lost only once. Their supporters were very appreciative. I received a standing ovation for some of the saves I made in those games.

John was very meticulous and left me under no illusion as to what he expected from me. We shared a professional, player-manager, relationship rather than a pally friendship. He wanted me to claim crosses and he emphasised, over and over, the importance of keeping possession. When I look back at the old footage from that time, it is noticeable just how often I threw the ball out. Possession was vital to John and we played enormous amounts of keep-ball and quick, one-touch passing, at Chadwell Heath.

We had some real ding-dong battles in training and I was paired against Trevor Brooking once and kicked holes in him because I just couldn't get the ball. Even those players who weren't brought up in the typical West Ham way – Keith Robson, Mick McGiven, Keith Coleman and Bill Green – learned very quickly and added their own brand of grit to John's style of play. Along with Billy Bonds, who didn't take any prisoners, full stop, we had some very competitive training sessions.

I used to socialise with Kevin Lock, Tommy Taylor and John McDowell, who were all at the younger end of the age scale. I travelled in from Chelmsford with Alan Taylor. He would pick me up at the Army and Navy building.

Around Christmas 1977, things were starting to get really

bad. My form had dipped, mistakes had set in and we were losing far too many matches. John pulled me to one side and told me he was going to give me a rest and play Bobby Ferguson instead. He felt I needed some time to get my head together. He said: "Take your wife out for a really nice meal and bring me the bill."

My final match for West Ham, came against Sunderland at home in a 3-3 draw. I can still hear the ironic cheering whenever I caught the ball. I remember that quite vividly. It wasn't a nice experience towards the end of my time at West Ham. I wasn't mature enough to find the right coping mechanisms to handle it. In those days you were left to fend for yourself. I don't recall John giving me any advice on the situation. Those fans in the Chicken Run really did have it in for me. Upton Park was not an easy place to play when that crowd was on my back. On reflection, I was trying too hard to improve things. I should have been trying to relax a bit more. When you hear that level of jeering from your own fans, you start to think that it might be time to move on. Having said all that, I loved my time at West Ham and it is still my club. Ron and John nurtured a love of football in me and showed me how to get the best out of certain type of players. That insight has kept me in good stead in my own coaching and scouting career. Ron and John understood how the game should be played. They knew there was no point trying to re-invent the wheel. They viewed football as a simple game, but today it seems to have been complicated by coaches and players.

West Ham was one of the first club's to have a goalkeeping coach. When I arrived in 1971, Ernie Gregory looked after Peter Grotier, Bobby Ferguson and myself. We used to have goalkeeping sessions together. Ernie was the reserve team coach, too.

John bought Phil Parkes in 1979. One week earlier, I had moved into a brand new house in Danbury, Essex, with a much bigger mortgage. Then, all of a sudden, the bottom dropped out of my world. West Ham paid a record fee for Phil, so I knew the writing was on the wall. The unfortunate thing from my point of view was that I didn't get on with Eddie Baily, who was John's chief scout. I blame some of what happened to me at West Ham on Eddie Baily rather than anyone else. He certainly had a voice on my fate at the club. I had no axe to grind with John and, in the end, the signing of Phil Parkes was a very good decision.

I blame myself for most of what happened to me at West Ham because I was too immature to handle the bad times when they came. I'd had the FA Cup experience, the European campaign and had been voted Young Player of the Year. Ron had told the press that I'd be West Ham's goalkeeper for the next ten years and all that was obviously terrific. It was a meteoric rise and a series of great memories. When the mistakes starting to creep in and my confidence dipped, I couldn't handle the pressure and criticism. In today's game there are Psychologists and various other support systems to help a player through that situation. I certainly could have benefitted from some level of help from the club but it simply wasn't like that back then.

What I find very frustrating is that I thought my career would end up being book-ended by West Ham. I started as a player in the early 1970s and, 35 years later in 2006, became assistant manager of the club, under Alan Curbishley. A nice 10-years stint alongside 'Curbs' would have done me nicely, but, for whatever reason, we weren't given enough time to implement our plans and ideas. We ended up leaving the club after just two years. Sadly, time is one thing a manager isn't given these days.
Mervyn Day

Following are some memories of 'Merv the Swerve:'

At the peak of his powers, Mervyn was a better keeper than Phil Parkes. After the 1976 European Cup Winners Cup final, John Lyall moved Billy Bonds back into defence alongside Tommy Taylor. A lot of mistakes were made and Merv went from being the best young talent in the land to a total wreck. Three years after the successes of 1975-76, Merv, Keith Coleman, Tommy Taylor, Kevin Lock and myself had all left the club. That seems very strange to me.
John McDowell

Merv never got overtaken on the A12! He bought a Ford Escort Mexico and bombed to and from training every day, leaving everything in his wake.
Kevin Lock

Player of the Year runner-up to Billy Bonds

Despite Merv's acrobatics, this one found the net

I got on really well with Merv and had a chat with Jimmy Bloomfield to bring him to Orient when his time at West Ham was over.
Tommy Taylor

We called him 'Donny Day' after the singer, Donny Osmond. He started appearing in various girly magazines as a bit of a pin-up. We gave him a lot of stick but I think he quite liked it because he had a bit of an ego.
Pat Holland

I took the photos at Mervyn's wedding in Great Baddow.
Steve Bacon

I watched the away leg of the Eintracht Frankfurt match recently and he was fantastic. He could have easily played for England.
Keith Robson

Merv and I hit it off and became room-mates at West Ham.
Alan Taylor

He always calls me the 'Gas man' because I worked for the gas board before I turned professional.
Anton Otulakowski

Mervyn always claims that I taught him how to drink at West Ham.
Bill Green

An outstanding young goalkeeper. Absolutely outstanding. Good presence, good reactions, good communication and a good shot stopper. We thought the world of him.
Mick McGiven

Mervyn (left) with his predecessor, Peter Grotier and successor, Phil Parkes (right)

2 – KEITH COLEMAN

"There was something magical about those European nights. The matches against DenHaag and Eintracht Frankfurt were incredible experiences. The Germans had a very good side and almost scored very late on so we only just scraped through."

Born: Washington, County Durham, May 24, 1951 • **Position:** Right-back • **Games played for John Lyall:** 85 (1974-1977) **Games played for West Ham United:** 122 (1973-77) • **Honours:** 1975 FA Charity Shield runner-up, 1976 European Cup Winners Cup Runner-up • **First game under John Lyall:** August 24, 1974 v Everton (h) L 2-3 (Bonds, McDowell – Royle, Latchford, Harvey) Att: 22,486 • **West Ham United:** Day, **Coleman**, Lampard, Bonds, Taylor T, Lock, Holland, Paddon, Gould, McDowell, Best. • **Everton:** Lawson, Darracott, Seargeant, Clements, Lyons, Hurst, Buckley, Harvey, Royle, Latchford, Connolly.* Sub: Pearson.*

Keith Coleman was signed from Sunderland by Ron Greenwood in September 1973. The fee was £20,000. He played 15 matches at right-back with the great Bobby Moore and his finest moment in the Hammers shirt came in 1976, against Anderlecht in the final of the European Cup Winners Cup. Keith still possesses both the Number 2 shirt and his runners-up medal from that special night in the Heysel Stadium: "There was no better atmosphere than those midweek matches, under the floodlights at Upton Park. The Chicken Run was full of characters and I received a few heckles: "Coleman, you're not mustard today," is one I remember!

Keith remains one of only 23 Hammers to have played in a major European final, but sadly, he did miss out on two FA Cup finals - the first, whilst playing for Sunderland in 1973, when the Mackems registered an unlikely victory over Don Revie's all conquering Leeds United. The second, when West Ham United beat Fulham 2-0 in the 1975 final. John McDowell wore the Number 2 shirt that day.

Despite playing in over 80 matches during the John Lyall era, the experience had its ups and downs. Contemporary press reports show that in early 1975 Keith asked for a transfer. He was quoted at the time as saying: "I have been in and out of the first team for two years. It destroys your confidence and I want to play permanent first team football." He eventually joined Belgian club Mechelen in 1978 before

returning a year later to play for Darlington.

Coleman was one of several players from the North East of England to ply their trade at West Ham. Mick McGiven, Pop Robson, Keith Robson and Bill Green made up a group of five. Damagingly, a newspaper ran an article about a North-South divide amongst the players and John Lyall took umbrage at the thought that one of his players could be involved in leaking such a story. Unfortunately for Keith, he was falsely accused of facilitating the bad press: "I had nothing to do with the newspaper article but John blamed me! Our relationship was ruined. I won't disrespect what he did for the club, but I do not want to contribute any more. Sorry but that is the way I feel."

Keith continues to enjoy his retirement near Pathos in Cyprus where he has been living since 2013.

He returned to Upton Park in May 2016 for the visit of Swansea City - the last ever Saturday match at the Boleyn Ground. Despite the 1-4 defeat, Keith caught up with his old pals Keith Robson, Alan Taylor and Ronnie Boyce.

Following are player recollections of Keith along with some photos from his time with the Hammers:

He was a solid right-back and our paths crossed again after our careers were over. I was running the Leisure Centre in South Woodham Ferrers and he was running one in Shenfield High School. **John Ayris**

In action against Brian Talbot of Ipswich Town, October 1976

Keith was one of the married guys at the club so I didn't see too much of him. We did go out occasionally during trips abroad. Another good lad from the North East.
Billy Jennings

Keith was a steady full-back, a quiet type who got on with things.
Pat Holland

I liked Keith. He was good pals with Mick McGiven. John would set up training sessions between the North and South. Keith, Mick, Robbo, Pop and Bill Green would play for the North.
Alan Taylor

Steady full-back. Luckily for me, he wasn't a left-back otherwise I wouldn't have played the few games I did!
Alan Wooler

He joined West Ham shortly before me. As a right-back he suffered a bit with a lack of pace on the one-v-ones, but loved to get forward and had good crossing ability.
Mick McGiven

He was quiet and I mistakenly thought he would be easy to beat because he looked like slow motion. But I was wrong. He was very sharp at right-back.
Yilmaz Orhan

A good guy who worked hard and earned his place in the European Cup Winners Cup final.
Keith Robson

Back at the old place one last time, May 7 2016

3 – FRANK LAMPARD

"John was an outstanding manager and deserves all the accolades he receives. I've got a lot of respect for him and his family."

Born: East Ham, London, September 20, 1948 • **Position:** Left-back • **Games played for John Lyall:** 426 (1974-85)

Games played for West Ham United: 670 (1967-85) – 2nd on the all-time appearances list behind Billy Bonds • **Goals:** 22

Honours under John Lyall: 1975 FA Cup winner, 1975 FA Charity Shield runner-up, 1976 European Cup Winners Cup runner-up, 1980 FA Cup winner, 1980 Charity Shield runner-up, 1981 Second Division winner, 1981 League Cup runner-up.

First game under John Lyall: August 24, 1974 v Everton (h) L 2-3 (Bonds, McDowell – Royle, Latchford, Harvey). Att: 22,486

West Ham United: Day, Coleman, **Lampard,** Bonds, Taylor T, Lock, Holland, Paddon, Gould, McDowell, Best.

Everton: Lawson, Darracott, Seargeant, Clements, Lyons, Hurst, Buckley, Harvey, Royle, Latchford, Connolly.* Sub: Pearson.

Frank Richard George Lampard registered one of the greatest careers in the history of West Ham United football club. Along with Billy Bonds and Trevor Brooking, he won the FA Cup twice and his 670 appearances in the claret and blue, places him second, behind Billy Bonds, on the all-time list. He also has one of the greatest songs sung after him – 'I'm dreaming of a Lampard special, just like the one at Elland Road.' (To the tune of White Christmas).

When John Lyall took over the reins as first team manager in 1974, Frank had been at the club for 10 years: *"I grew up in Canning Town and the choices weren't that great. Kids tended to work in the Docks, rob a bank or play football! I always wanted to be a footballer and signed apprentice forms for West Ham in 1964."*

Lampard made the Number 3 shirt his own over a 15-year period and, after hanging up his boots, coached under Bobby Moore at Southend United in the mid-1980s, and, between 1994-2001, was assistant manager to brother-in-law, Harry Redknapp, back at West Ham. *"We applied a lot of what we learned from Ron Greenwood and John Lyall in our training sessions because that's what we'd grown up with."*

Lampard's son, Frank junior, also began his career at Upton Park, before moving to Chelsea. It was at Stamford Bridge where he achieved the accolade of becoming the club's all-time leading goalscorer with 211 goals - a sensational achievement from a midfielder. Young Frank's 106 caps for England fell respectively short of Bobby Moore's 108, with whom his father had played alongside on over 200 occasions.

The Lampard's are one of only seven father and son pairings to have played for West Ham United. The other six are the Barrett's (Jim and Jim jnr), the Brown's (Ken and Kenny), the Lansdowne's (Bill and Billy), the Potts', (Steve and Danny), the Moncur's (John and George) and the Lee's (Rob and Elliot).

Frank continues to work in the world of property and, as always, was very generous with his time to talk about John Lyall:

John learned a lot about the game from Ron Greenwood but had a gritty determination all of his own. They were cast from the same mould but had different temperaments. Ron was the great tactician who created the framework for his players. John continued with that framework but also put a little bit of fright into his players in order to succeed.

I had a good relationship with John. I was a lot like him in many ways. I knew what I wanted and where I wanted to get to and believed in hard work and determination to achieve my ambition. Football didn't always come natural to me, so I had to put in the hours of effort to make it happen. John's

Frank enjoying FA Cup success in 1975

work ethic was very similar. He never got too animated either. He might have been excited inside but he didn't tend to show it. He never gave too much away.

The three senior professionals at the time were Trevor Brooking, Billy Bonds and myself. We had a special rapport with John and he would discuss certain things with us which he wouldn't share with the others. He knew we were committed, hard-working and ambitious and he allowed us to do our own thing. We didn't abuse his trust.

John helped me to improve my game at a very young age. I was about 17-years-old and was playing ok but lacked a yard of pace. He was coaching under Ron at the time and called me in to his office and suggested that I wear a pair of sprinting spikes. So that's what I did. I started sprinting over 10 and 20 yards to build up my speed. That was the making of me and really pushed my game forward. I had so much belief in those spikes that I bought young Frank a pair when he was a young boy to help improve his quickness of the mark. He'd spend 30 minutes every day over at Chadwell Heath doing spike work. That all goes back to John.

John was a good man with a lot of feeling for people. He was approachable and wanted to help his players on any level. He was a problem solver and liked to find solutions for people, whether they were related to football or life. Through that approach he gained the confidence and trust

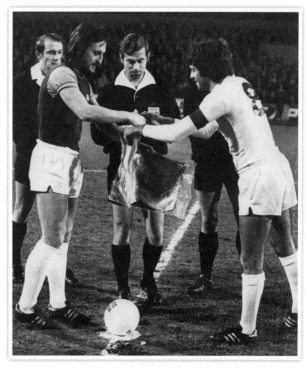

Captaining the Hammers against Fiorentina in the 1975 Anglo Italian Cup final, Decemeber 1975

I'm dreaming of a Lampard special, just like the one at Elland Road...

of all his players. It is hard for the modern day manager to create a culture like that because nobody is given any time these days. The day a manager is appointed is the day the countdown to getting the sack starts.

John liked to see his players every morning and would sit at a table near the entrance to the changing rooms at Chadwell Heath. He'd sit there with Ronnie Boyce and Bill Lansdowne and make a point of saying good morning to everyone. He was probably seeing what shape they were in and if they'd had a heavy night. It's funny because Harry Redknapp and I did something similar when Paolo Di Canio was at West Ham. If Paolo came in happy and full of life we'd know that training could start immediately and everything would be ok. Sometimes, if he came in with the world on his shoulders things would take a bit longer to get started!

John made me captain on a few occasions. After Bobby Moore left the club in 1974, Ron Greenwood had to make a decision about his successor for the captaincy. It was between me and Billy Bonds and obviously Billy got it. If ever Bill was injured, John usually gave me the captain's responsibility which I really enjoyed. I always felt I was captain material. He made me captain for the Charity Shield in 1975 which was a special moment.

During the 1980 FA Cup run I was left out of the first semi-final against Everton at Villa Park. However, John brought me back in for the replay and I'm pleased he did. The winning goal in the replay was my biggest moment over an 18-year playing career at West Ham. People often asked me what I

was doing so far up the pitch and I answer by simply saying that I was too knackered to get back! An even stranger event in my book was Trevor Brooking taking the throw-in which led to my goal. When have you ever seen Trevor take a throw-in? He must have been more knackered than me!

I returned to West Ham in 1994 as assistant manager under Harry Redknapp. We used a lot of the teachings of Ron Greenwood and John Lyall. That is all we knew and it had proven to be successful back then so we maintained those traditions through our training sessions at Chadwell Heath. They call it sport science these days but the fundamentals haven't changed.

It's great that we still have reunions of West Ham's great Cup winning teams. The fans never forget those days and they still want to hear the stories. The players are a great bunch of lads, good boys, led by a terrific manager. They deserve all the credit they get.

Frank Lampard

By the time I went to West Ham Frank had seen it all and done it all. He helped me with my own game and although he didn't have any pace he had a good footballing brain which is why he stayed at the top for so long.

Steve Walford

I've never known anyone to put as much hard work into improving his game as Frank. Even when training was over he'd ask some of the younger lads like Joe Durrell,

Patsy Holland or myself to stay behind and run at him. He was always thinking about ways to improve. He was a talented footballer, not the best, but through hard work and dedication he earned two England caps and became a West Ham legend.
John Ayris

I liked Frank, he was a hard tackler and a straight talker. We had a few beers in his pub, The Britannia, with the old ticket tout, Terry Creasey.
Derek Hales

He was so dedicated. He wasn't blessed with pace but would put on the spikes and made the best of what he had. He gave it his all. A dedicated professional and workaholic.
Ron Boyce

Frank was really good to me at West Ham. He was good friends with the Curbishley brothers, Alan, Paul, Billy and Alfie. Billy was the manager of The Who and Alfie ran the Lord Stanley near the ground. Frank owned the Britannia pub in Plaistow. We'd often pop in there and Frank would always make sure he bought us a beer and looked after the lads.
Phil Brignull

Frank gave me a lot of advice and little tips about improving my game. He also owned a couple of bars and I liked a drink so that worked quite well, too! Billy Lansdowne jnr
When I first started training with West Ham Frank would often give me a lift home to Canning Town. He'd pop in to see his mum in nearby Malmesbury Road. We had mutual friends in Terry and Pat Creasey so had quite a bit in common.
Alan Curbishley

A great pro. If you wanted to sum up Frank you only have to look at how he behaved on the cross country runs. If anyone was trying to overtake him he would rather elbow them into the bushes than be overtaken. That was Frank all over.
Pat Holland

I'd often go with Frank and Graham Paddon to the William the Conqueror in Manor Park for a couple of pints.
Keith Robson

When I first came down from Barnsley I really struggled with Frank's Cockney accent. He invited me to play squash and I asked him to repeat what he had said three times! I'd like to catch up with Frank. We got on well at West Ham and played quite a bit of squash together – eventually!
Anton Otulakowski

One of only three Hammers to win the FA Cup twice, May 1980

Frank was someone I looked up to at West Ham. He put more effort into his training than any other player. I could talk to him about any aspect of the game and he'd try to help.
Alan Taylor

Frank could have played anywhere across the back four and should certainly have got more than his two England caps. The one game which sticks in my mind was against QPR at Upton Park. Dave Thomas played on the right-wing for them and was a good pal of mine. I'd known him since I was a young kid - we were like brothers. Anyway, the match kicked off and the ball went out wide and Frank just went straight through Dave and clattered him into the old West Stand.
Mick McGiven

I still have scars on my left ankle from training with Frank. I show my friends and tell them they belong to Frank Lampard.
Yilmaz Orhan

Reliable, quite private and a winner.
Alvin Martin

Frank and I have known each other for a long time and we are best of friends. Everyone remembers the goal he scored against Everton in the 1980 FA Cup semi-final replay at Elland Road, but he also scored a very important goal at Upton Park in the European Cup Winners Cup quarter-final against Den Haag. I could talk all day about Frank because he's a great mate of mine.
Rob Jenkin

Frank was always good to me and I used to visit his house and got on well with his family. I took photos at his pub, The Britannia, in Plaistow and also when he opened his nightclub, Reflections.
Steve Bacon

We were playing head tennis at Chadwell Heath when Frank asked me what my dad did for a living. "He's a fisherman," I replied. "Same fing innit?" came Frank's lightning quick reply. When I asked him what he meant, he explained: "Well, you've gotta get 'em in the net, aint ya?" I still laugh about that now.
George Cowie

Frank had so much faith in my ability. He'd pass the ball to me when I was being marked by two men.
Alan Devonshire

One of 77 Hammers to have played for John Lyall and one of 89 to have played with Bobby Moore

4 – BILLY BONDS

"John ran the club from top to bottom. I don't recall ever talking to him about transfers, tactics or anything like that. Today, they call men like John Lyall: 'Old school' or 'Old fashioned manager'. What they actually mean, is that John did the work done by 50 men in today's game."

Born: Woolwich, London, September 17, 1946 • **Position:** Defender/Midfielder • **Games played for John Lyall:** 477 (1974-1988) **Games played for West Ham United:** 799 (1967-88). First on the all-time appearances list. • **Goals:** 59 (22nd on the all-time list) **Honours under John Lyall:** 1975 FA Cup winner (captain), 1975 Hammer of the Year, 1976 European Cup Winners Cup runner-up (captain), 1978 First Testimonial (v Tottenham Hotspur, 21,081) 1980 FA Cup winner (captain), 1980 Charity Shield runner-up, 1981 League Cup final runner-up, 1981 Second Division champion (captain), 1987 Hammer of the Year, 1990 Second Testimonial (v Tottenham Hotspur, 10,443) • **First game under John Lyall:** August 24, 1974 v Everton (h) L 2-3 (Bonds, McDowell – Royle, Latchford, Harvey). Att: 22,486 • **West Ham United:** Day, Coleman, Lampard, **Bonds,** Taylor T, Lock, Holland, Paddon, Gould, McDowell, Best. **Everton:** Lawson, Darracott, Seargeant, Clements, Lyons, Hurst, Buckley, Harvey, Royle, Latchford, Connolly.* Sub: Pearson.

William Arthur Bonds established a whole swathe of records during his 21-year span as a player at West Ham United. His legacy of 794 appearances, two successful FA Cup victories (both as captain), two Testimonials and four Hammer of the Year Awards - with a noteworthy 16-year gap between the first, in 1971, and the last, in 1987 - is highly unlikely to be bettered for some considerable time to come.

Bonds is the last player to captain West Ham United to a major European final – versus Anderlecht in 1976 – and, on April 30 1988, became the club's oldest ever player, when lining up for his final match, at The Dell, Southampton, aged 41-years and 226 days. He also sits in 22nd position on the all-time scorers list at West Ham with 59 goals.

In one spell over Christmas and New Year during the 1987-88 season, 41-year-old Bonds played four games in eight days. No wonder contemporary press reports referred to him as 'Rambo', the all action hero. To the Claret and Blue faithful he is one of the most enduring heroes of all-time.

Bonds was John Lyall's longest serving captain and maintained the very high standard set down by his predecessor and World Cup winning captain, Bobby Moore.

Between them, they lifted the greatest haul of trophies in West Ham United's history - by some considerable distance.

Billy continues his role as a devoted family man and his legendary prowess as an endurance runner continues to keep him in good stead – only these days, it concerns the early morning school run with his grandchildren!

At 71-years-of-age, Billy is enjoying retirement with wife Lynne and they share their time between Chislehurst, Kent and their holiday home in Dorset. He occasionally attends various West Ham United reunions and is feted by Hammers' fans wherever he goes.

Once again, Billy was most generous with his time to share his memories of John:

I was signed by a great coach in Ron Greenwood, but played most of my career under John Lyall, who, under Ron's tutelage, matured into a great coach. Like Ron, he should have managed England. I think he would have been a terrific England manager, there is no doubt about that.

The main difference between the pair of them was that John was more wired into his players than Ron and could be a lot stricter. Too many players got away with far too much under

With Frank Lampard and the FA Cup in 1975

they wanted their teams to play. Once John was appointed first-team manager and established the role as his own, he was the best manager I played under.

John began his own playing career at West Ham in the 1950s and had learned from some great footballing characters such as Malcolm Allison, John Bond, Malcolm Musgrove, Noel Cantwell and Phil Woosnam. It makes me appreciate that he really did have all the right influences to be a top class manager. Place Ron Greenwood at the top of that list, add John's own innate talent and there is little wonder that he knew his trade so very well.

When I joined the club in 1967, John was coaching the kids and had an office at the training ground in Chadwell Heath. Most mornings, the first thing I saw was Ron, John and Bill Lansdowne, sitting around a table discussing football. When John took over in 1974, the club was going through a few changes. Bobby Moore had just left for Fulham and Ron had given the honour of club captaincy to me. John saw no reason to change this when he took over a few months later and we developed a close understanding. The relationship between manager and captain has to be one of great strength, trust and respect. I felt John and I were very strong together. I was his voice out on the pitch and he would get things through to me if he felt we needed to change anything. I made sure everyone knew what was required of them so that we were all pulling in the same direction.

John's training sessions were brilliant, just like Ron's before him. I never left Chadwell Heath thinking: "That was boring." Far from it. They were exciting, varied, inventive and strenuous. Both Ron and John were innovators. An example of John's way of looking at things differently can be seen around the options a player faces when getting to the byline. Normally, a player would either float a cross into the six-yard area, or strike it, low and hard, across the box. John gave us another option - playing the ball back to the edge of the 18-yard box for someone to have a crack at goal. It is something you see all the time in today's game but John had been setting up dedicated sessions in the 1970s.

It is interesting to note that I see tactical play in today's game which Ron and John simply never believed in. They certainly wouldn't have advocated an offside trap. They wouldn't have seen that as having any entertainment value, at all. They would have viewed it as bad for the game. I think John tried it once during a pre-season tournament in Germany in the early 1980s. We got slaughtered by a very handy Ajax side which included Ronald Koeman, Jan Molby, Jesper Olsen and Marco Van Basten. John never tried it again!

John set up some great five-a-side matches in the gym at Chadwell Heath. He made it more difficult by not allowing anyone to play the ball off the wall. It meant that you had to

Ron. Furthermore, Ron wouldn't compromise on the way he thought the game should be played, whereas John was a bit more flexible. Even after substitutes were introduced in the mid-1960s, Ron rarely used them. I think John realised that you couldn't go out and play the perfect game every week and tried to change things around a bit more.

One big change I noticed when John took over was that we didn't concede as many goals from set plays, particularly corners. We shipped far too many goals from corners under Ron, whereas John would give us specific instructions about where the threat would come from and who we needed to be marking. This is only a small point because they were two great coaches but John just had that little bit of steel and flexibility in his approach to the game.

Both Ron and John shared the same philosophy in that they wanted West Ham United to play entertaining, attacking football. When Ron played me at right-back, he always encouraged me to run with the ball and make overlapping runs. When I played centre-half, he wanted me to bring the ball down and run into the midfield. Similarly, in midfield I could get beyond Trevor Brooking and support the attack. John was the same when he took over because that is how

The man for the big occasion

be really precise with your passing, control and the timing of your runs. A little tweak like that really made you think about the game in a different way.

John could easily coach any of the top clubs today. The notion of John, with unlimited financial resources at his mercy, is something very thought-provoking, indeed. However, because West Ham United was run on a shoe-string, John needed an extremely good eye for seeing the potential in a player. The club couldn't afford the finished article so John had to find players he thought could benefit from his coaching skills. That is why scouts like Wally St Pier and Eddie Baily were very important to John. Nowadays, of course, the money sloshing about in the game means that clubs like Chelsea and Manchester City are fielding 'cheque book' teams. In such a position of unlimited resources I wonder which global talent John would pencil in on his team sheet? If you look at West Ham in the Greenwood and Lyall era there were always three of four great players, but the squad around them wasn't strong enough which is why the trophies they won during that era deserve the utmost credit. Sadly, it is also the reason why West Ham didn't win the league title.

John was very constructive in everything he did. Some managers just rant and rave and go off on tangents, completely losing it and confusing their players. John wasn't

anything like that. He was methodical and talked sense. When John delivered a team talk, everyone listened. We all believed in what he was saying and what he was trying to achieve. Even if anyone played badly, John was constructive in his criticism. His point of view made sense, was easily understood and offered knowledgeable advice. Sometimes, when the performance was particularly bad - like it was up at Leicester City once - John kept us all behind in the dressing room for well over an hour. We usually stuffed Leicester but, on this occasion, we'd had a bad day up there. We were sitting in our dirty strip, sweat dripping on the floor, but John wouldn't let us even take a shower until he had got all his points across. He wasn't slagging people off or throwing things around. He was just calmly making his points – and there were a lot of them! John was a great talker and could easily spend any amount of time discussing football. He offered well informed opinion based on a lot of experience, which is why Alex Ferguson thought the world of him.

In the early 1980s, West Ham went up to Aberdeen for a pre-season tournament. They were flying high under Alex Ferguson and had just won the European Cup Winners Cup, beating Real Madrid in the final. Alex was very respectful to John and was keen to discuss football with him. Alex rated John very highly.

As a player, John knew I didn't really need encouraging.

He generally left me alone to get on with things. He knew I was trying to give 100% in every game and that never changed throughout my time at the club. I think the players who upset John were those who made mistakes which were thoughtless and damaging to the team.

I was never fined by John even though I was sent off once during his time in charge. It happened against Birmingham City before the 1980 FA Cup final, after an altercation with Colin Todd. John viewed it as an honest mistake made under very heated circumstances. Thankfully, the Football Association panel was as forgiving as John so I was able to play against Arsenal at Wembley.

After West Ham lost to Stoke City in the League Cup semi-final in 1972, I started to think that my chance of playing at Wembley had gone. The fact that I went on to lift the FA Cup, not once, but twice, is just wonderful. It was different back then because, as a kid, the only thing you thought about was winning the FA Cup. It was more important than winning the league or triumphing in Europe, for that matter. The FA Cup was the trophy everyone wanted to get their hands on. There was a time when it was the only game shown live on television. It had a magical quality.

The first FA Cup final I watched was the Stanley Matthews classic in 1953 between Blackpool and Bolton. I was six-years-old and completely transfixed by the FA Cup from that moment on. I often pretended to lift the cup in my back garden. Sadly, it has lost a lot of its lustre nowadays, which is a crying shame. When West Ham won it in 1975 and 1980, I think everyone in the East End and beyond turned out to see us bring the FA Cup back to East Ham town hall. Memories like that never fade. Of the two FA Cup finals, the victory over Arsenal gives me most satisfaction. It was John's finest moment as a manager.

Looking back on my own career, that 1980-81 team was the best I played in. John built that squad. He signed David Cross, Alan Devonshire, Phil Parkes, Stuart Pearson and Ray Stewart. He also helped Geoff Pike, Alvin Martin and young Paul Allen progress through the ranks from young apprentices to first team pros. That leaves just Frank Lampard, Trevor Brooking and myself from Ron Greenwood's era. There were no posers in that side, no big egos. They were a great group of lads who John had moulded in the right way. We were virtually unbeatable for a couple of years. There was plenty of skill in that side and also a lot of leaders, too. The defence was really strong and we didn't take any nonsense from anyone. We all pulled our weight and got hooked on the winning habit.

I hadn't watched the 1980 FA Cup final until a couple of years ago at a reunion. We looked comfortable throughout the whole match and kept our passing game together. It was a terrific team performance and John demonstrated great tactical awareness. He beat Arsenal at their own game by keeping a clean sheet and wining by the only goal. That has

West Ham v Birmingham City. David Cross takes the diplomatic approach while Billy has other ideas, April 1980

With the FA Cup in 1980

regained a bit of pride in front of 80,000 fans. An interesting footnote to the Tbilisi experience came when I visited Upton Park during West Ham's last ever season at the Boleyn Ground in 2015-16. I was in the Director's room sitting next to a gentleman who had travelled over from Georgia, where Tbilisi play. He said that was the greatest side ever to come out of the old Soviet Union. They went on to win the European Cup Winners Cup that year, beating Carl Zeiss Jena, 2-1. He told me that David Kipiani, who was scintillating at Upton Park, died in a car crash. He was only 49-years-old. A lot of West Ham supporters generally agree that Tbilisi were the best side to play at Upton Park. As good as they were, I still think it is debatable, because there were some tremendous teams from Liverpool and Manchester United to play at the Boleyn Ground down the years.

As much as it was great to play in the Bernabeu Stadium - against Real Castilla - in the earlier round of that European Cup Winners Cup campaign, the occasion didn't leave me with a great memory - everything went badly wrong. Our performance on the pitch was diabolical and the fans were fighting in and around the stadium. We knew we had let ourselves down as a club but thankfully, we slaughtered them at home in front of a couple of hundred fans. The 'Ghost Match' I think they call it and that is exactly what it felt like. I watched the highlights on the TV and could hear all the swearing and shouting from the players. I even heard myself shouting: "Effing good goal, Pikey!"

We were all stunned when we heard the news about John getting sacked. I was at Chadwell Heath with Mick McGiven and Ronnie Boyce. It was hard to take in, a complete shock. The decision was a bad mistake and I don't think the club has ever been the same since. I spoke to John quite a bit at the time and he was clearly very disappointed and didn't want to go anywhere near the place again. It hurts me to think about how John was let down like that.

It really was the worst thing to happen to the club. The logical thing would have been to bring in a younger manager when the time was right, keeping John at the club in a consultative role. That had worked previously with Ron Greenwood. A lot of people said I was the best person to follow in John's footsteps. I would have relished the opportunity to have worked with him. However, I wasn't thinking about that at the time, because John was only 49-years-old and should have had years left as manager of West Ham United. Sadly, the opportunity didn't arise but I know we trusted each other implicitly so it would have had a good chance of working really well.

Instead, they brought in Lou Macari and although he was fine with me, a lot of the other players didn't like him. John and Lou were chalk and cheese so it was always going to be difficult for Lou with that particular group of players.

been an Arsenal trademark for years, but John made sure it ended 1-0 to the Hammers.

John enjoyed the challenge of pitting his wits against European teams. We had a great run to the European Cup Winners Cup final in 1976 against Anderlecht. They had Rob Rensenbrink, Arie Hann, and Francois Van der Elst and were a top quality side. Rensenbrink tore us apart in the second half. 1976 was the first of three consecutive finals for them in that competition and they won two of them. That shows just how good they were. I think the game turned on Frank Lampard's under hit back pass on the stroke of half-time. I'm not blaming Frank because it could have happened to me or anyone else. I think he stubbed the turf and didn't get a clean connection on the ball. It was no disgrace to lose to them, it was just one of those things.

The Dinamo Tbilisi side from 1981 was one of the best I ever played against. They were deadly on the break and Gutsaev, Shengalia, Chivadze and Kipiani totally destroyed us. They beat us 1-4 in our own back yard. To be fair to John, he hadn't received any reports or analysis on Tbilisi before the first leg at home, so he was managing in the dark as far as tactics were concerned. It was a testament to his coaching ability that once he had seen them play, we went out to Georgia and beat them 1-0. We were never going to claw it back completely, but we

Introducing long ball football was never going to work in a John Lyall culture. I was surprised that Lou advocated such a direct style of football, given his playing experience with a very cultured Manchester United in the 1970s.

After I replaced Lou as West Ham's manager, I remember seeing John at Ipswich Town where he was managing. I had just brought in Harry Redknapp as my number two and John pulled me to one side and said: "What the bloody hell have you done? Why have you brought him in?" I explained that we were old pals and that he was doing a great job, but John just looked at me and said: "I hope you don't live to regret it." He was right there.

The last time I spoke to John was at a West Ham reunion in Canary Wharf. All the players from his two FA Cup winning sides returned for a very special evening. John couldn't believe just how much respect both the players and fans had for him. It is strange really because Bobby Moore was a bit like that. Some players and managers lose sight of their place in a club's history. The fans and the players never forget but that night John told me just how amazed he was at the reception and treatment he had received.

I was sitting in my study at home when I got a call from Ray Stewart informing me that John had died. Obviously, I was stunned and it just dominates your thoughts for a long time. I thought the world of him.

At John's funeral, his brother came up to me and said: "John thought so very much of you." It was a lovely thing to hear and John knew the feeling was mutual. I played for him. I played for John.

Billy Bonds

The list of memories about Billy is endless:
What an asset! A 100% diamond of a player. Everyone learned so much from Billy and his attitude to the game. His shirt was wringing wet after every one of his 794 games for the West Ham.

Ron Boyce

The legend himself! They threw away the mould when they made Bill. He could play midfield, up front centre-back and right-back. Completely dependable, committed, loyal and a winner. My idol growing up was Dave Mackay and Billy was every bit as good as him.

Mick McGiven

A fantastic role model for all footballers. When you see the dross that's been allowed to pull on the England shirt in recent times, it makes you wonder how Billy never got 50 caps, let alone one. When you think about Andy Carroll today, and all the matches he has missed through injury, it really does underline, just how resilient a player Billy was.

Almost 800 games says it all. He had to be at death's door to miss a game for West Ham.

John Ayris

Bondsy was probably the most professional player I ever played with. He gave 120%. We had a guy at Charlton called Keith Peacock who was a pro through and through and any club is lucky to have players like them. Bondsy had such great commitment, could run forever and was always reliable. He never had a drink or went out with us after a game, but he always did more than anyone else. West Ham were lucky to have him.

Derek Hales

I've spoken to Stuart Slater and Pottsy about this. Because we had trained and played with Bondsy while John was in charge we were ready to run through brick walls for Bill when he became West Ham's manager. When I joined West Ham, he was in the twilight of his playing career, but you would never have known it. His attitude and the way he trained just left everyone in total respect for him. What a player and what a man! If you had him on your team in training you were guaranteed to win. Guaranteed.

Kevin Keen

I joined West Ham in 1974 and Bobby Moore had just left so I never got to play or train with the great man. However, I did play with Billy Bonds and he is my Bobby Moore, my number one. I was a flash little 16-year-old Scouser when I joined West Ham United and Bonzo would boot me around a bit to keep me in line. He showed me the ropes and we started playing alongside each other in the first team. I always felt there was a good rapport between us and I was always led by him. I was never as good a captain as Bill but I learned a lot from him. I'd like to think that I was a tiny proportion of the great captain we had in Billy Bonds.

Alvin Martin

I remember he lost his driver's licence once, so I picked him up at Beckton flyover on the way to training at Chadwell Heath. On one occasion, Bill wasn't there, so, I panicked and drove off. He ended up being late for training and all I can remember is being held up against a wall with Bill's hands around my neck!

Pat Holland

I think Billy Bonds preferred playing in midfield. He enjoyed being in the thick of things.

Alan Curbishley

Bonzo was absolutely superb. Easily the best player I played

The final encounter between Billy Bonds and John Lyall, The Britannia Hotel, Isle of Dogs, 2005

with, without a shadow of a doubt. He was just heart and soul West Ham. He would have run through a brick wall for West Ham and you can't say that about many since Billy.
Keith Robson

The hardest and most honest man I ever played with.
Greg Campbell

A great, great leader. I've got a lot of respect for Billy. He played behind me and was so professional and dedicated. He talked to me on the pitch helped me more than anyone.
Alan Taylor

People often talk about Bill's bravery and leadership but he could also play one-touch football with the best of them.
George Parris

Trojan.
Alan Wooler

A wonderful athlete, a wonderful player and a great man. One Christmas we played in defence together, in a match up at Birmingham City. I kicked Kenny Burns from pillar to post and Bill kicked Trevor Francis from pillar to post. I think we nicked a 0-0.
Bill Green

I tried to model my game on Billy's because he threw himself around and always seemed to be in the thick of the action. He gave me a lift home through the Blackwall Tunnel when I was a young apprentice. It made my day because I was so

in awe of him. It was great to see him at the London Bridge Hilton for a reunion of the FA Cup teams a few years back.
Keith McPherson

Hero.
Alan Dickens

He has always been a man of few words. When I was in prison he sent me a letter which simply said: "Thinking of you – Bill."
Mark Ward

I hold Billy in as high regard as John Lyall. He gave me my first chance to coach so I'm forever grateful to him for that. How is it even possible to play for that long with that much enthusiasm?
Paul Hilton

He used to say that if I had any trouble with anyone on the pitch just let him know and he'd sort them out.
Kevin Lock

Mr West Ham. Simple as that. Billy Bonds and Trevor Brooking were the masters of the old place.
Tommy Taylor

Billy's farewell to The Boleyn Ground

05 – TOMMY TAYLOR

"John was a nice man, a good coach and he looked after his players."

Born: Hornchurch, Essex, September 26, 1951 • **Position:** Centre-half • **Games played for John Lyall:** 228 (1974-79)

Games played for West Ham United: 397 (1970-79) • **Goals for West Ham United:** 8

Honours under John Lyall: 1975 FA Cup winner, 1975 FA Charity Shield runner-up, 1976 European Cup Winners Cup runner-up

First game under John Lyall: August 24, 1974 v Everton (h) L 2-3 (Bonds, McDowell – Royle, Latchford, Harvey). Att: 22,486

West Ham United: Day, Coleman, Lampard, Bonds, **Taylor T,** Lock, Holland, Paddon, Gould, McDowell, Best.

Everton: Lawson, Darracott, Seargeant, Clements, Lyons, Hurst, Buckley, Harvey, Royle, Latchford, Connolly.* Sub: Pearson.

Thomas Frederick Taylor is one of only 30 Hammers to have won an FA Cup winners medal. Hornchurch-born Taylor was signed from Leyton Orient by Ron Greenwood in 1970. However, he played more than half of his 397 club appearances under John Lyall. If the 2-0 FA Cup final victory over Fulham stands as Tommy's highest point in football, the defeat against Anderlecht in the final of the European Cup Winners' Cup, a year later, was the lowest. After some deliberation, Tommy comments: "The FA Cup run in 1975 was great, but the European campaign the following season was equally as good. We should have beaten Anderlecht in the final and I firmly believe that John Lyall should have replaced Frank Lampard with Kevin Lock at half-time."

Taylor formed Bobby Moore's final central-defensive pairing at West Ham United and, despite gaining 12 England under-23 caps, could not emulate his mentor by gaining full International honours.

In 1979, Taylor returned to Leyton Orient to see out his playing career before entering the world of coaching. To date, Taylor has managed no fewer than 13 different football clubs, and is in no mood to take it easy just yet: *"I'll never retire, because if you retire you die. I've coached all around the world and had a lot of fun along the way. You can't ask for more than that. All those training sessions with Ron and John at Chadwell Heath have kept me in good stead!*

Another ex-Hammer - Jimmy Bloomfield at Orient - was a big influence, too."

Regardless of where Tommy Taylor next applies his considerable knowledge of the game, he can always reflect on the fact that the two most successful managers in the history of West Ham United combined to select him on almost 400 occasions. Such experience should always find a home in football.

Tommy gave the following interview from his home in Northampton:

John was very hands on and would never delegate training sessions to others. He was out there, in all weathers, setting the drills and coaching the players. He was happy to let everyone do their own thing as long as they were doing it properly. If you can't master the basics, you can't play football and John knew that all too well.

I've coached quite a few teams around the world and definitely benefited from the very good coaching advice given to me by Ron Greenwood, John Lyall and Jimmy Bloomfield. They were so good at ensuring their players understood the basics - first touch, one and two-touch, short passing, long passing, give and go, those basic, but vital skills. It is amazing how many players can't perform those simple tasks, even at the highest level. They say football has changed, but you still have to control the ball, pass the

Scoring against Aston Villa at the Boleyn Ground, October 1977

ball, head the ball and take corners and free kicks. Ron and John drilled that into every player at West Ham United and they were all the better for it. The only thing that has really changed in the modern game, is the level of fitness. Diet and training have both improved considerably but what is the point of running fast and forever if you can't trap a ball?

I played almost 400 games for West Ham and probably played a few more for John than I did for Ron. They were different people altogether. I enjoyed myself equally under both men. Ron left John a very good team and John progressed from there. John added his own ideas and players into the mix but he also had some good old heads to help him along the way. Any manager who has both Billy Bonds and Trevor Brooking on his team sheet has got a chance.

I really enjoyed the one-touch training sessions at Chadwell Heath. John was always tweaking something ever so slightly to make it more interesting. For example, he would decrease the size of the playing area so that things happened that bit quicker. It was very fast and very intense. Another time, we'd play two-touch football in the grids, with three-on-three players or four-on-four. I loved those sessions because I was usually in very tight situations and had to be alert all the time. Good touch, sharp awareness and knowing what to do before you received the ball was the essential survival kit in those grids!

I always wanted to wear the Number 6 shirt, but Bobby Moore basically had it tattooed on his back! I ended up wearing the Number 5. I liked to play the ball out of defence and run with it into midfield. I thought my passing was good

and I had good pace. I read the game well and was also a good communicator on the pitch. I talked to everyone, which is a useful trait to have on any football pitch. Some players are very good players but very quiet, while others are not so good but very noisy. I like to think I possessed the good bits

Getting to grips with Everton's Duncan McKenzie, February 1978

FA Cup immortality

from each of those extremes!

I never once saw John Lyall lose his temper but I did see Ron Greenwood lose his. He caught both Ronnie Boyce and Harry Redknapp sharing a cigarette at half-time! Ron was so angry and looked at Harry and said: "Any chance of you putting in a cross in the second-half?" Harry took a puff and replied: "They're kicking lumps out of me, Ron!" Boycey backed him up but Greenwood went into a rage and shouted: "If you don't put a cross over in the first five minutes I'm taking you off!" Sure enough, Harry was sitting on the bench six minutes into the second half!

The defeat against Anderlecht in the European Cup Winners Cup final was a crushing disappointment. In the first-half we were in control of the game. We won plenty of corners and took the lead. Unfortunately, we conceded a couple of silly goals but at 1-2 down I volleyed a shot from about 20-yards which was flying into the top corner. It was the sweetest volley I'd ever hit and felt certain it was flying in, but somehow their keeper clawed it away. Even though Keith Robson headed us level soon after, we soon got completely overrun. It was a very good match, but we should have won. I've still got all my medals and cup final shirts.

John was very fortunate in that he didn't really have one bad egg in the camp. He had a good blend of young and old pros, who could play the game the way he wanted it to be played. That is half the battle as a manager. I don't know if John ever had to fine anyone but I certainly wasn't fined. I was never sent off during my time at the club. Anyway, I didn't earn enough money for him to fine me! West Ham were the worst payers in the world. They were tighter than a duck's arse! It was a great club, with great players, but really tight with money. Having said that, I wouldn't change a thing from my playing career. I had such a good time and got on really well with John McDowell, Kevin Lock and Pat Holland. We had a lot of fun together. Money just wasn't the main motivator back then.

During the summer of 1977, a few of us flew out to the United States to play in the Major Soccer League. It was the heyday of soccer in the States and I played for Team Hawaii along with Pat Holland, Keith Robson and Keith Coleman. I think John was happy that we went, because we were all as fit as fleas when we came home. I was certainly in better shape than I'd ever been.

During my early years at West Ham United, I played quite a few times for England under-23s and a full England cap seemed inevitable. In fact, Alf Ramsey came up to me once and said: "Tommy, if you didn't mess around so much on the pitch, you would be my Number 5." The truth of the matter, was that I liked to have a bit of fun out on the pitch. I felt I could mess around and still play well, so didn't see it as a problem. Some people will probably say that I mucked around a bit too much at West Ham, but I don't think it ever affected my performances on the pitch. Unfortunately, it clearly cost me an England cap.

In 1979, I'd been at West Ham for nearly 10 years and felt that I needed a change. I didn't think about a Testimonial match because I just wanted to try something different. John seemed happy to let me go, but it was an easy decision, because he knew that Alvin Martin was coming through the ranks, so there was no great urgency for John to convince me to stay. I ended up returning to Orient for a few more years before a spell with Deerschot in Belgium.

I wasn't surprised when John was replaced by Lou Macari. Obviously, I wasn't at the club at the time, so I don't know the full details, but nothing surprises me in football anymore. It's all about money, winning and making sure the fans keep coming through the turnstiles. The board will never like it when supporters start calling for a manager to be sacked. They worry about falling attendances and, at the time, West Ham's attendances were as low as 14,000. For all the great things that John Lyall did for West Ham United, the fans were calling for his head in the end. Very sad, but very true.

Tommy Taylor

Final whistle in Brussells - Tommy wipes away the tears after defeat to Anderlecht, May 5, 1976

A few memories of Tommy:

Tommy was a dominating player, but he could be a bit carefree at times. He carved out a good career for himself as a player and a coach.
Ron Boyce

He was the spoilt brat. A fantastic footballer who had his career path laid out in front of him and knew exactly what he wanted to do. He always loved to play tricks and practical jokes on others but was less keen when he was on the receiving end.
John Ayris

Tommy was a talented player but should have been a lot better. Bobby Moore wrote about him in his book and mentioned that he didn't fulfil his potential.
Pat Holland

Whenever we played keep-ball in training, I was always paired with Tommy. I was quite lively and had a bit of pace so he would try and kick holes in me and do anything to stop me running about. I've got a lot of stud marks down my shins from those sessions with Tommy.
Alan Taylor

I found Tommy very intimidating and he gave a lot of the

youngsters a tough time. I remember him saying to John Lyall that if he wanted to get Pikey to make runs in the box he'd better leave a trail of doughnuts there! He went in hard in training when it wasn't necessary. I played alongside him and he'd always give me a lot of stick.
Phil Brignull

Tommy was very good to me at West Ham. He invited me to his house for Christmas Day and I had a fantastic time with all his family. His mum and dad were there and his wife, Pat, was brilliant. So sad to hear the news that she passed away recently.
Keith Robson

A cracking fella who gave me a lot of helpful advice.
Alvin Martin

Tommy was a typical Londoner - full of life. We got on well even though we were competing for the same position at centre-back. Tommy gave me my nickname, 'Jolly'. At first I felt that the players must have thought I was a right miserable git but then it was explained to me about an advert with the 'Jolly Green Giant.'
Bill Green

I loved Tommy to bits. He was a very good player. Strong in the air and strong in the tackle. He could hit a pass 60-yards to feet but he just lacked a bit of concentration and could fall asleep during a game. A bit too easy-osy.
Mick McGiven

Tommy today

6 – KEVIN LOCK

"John was the best manager I played for and one of the nicest guys you could wish to meet. He was a brilliant coach and tactician. I have only great things to say about him."

Born: December 27, 1953 Plaistow, London • **Position:** Left-back/Centre-half • **Games played for John Lyall:** 127 (1974-77)

Games played for West Ham United: 165 (1972-77) • **Goals:** 2 • **Honours under John Lyall:** 1975 FA Cup Winner, 1975 Charity Shield runner-up, 1976 European Cup Winners Cup (unused substitute)

First game under John Lyall: August 24, 1974 v Everton (h) L 2-3 (Bonds, McDowell – Royle, Latchford, Harvey). Att: 22,486

West Ham United: Day, Coleman, Lampard, Bonds, Taylor T, Lock, Holland, Paddon, Gould, McDowell, Best.

Everton: Lawson, Darracott, Seargeant, Clements, Lyons, Hurst, Buckley, Harvey, Royle, Latchford, Connolly.* Sub: Pearson.

Kevin Joseph Lock grew up in Jenkins Road, Plaistow, and played for his local team, West Ham United – the club he loves. He was signed by Ron Greenwood and, in his formative years as a player, lined-up alongside the legendary Bobby Moore. Like Moore he is one of only 30 Hammers to have won an FA Cup winners medal.

Lock received tremendous support from his parents and a wry smile appears as he remembers a couple of amusing family stories: *"My dad, Tom, was a good footballer and played for the army. QPR wanted to sign him but his mum wouldn't let him. "Go and get a proper job!" she told him. Sadly, he passed away in 1973, which was a devastating blow. My mum, Kitty, continued to watch me play up and down the country. She took the supporters' coach to the away matches and sat with the mothers of both Frank Lampard and Billy Bonds. My mum hated Billy Bremner of Leeds United and used to shout abuse at him up at Elland Road! She also provided accommodation for West Ham players. Her address was 70 Jenkins Road and Alan Taylor lived there for a while after he joined the club. Coincidentally, I was talking to Mark Noble at the Hammer of the Year Awards in 2016, and he told me that he grew up in Jenkins Road, too."*

Lock won England Under-23 honours but narrowly missed out on a full England cap - he was an unused substitute in a European Championship qualifier against Portugal. Ironically, he was also an unused substitute in the 1976 European Cup Winners Cup final against Anderlecht and our imaginations will have to mull over the consequences of him playing, and winning, in both of those matches.

Lock left West Ham United in 1978, after Fulham secured his services for £60,000. He ended his career at Southend United and, like so many contemporary footballers, entered the pub trade – running the Prince of Wales in Mountnessing.

Today, Kevin lives in Maldon and works as a highly respected usher at Chelmsford Magistrates Court. He is a season ticket holder at the London Stadium and, in September 2017, attended a reunion of the 1975 FA Cup winning team at the London Bridge Hilton Hotel.

Kevin is no stranger to holidaying abroad and enjoys the relaxed ambiance offered by both Spain and Portugal. Thankfully, he was able to squeeze in this interview in between trips!

Both Ron Greenwood and John Lyall were not only pioneers at West Ham United, they also laid the foundation for a lot of the coaching which is taught in football today. They were very continentally minded, had a thirst for knowledge but never lost sight of the basics.

John was appointed first team manager after a couple of games into the 1974-75 season. It was from that time when I really developed as a first team regular. John played me in every match that season which amounted to 53 appearances.

I got to know John quite well during a tour or the United States in 1971. Me and Johnny Ayris were the two youngsters chosen to join the first team. We travelled to Boston, New York and ended up in Bermuda, where Clyde Best's dad looked after us all. That was the ice-breaker in my relationship with John and we got on well from that time on.

John's training methods involved a lot of work with the ball. He placed great emphasis on control and passing. I'd like to think I was a composed, ball-playing, defender. That is certainly how John developed me as a player.

John was by no means a soft touch. He knew how to get his point across without shouting or throwing things around. His comments were designed to correct mistakes and eliminate any imperfections that he had noticed during a match. He would never slag off anyone for the sake of it. John always put his point across constructively and calmly, which I preferred. I played for managers who just shouted very loudly and I used to just zone out. I couldn't listen to what they were saying because it was just a loud noise. Players generally know when they are not playing well, they don't need anyone screaming at them to make them play better. John knew that his players were trying their hardest, he just needed to point out a little thing here and there to keep us all on top of our game. We wanted to do our best because we were professionals and loved the club. It made a significant difference to our money if we did well, too. Our appearance money and win bonus could double our wages so we worked hard at our game to ensure selection. We were not like many of the players today who don't give a damn about the club and are just happy to pick up their huge salaries. Playing, competing and winning makes no difference to their financial security.

Enjoying the feeling of being an FA Cup winner

In aerial combat with Brian Kidd of Arsenal during the FA Cup quarter final, March 8 1975

John was always very encouraging. He would say things like: "Don't be afraid to receive the ball. Think about what you are going to do with it. Have the confidence to bring it out from the back." If you tried to do the right thing, and it went wrong, he would never criticise you. John was naturally positive, filled his players with belief and liked to play positive, entertaining, football. We never played the offside trap. It just wasn't how the game should be played in John's eyes. There wasn't one offside in the 1975 FA Cup final. John would never set up his team in a defensive format. Not like in today's game where teams can have seven or eight defensive minded players. If you look at West Ham United's midfield players in the 1970s – Trevor Brooking and Graham Paddon – they didn't think defensively at all. They were flare players, creative thinkers who ensured forwards, like Pop Robson, had plenty of chances. Even Billy Bonds, who was a great defender, went marauding forward and often got ahead of Trevor in order to set up and score goals. Billy scored over 60 goals for West Ham, which is another incredible achievement from the great man. Basically, we had players who wanted to play. John McDowell and Tommy Taylor were great ball-players. We never had a stopper or anyone like N'Golo Kante at Chelsea or Nemanja Matic at Manchester United. They just break up the play and destroy any movement in midfield. That wasn't the John Lyall way. He certainly wouldn't have

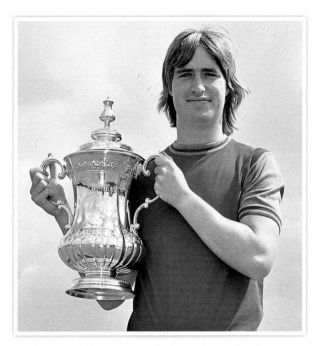

Holding the FA Cup at Chadwell Heath, August 1975

was never fined or disciplined by John.

John put me on the bench for the European Cup Winners Cup final against Anderlecht. It was strange that he didn't bring me on at half-time when Frank had to go off with an injury. Whenever I talk to Trevor Brooking about it he always agrees that it should have been a straight swap – me on for Frank – because I was a left-footed defender and the obvious choice.

Even when I wasn't being selected for those key games, John was always available to discuss anything that was on my mind. His door was always open and he was a very good listener and always gave honest answers. There were plenty of managers who said things they didn't mean or offered deals they had no intention of honouring, but John was the polar opposite of such behaviour. Even if it was bad news, he would tell you face-to-face. Furthermore, I think his honesty and respect was reciprocated. John received a lot of loyalty from his players.

I scored two goals while I was at West Ham. The first was against Everton - I chested it down and half volleyed it in. The second was against Queens Park Rangers - I shot home from the edge of the box. When I worked with Dave Webb at Southend United I pulled his leg about that goal because I had a picture of Dave trying to block the shot, unsuccessfully. Dave wasted no time reminding me that I'd scored an own goal in that same match, too!

I always found Joe Royle of Everton very difficult to play against and the toughest duo were John Toshack and Kevin Keegan of Liverpool. Toshack was so strong in the air and Keegan used to buzz around all over the pitch. With some strikers it was possible to stand around and have a chat, but never with those two.

It absolutely broke my heart to leave West Ham. I didn't want to leave, but circumstances dictated otherwise. John knew it was hard for me to move on and tried to keep the situation upbeat. My only regret in football is that I didn't spend my whole career at West Ham United. It was a bit of a culture shock playing in the lower leagues but I do remember returning to West Ham with Bobby Campbell's Fulham and beating them 1-0, which was a bitter sweet moment, because West Ham were still my club.

I am so pleased the players at West Ham during that era have the chance to share their memories of John because there will be so many positive things said about the man. Sadly, he was treated atrociously by the club so John's legacy, as seen through the stories of those who played for him, will be a fitting tribute. He deserves so much recognition.

I finished my playing career at Southend United under Bobby Moore and he asked me to help coach the kids there. I passed on a lot of John's advice and coaching methods to Southend's young players. It took me back to that time when John had

tolerated players who lacked ambition to create, or contribute something positive. Nowadays, players are happy not to play. The slightest niggle and they'll take a month off, being massaged. I travelled to London with Trevor Brooking to have injections in our groins so that we could play. Billy Bonds was not fully fit for the 1975 Cup final, but there was no way he was going to miss that game.

I think the 1975 FA Cup final was the happiest I ever saw John. One of the nicest things I remember, came after that final, when John was interviewed on television by Brian Moore, the well-known football commentator. They started discussing my performance, and John said that, not only had I played well, but I had been consistently very good all season.

In contrast, the most disappointing memory, came before we played Eintracht Frankfurt in the away leg of the 1976 European Cup Winners Cup semi-final. John called me in and told me that I wasn't going to play. It was a real blow because I'd played in both legs of the quarter-final against Den Haag. Curiously, John told the press that I wasn't in the right frame of mind, which caused my family a great deal of anxiety. They thought something serious had happened to me but it was simply John's decision not to play me. I was fine and fit and ready to play. I found it hard to get upset or angry with John, because I felt we had a strong and honest relationship. I always tried my best for him in training and on the pitch. I wasn't a wild kind of guy who went out clubbing and drinking all the time. I was a dedicated professional. I

Trying to contain the great Kevin Keegan of Liverpool

taught me as a young kid, on the forecourt, in the shadow of the main stand at Upton Park. We only had street lighting on that forecourt so after dusk it was hard to see anything.

The last time I saw John was at a reunion of his cup teams at the Britannia hotel in London's Docklands. We had a chat and he said I hadn't changed at all.

I was devastated when I heard the news that John had passed away. He had been a massive influence on my life. I reacted in the same as when I'd heard Bobby Moore had died – I cried.
Kevin Lock

Locky is a good mate of mine, a lovely man. Tommy Taylor Locky was a natural footballer and a very good player. Probably not as vociferous as he should have been, but that was his personality. He spoke through his football rather than shouting and hollering. **John Ayris**

Kevin was a proper West Ham United player, a pure footballer. Sadly, he was another to be hampered by comparison with Bobby Moore.
Billy Jennings

I like Kevin a lot. He had a purple patch when we won the FA Cup in 1975, but was never really the same player after John dropped him for some important European matches the following season.
Pat Holland

I think John Lyall slipped up in the European Cup Winners Cup final against Anderlecht. He should have brought on

Locky when Frank Lampard got injured. I would say that was the only mistake John made while I was at West Ham.
Keith Robson

After I joined West Ham, I stayed with Kevin Lock's mother in her high rise flat, not far from the ground. Kevin regularly popped round to see his mum, of course, so we spent quite a bit of time talking about football.
Alan Taylor

The thing I remember about Locky, apart from him being a decent player, was his ability to forge autographs. He could do Bobby Moore, Geoff Hurst and Martin Peters, no problem.
Bill Green

Kevin was a player with very good positional sense and a great left foot. He read the game very well and was an educated player. He had obviously watched and learned from Bobby Moore, but Kevin was still very much his own player.
Mick McGiven

Kevin Lock and Tommy Taylor were a very strong defensive partnership and, in my opinion, the best in the league. On their day they were untouchable.
Yilmaz Orhan

If you wanted a reliable player, Locky would be your man.
Ron Boyce

Locky back at The Boleyn Ground during the last ever season, 2015-16

7 - PAT HOLLAND

"I had been in and out of the FA Cup run of 1975 but on the Monday before the final versus Fulham, we were playing Arsenal in a league match. John called me into his office and said: "You're playing tonight and you're starting in the final on Saturday. Don't let me down!"

Born: Poplar, London, September 13, 1950 • **Position:** Winger • **Games played for John Lyall:** 218 (1974-1981)

Games played for West Ham United: 304 (1969-1981) • **Goals for West Ham United:** 32

Honours under John Lyall: 1975 FA Cup winner, 1975 FA Charity Shield runner-up, 1976 European Cup Winners Cup runner-up, 1980 Charity Shield runner-up, 1981 Second Division Championship, 1984 Testimonial v Tottenham Hotspur. Att: 6,421

First game under John Lyall: August 24, 1974 v Everton (h) L 2-3 (Bonds, McDowell – Royle, Latchford, Harvey) Att: 22,486

West Ham United: Day, Coleman, Lampard, Bonds, Taylor T, Lock, **Holland,** Paddon, Gould, McDowell, Best.

Everton: Lawson, Darracott, Seargeant, Clements, Lyons, Hurst, Buckley, Harvey, Royle, Latchford, Connolly.* Sub: Pearson.

Patrick George Holland is one of the great names in West Ham United's history. The shy but fearless winger played the vast majority of his matches under John Lyall, having been given his first-team debut, at home to Arsenal, by Ron Greenwood in 1969.

But for a succession of injuries, Poplar-born Pat would doubtless have made many more appearances and may not have missed out on both the 1980 FA Cup final and the following season's League Cup final. His testimonial against Tottenham Hotspur in 1984 was a fitting tribute to a loyal servant and his recollections of John are full of heartfelt sincerity. His affection for the man is unequivocal and when Patsy talks about John Lyall it is a joy to listen.

Nowadays, Pat continues his scouting role at Arsenal and, like all ex-Hammers to have pursued a career in scouting – John Cartwright, Eddie Presland, Roger Cross, and the much-lamented Peter Brabrook, to name but a few - his West Ham United experience has served him well.

Living with wife Jeannette in Upminster Pat had the following recollections of John:

It was Tuesday night when I first trained at West Ham United in the late 1960s. I was met by this man in a red Umbro track suit who introduced himself as John Lyall. He was my first introduction to coaching. It was the best possible start. I've never forgotten him.

I almost never played for John because I was part of the deal that was going to bring Graham Paddon to West Ham from Norwich City. Ron Greenwood had agreed to pay them £180,000 and I was going to make up £60,000 of that. I reluctantly agreed to go because I was courting my future wife, Jeannette, at the time so could have done without the upheaval of leaving London. Then, unbelievably, the weekend before I was due to go, their manager Ron Saunders went to Manchester City so I felt like I would be walking into a hornet's nest at Norwich. It was an unsettling time but, John Bond came in as Norwich boss. He didn't want me and that suited me down to the ground. I ended up staying at West Ham and Greenwood put me on the sub's bench for a cup tie against Hereford United. It was Bobby Moore's final game for the club and I came on and played really well. I scored a header but it was disallowed because Clyde Best was offside – again! Then I went on a mazy run and equalised in the closing minutes. From that moment on, the whole atmosphere changed for me and I stayed at West Ham for another seven years.

One of the best memories I have of John came the week before the 1975 FA Cup final. I'd played in most of the matches in the earlier rounds but had picked up an injury in a league match against Newcastle. Alan Taylor had come in for the sixth-round match at Arsenal and couldn't do anything wrong, so John wasn't likely to drop him. I was only a sub for the two matches against Ipswich Town in the semi-final even though I had been starting in the league games. I had been in and out of the FA cup run but on the Monday before the final we were playing Arsenal in a league match, John called me into his room and said: "You're playing tonight and you're starting in the final on Saturday. Don't let me down!" We ended up beating Arsenal 1-0 and I remember putting both Peter Storey and Alan Ball up in the air. I must have been so high on the news that I was trying to win every ball by fair means or foul! John showed such faith in me and I don't think I let him down in the final.

The following year I picked up a hamstring injury and missed both legs of the European Cup Winners Cup quarter-final against Den Haag. By the time we played Eintracht Frankfurt in the semi-final, I was fit again but wasn't sure if

John was going to bring me back in. He called me over as I was getting off the bus after our training session in Germany and asked me how my leg was and I told him it was fine. He said: "Are you sure?" and I assured him that everything was fine. "Good," he replied. "Because you're in the team for Frankfurt." I ended up playing in both legs of the semi-final and the final itself.

He had so much belief in me, which is what I needed because I could get low on confidence sometimes. I think he knew what he was going to get from me. He had some good players but he probably felt I offered the team a bit more stability when we didn't have the ball. Jimmy Neighbour was a better player than me technically but I think John felt I gave him a better balance, which he liked. Even in 1980 when I had missed every match in the FA Cup run, he brought me back in for the semi-final against Everton. Unfortunately, I picked up another bad injury and missed out on both the semi-final replay and the final itself.

I was a good pro but lacked so much confidence it was untrue. That is where I think I lost Ron Greenwood's belief in me. He tried hard with me when I was a kid but I couldn't see it at the time and gradually he lost patience, whereas John knew me inside out and got the best out of me. There is a perfect example to illustrate this fundamental difference between Ron and John. We were playing Sheffield Wednesday at home. I was getting plenty of stick from the Chicken Run. I scored and we won 2-1 but the insults just didn't stop. After the game I called John into this little room near the tunnel and said: "That's my lot. I've had enough. I want away. Just find me anything and I'll go." John asked me if I was sure and then said: "Okay, come and see me tomorrow." The following day he said he had some interest from a team up north and that I should think about it. I wasn't keen on a move up there and he knew that only too well. The next day, he asked me if I'd made my mind up and then put his arm around me and said: "Now listen here, if you weren't a player you'd be in that Chicken Run handing out just as much stick as the rest of them. It doesn't matter what they say, I'm keeping you out on that pitch. Just get on with it." That is all I really wanted to hear, a vote of confidence in my ability. Ron couldn't give that.

John was terrific in the dressing room. He never raised his voice, although I can recall a match when he lost his temper. We played at QPR on Boxing Day 1980 and lost 0-3 on their artificial turf. In the dressing room afterwards John was so angry. He said: "If that is how you are going to play then I am going to get my cheque book out and make a few changes." He was swearing and was so angry but the following day we went out and beat Orient 2-1 at home. I scored and Paul Allen got one, too. Back then, making changes to a team was the last thing you wanted to hear because being

FA Cup jubiliation with Billy Bonds and Kevin Lock, May 3 1975

John Lyall by Patsy's side during the highs - Wedding Day celebrations in 1975

selected was the only thing that mattered. Nowadays, players are happy to pick up their money and never play but it wasn't like that back then. You always wanted to play and you always wanted to play well. It affected your mood when you weren't playing or your form dipped.

There is so much missing from John's approach to coaching in today's game; creative coaching, making the youngsters think about the game and showing so much belief in professional footballers. I think the FA has a lot to answer for. They rely too heavily on buzz words and formats. Young kids are now taking their coaching badges at University and going straight into the game ahead of pros, who have so much experience, which simply isn't being passed on to the extent it should be.

West Ham United was a fantastic club for coaching. Ron set up a great culture and John carried it on. In terms of the standard of coaching I don't think you can split them. They both had great strengths. John introduced me to coaching when I was 17 years-old. I used to help him coach the schoolboys at the ground and at Chadwell Heath. Later on, I had my own centre at Tilbury where I would coach on Tuesdays and Thursdays. Alan Curbishley and Paul Brush had similar places in Plaistow. It just seemed second nature to most West Ham players to get involved in coaching. Learn it, use it, and pass it on.

In terms of the 1976 European Cup Winners Cup final, I always preferred to play centre-midfield and I felt I wasn't as involved as I could have been in the first half when I was playing on the wide right, even though I had scored our first goal. John's changes at half-time were good for me and ones

with which I was happy. However, with hindsight, I suppose you can look back on it and say that it might have been better to bring in Kevin Lock once Frank Lampard had gone off injured and left McDowell in midfield where he had been playing well. It's easy to point the gun at John's decision but I've never looked back on it with any criticism. I know a few of the players were not happy with the changes but nobody was playing in a position, where they hadn't played before.

I had my ups and downs with John but all families do and there was never anything major. In fact one memory raises a laugh even now. John used to fine us five pounds if we were late for training. I travelled in from Upminster and was late to Chadwell Heath one day and was really cursing my luck. Then I noticed the side door had been left ajar so I sneaked in. John used to sit near the front entrance with Boycey, Mick McGiven and Tony Carr so I thought I had got away with it but when I looked up John was there holding up his hand showing all four fingers and thumb. All he said was: "Five. And I want it this morning!"

The real measure for me, which brings home what a great man John was, comes from when you talk to those players, who came into the club from up north. I had been there all my life so hadn't known any different but if you talk to Bobby Gould and David Cross about John Lyall they absolutely love the man.

He could handle most situations and I remember at Ronnie Boyce's testimonial all the players and their wives were invited into the boardroom. I don't recall it happening on any other occasion. Anyway, John saw my wife Jeannette who was working at Alfred Marks at the time. "Still working,

Jeannette?" John said. "John, on the money you're paying my old man, I'll be working well into my sixties!" she replied. Afterwards, John came over to me and said: "I've just been given a b******* by your wife!" Now, for her to talk to him like that and for him to take it in the right spirt underlines just how much respect there was between everyone at the club.

There were a few years between my final game for West Ham and my testimonial. It would have been better if it had happened sooner as I had already left the club and was Youth Team coach for Orient. But I came back for the match which was against Spurs. All credit to Peter Shreeve who brought the team that was going to play Anderlecht in the UEFA Cup final a few days later. It was very risky and would never happen today but they went on to win the Cup so it didn't have any adverse effect. Over 6,000 turned out for my match but I'd worked really hard to ensure my testimonial year helped me financially.

John was just like a footballing dad to me. I was so lucky because I absolutely loved football and found a bloke, who gave me an education in the playing and coaching of the game. I was lucky to find a mentor for something I was passionate about. I found a great one in John.

I remember a funny story when John brought Bill Nicholson to West Ham in a coaching role. Bill was obviously Spurs through and through and we were playing Ararat Erevan in the European run in 1976. John asked him to deliver the team talk. Bill said: "And when we get them back to White Hart Lane!"

John and myself didn't always see eye-to-eye. I remember when he dropped me for the FA Cup quarter-final against Aston Villa in 1980 and he brought in Geoff Pike. At the time, my mum was working in a little leather factory down in the East End and I was knocking out a few of their coats at about £20 a time. I was always selling something like music cassettes or TVs. At training one day John pulled me to one side and asked if I could get one of those coats for his son, Murray. "How much are they?" he asked. "£20." I replied and he asked me to get him a medium size. A little while later he told me he was dropping me for the Villa tie, so on the Monday after the match I went and saw him in his office. "What are you doing here?" he said. "I've already told you why I dropped you." Both Ron and John always said to the players that they wouldn't leave their office until they were happy. I told him I wasn't happy. We had a discussion about it but I still had the hump and when I walked out I told him that his leather jacket was now going to cost him £30!

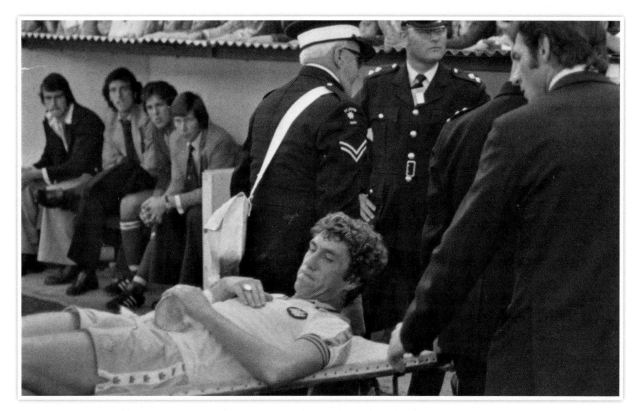

John Lyall by Patsy's side during the lows - stretchered off after another injury

"Well, you can keep it!" he shouted after me. The next day we had a laugh about it. "You Cockneys are all the same!" he laughed. I think he liked people with a good sense of humour.

I don't think John had his favourites. Some have said otherwise but I think he always picked his best side. He had great respect for Billy Bonds and Trevor Brooking and rightly so because they were great West Ham United players. Bill would sit in with John on Fridays and discuss team matters and the side he had picked for Saturday. I remember being in the dressing room a few days before the European final in 1976 when John walked in. Alan Taylor, who was in the bath, kept asking him over and over again if he was starting against Anderlecht but John just replying that he didn't know and that he hadn't decided on the starting line-up. "Wait and see," he kept saying but Alan was persistent: "But John, I need to know," he urged but John just wouldn't give in.

I had quite a few wingers to contend with during my time at West Ham. Ron Greenwood brought in Bertie Lutton while John signed Jimmy Neighbour and nurtured Paul Allen through the ranks so I always had someone competing for my position which wouldn't have happened if I'd been a favourite. The one signing that would have really bothered me was when they were within inches of signing Steve Coppell in the late 1970s. He came down and looked at houses and it was pretty much a done deal. I would have battled to keep my position, of course, but that would have been a tough one.

John demonstrated loyalty and commanded loyalty in return. I remember when I made my comeback after a broken leg and the same player tried to break it again. John was incandescent with rage. He drove me home that night after the match and I still had my kit on. We didn't have the Number 7 shirt for the next match because Jeannette was still washing it!

After I left West Ham I didn't see John for a while but we bumped into each other during a South East Counties evening and kept in touch. After West Ham sacked him, Terry Venables brought John to Spurs, where I was looking after the youth and reserve teams. He didn't stay long because he got the manager's job at Ipswich Town and, from then on, we spoke to each other virtually every week. We would talk about everything and, in particular, the development of young players. He was such a tremendous help to me and it was a great shock when he passed away. I was on my way to a youth game at Coventry when I heard the news and I just sat there in disbelief, very emotional. I called up Billy Bonds straight away and then just tried to come to terms with the news. It really upset me. It was a very difficult time.

I went to the private funeral in the morning, along with a few others such as Sir Alex Ferguson, Phil Parkes and Ray Stewart. It was a very touching affair. It may sound a bit strange but I wrote a letter addressed to John to thank him for all the help he had given me in my career. When Yvonne read it she said they were going to put the letter in the coffin with John because they felt the way I spoke about him was very touching. In the afternoon, we all went on to Ipswich Cathedral, where John received the tremendous turn out he deserved.

Pat Holland

Scoring against Chelsea at Stamford Bridge, November 1979

There was no shortage of comments about Patsy:
John loved Patsy for his honesty, endeavour and loyalty. That is the magic triangle of character traits for all the great West Ham United players. I view Pat Holland in the same way I look at Billy Bonds. He could play on the left, on the right, in the middle and he gave you everything. He loved playing for West Ham. Irreplaceable.
Mick McGiven

I had curly hair like Patsy, but mine was natural so I used to pull his leg that he'd permed his!
Rob Jenkins

He was my mate. We got on like a house on fire. He was a workaholic and so resilient to come back from all those injuries he suffered. What he has gone on to do in the coaching and scouting world is also testament to his hard work and great knowledge of the game. He learned a lot from Ron and John and has put it to good use and benefited many others, which is how the game should work.
John Ayris

He was a bits and pieces player when I was at the club. Pat loved to shimmy down the wing and like most wingers had his good games and his bad games, too. Derek Hales
Patsy was a proper old pro by the time I met him. He'd sit down with you and pass on his experience and advice.
Greg Campbell

Patsy gave me my nickname - 'Whizz.' We were playing up at Middlesbrough and the headline in the local paper was: 'Will the whizz kid play?' Patsy saw it and, since then, everyone from that era calls me 'Whizz'.
Alan Curbishley

Another unsung hero at West Ham. A proper West Ham man, a workaholic and an all-round gentleman. Keith Robson
I played in the game against Notts County, when he picked up his injury. Patsy was the bravest winger I ever saw.
Paul Brush

I loved Patsy. He had a lot of time for the young players at West Ham.
Phil Brignull

Always a good laugh in the dressing room and made training sessions really entertaining.
Alan Taylor

He worked his socks off for West Ham.
Alan Wooler

He's got my cup final shirt!
Bobby Gould

What a consistent character. Pat never changed from the moment I first met him in the 1970s. A super guy and I really like him. He works for Arsenal so our paths cross quite a bit.
Bill Green

I don't think I have met a nicer guy than Pat Holland. Always happy, but a little shy. He would turn red sometimes when people spoke to him. A real gentleman.
Yilmaz Orhan

Patsy invited me along to the opening of his wine bar, Hollands, which is directly opposite Shenfield station. He's a lovely guy and a bit of a practical joker. Once, I was taking a team photo when I noticed everyone was laughing. Patsy was wearing a ridiculous bobbly contraption on his head!
Steve Bacon

Patsy used to take the training on the forecourt outside the stadium on Tuesday and Thursday evening. I really enjoyed those sessions. Alan Dickens

A proper West Ham grafter. Patsy would run all day for you. A good laugh and a great fella to have in the dressing room.
Ron Boyce

Patsy was, and still is, a work horse. I think Frank Lampard was lucky to have him on his side of the pitch because he defended more than Frank!
Tommy Taylor

Patsy back at the Boleyn Ground during the last ever season, 2015-16

8 – GRAHAM PADDON

"The finest goal I scored in my career came up at Molineux. It was a blustery day and I dribbled the ball into their half. I thought: 'I'm going to have a go."

Born: Manchester, August 24, 1950 • **Died:** November 19, 2007 • **Position:** Midfield

Games played for John Lyall: 124 (1974-1976) • **Games played for West Ham United:** 152 (1973-76) • **Goals:** 15

Honours under John Lyall: 1975 FA Cup winner, 1975 FA Charity Shield runner-up, 1976 European Cup Winners Cup runner-up

First game under John Lyall: August 24, 1974 v Everton (h) L 2-3 (Bonds, McDowell – Royle, Latchford, Harvey). Att: 22,486

West Ham United: Day, Coleman, Lampard, Bonds, Taylor T, Lock, Holland, Paddon, Gould, McDowell, Best.

Everton: Lawson, Darracott, Seargeant, Clements, Lyons, Hurst, Buckley, Harvey, Royle, Latchford, Connolly.* Sub: Pearson.

Graham Charles Paddon was signed by Ron Greenwood for £170,000 from Norwich City. The three years he spent at Upton Park – 1973-76 - yielded an FA Cup winners medal and a European Cup Winners Cup runners-up medal.

Manchester-born Paddon made 147 appearances for West Ham United. He left a positive impression on everyone who saw him play. 'Stylish,' 'Exceptional,' 'Talented,' and 'Magnificent' are the most-used adjectives when describing Paddon's midfield capabilities.

He scored in 14 different matches for the Hammers and ended up on the winning side in 13 of them. Ironically, the exception came in the away leg against Eintracht Frankfurt, which many consider to be his best goal for the club.

In 2006, I interviewed Graham for an article celebrating the 40 year anniversary of the European Cup Winners' Cup final against Anderlecht. During our telephone conversation, he described his goal against Eintracht Frankfurt on March 31, 1976: "Before the game, Bobby Ferguson bet me a bottle of whisky that I wouldn't score. After eight minutes I was wheeling away having put us ahead. To his credit, Fergy paid up." During that interview, Graham also described a goal he scored against Wolverhampton Wanderers on September 27, 1975: "The finest goal I scored in my career came up at Molineaux. It was a blustery day and I dribbled the ball into their half. I thought: 'I'm going to have a go,' and the ball flew into

the net. My good friend, Willie Carr, was in the Wolves team that day and I've enjoyed reminding him of it down the years!"

Graham lived for football and, when he was no longer involved, struggled to cope with life outside of the game. On November 19, 2007 he suffered a fatal heart attack in his bed. He was 57.

In 2014, Heather Paddon, Graham's daughter, created a very touching film tribute to her father. (https://vimeo.

Collecting an Evening Standard Player of the month award from Ron Greenwood and John Lyall, November 1974

Wielding his left foot against Coventry City at Upton Park, November 1975

com/98456323). His fellow midfield maestro, Trevor Brooking, features in it.

Following are memories of Graham and photos from his time at West Ham United:

My dad's years at West Ham were the best years of his life. He embraced being in the East End, respected the people and they really warmed to him. He was very close to Frank Lampard, Keith Robson Pat Holland and Billy Jennings.
Guy Paddon

Graham was a smashing bloke and had a lovely left foot. West Ham's midfield was all the better for it. Both Graham and Trevor Brooking were like poetry on the pitch. The only trouble was neither of them wanted to defend, which put more pressure on me in central defence! Whenever I had the ball I would just give it to Graham or Trevor and let them get on with it.
Tommy Taylor

In 2006, Graham attended the reunion of West Ham's cup winning teams at the Britannia International hotel in London's Docklands. He chatted with John Lyall that evening but, sadly, just like John, it was Graham's last public appearance in a West Ham environment.
Tony Gale

He was a proper West Ham player. Always wanted to bring it down and play football. He was very skilful and he looked the part. Left-footed players always look more elegant than right-footed-players.
John Ayris

He joined West Ham shortly after me. He was unfortunate to have played in an era of so many outstanding midfield talents. Graham was a stylish player. He could create, he could tackle

and had a magnificent left foot. A very talented player.
Mick McGiven

Graham was a good friend and we'd go out socialising with Keith Robson and Frank Lampard.
Billy Jennings

Graham was a good looking guy. Very quiet but loved a beer and a bird.
Rob Jenkins

An unsung hero. He had fantastic ability and was such a workhorse. He was absolutely brilliant. He scored one of the best goals I've ever seen, against Eintracht Frankfurt out in Germany. It was the semi-final of the European Cup Winners' Cup which was the perfect stage for Graham's talents. He hit it from miles out and it just flew in. What a player!
Keith Robson

I played with Graham at West Ham United and Norwich City. He was very experienced, very dedicated and an outstanding player.
Alan Taylor

He loved the game and that showed in the way he played.
Alan Wooler

He was a very good player and could have been even better. I saw him a lot after our playing careers were over. He was scouting and coaching at Portsmouth and other places. What a shock that was when I heard the news that he had died.
Bill Green

Behind Billy Bonds prior to the European Cup Winners' Cup final against Anderlecht at the Heysel Stadium, May 1976

9 – BOBBY GOULD

"After I won the FA Cup with Wimbledon in 1988, John sent me a telegram. It read: "Start playing football!"

Born: Coventry, June 12, 1946 • **Position:** Striker • **Games played for John Lyall:** 45 (1974-75)

Games played for West Ham United: 62 (1973-75) • **Goals:** 19

Honours under John Lyall: Substitute in 1975 FA Cup final, 1975 FA Charity Shield runner-up

First game under John Lyall: August 24, 1974 v Everton (h) L 2-3 (Bonds, McDowell – Royle, Latchford, Harvey). Att: 22,486

West Ham United: Day, Coleman, Lampard, Bonds, Taylor T, Lock, Holland, Paddon, Gould, McDowell, Best.

Everton: Lawson, Darracott, Seargeant, Clements, Lyons, Hurst, Buckley, Harvey, Royle, Latchford, Connolly.* Sub: Pearson.

Robert Hewitt 'Bobby' Gould scored the first hat-trick of the John Lyall era – against Tranmere Rovers - in September 1974. The Daily Mirror awarded him the Player of the Month award for September, 1974 – Lyall's first full month in charge. He is also one of the very few Hammers to have played football in the league, FA Cup, League Cup, European competition and the Charity Shield.

Ironically, the 1975 FA Cup final, when Gould was left on the bench as a frustrated unused substitute, has come to define his time at West Ham United: *"I hold a record in football as the only player to have won two FA Cup medals without getting on the field of play – the first with West Ham in 1975 and the second as manager of Wimbledon in 1988"*

After an illustrious career as both a player and manager, Gould entered the world of media and is best remembered as, 'The Gouldfather,' on talkSPORT's Friday night radio show, The Sports Bar, with Andy Goldstein. In 2016 he retired from the show. *"I'm a free spirit nowadays"* jokes Bobby.

Having been signed by Ron Greenwood and coached by John Lyall, Bobby has the utmost respect for both men. Like so many from that era, he is disillusioned by the current incarnation of the great game: *"I'm disappointed with the modern game because the ball goes sideways. I call it crab football. How can you have 40 passes but not have a shot on goal? John Lyall would never have tolerated that at West*

Ham. It's not for me, either."

In September 2017, Gould attended a reunion of John Lyall's 1975 FA Cup winning team at the London Bridge Hilton Hotel. *"What a terrific night! Great to see the players and the fans still passionate about that special time in the club's history."*

Scaling the heights against Newcastle United, February 1975

Getting kitted out for Wembley in 1975

Following are Gouldy's recollections of John Lyall:

I thought John was very brave to take over from Ron Greenwood. They were a very big pair of boots to fill and it could have all gone horribly wrong. I'd been signed by Ron for £80,000 but I learned a lot from John. I was 28-years-old when I joined West Ham United. I'd been a professional for 10 years so I couldn't believe my luck when I was got the chance to play for West Ham United. How could I turn it down? When I got home, my wife Marjorie asked me about the wages but I honestly didn't know because they hadn't been discussed!

I didn't realise there was so much more for me to learn until I started training with Ron and John. One of the things John liked about me was that I was so willing to learn at 28. If I'd signed for West Ham as a 20-year old I have no doubt that I would have played for England. The technical coaching at West Ham was the best in the game.

It was a dramatic moment when Ron handed over the reins to John. We had just been well beaten by Manchester City at Maine Road. Ron was in the dressing room but he started walking towards the door as he was talking to us: "I'm going to hand over to John now," he said. We were all a bit confused. Before he walked out he said: "John will be manager of West Ham from this point on." We were completely gobsmacked and were looking at each other in disbelief. From that point on, Ron was always in the background and left John to diligently apply his own interpretation of the game. John became successful in his own right.

John had a storming first season and at the end of it I found

myself sitting on the bench at Wembley for the 1975 FA Cup final. We were cruising at 2-0 and I desperately wanted to get on, but time was running out. I started the worst coughing fit any man has ever had. I was desperate for John to look round so I could urge him to put me on for five minutes. He could be very stubborn and so I never got my chance. I did get a medal but it's not the same if you don't play.

Ironically, John picked me for the Charity Shield against Derby County but ended up substituting me! It was funny because he took off both me and Billy Jennings and we went straight down the tunnel and jumped in the bath. Then it occurred to us that we'd have to collect our medals, so we quickly got changed and ran back out!

I scored my fair share of goals for West Ham including a hat-trick against Tranmere Rovers. John was mad at me that night because the third goal came from a penalty which Billy Bonds normally took. The thought of glory got the better of me and I grabbed the ball from Bill and told him I was going for my hat-trick. I looked across and I could see John pointing at me and shouting: "Don't let him take it!" I just turned on a sixpence, ran up and slotted it home. I've still got that ball to this day.

John took me out to Ararat Erevan to play in the European Cup Winners' Cup and I roomed with Trevor Brooking. In the middle of the night he jumped out of bed because it was full of cockroaches. His nickname was Boogaloo but it was Bugaloo that night! There was nothing glamorous about that European tour.

All the players at West Ham had great technical ability and that was drummed into them every day by John and

In the thick of things against Manchester United, October 1975

his coaching staff. Captain Bonzo was immense and Trevor Brooking's ability with the ball was outstanding. It was a great time to be at the club. There were a lot of great characters. I took Keith Robson under my wing and also enjoyed being around 'Jilly Jennings' and Mick – 'Coco the Clown' – McGiven. The fans were great as well. The Chicken Run was a very special place. I played down the wing in front of them and loved every minute of it.

Towards the end of my playing career John offered me an opportunity to join the coaching staff at West Ham. Ron had taken the England job and I had left West Ham and returned to Wolves for a couple of seasons. John saw an opportunity and invited me to be part of his coaching team. I turned him down because I wanted to carry on playing and, after leaving Wolves, had spells at both Bristol Rovers and Hereford United. It was probably the wrong decision and who knows what could have been achieved if I'd been part of John's team? I had a lovely relationship with him and, when I entered management, would call up John because he was a soothing influence and good at providing perspective. We also had something in common – we both had a nasty streak in us.

In my own management career I told everyone that if they could play one-touch football like West Ham, they could play anywhere in the world of football. Mark Hughes was the best one-touch player I ever coached, when I was in charge of Wales. John Lyall used to say that the art of one-touch football was to play the ball at the very last second.
Bobby Gould

He didn't have great technical ability but he worked so hard for the team and found so much space in the box.
Ron Boyce

He always slaughters me whenever we see each other. No matter who is around he always shouts out that I have his Number 11 shirt from the 1975 FA Cup final.
Pat Holland

Gouldy was a character. He sold the odd car here and there and I agreed to buy one. Then, all of a sudden, I'd gambled all my money away, so that was that!
Keith Robson

He had a great sense of humour and it was terrific to see him back at Upton Park during the final season. He is as bubbly as ever and a super guy.
Alan Taylor

A tough and hardened player and a tough and hardened coach.
Alan Wooler

Along with Billy Jennings, Bobby was one of the best headers of the ball at the club. His timing was excellent.
Yilmaz Orhan

He was coming to the end of his playing career when he joined us, but he was so energetic and hard working. He was Mr Perpetual Motion. He worked the flanks so well and always got in the box and amongst the goals.
Mick McGiven

I absolutely loved Gouldy. He was a tremendous character. Larger than life and gave 100%. A magic guy. The great Bill Shankly of Liverpool said he couldn't trap a bag of cement and Bobby still laughs about it today.
Rob Jenkins

With his 1975 FA Cup final shirt

10 – JOHN McDOWELL

"Wally St Pier spotted me, Ron Green-wood signed me and John Lyall coached me. That was my introduction to West Ham United and it was a club renowned for giving youngsters a chance. Ron dreamed about idealistic football. John lived in the real world."

Born: East Ham, London, September 7, 1951 • **Position:** Right-back • **Games played for John Lyall:** 144 (1974-1979)

Games played for West Ham United: 303 (1970-79)

Honours under John Lyall: 1975 FA Cup winner, 1975 FA Charity Shield runner-up, 1976 European Cup Winners Cup runner-up-

First game under John Lyall: August 24, 1974 v Everton (h) L 2-3 (Bonds, McDowell – Royle, Latchford, Harvey). Att: 22,486

West Ham United: Day, Coleman, Lampard, Bonds, Taylor T, Lock, Holland, Paddon, Gould, McDowell, Best.

Everton: Lawson, Darracott, Seargeant, Clements, Lyons, Hurst, Buckley, Harvey, Royle, Latchford, Connolly.* Sub: Pearson.

John Alfred McDowell had already made over 150 appearances under Ron Greenwood by the time John Lyall took over first team responsibilities at West Ham United. East Ham-born, McDowell, had taken the path of Shaftesbury primary school, Sandringham Road secondary school as well as playing for both Newham and Essex before Wally St Pier secured his signature for the Hammers in 1967.

McDowell's highs and lows at West Ham all occurred while Lyall was at the helm. His performance in the 1975 FA Cup final was exemplary, while the events of the European Cup Winners Cup final the following year continue to torment. One of only 89 Hammers to have played with Bobby Moore, one of only 30 Hammers to have won the FA Cup and one of only 23 Hammers to play in a major European final, John McDowell, easily secures his place in the illustrious chapter of West Ham United's history.

After leaving West Ham in 1979, spells at both Norwich City as a player and Bristol Rovers as a coach were followed by a lengthy stint as a Sales Director. In 2002, John and his wife, Carol, moved to Tenerife where they ran an English supermarket in Playa de las Americas.

Nowadays, John splits his time between England and Spain and his five children have ensured plenty of grand-parenting responsibilities. Like many ex-pros from his era, John has had two hip operations and doesn't spend as much time on the golf course as he would like.

In September 2017, McDowell attended a reunion of the 1975 FA Cup final team at the London Bridge Hilton Hotel. It was his first public appearance in a West Ham setting for some time and the fans welcomed back one of their cup heroes.

Talking West Ham with John is always thought provoking and discussing John Lyall was no exception:

When John took over the first team in 1974 I felt we had a close bond. Our playing careers were quite similar in that we both got into West Ham United's first team quite young. He was a left-back while I was a right-back and we both gained England Youth caps. Sadly, we both had our careers curtailed by knee injuries, too.

By all accounts John was quite a hard, aggressive player so I felt we had a lot in common. He liked the physical side of the game and didn't take a dim view when I stopped Les Barrett going clear in the 1975 FA Cup final. Don't get me wrong, John still wanted to see nice football and pretty patterns of play but, like Ron Greenwood before him, he knew that everything started with the pass. Trevor Brooking could never have received the ball sideways-on if the ball hadn't been perfectly passed on the blind side of the player marking him.

I am probably the one West Ham United player who has lived closest to the Boleyn Ground in the entire history of the club, certainly if you draw a straight line from Plashet Grove, where I grew up. Until I could afford my first car – a red Austin 1100 which was a pile of crap! – I used to rely on old Jimmy Barrett's mini-bus which picked us up at the ground and took us to Chadwell Heath. Jim was hilarious, a real character.

When I first went to West Ham as an apprentice in 1967 John was in charge of all the juniors and the Youth team. In the late 1960s, all training sessions were dictated by Ron. The West Ham way was Ron Greenwood's way and we spent hours and hours passing the ball backwards and forwards, from 10-yards, 15-yards, 20-yards, 30-yards and so on. Left foot, right foot, left foot, right foot, it had to be delivered properly, not too high and with just the right amount of weight. It was all about muscle memory. Ron would be patrolling Chadwell Heath saying: "That's not right, that's not right." You just kept doing it over and over again. John was seeing this every day and absorbing everything. Once the rhythm set in, it was like poetry in motion. In the end, I could collect the ball from our keeper Bobby Ferguson or Peter Grotier, run a few steps and without even looking, clip the ball in knowing that it would land at Geoff Hurst's feet. I remember playing Sheffield United, who were newly promoted and top of the league. It was a League Cup quarter-final and we won 5-0. For twenty minutes in that game we were unplayable and probably produced the best football I can remember being involved in for any team. We absolutely tore them to bits. I can remember playing games in the first team where every player was home grown and that was in the highest division of the English league. Nowadays, you're lucky to get one.

The art of a good manager as far as I'm concerned is one who looks at his players' strengths and weaknesses and creates a system to get the best out of them. Not the other way round where you have a system and you try and fit players into it.

I always played to win and all this nonsense about it's the taking part that's important doesn't wash with me. As much as I wanted to win, something happened early on in my time at West Ham which, on reflection, partly explains why we never challenged for the title.

I can't remember the game but their striker was clean through on goal when I pulled him back and conceded a free kick. I picked up a booking but as Robbie Savage would say: "I took one for the team." Afterwards, Ron was livid and pulled me to one side and said I would never play for West Ham United again if I ever repeated that behaviour. I was never a malicious player and certainly wouldn't go out with the intention of causing physical harm to any player, but I saw nothing wrong with pulling someone back, tripping them up or spinning them around if it helped to prevent a goal. Those things are quickly forgotten and it is the result that counts, but Ron would never support such a view.

John and I had our rows. After a game, if we had lost or I had played badly I was a nightmare. I wouldn't listen to anyone. If someone tried to dig me out for something that had happened I would just go for them. I was so wound-up, anything could trigger my temper. It didn't even matter if it was my fault or not. It wasn't anything physical but I would forcefully defend my position. John knew it was pointless trying to communicate with me after a game and usually left me alone but called me into his office on the Monday to explain his take on things. I was the same before the game, I just wanted to be left alone so that I could sit on my own with my head in my hands and visualise the first five minutes of the game. When the players saw me like that they knew not to come near me. Once I'd thought about the player I was marking and how I was going to play against him, I was alright and could get on with things. Having said that I was one of those players who would have benefited from the level of analysis we have in today's game. Sadly, that was lacking back then. Personally, I got a lot more of that at Norwich City where Mel Machin and John Sainty were part of John Bond's coaching staff. Mel, who had been a defender himself, gave me some very good advice about my game.

The best goal I scored for West Ham was against Newcastle United in 1979. I actually got two that day, both with my left foot. The second one was the best, a half-volley from about 25-yards which just flew into the bottom right corner at the North Bank end. It stayed about a foot or so off the ground the whole time. It was the sweetest ball I think I ever struck. They showed it on The Big Match the following day.

People say that I never went as far in the game as I should

Scoring against Newcastle United at The Boleyn Ground, March 1979

have done and I don't know whether they mean that because of my injury or something else. I would say 60% was due to my injury, 20% was down to the management not giving me the correct advice to fulfil my potential and the other 20% was down to me. I watch old West Ham games now and notice that my positional sense could have been better. I could have got closer to the winger but I cannot recall anyone at West Ham - whether it was Mooro, Ron or John - turning round to me and making me aware of that. I may have a selective memory, of course, but Ron and John addressed all the defenders in training rather than working on the strengths and weaknesses of the individual.

I think I got quite close to earning an England cap. If Alf Ramsey had stayed in the England job I am fairly certain I would have got one but Don Revie came in and he didn't fancy me. I remember he called 40 players to Lilleshall and I was one of them. Trevor Brooking went, Billy Bonds went, Tommy Taylor, Kevin Lock and I'm fairly certain Graham Paddon went, too. Anyway, he didn't pick me and my old adversary, Steve Whitworth, took the right back shirt instead. Later on I heard that Revie never felt that I got close enough to wingers but that was my way. I always felt I had enough pace to stop most wingers regardless of how closely I was marking them, with the exception of Steve Kindon of Burnley of course! His pace was unreal.

I was unhappy with the way it ended for me at West Ham. I had picked up an injury to my right knee and they couldn't find out what was wrong with it. It had happened during a pre-season friendly out in Spain in 1976. I can remember it as clear as day. The winger was coming at me with the ball so I showed him the line and he went for it. I slid in and took the

Getting the better of Arsenal's Alan Ball at Highbury

ball from him but he landed in a heap on my knee. At the age of 25 I was never going to be the same player again. There were no MRI scans in those days and an X-ray didn't show much at all. I could run, I could turn but I couldn't accelerate to full power. My knee just wasn't coming through quickly enough. Behind the knee is the Popliteus muscle and I've heard that this is vital when trying to reach 90% or 100% running capacity. Mine had been completely torn away. I was out for a year and a lot of soul-searching, blood, sweat and tears went into fighting my way back to full fitness. I then had to have my cartilage removed which delayed my return even further and I feel that I never made it back to the type of player I had been between, say, 1973-76.

My ideal situation at West Ham would have been for me not to have got injured and perhaps, just as important, Frank Lampard not to get injured in the 1976 European Cup Winners Cup final. Furthermore, I would like to have had a Testimonial and stayed at the club for the 1980 FA Cup final. The absolute utopia would have been Alf Ramsey staying on as England manager and giving me a few England caps, too. In fact, Ron may well have done the same had I not been injured when he took over the national side in 1978. We'll never know, will we? I probably didn't do my England chances any good in that I liked to play in different positions. My preferred position, believe it or not, was midfield.

In terms of John's strengths, he was West Ham United through and through and I'm sure that everything he did had the best intentions for the club at heart.

In terms of weaknesses, I'm not sure whether he was he tactically astute. I'm not sure the game was played that

One of only 30 Hammers ever to win the FA Cup

way in those days. I can't remember too much in terms of systems, the way we were going to play and what we were going to do. Yeah, we had certain things – if we were playing Arsenal it was my job to mark Alan Ball and if we were playing Spurs it was my job to mark Martin Peters – but John probably wasn't as innovative as Ron Greenwood but, then again, I don't think many people were.

I certainly feel John got it badly wrong in the European Cup Winners Cup final in 1976. His decision not to replace Frank Lampard with Kevin Lock – a left footed defender for a left footed defender – cost us the match in my opinion. To bring on Alan Taylor and move three other players to accommodate him didn't make any sense at all. We were still in that game and had been causing Anderlecht a lot of problems. We were completely over-run after that substitution. If John made all those changes at half-time in Brussels for the good of the team, then I respect him for that. But, if he made those switches to accommodate a player with whom he had a prior agreement then I withdraw my respect. John Lyall made the wrong decision in that final and no one will convince me otherwise. His decision was not the best thing for the team. Let's win the game first and bring on anyone who you want to receive a medal with a couple of minutes to go. If he thought Alan Taylor was the best person to play, why didn't he start with him? Locky had played in Frank's position numerous times and although he wasn't the quickest he did have other attributes. If you look at the first half, Anderlecht were not causing us any problems down our left side. The irony is that if Frank had been injured after 20 minutes I think John would have brought on Locky because there would not have been sufficient time to communicate all the information to change four positions. The fact it happened on the stroke of half time gave John the opportunity to make those dramatic, ill-fated, changes.

It was a watershed in my relationship with John and I think he only really had his own team after he'd moved me, Tommy Taylor and Kevin Lock on. Along with Mervyn Day, we were the last remnants from the Greenwood era, apart from Trevor, Frank and Bill of course.
John McDowell

Following are various comments from John's former team-mates and other notable personalities from the John Lyall era:

I remember talking to John Lyall about Johnny Mac and he thought he could have been a top, top player. He was a creative player. Sadly, we were playing in Spain against Santander in a pre-season friendly and I played a ball to him but I left it short and their player went right through him and injured his knee. He was never really the same after that.
Pat Holland

I liked John and played with him at Norwich City as well. If he had anything to say he would never hold back. He played the game the right way, he took a few risks but he was a very good player.
Keith Robson

Johnny Mac was an honest player but his form could blow hot and cold. We lived near each other in Hornchurch.
Ron Boyce

John loved his golf and both he and Tommy Taylor would get the golf balls out at Chadwell Heath and practice their swing.
Alan Taylor

A very good attacking player who had everything to be an England international.
Mick McGiven

I tell you now. You did not want to beat John McDowell. You would lose your legs!
Yilmaz Orhan

I used to kick about with Johnny Mac, Tommy T and Patsy the monkey! All great lads.
Kevin Lock

John should have played for England, not just once but all the time. A great full-back.
Tommy Taylor

Johnny Mac holding up the 1976 European Cup Winner's Cup final programme

11 - CLYDE BEST

"John was a great guy. He was very fair to everybody and he tried hard to ensure his players played the game the right way. I thought he was a brilliant teacher because he taught his players the basics."

Born: Somerset, Bermuda, February 24, 1951 • **Position:** Striker • **Games played for John Lyall:** 28 (1974-76)

Games played for West Ham United: 221 (1969-76) • **Goals:** 58 (Joint 24th with Stanley Earle on the all-time list)

First game under John Lyall: August 24, 1974 v Everton (h) L 2-3 (Bonds, McDowell – Royle, Latchford, Harvey) Att: 22,486

West Ham United: Day, Coleman, Lampard, Bonds, Taylor T, Lock, Holland, Paddon, Gould, McDowell, **Best.**

Everton: Lawson, Darracott, Seargeant, Clements, Lyons, Hurst, Buckley, Harvey, Royle, Latchford, Connolly.* Sub: Pearson.*

Clyde Cyril Best was signed by Ron Greenwood in August 1969 and became one of the most popular characters in West Ham United's history. He spent seven years at the club and scored 58 goals, which keeps him comfortably ahead of 21st century strikers such as Paolo Di Canio (50), Jermain Defoe (41) and Bobby Zamora (40).

Following his time at Upton Park, Clyde took his talents overseas, first in the North America Soccer League with both Tampa Bay Rowdies and Portland Timbers, and then to Holland, where he spent a season with Feyenoord. He played out his career in America's Indoor Soccer League, before eventually hanging up his boots in 1984.

In December 2016, Clyde visited these shores from his native Bermuda. The purpose of his return to his spiritual home in London's East End, was to launch his Autobiography titled: The Acid Test. It is a thrilling occasion when Clyde is in town. He always takes the time to visit so many of the people from his West Ham days - Carol Charles (wife of John 'Charlo' Charles), Rita (Clive and Charlo's sister) and his good friend Alan Olsen, too.

Today, Clyde is a man of leisure: *"I've retired from working at the Westgate Correctional Facility in Hamilton. I'm 66 now so spend my days watching sports and going out when I want to. I try not to do too much these days but hope to get over to West Ham and see everyone in the not too distant future."*
Following are his reflections of John Lyall:

John was a great guy. He was very fair to everybody and he tried hard to ensure his players played the game the right way. I thought he was a brilliant teacher because he taught his players the basics. John would have been disappointed not to win the league and I always tell people that the quick, open, attacking football that West Ham played in those days, would be well suited to today's game. I am in no doubt that under today's rules and conditions, West Ham would have won the league. I am convinced of that.

I was disappointed that John didn't pick me to be more involved in the 1975 FA Cup final run. In the end, I only played in the two matches against Swindon Town in the fourth round. We drew at home and beat them in the replay at the County Ground. At the time, John was deciding between Patsy Holland, Bobby Gould and myself. In the replay we won 2-1 and I set up the winner for Patsy which was one of the great ironies during my stay at West Ham. It helped get us through to the next round but I never played another game in that great cup run. Patsy, of course, went on to play a key part in the final. There were only 12 players allowed to be involved in the final so it was a lot different from today with so many more substitutes.

The first thing John did when he became manager was to sign Billy Jennings, Keith Robson and Alan Taylor – three strikers! I think he was trying to send me a message! It didn't bother me at all because there is no point playing football if you are going to be afraid of someone taking your place. That means you are not willing to fight for it. No fight, no

Clyde had played with the best before John Lyall was appointed manager. - L-R Mordechai Spiegler, Bobby Moore, Clyde, Geoff Hurst and Jimmy Greaves

point. I knew I had to work harder and show more application to ensure I earned my place in the team. I recognised the territory anyway because a few years earlier, Ron Greenwood had brought in Jimmy Greaves, Pop Robson and Ted MacDougall, so I'd been fighting for my place all along.

John was happy for me to stay at West Ham but I wanted to go. I thought there was an excellent opportunity for me to play in the United States of America and to help progress the game over there. It felt like the right time to leave. I had offers from other clubs in England, but I didn't want to play for anyone else. West Ham was my team and will always be my team.

I also had a season playing for Feyenoord in Holland and Dutch football at the time was probably the best in the world. It hurts me to see how much it has fallen from grace these days. I remember coming back to West Ham and sitting with John in his office and describing how club's out there trained twice every day and not once which was the norm for most clubs in England.

I still watch every West Ham game from my home in Bermuda. It was great to see them beat Spurs in the League Cup, coming from 0-2 down to win. Not many teams have done that against a very good Tottenham side. I still think the team lacks a bit of heart. That's why I loved Billy Bonds, because he was all heart and brim full of passion. Any West Ham team needs someone like him out there.

I've never seen a West Ham team lay down like the one which lost at home to Brighton 0-3. Never in my whole life. When their midfielder, Jose Izquierdo, cut in and scored that goal from distance I could hear John Lyall's voice: "Why did you let him come inside on his stronger foot? You know that

his left foot is weaker, so push him to the outside." Both Ron and John would have been disgusted by that because it is such an elementary part of defending. They devoted their lives to the basics of the great game.

I scored 58 goals for the first team but the one which gives me the most pleasure came when I scored for the 'A' team at Chadwell Heath. John Lyall was the coach and I hadn't been at the club that long. Keith Pointer played the ball in to me and I back-heeled it over the defender's head, ran around him, and volleyed it into the net with venom. John said it was the best goal he'd ever seen in his life. Even the players stopped and clapped! That is the goal which gave me the most pleasure.

Ernie Gregory taught me not to show any mercy towards goalkeepers. In training he would stand in the goal and shout at me to knock him over. He would taunt me so I would kick the wind out of that ball!

John was a fantastic person and I'm glad that I had the chance to have him as part of my football career. He was a great coach and I learned a lot from him. Men like Ron Greenwood and John Lyall are sorely missed in today's game. There are not many with football brains like they had. It was a treat to be in their company and at a club like West Ham, which had great players. Martin Peters, Geoff Hurst, Bobby Moore, Trevor Brooking, Billy Bonds... the list goes on. If I had to do it all over again, West Ham would still be my club.
Clyde Best

Some player comments about Clyde:

Clyde would be worth a fortune in today's game. He could

John Lyall knew he had a target man at his disposal - Clyde challenges Chelsea's John Phillips at The Boleyn Ground, March 1974

Clyde taking on future West Ham United coach, Frank Burrows of Swindon Town. FA Cup 4th round, January 1975

hold it up, beat players on the floor and in the air. He could out-muscle anyone and scored tap-ins and bullets from 25-yards. The only thing he lacked was stamina. Good old Clyde!
Mick McGiven

We called him the 'Honey Monster' because of his imposing physique. He always played the ball with the outside of his foot and no one could get near him.
Tommy Taylor

Clyde had a lot to contend with when he first came over. He was a strong, powerful lad and a good finisher. He overcame all the difficulties and became a fan favourite. His name will live long in the club's history.
Ron Boyce

West Ham thought they had a world beater in Clyde and he was a good player and did well for West Ham - but he was too nice. He needed to be angry to really produce his fine talent.
John Ayris

I made my debut up front with Besty. He was a great lad and we roomed together a couple of times. I would love to see him again.
Billy Jennings

If you gave him a chance, he would score. That was Besty. I felt sorry for him when we were sitting next to each other in the stands at Wembley for the 1975 FA Cup final, because

he'd played in an earlier round.
Keith Robson

It is always lovely to see Clyde when he visits from Bermuda. I learned a lot from him about the role of a striker and I've got a lot of time for him.
Alan Taylor

When he was in full flight it was hard to stop him. You wouldn't want to get in this way. He was very sharp for his size.
Yilmaz Orhan

Clyde was so funny during pre-season training. He'd wear black bin liners and cotton wool to help sweat off the pounds during the runs around Epping Forest. Then he'd call a taxi at the first phone box!
Alan Wooler

One of life's nice guys. A top bloke. He did really well, but then suffered with his confidence a bit. After he left West Ham our paths crossed in America where he was playing for the Portland Timbers and I had a spell with Team Hawaii. We saw each other at Peter Brabrook's funeral in December 2016. It was so good to catch up with him.
Pat Holland

Visiting from Bermuda to launch his Autobiography - 'The Acid Test,' December, 2016

12 – JOHN AYRIS

"I'm sure he had his favourites but he made you feel that you were a favourite."

Born: January 8, 1953, Wapping, London • **Position:** Right-wing • **Games played for John Lyall:** 21 (1974-76)

Games played for West Ham United: 69 (1970-76) • **Goals:** 2

First game under John Lyall: August 31, 1974 v Newcastle United (a) L0-2 (Tudor, MacDonald) Att: 30,780

Newcastle United: McFaul, Craig D, Clark, McDermott, Keeley, Howard, Burns, Nattrass, MacDonald, Tudor, Hibbitt.

West Ham United: Day, Coleman, Lampard, Bonds, Taylor T, Lock, Holland, Paddon, Gould*, McDowell, Best. Sub: **Ayris.***.

John Patrick Ayris is a member of a quirky, four-man, club of West Ham United wingers, all of whom grew up in the borough of Tower Hamlets. The others include Harry Redknapp and Pat Holland (both Poplar boys) and Stepney-born Joe Durrell, a life-long friend.

John is another to have been signed by Ron Greenwood and coached by John Lyall. By the time Lyall took over first team duties, in August 1974, the two Johns had known each other for several years and had developed a great mutual respect. John will be forever associated with a career-damaging challenge from Ron 'Chopper' Harris of Chelsea in September 1971. Enough time has passed for John to apply his sparkling wit to the memory, and when asked if he has ever discussed the incident with the Chelsea hard man, he replied: "I sent him a Christmas card once, asking for my lung back!"

John works at South Woodham Ferrers Sports Centre in Chelmsford and occasionally arranges mini West Ham reunions for his former teammates at youth, reserve and first team level. Both, The Sutton Arms in Hornchurch and Nathans Pie and Mash shop in Barking Road, are proving to be popular venues. His former team mates, Kevin Lock, Joe Durrell, Barry Barnes, Ray Fulton, John Watson and Jimmy Brown catch up on the old days, along with former club physio, Rob Jenkins, too. Long may it continue!

Following are his reflections of John Lyall:

I first met John when I joined West Ham as a 14-year-old schoolboy. I was invited along to a training session on the forecourt at the ground and I spotted him wearing a claret track suit with the biggest quiff in the world! He became my Youth team manager and then, after 1974, my first team manager.

He was one of the nicest men I have ever met. He was very friendly, knew what he was talking about and was very encouraging with the youngsters. He was Youth team coach when I joined, and looked after what I lovingly refer to as: 'the Cockney Mafia.' – Me, Joe Durrell, John Watson, Patsy Holland and Barry Barnes. So, very early on in my friendship with John, he had to put up with a lot of East End mischief and mickey takers, but he took it all in his stride.

John visited my mum and dad in Wapping to get me to sign for West Ham. My dad, John, was a Docker and my mum, Mary was a barmaid: "She earned the money in The White Swan at one end of Wapping High Street and he'd be lose it in the betting shop at the other end!"

I was very fortunate to have John Lyall as my first real coach in the youth team at West Ham. He had this ability to bring out the best in people. I think he liked wingers, especially young wingers with a bit of gumption. John played left-back in his day and faced quite a few quick and tricky wingers, so he had first-hand experience on what made a good one.

His training sessions were fantastic. It was mainly all with the ball. I remember when I left West Ham and went to Wimbledon, it was three weeks before I even saw a ball! Everything made sense with John. He explained the reason behind everything he was trying to achieve. He wouldn't just say this is what I want you to do. He would say this is what I want you to do because... and then go on to explain the detail and importance.

John's man-management skills gave him the edge over Ron Greenwood. Maybe this was because he was a bit younger and associated better with the younger generation. In the dressing room he was terrific. He could command your attention without having to shout or remonstrate. He usually had something worthwhile to listen to. The senior pros at the club were immersed in this culture and passed it on to the young kids coming through. Consequently, the club developed in the right way.

One of my overriding memories of John came after I left West Ham. I had agreed to join Wimbledon, but as soon as I got there I realised I had made a mistake. I really didn't know what to do and John was the first person I turned to. He was so understanding and immediately invited me down to his house in Abridge. We had a cup of tea and a chat and a heart-to-heart. Afterwards, he arranged for me to have a trial at Brentford with Bill Dodgin. This gave me the direction I needed and removed all the worry I had about the move to Wimbledon. It was the nicest thing.

With Pat Holland after the 1976 European Cup Winners Cup final defeat against Anderlecht

In action against Fiorentina, with Alan Taylor on hand. Anglo Italian Cup Winners Cup final, December 1975

When I see some of the clowns on the television nowadays and listen to the rubbish they talk about, it only goes to underline just how lucky I was to have played my football under Ron Greenwood and John Lyall, alongside the likes of Bobby Moore and Billy Bonds. It was very much a question of right time and right place for me.

Whenever I have coached players or spoken to players, I have used Ron and John's teachings. Receiving the ball sideways on is a good example of this. Never receive the ball square on as this leaves you with too much to do. Being sideways on means you are already on your way. Another one is to play it simply. Pass with the inside of your foot, drop your shoulder when volleying the ball. There are so many.

Ron and John thought things through a lot more than today's managers and, even though you have to admire the athleticism and pace of the game today, there doesn't seem to be the same design and planning as there was when I played. It does make me chuckle because the media salivate over modern day coaches such as Pep Guardiola and Jose Mourinho, but they haven't introduced anything that wasn't taking place at West Ham United forty, fifty years ago. How they can talk about football nowadays and ignore the contribution of great men like Lyall and Greenwood, Bill Shankly and Bob Paisley at Liverpool and Matt Busby at United is beyond me. It probably explains why the England team is in such a state.

I was absolutely gobsmacked when they sacked John.

One of John's occasional West Ham reunions - Nathan's Pie and Mash shop with L-R Joe Durrell, John, Barry Barnes, Alan Stephenson and Rob Jenkins, 2016.

Completely dumbfounded. It made no sense at all and they have never really replaced him. They have had partially successful managers, but sadly, that magical culture brought to West Ham by Ron and John has been so diluted you'd be hard pressed to find any of it all, nowadays.

I attended an event in South Benfleet in 2016 to mark the tenth anniversary of John's death. What came out from that evening was just how well liked he was, what a lovely man he was and how he treated each player fairly, with honesty and respect. I'm sure he had his favourites but he made you feel that you were a favourite. That's why he is so highly regarded and sorely missed by so many.

Ron gave me my opportunity but John taught me all I needed to know to get that opportunity.
John Ayris

Following are some player reminiscences of John:

You don't see many wingers like John in the modern game. He was enthusiastic, had very quick feet and he could drop his shoulder so defenders never knew if he was going inside or outside. Nowadays, there are too many functional players who don't have the capability of going one way or the other because they can't play with both feet.
Mick McGiven

John is a lovely fella and was a pin up boy at West Ham. He took my place for a while but Ron Harris caught him, which set him back. We went out socially together and often met up in the East End for a drink. He's always had a great sense of humour.
Pat Holland

John was a typical West Ham character. A really lovely bloke. I saw him at one of the last games at Upton Park. He looks fitter now than he did when he played!
Keith Robson

You were always guaranteed a laugh with John. He was usually full on in the dressing room with Patsy Holland and Trevor Brooking.
Alan Taylor

Tell him thanks for coming off against Stoke City so that I could make my debut! It happened 37 minutes into the game so I got a good run out, or should I say run around because we lost 0-3!
Alan Wooler

I've got a photo of John and me at Chadwell Heath. It is a little and large type of photo. It was good to see him at the final game at Upton Park against Manchester United. He's a good fella and West Ham through and through.
Bill Green

He was a little speedy Gonzales and a very good crosser of the ball! He was a good friend to me and had a great personality. He has the ability to make people laugh.
Yilmaz Orhan

I love the rat! He's always laughing. Even when he isn't laughing he looks like he's laughing! I always tell him that it was his fault that Chopper Harris put him over the wall because he was a cocky little git. He used to go past players and laugh at them. I thought he was a very good player and it was a shame what happened.
Kevin Lock

Farewell to the Boleyn Ground, 2016.

13 – BILLY JENNINGS

"When you share a magical time with a manager it stays with you forever."

Born: Hackney, London, February 20, 1952 • **Position:** Striker • **Games played for West Ham United:** 125 (1974-1979)

Goals scored: 39 (Joint 46th with Brian Dear on the all-time goal scorers list)

Honours under John Lyall: 1975 FA Cup winner, 1975 FA Charity Shield runner-up, 1976 European Cup Winners Cup runner-up

Debut: September 7, 1974 v Sheffield United (h) L 1-2 (Jennings – Woodward, Dearden) Att: 20,977

West Ham United: Day, McDowell, Lampard, Bonds, Taylor T, Lock, Ayris, Paddon, **Jennings,** Holland, Best.

Sheffield United: Brown, Badger, Hemsley, Eddy, Colquhoun, Franks, Woodward, Speight, Dearden, Currie, Field.

William John 'Billy' Jennings belongs to a select group of Hammers who have scored on their first team debuts. Up until the 2016-17 season there had been 93 scoring debutants in West Ham United's history and Jennings' strike against Sheffield United, in September 1974, has secured his place on that list.

The fourth most expensive player in the club's history at the time, Billy was signed from Watford for £110,000. He was the first player to join West Ham United following the news that John Lyall had replaced Ron Greenwood as first team manager on a permanent basis. He enjoyed a flying start, scoring five goals in as many games.

Billy's finest moment in a Claret and Blue shirt came away against Den Haag in the European Cup Winners Cup campaign of 1975-76. West Ham were trailing 0-4 at half-time before spring-heeled Jennings scored a brace to set up a thrilling, and successful, quarter-final, second leg at Upton Park.

An Achilles injury restricted his appearances and he signed for Leyton Orient in 1979. He later worked as a football agent for Premier Management International and represented former West Ham United midfielder, Hayden Mullins.

Nowadays, Billy is easing himself into retirement: *"I've been an agent for 30 years and still go to football but the game is changing beyond all recognition and West Ham United is completely unrecognisable in terms of the infrastructure. I'm*

Jennings with John Lyall in September 1974

taking a step back because it is very difficult to compete in the agency business at my age. I've got a few clients but I'm not as active as I used to be. My circuit is League One and League Two – so I cover a few games in those divisions."

Billy attended a John Lyall tribute in South Benfleet in 2016 and was readily available for interview once hearing about the book:

John took over first-team affairs at about the time I joined the club. I believe I was his first signing shortly followed by Keith Robson and Alan Taylor - Quite a transfer haul in the space of a few weeks. I was only a young kid and was playing under Kevin Keen's dad, Mike, at Watford when Ron Greenwood came in for me. I remember meeting Ron in his office to discuss my transfer and then, afterwards, John took me on a tour of the ground. We went out on the pitch and he was telling me all about West Ham. I was coming from the Third Division and, although I was an East End boy, from Hackney, I'd never been to Upton Park before. It was all very exciting and full of potential and as a youngster I was a bit in awe of it all.

The day I signed there was a bit of a press event on the pitch. Keith Robson had also joined the club by then and it really was an exciting time.

Both Alan Taylor and I had come from a lower level so everything was really new to us. Watford wasn't a bad little club. We didn't have a training ground as such so even though West Ham didn't have the greatest facilities they were still a big step up from what I had been used to.

My first day's training was in a gym at Redbridge and there is a lovely photo of me, Billy Bonds and John from that day. The training was a blend of Ron's technical side and John's motivational side which was a great combination.

I think John liked his players to put in a good shift and I always gave 100% so I suspect he liked that about me even though I wasn't as silky a player as some of the others at the club. I had scored a lot of goals at Watford and quite a few of them were in the air. In those days heading was a big factor in the game and I had a good spring and liked to score with my head. I'm sure that would have caught John's eye. Sadly, the art of heading hasn't travelled well in football today, and I know from my contacts in the game that training is concentrated on the ground. Very little time is spent on the art and technique of heading, which is a shame. We often played 4-3-3 and I was quite fluid across the front three, a bit like Keith and Alan really. We could all switch positions and even though I felt more natural down the middle I was also comfortable playing out wide sometimes. Whether it was luck or judgement John must have been pleased that we could co-exist as a three up front.

I had a fantastic start to my time at West Ham. I scored five times in my first five outings, including my debut. It couldn't have gone any better really. The first six weeks at West Ham were unbelievable and if ever you think things were meant to be, that seemed to be the case. It was a great time to join the club. They had a really good squad and it was the start of a new era. John has to take a lot of credit because it could have gone horribly wrong for him. Bobby Moore had moved to Fulham and Ron Greenwood had taken on a consultative role, so it could have easily unravelled very quickly. But thankfully it didn't and John steered that team to FA Cup success in 1975 and a terrific European campaign the following season.

It could've been so different for me, too, because I almost signed for Portsmouth before I joined West Ham but Mike Keen at Watford talked me out of it. I was all set to go because Pompey were a big club and they were offering big money for me. Thankfully, Mike believed in me and convinced me that West Ham were the best option. I feel it was written in the stars that I should sign for West Ham and be part of a successful FA Cup run during my first season.

John was quite a hard task master and always let his players know if they weren't performing as expected. That's why everyone respected him, because he was always trying to help improve you as a player. He did this in quite a calm manner and wasn't one to be throwing cups about or anything like that. He was building a team around Trevor Brooking, Graham Paddon and Billy Bonds in midfield and that really worked well for West Ham during my first couple of seasons. John had developed the right blend of skill and steel so he would have been happy to facilitate the entertaining play expected of West Ham United.

I felt I gave John a good return during my time at West Ham. He brought me in to score goals and I managed to get 39 in total. It would have been more but for a couple of injuries. People often recall the two I scored out in Holland against Den Haag because we were 0-4 down at half time. Those goals got us back into the tie which we finished off at home, 3-1. We went through courtesy of my two away goals. If we had gone on to beat Anderlecht in the final then maybe they would have been the pick of the 39 but I would have to pin-point a hat-trick I scored against Stoke City. It came during my second season and were against Peter Shilton, who was one of the best keepers around at the time. We also ended up winning the game which was shown on telly so I'm very fond of that day because everything went so well.

I also scored a goal in our winning FA Cup run – against Swindon Town at home in the fourth round. It helped to earn us a replay so it was quite an important one. It would have been nice to have scored in the final but I did get an assist for one of Alan's goals which is nice to see from time to time. I didn't get much sleep the night before because I was so nervous. I'm very proud to have played in every round that year. There have been better players than me never to have played in an FA Cup final so I'm very happy to have played a small part in West Ham United's history.

I'd never played with or against Bobby Moore before that final, so to be on the same pitch as someone as great as him was extra special. I hope my children and grandchildren mention that around the dinner table from time to time in years to come because it is not often I get mentioned in the same sentence as Bobby Moore!

The open top bus journey back to East Ham town hall on the Sunday was a bit special, too. I had never experienced anything like that. The amount of people who turned out to line the streets of the East End was unbelievable and it was one of those days of pure happiness. I remember more from that Sunday than I do from the final itself! I was pleased for John because he was a young manager – only 35 at the time – and you could see it meant as much to him because he was a West Ham United man through and through.

Sadly, we couldn't repeat that success in the European Cup Winners Cup final the following year but I think John got his tactics right throughout that run and if we hadn't conceded from Frank Lampard's back pass and gone in at half-time 1-0 up, then I think we would have gone on to win the game. I think that we should have been 2-0 up in that first half because we had the chances but I believe we lost to the best team in Europe at the time in Anderlecht and we had our fair share of good fortune in the earlier rounds. We could have easily lost to Den Haag in the quarter-final or Eintracht Frankfurt in the semi-final. Some say John should have simply brought on Kevin Lock for Frank Lampard but that is a matter of opinion. Conceding that goal so late in the first half would have forced John to completely change his half-time talk which must have been difficult.

One thing I will say is that everyone at the club believed in what John was trying to achieve. You felt he was trying to

Enjoying FA Cup final glory with Pat Holland, May 3, 1975

The second of Billy's headed goals away at Den Haag, March 1976

improve you as a player. The fans loved him and some of those cup nights under the lights are testimony to that. That must be something the fans miss about leaving the Boleyn Ground. I felt the noise generated by the crowd was easily worth a goal to us. You could see the fear in the faces of some of those European teams we played. They felt the heat coming off the Chicken Run and they just didn't like it. Most fans I speak to always claim the semi-final match against Eintracht Frankfurt was the best they ever saw over there so to have been a part of that is a very special memory for me, indeed.

John was always very fair to me, especially after I completely severed my Achilles at home to Queens Park Rangers at the start of the 1977-78 season. That injury forced me out of action for a year but John was very encouraging and I am grateful that he stood by me and gave me the chance to wear that Number 9 shirt again. Sadly, I had lost a bit of pace and I wasn't the same player. The injury was to my left leg and that was the leg I used to propel myself from when getting up to head the ball. All those years of putting

pressure on it to generate that extra spring had finally taken its toll on the tendon. I was never really the same after that.

Another big contributory factor to my departure was the arrival of David Cross and Pop Robson who had struck up a good strike partnership. I knew it was going to be tough. Having said that, I had played well in a couple of pre-season friendlies up in Scotland and started to feel like I was in John's thoughts once again. Then, one day he called me in for a chat and told me that Orient had made an offer which the club had accepted. When I heard that, it rocked my world. I was only 26 but already surplus to John's requirements so I went and spoke to Jimmy Bloomfield who was a lovely man, a wily old fox. I wanted to think about it but Jim wasn't going to let me go which, with hindsight, was a pity because if I had taken the time to think about it in a little more detail, I probably wouldn't have gone. John didn't put any pressure on me and said I didn't have to leave West Ham. He left it up to me so I have no axe to grind with him on any level.

No disrespect to Orient but a month after signing I realised

One of only 30 Hammers to win the FA Cup

I had stepped down a level in terms of training, players, facilities and pretty much everything else! I just had to get on with it really so that's what I did. I hadn't played any kind of football for a year so I was keen to get back playing regularly and that's what I got at Orient.

I didn't see much of John after I left the club and apart from looking out for their results I had nothing to do with West Ham. I hadn't been a West Ham fan even though I was an East End boy so when John was sacked I didn't really have any strong opinions on the matte,r even though I had the utmost respect for him.

I do regret not going to his funeral, especially as I had been his first signing and having enjoyed a tremendous couple of years with him. I hadn't seen him or spoken to him for such a long time and thought it might be a little bit hypocritical. I now know that to be a mistake on my part.

I hold John in very high regard and it was partly due to the fact that I missed his funeral that I made the effort to show my respects by attending a tribute evening to John in 2016. It took place at South Benfleet to mark the tenth anniversary of his death. He helped me adapt to football in the highest league and changed my life really so I'll always be grateful to him for that.
Billy Jennings

Following are some player recollections of Billy:

He had two very good seasons at West Ham and possessed fantastic spring in the air. He was the bachelor at the club and the ladies loved him.
Pat Holland

Billy was unbelievable in the air. He must have only been about 5 feet 9 inches but I could swing that ball in as high as I liked knowing that he would be the first to get his head on it. Absolutely brilliant!
Keith Robson

We were both strikers and Billy was someone I could really talk to about the game more than anyone else. A great, great friend and someone I enjoyed playing with.
Alan Taylor

He scored quite a few memorable goals for West Ham but I think his hat-trick against Stoke City's Peter Shilton - a top quality goalkeeper - was his finest achievement on the pitch. Two of them were headers.
Rob Jenkins.

He would jump for the ball and not come down! Alan Wooler I've always got on well with Billy and saw him at the final match at Upton Park. He used to call me up from time to time as part of his work as an agent, introducing new players to me.
Bill Green

Billy was an intelligent player, who was always in the thick of the action and could score goals with either foot. He wasn't the strongest, didn't like a challenge, but knew how to lose his marker in the box.
Mick McGiven

The smallest centre-forward you are ever likely to meet but he won everything in the air. Unbelievable!
Tommy Taylor

At a reunion in 2016 with Alan Taylor and Billy Bonds

14 – TREVOR BROOKING

"There are so many similarities between Ron Greenwood and John Lyall but the one which must be emphasised above all others is their honesty. Every player who passed through West Ham United between 1961 and 1989 knew exactly where they stood."

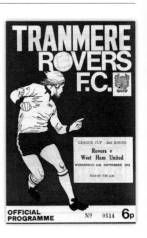

Born: Barking, London, October 2 1948 • **Position:** Midfield • **Games played for John Lyall:** 395 (1974-1984)

Games played for West Ham United: 643 (1967-84) • **Goals scored:** 102 (10th on the all-time list) • **Honours under John Lyall:** 1975 FA Cup winner, 1975 FA Charity Shield runner-up, 1976 European Cup Winners Cup runner-up • **Games played for England:** 47 (5 goals) – 3rd West Ham England International behind Bobby Moore (108) and Geoff Hurst (49). Martin Peters won 33 caps as a Hammer. **Honours under John Lyall:** 1975 FA Cup winner, 1975 FA Charity Shield runner-up, 1976 European Cup Winners' Cup runner-up, 1976 Hammer of the Year, 1977 Hammer of the Year, 1978 Hammer of the Year, 1978 Testimonial v An England XI, 1980 FA Cup winner, 1980 Charity Shield runner-up, 1981 Second Division Champion, 1981 League Cup runner-up, 1984 Hammer of the Year. • **First game under John Lyall:** September 11, 1974 v Tranmere Rovers (a) D 0-0. Att: 8,638

Tranmere Rovers: Johnson, Matthias, Flood, Moore, Philpotts, Veitch, Coppell, Palios, Young, Tynan, Crossley.

West Ham United: Day, McDowell, Lampard, Bonds, Taylor T, Lock, Ayris, Paddon, Holland, **Brooking**, Best.

Trevor David Brooking scored the single most celebrated FA Cup goal in the history of West Ham United. Ronnie Boyce's winner in the 1964 FA Cup final and Alan Taylor's double strike against Fulham in the 1975 FA Cup final, have all unleased an endless claret and blue joy that has reverberated through the ages. However, Brooking's 13th minute header, past Pat Jennings of Arsenal in the 1980 FA Cup final, sits above them all. As a consequence, he enjoys god like status in the minds of all West Ham United fans. Deservedly so.

It could have all been so very different. It is unthinkable in the modern game that someone with the natural ability of Trevor Brooking would stay with a relegated club. But that is exactly what Brooking did back in 1978, following West Ham's loss of their top flight status. For Brooking to spend three seasons in the second tier speaks volumes about his relationship with John Lyall.

Signed by Ron Greenwood as an apprentice professional on July 24, 1965, Brooking enjoyed a 17-year playing career at West Ham and, despite being moulded very much in the Ron Greenwood style, played the majority of his 643 games for the club under John Lyall.

When taking the decision to make the 1983-84 season his last at West Ham, there were numerous tributes to his career aired on television. On one occasion, a young girl, obviously traumatised by the thought of life without Trevor gushed her grief-stricken mind in front of the cameras: *"Without Trevor Brooking,"* she cried, *"West Ham are never going to win another game!"* I laughed at the claim back then but now realise that if she had used the word 'trophy' instead of 'game,' her words would still stand tall today.

Now 69, Trevor has finally embraced retirement after a dazzling career in football. In 2004 he was presented with a Knighthood for his services to sport.

"I like to play a round of golf and it is always good to catch up with the lads at the various reunions which take place each year."
I had a bit in common with John. We both grew up in the

Adored by the fans, Wembley 1975

East End and our fathers had worked for the police force. He had a strong Scottish heritage and always maintained a high regard for Scottish footballers. He saw character traits in them which existed in himself – hard work, discipline and a bit of steel.

John had the utmost respect for Ron Greenwood and viewed himself as a Greenwood disciple. He continued so many of Ron's beliefs but also added his own ideas. He tried to maintain the emphasis on stylish, attacking football, but wanted to introduce a stronger defensive culture. He brought in players like Phil Parkes, Ray Stewart and Alvin Martin, all of whom served him well and added to his success as a manager.

It should be remembered that John had been at West Ham for almost 20 years before he became first team manager. He'd played in the first team until he was 23. He then worked for Eddie Chapman in the office, helping out with payroll and all manner of administrative tasks. After that, he was put in charge of coaching the younger kids which took him a big step closer to the influence of Ron. In 1971 he was made assistant manager and was the only candidate for the main job once Ron had decided to take a step back from first team affairs. It is hard to imagine a more qualified man for the position of manager of West Ham United.

He certainly hit the ground running, winning the FA Cup in

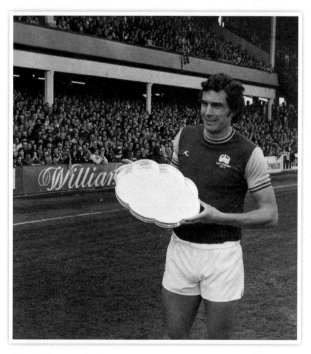

One of five Hammer of the Year awards - 1972, 1976 (above), 1977, 1978 and 1984

The first of two FA Cup successes, May 1975

both very special. It has been said that on each occasion, upwards of 250,000 West Ham fans lined the streets of the East End to see the open-topped bus journey to East Ham Town Hall. We boarded the coach at Stratford Broadway and trundled along for a couple of hours – we passed hospitals where the patients were being wheeled out, babies were being held up crying their eyes out and every pub was full to the rafters. It was totally awesome.

I had a very strong relationship with John. He came along to so many special occasions in my life – birthdays, family occasions, awards evenings, to name a few. When I was made a freeman of Brentwood, John was there along with Martin Peters and Brian Dear. It was typical of the support he had given me throughout my career.

West Ham fans probably look back on those John Lyall years and think they were quite well off. A couple of FA Cups, a European final and a League Cup final looks quite bountiful as we approach 40 years without winning anything.

Trevor Brooking

The words flow easily when talking about Trevor Brooking:
It's hard to find words to describe Trevor's talent. He was simply unbelievable. He was so consistent and played just as well in friendly and practice matches, as he did in the first team. There were so many plusses to his game I've lost count!

Ron Boyce
Trevor was so good for me at West Ham. He'd receive the ball with either foot and could dribble around the penalty area, in those penetrating spots where you can cause a lot of damage. He could cross the ball, flick the ball and chip the ball with the inside or outside of his foot. He could pass to wherever he wanted and I was quite good at reading what

his first season and a thrilling ride in Europe during his second season.

The goal against Arsenal to win the FA Cup was my finest moment at West Ham. I know it was John's, too. The ball went to Dev out on the left. I knew he'd make his run to the by-line and put a cross in. I jogged into the box, hoping that Dev's cross would avoid big Pat Jennings in the Arsenal goal. As it happened, Pat got a hand on it and put it beyond the far post. Obviously, my initial run came to nothing so I stood there with my hands on my hips taking a breather! Afterall, it was a very hot day and we'd been playing for 13 minutes! Almost immediately, Crossy had a shot which hit Willie Young and went out to Stuart Pearson. As we all know, strikers will not pass and 'Pancho' was no different. He had a shot and it was going across the goal, so I managed to adjust myself and carefully steer the ball into the net. Every Arsenal fan I've met since says it just hit me on the head, but this was a move that we'd rehearsed in training many times!

The Sunday after the FA Cup finals in 1975 and 1980 were

The giver of hope - ECWC final v Anderlecht, Brussels, 1976

he was going to do, which is why I had so many chances and scored the goals I did.
Bryan Pop Robson

Trevor decided when to pass the ball. I'd be calling for it, thinking I was in the right place at the right time to receive it, but he would often wait that bit longer. When he did put me in, he's decision when to pass was usually right. He only ever wore moulded studs, his balance was that good. When Trevor was working at the Football Association, I saw a lot of him. At one function, Claudio Ranieri was on our table and he was so excited to see Trevor. There was a bit of the starry-eyed fan meeting his hero. I work with a lot of senior football ambassadors around the world and they often talk about Trevor's goal for England against Hungary when the ball stuck in the stanchion.
Bobby Barnes

Sir Trev used to call me Stefan and followed it with his trademark laugh. I did a lot of photography for Trevor, at his house when his kids were born, and also when he and his wife, Hilkka, ran a business called Colebrook Plastics. We go back a long way and I am grateful to him for coming along to a benefit evening which was organised for me in 2016.
Steve Bacon.

I felt like I should've bowed in his presence because he was just like royalty at West Ham.
Steve Walford

He wasn't your archetypal Barking boy! He was a posh lad and what a player! He couldn't head the ball, and had little or no pace, but what an astonishing talent. I think he learned a lot from Ronnie Boyce because Boycey was another player who used to let the ball run across him to gain a yard.
John Ayris

Sheer class!
Derek Hales

He was in his pomp when I was at West Ham in the late 1970s and into the 1980s. He was a big star for England at that time, too. A phenomenal player and a really, really good guy. We share the same Birthday, only 12 years apart.
Phil Brignull
I think he decided to pack it all in once he saw me turn up!
Paul Hilton

We were always told to give the ball to Trevor and that is basically what I did while I was at West Ham!
Anton Otulakowski

When defeat hurts - Final whistle v Anderlecht, May 1976

The boy from Barking gained 47 caps for England

Running the show against Arsenal in the 1980 FA Cup final

Lest we forget...

I never got to know Trevor that well. He stayed within the boundaries of sensible behaviour so it was difficult to really get to know him.
Billy Jennings

When I was a kid, I had pictures of Trevor Brooking and Billy Bonds on my bedroom wall from Shoot magazine. Paul Brush Magician.
Alan Dickens

The biggest compliment I can give Trevor is that people knew exactly what he was going to do and they still couldn't stop him. Along with Bonzo, he was the best I played with.
Alan Devonshire

I hold the distinction of making Trevor swear. We were playing in a reserve game and he ran towards me to collect the ball but I didn't give it to him so he swore in frustration. There is always a first for everything!
Ray Houghton

What an unbelievable player! He could cross the ball from anywhere. He scored our third goal against Eintracht Frankfurt in the semi-final and it was just mesmerising. The way he cut inside and slotted it home was just sheer class. Keith Robson He liked playing table tennis against me because I was fairly decent. Neither of us was anywhere near as good as Pop Robson, though.
Dale Banton

Trev had control of the ball without touching the ball.
Greg Campbell

Great, great ability on the ball. He helped set up quite a few of my goals and it was all about timing with Trevor. He was

With wife Hilkka and the FA Cup

Brooking saluted a goal on 102 occasions for the Hammers

With son Warren - last ever Saturday match - Nottingham Forest, May 1984

great at finding me when I was making my runs through the channels. They didn't keep records of assists back then, but I imagine Trevor would have been top of the charts. He was the player I fed off most.
Alan Taylor

The Maestro.
Alan Wooler

I knew he was a very good player, but I didn't know just how big and strong he was. It was very hard to get the ball off him in training. He was so good at keeping defenders at arm's length. I saw a lot of him at various matches up and down the country when he was working for the FA.
Bill Green

An artist. He put those beautiful crosses in and that is something you never forget. I'm 62 now so it's easier to be like him when I play football. I walk around the pitch putting in good crosses and setting up goals!
Yilmaz Orhan

Mr Elegance. His shielding of the ball, and swivelling of the hips, allowed him to place a pass or a cross with either foot. His shimmies, shots and vision made him a very exciting player, indeed. Absolutely brilliant!
Mick McGiven

Top, top drawer. I remember my first training session with the first team. I was 17 and kicking a ball around with Bobby Moore, Geoff Hurst and Martin Peters. When I got home, my dad asked me who I thought was the best player and I answered: "Trevor Brooking."
Pat Holland

John Lyall's captain and midfield supremo, April 2016

15 – KEITH ROBSON

"If John Lyall was here today he would say I was a good player who went down the wrong road."

Born: Hetton-Le-Hole, County Durham, November 15, 1953 • **Position:** Striker

Games played for West Ham United: 89 (1974-1977) • **Goals scored for West Ham United:** 19

Honours under John Lyall: 1975 Charity Shield runner-up, 1976 European Cup Winners Cup runner-up

Debut: September 19, 1974 v Tranmere Rovers League Cup 2nd round replay (h) W 6-0 (Bonds 2, Gould hat-trick, Ayris) Att: 15,854

West Ham United: Day, McDowell, Lampard, Bonds, Taylor T, Lock, Ayris, Paddon, Gould, Brooking, **Robson K.**

Tranmere Rovers: Johnson, Matthias, Flood, Moore, Philpotts, Veitch, Coppell, Palios*, Mitchell, Tynan, Crossley. Sub: Webb.*

Keith Robson was born the son of a coal miner and grew up in Caroline Street, Hetton-Le-Hole, in County Durham. His father, Thomas, later worked in the Appleton distillery while his mother, Lillian, helped to raise Keith, his two brothers, Alan and Bob and their sister Lillian.

West Ham United paid £60,000 to Newcastle United for his services and with five goals in his first five games it looked as though both 'Robbo' and the Hammers were destined for great things. Unfortunately, a combination of injury and an over indulgence in the wilder side of professional football, meant that Keith didn't really fulfil his potential in the East End.

Having played in the third, fifth and sixth rounds of the 1975 FA Cup run, it was a bitter disappointment for Keith to miss out on the Wembley final, against Fulham, due to injury. Subsequently, he did demonstrate his talent for scoring vital goals, in both the semi-final and final of the European Cup Winners Cup the following season.

Robson's goal against Eintracht Frankfurt in that semi-final second leg is widely regarded as one of the greatest in the club's history. It must have also been a huge relief to Keith, who had failed to score in his previous 25 matches for the club. Along with both Alan Sealey and Pat Holland, he is in a very select trio of Hammers to have scored in a major European final.

Sadly, after one drink-driving ban too many, John Lyall eventually lost patience with Robbo and he was sold to Cardiff City in 1977 where he joined up with former Hammer, Jimmy Andrews. Keith eventually played out his career at Norwich City and Leicester City but his heart will always be with the Hammers.

Keith holds the dubious distinction of being the only West Ham United player to be banned from driving while being banned from driving! Not since John Dick – West Ham's prolific striker from the 1950s - has a West Ham goal getter enjoyed gambling so much and the local betting shops were another banned territory for the loveable Robbo.

Nowadays, Keith lives in Norwich with wife Karen and is an apron hand at the city's airport where he mainly looks after passengers for Bristow helicopters. He is regularly invited back to London Stadium to host the various lounges for the claret and blue faithful. His happy-go-lucky take on life and first-class company make him the perfect man for the job. Long may it continue!

One of West Ham's great characters, Robbo's recollections of John Lyall were tinged with no small amount of regret but thankfully, his left foot has ensured his place in the important side of West Ham United's history.

When I was a young kid, I played for a junior side and was sent to clubs all over the place for them to run their eye over

John Lyall with his two new strikers - Keith Robson and Billy Jennings

me. I went to Liverpool, Aston Villa and Coventry City. Then Alan Brown, the Sunderland manager, came to my house and invited me to train with them. The next day I missed the bus and didn't make it. I was playing a match the following evening and Joe Harvey and Keith Burkinshaw, the Newcastle manager and coach came along and I scored a few goals. In no time at all, I was playing for Newcastle United which didn't go down well in my village- Hetton-Le-Hole - because they were all Sunderland supporters. I was playing with the likes of Terry McDermott, Malcolm MacDonald and John Tudor.

The West Ham connection started after a game against Liverpool. I was walking along the street on my way back to Hetton when I noticed Ron Greenwood. I recognised him and we looked at each other.

I think he had come up to see a winger named Stewart Barrowclough, but on Monday morning Joe Harvey called me into his office and told me that two clubs had made an offer for me and that one of them was a very good footballing side – West Ham United. He didn't even tell me the name of the other team! At that time I had only ever been to London once, to watch a rugby match at Twickenham.

I moved down in September 1974 and the club put me up in a hotel in Kings Cross. It was either Bill Lansdowne or Rob Jenkins who picked me up to take me to West Ham

but a huge boil came up on my leg so I couldn't play against Sheffield United on the Saturday which should have been my debut. It was a pity because I was so fit from having been playing in Newcastle's first team.

They moved me to a hotel in Wanstead Flats for a few weeks before I eventually stayed in digs on Lonsdale Avenue, East Ham. My landlady was called Nell. There were so many nice people at West Ham it was like a dream come true. Bill Lansdowne, Albert Walker, Ernie Gregory, Rob Jenkins, Ronnie Boyce, Mick McGiven, they were all different class. The whole place was like a family.

I found John a very nice but very quiet man. I probably gave him a lot more trouble than he deserved.

My debut came at home to Tranmere Rovers in the League Cup and I remember being a bit worried because I'd seen us play the first game up in Birkenhead and John had selected Clyde Best up front alone. Now, playing one up front is no good to anybody but John changed it for the replay and we won 6-0 - It could have easily been 10. He played me out wide on the left which I didn't mind. To be honest it was really easy playing in that West Ham side with Billy Bonds, Trevor Brooking and Graham Paddon.

I had a storming start in the league, too. I scored five goals in my first four league matches. We beat Leicester City 6-2 at home on my league debut and Birmingham City 3-0 at home. Then we went to Burnley and won 5-3. I got two in that one, before drawing 2-2 at home to Derby who went on to win the league that season. I couldn't put a foot wrong. I think we were bottom when I joined but we went on a really good run and looked like a very decent side. We only lost one league game in my first 16 starts. We lost our league form a bit once that great 1975 FA Cup run got under way but on our day we could have beaten anybody.

I thought I had good control, mainly left footed but I was very good in the air as well. My pace was okay but I picked up a bad injury away at Birmingham – a massive haematoma in my leg – and I lost a yard of pace from that point on. I remember the incident well. I played a one-two with Trevor Brooking and their centre half, John Roberts, clattered into me and gave me a dead leg. It wasn't until after the game that I realised how bad it was. My leg just came up like a balloon. I had to use crutches for a while and was out for ages. That was in March, 1975 and I didn't return until the start of the 1975-76 season. Obviously, I missed out on the FA Cup final against Fulham and to be fair, Ron Greenwood was more sympathetic towards me than John. I'd made a daft decision to play in a charity match during my recovery. It was against the Metropolitan Police and I got clattered which set be back and ruled me out completely. The week before the final, I was included in a reserve team to face Arsenal and Bill Lansdowne said to me: "Give it 45 minutes and see how you feel." At half time I could feel it swelling up so he took me off. I ended up watching the final in the stand sitting next to Clyde Best. It was such a bad game I could have fallen asleep and woken up when it was over. To be honest, I thought the club might've sorted me out with a medal. After all, I'd scored the winner in the 5th round against QPR, but all I got was John putting his arm around me and saying: "Don't worry, we'll win the European Cup Winners Cup next year."

The training at West Ham was completely different to Newcastle. Up there we did a lot of weights and a lot of running but with John it was so much more technical. We did everything with the ball and it was very tactical. We used to play in a gym over at Redbridge and some of the football we played in there was unbelievable. The one-touch, two-touch football was absolutely brilliant. The training was just so much better at West Ham.

The European games were so different to the league matches. They were a lot slower with more possession ball. The atmosphere was fantastic. The fans at Upton Park were just incredible and, to be honest, those games gave me a bit of a lift. I'd scored in the early rounds against Reipas Lahden and Ararat Erevan but then I went into a real slump. It was totally my fault because I just lost it in my head. I was drinking too much, socialising too much and got in with the

Squaring up to Bethnal Green's World Welterweight Champion, John H Stracy

wrong crowd and didn't know how to get out of it. My dad had passed away just before I'd come down from Newcastle and we were really close. He'd seen all my matches.

I wasn't the type to sit at home every night and just loved to drink and gamble. At Newcastle, I was on £50 a week and then I was on £100 a week at West Ham which went up to £160-a-week. That was very decent money back then and I used it for all the wrong things. I completely lost my focus. John really helped me out even though I was letting him down. I'd been done for drink-driving and had lost my licence. I ended up staying with John and his wife, Yvonne, for a few weeks just to sort my head out. He had such a lovely family and if I'd stayed with John I probably would never have left West Ham. John did as much for me as he could but I let myself down. He'd drive me into training every day and his wife would say: "What a lovely lad, I can't believe you've got any problems with him." But I wasn't in a good place and all credit to John, he stood by me.

I can't even remember him fining me but then again I never used to check my wages. It was just in one pocket and out the other. He let me go back home to Newcastle most weekends and gave me Mondays off to make it easier. He was so very, very fair to me and I abused it, really. They always say that if you get your time again you'd do it all differently and I would but you don't get your time again, do you? If I'd carried on behaving as I did when I first arrived I think I'd have been a very decent player with a very decent record at West Ham.

I went 25 games without a goal but John never lost faith in me and when I did score it was the goal everyone always talks about – against Eintracht Frankfurt at home. If you listen to the commentary, Brian Moore says it's my first goal since November. I couldn't believe that when I heard it recently!

John always encouraged me to play my natural game. He loved to entertain and he brought players in who he thought could entertain. He was definitely one of the best coaches I played for along with John Bond at Norwich City. They were very similar in their approach to how the game should be played. Lyall was a lot more laid back than Bondy who would give you both barrels when he wasn't happy! West Ham was easily the best team I played for.

When I first arrived, I was always in the box, always looking to score and being involved in the penalty area. The crowd will always take to someone like that. John wasn't the type to tell me about the strengths and weaknesses of the defenders I'd be going up against. He probably knew it would worry me too much! When I went up against the likes of Liverpool's hard man - Tommy Smith - it meant nothing to me and played my game, not his game.

After the final against Anderlecht my behaviour didn't improve and I ended up leaving West Ham under a cloud. I think John knew he'd tried everything he could and my last game for West Ham came in 1977 against Sunderland. We were thumped 6-0 at Roker Park and on the following Monday,

Ron and John called me into the office and just like that I was moved on. They told me that the club had accepted an offer from Cardiff City. Alan Sealey was the coach there and he had obviously spoken to John about signing me. I remember Alan saying: "Why do you want to play in the reserves when you could walk into our first team?" So, I was at West Ham one minute and gone the next. It didn't take long for me to realise what I'd left behind and I was looking out for West Ham scores every week. I missed the place so badly.

The last time I saw John was at a reunion in London's Docklands on the Isle of Dogs. We had a chat and I'm so pleased to have that as my last memory. It was a special evening and John really enjoyed seeing so many of the players he'd been in charge of at West Ham.

Some of Keith's West Ham colleagues had the following memories of him;

He gave 100% and the crowd loved him for it. Ron Boyce
He was a great laugh, had lots of ability and was a good lad but a bit of a nut case!
John Ayris

It wasn't a great idea to put him in rented accommodation above a bookies!
Pop Robson

We became close friends because we joined the club at the same time, were both single and went out socialising together. He was quite mad as everyone always says about him but you couldn't help but love him and we gelled really well. I liked playing up front with Robbo because he was a big lad with fantastic ability and could hold the ball really well.
Billy Jennings

He is a charming man. He has a great love of the club and is always very passionate about the current team. West Ham runs right through him. For me, he didn't fulfil his potential because he had a lot of very fine attributes; a very good left foot and great heading and tackling ability. He didn't have great pace but he could play up front and out wide.
Pat Holland

Robbo is a great, great bloke and I've always got a lot of time for him. I was born a day before him on November 14 1953 but we always get confused and argue about who is the eldest. Along with Billy Jennings, we all signed around about the same time and all did well for West Ham.
Alan Taylor

Robbo was mad but everyone loved him. I remember all the

Robbo leaves the pitch after his wonder goal against Eintracht Frankfurt, March 1976

Robbo's headed goal makes it 2-2 against Anderlecht - the last Hammer to score in a major European final

wives and girlfriends felt so sorry for him when he missed out on the FA Cup final. He kicked Tommy Smith of Liverpool once. It happened really early on and Tommy Smith spent the rest of the game trying to get him back. Robbo had this trick he used to play on the pitch. He did it to Paul Reaney once up at Elland Road. He had the ball at his feet but would suddenly stop and throw up his arms in exasperation as if the ref had blown his whistle. He would then bend down to pick up the ball but dashed passed Reaney instead. The Leeds fans went mad!
Kevin Lock

A few years ago I went back with my dad to watch a game at West Ham. It was against Arsenal and we were in the Di Canio lounge when Robbo came over and made a fuss of us. He was working as a club ambassador. We had a nice chat and afterwards he said to my dad that I was one of the unluckiest players to be released by West Ham. Whether or not he meant it I don't know but my dad never forgot it. Some of the goals Robbo scored for West Ham were amazing. A lovely guy.
Alan Wooler

I like Robbo, but he was his own worst enemy. He would give you the coat off his back and people took advantage of him. He had the bad footballer's habits of drinking and gambling. I remember seeing him pick up his wages and going straight to the bookies

opposite The Boleyn pub, putting it all on the favourite and doing the lot. Then he'd borrow £20 and win a few hundred at the dogs in the evening. Easy come easy go, that's Robbo.
Bill Green

A mad, lovely man who would do anything for anybody - and he could play.
Tommy Taylor

Keith with Pat Holland - the last Hammers to score in a major European final

16 – ALAN TAYLOR

"Ron and John gave me my chance to play top flight football and there was nothing better than scoring in front of a full-house at Upton Park."

Born: Hinckley, Leicestershire, November 14, 1953 • **Position:** Striker

Games played for West Ham United: 124 (1974-79) • **Goals scored for West Ham United:** 36 (Top 50 on the all-time West Ham United goal scorer list) • **Honours under John Lyall:** 1975 FA Cup winner, 1975 Charity Shield runner-up, 1976 European Cup Winners Cup runner-up • **Debut:** December 7, 1974 v Leeds United (h) W 2-1 (Gould, Jennings – McKenzie) Att: 39,562

West Ham United: Day, Coleman, Lampard, Bonds, Taylor T, Lock, Jennings*, Paddon, Gould, McDowell, Robson. Sub: **Taylor A.***

Leeds United: Harvey, Reaney, Cherry, Bremner, McQueen, Madeley, McKenzie, Clarke, Jordan, Lorimer, Yorath.

Alan David Taylor was one of three strikers to join West Ham United after John Lyall had been appointed first team manager in 1974. It was a statement of intent from a club which had always prided itself on entertaining, attacking football.

Little could John have known that the £40,000 paid to Rochdale for the waif-like Sparrow's services would provide such a thrilling return in his first season.

No player in FA Cup history has scored two goals in the sixth round, semi-final and final but that is exactly what Alan achieved in 1975. The two goals against Arsenal at Highbury in the sixth round were Taylor's first for the club. He eventually went on to score six goals against the north London rivals during his time at West Ham, something that hasn't been equalled by any Hammer since. Indeed, in the games when he netted his 36 goals for the club, West Ham only lost twice and never at home. What a talisman!

Sparrow enjoyed the highlights of FA Cup success and a thrilling European campaign but injury began to restrict his first team appearances. He enjoyed five years at Upton Park before becoming something of a journeyman, scoring goals for Norwich City, Cambridge United, Hull City, Burnley, Bury and Vancouver Whitecaps in the North American Soccer League.

Living with wife, Jeanette, Alan currently works as a pall-bearer and part time newsagent in Norwich, having previously run both a milk round and his own shop in the city. Having regularly hosted the lounges at the Boleyn Ground he continues this ambassadorial role at the London Stadium.

Alan had the following memories of John:

Both Ron Greenwood and John Lyall had been watching me at Rochdale, but the first I knew of this was in November 1974 when Rochdale played at Northampton Town. They both came up to watch me play. It was Guy Fawkes Night and they obviously liked what they saw because, about a week later, I was a West Ham United player.

Chelsea had also keen to sign me but after that Northampton match, Walter Joyce, the Rochdale manager travelled down with me to West Ham and I ended up signing on November 14th, my 21st Birthday. I was scoring for fun up there and I think I'd got 10 goals in 10 games so that helped put me on a few club radars and thankfully, Ron and John came in for me. Back in those days both managers and scouts seemed to look at the lower divisions a lot more.

The timing of the signing was crucial, because I was due to play for Rochdale against Marine in the first round of the FA Cup so would have been cup tied at West Ham! Obviously my FA Cup achievements would never have happened.

When I joined West Ham I must say that I didn't know much about John Lyall at all. I knew of Ron Greenwood and I

knew West Ham was the type of club to give young talent a chance. Bobby Moore, Trevor Brooking, Frank Lampard had all come through the ranks to become household names. I remember being very excited coming from Rochdale because I was going to get my chance at a top-flight club. After a spell in a hotel I ended up staying in digs run by Kevin Lock's mum.

John was a real father-like figure. All the players looked up to him and I can't remember a time when he lost his cool. He may have taken you to one side and said a few words but his overriding concern was to improve you as a player.

I couldn't have asked more from John and West Ham United. My wages more than doubled, they were terrific with my move down to London, but, most important of all, I was going to play for a big club noted for playing entertaining football and that excited me.

John had tremendous knowledge and was always learning from the game. Our training sessions often addressed some of the points he had pulled out from the previous match. There were so many keep-ball and one-on-one sessions. His technical knowledge was very, very, good. He would sometimes work with just the strikers and discuss positional sense and when to make a run, that sort of thing. He was very considered in what he said. In the dressing room before, during or after a game, he would address the whole team. He wasn't the type to throw things or raise his voice. He was more concerned about getting his point across in a calm manner.

We were a young team at that particular time and through John and the experienced pros such as Billy Bonds, Trevor Brooking and Frank Lampard, we were given the best possible support about how to play the game. That is part of the reason I had five great years there.

John probably liked me for my pace above anything else but I'd like to think that the goals I scored were another big asset for both him and the club. I think he bought me as a winger but like Theo Walcott at Arsenal I was tried out in attack and started scoring goals. The interesting thing at the time was that John would play myself, Keith Robson and Billy Jennings and you couldn't really say that any one of us was a loft winger, right winger or a centre forward because we could play up there together and chop and change. John worked with us on that and we would alternate a lot during a game. I'd attack the near post sometimes while other times it would be Keith or Billy. The big problem I had was that I wasn't the biggest of guys and picked up my fair share of injuries. I just couldn't stay fit. A bit like Andy Carroll. He always tries his hardest and puts plenty of effort in but just seems to pick up injuries that keep him out for months at a time. It reminds me of my own experience.

I made my debut as a substitute against Leeds United but my actual first start came on Boxing Day, 1974, at Stoke City

With John Lyall after signing for West Ham in November, 1974

and I had to leave the game after an hour because I had done my medial ligaments after a tackle on Alan Hudson. I was out for quite a while and my first game back was against Newcastle United at home when I came on as sub. The following Saturday, West Ham were due to play Arsenal in the FA Cup 6th round. I had only just started my return to full fitness but on the Friday before the game, John pulled me into his office and told me he was going to start me at Highbury. I went home that night and had a terrible night's sleep. Highbury would have 50,000 packed in, a far cry from the 1,500 I'd been playing in front of at Rochdale, but I knew I couldn't let John down. This was my chance. The following day at the hotel, John announced the team and, on the coach journey to Highbury, Bobby Gould came and sat next to me. It was Bobby's place I was taking but what a gentleman he was. He wished me all the best and gave me great words of encouragement.

The six goals I scored in that cup run will stay with me forever; the first at Arsenal came when Graham Paddon chipped a ball at the far post and I finished it off. The second one I took a pass from Trevor Brooking and threaded it through the mud into the corner.

The first against Ipswich Town in the semi final was a header at the far post which I celebrated with Bobby Gould and the second was a shot from outside the area which found its way into the corner with about ten minutes to go. I remember being held aloft like a statue by Frank Lampard with my arms in the air.

The goals in the final at Wembley were not spectacular but they mean the world to me. The first came when I followed up on a shot by Billy Jennings and it ended up going through Peter Mellor's legs. The keeper made another mistake for the second and I just buried it.

The FA Cup run kick-started a good spell for me and I ended the following season as top-scorer at the club with 17 goals which was remarkable given that twelve months

Scoring through Peter Mellor's legs in the 1975 FA Cup final against Fulham at Wembley

earlier I was playing at Rochdale. I owe so much to John Lyall for that. He always had time to help and worked with all the players to address any little thing that wasn't quite right with our game. He was so encouraging and nothing was too much trouble. He made our concerns his concerns. He spent so much time with me, showing me when, and how, to make near post runs and how to open up my body when shooting. I was lucky to be coached by John and to play with the calibre of players around me. It was a tremendous time.

I know everyone remembers me for the six goals in that 1975 cup run but I almost won the Goal of the Season in 1977. It came at Highbury where we won 3-2. I got a couple and the winning goal was a flying header after Frank Lampard had out-muscled George Armstrong and whipped in a cross. To be fair it looked like a foul on Armstrong which is probably why they never gave the award to me. Terry McDermott of Liverpool won it, instead. He shimmied and chipped in against Everton.

I was quite unlucky with injuries and wish I'd had a better chance at representing England. Don Revie did call me up once to play for an England XI in Alan Ball's testimonial.

I was in and out of the West Ham side after our European campaign and when John Bond came in for me at Norwich City I felt like a fresh start might be the answer. The fact that my wife, Jeanette, is from Norwich made the decision that

bit easier. I had a year there before spending the best part of five years playing indoor soccer for Vancouver Whitecaps.

A good example of just how much John cared for his players came when I picked up an injury against Stoke City. I was new at the club, still living in the Post House Hotel at Epping, and finding it very difficult to get to the ground for treatment but John, who was living at Theydon Bois at the time, would pick me up every day and drive me in. That was just the type of bloke he was. You just don't forget people like John Lyall.

Following are some comments from Alan's former teammates;

Alan had five years at the club but it only took him two months to write himself into the club's history books forever.
Ron Boyce

He was as skinny as a twig. I still call him 'Sparrow' today. He came from Rochdale and scored six of the most important goals in the club's history. What a story!
Keith Robson

He used to pick me up in his red TR7. I was living in Stanford-Le-Hope and I think he was living in Billericay.
Kevin Lock

Alan enjoying the fruits of his unique achievement

We were very similar players, apart from the fact he was much quicker than me. A bit erratic at times but he carved out a special piece of West Ham history for himself so all credit to him.
Billy Jennings

I played a handful of games with him during the 1977-78 relegation season so I obviously didn't see the best of him. He jumped too high for my liking. If someone comes in with a tackle, there is no need to jump like a kangaroo is there?
Derek Hales

I think they called him Sparrow because he trained against me and I used to kick him up in the trees! In all seriousness, he had good talent, fantastic pace and could put in a good cross as well as scoring his own fair share.
Alan Wooler

He was probably the only one quicker than me over short distances. He had good technique and took his opportunities.
Yilmaz Orhan

Football can be a cruel game and a few mistakes can ruin a career. However, the other side of that coin is a run of scoring goals which can guarantee you a place in folklore and Sparrow has his place in West Ham's history.
Mick McGiven

Working in the lounges at the Boleyn Ground, May 2016

17 – ALAN CURBISHLEY

"John's end in football was a bit similar to Bobby Moore. He was available but nobody was using him. The mind boggles that such knowledge of the game wasn't put to greater use later in his life."

Born: Forest Gate, London, November 8, 1957 • **Position:** Midfielder • **Games played for West Ham United:** 96 (1975-79)

Goals for West Ham United: Five • **Debut:** March 29, 1975 v Chelsea (h) L 0-1 (Droy) Att: 31,025

West Ham United: Day, Coleman, McDowell, **Curbishley,** Taylor T, Lock, Jennings, Paddon, Taylor A, Brooking, Gould. Sub: Ayris.*

Chelsea: Phillips, Locke, Harris, Hollins, Droy, Hinton, Kember, Hay, Langley, Houseman, Cooke.

Llewellyn Charles "Alan" Curbishley was born the son of a Docker and grew up in Canning Town, just a brisk walk from the Boleyn Ground. He was one of six children, including three brothers, Bill, Alfie and Paul – another former Hammers Youth Team player - and two sisters, Della and Laura.

Alan had joined West Ham United at the age of 13 and, by the time John Lyall had given him his first team debut against Chelsea in March 1975, he was widely touted as one of the bright young hopefuls produced by the club's Academy.
In 1975, he helped an England Youth team win a UEFA tournament which launched the careers of Ray Wilkins, Glenn Hoddle and Bryan Robson. The rapid progression of those players ultimately compounded the frustration felt by Curbishley and his own lack of first team action at West Ham.

Remarkably, Alan formed part of a West Ham reserve side in 1975 which comprised 11 players that would all experience first-team football with the Hammers. The match was a 9-1 thumping of Swindon Town at the County Ground and the line-up was: Ferguson, Coleman, Wooler, Pike, Martin, McGiven, Ayris, Curbishley, Jennings, Coker and Orhan.

Unbridgeable differences with Lyall over team selection, resulted in Curbs leaving the club in 1979 and signing for Birmingham City. The fee was £225,000. It would be 27 years before Alan would once again become part of the claret and blue fabric, when he was appointed manager of the club in 2006. Along with Billy Bonds and Trevor Brooking

he is the third ex-player to manage West Ham from the John Lyall era.

Alan took the time to visit my home in Blackheath to discuss John:

My earliest memories of John Lyall are from when I was a schoolboy at West Ham, aged 13. He was the youth team coach under Ron Greenwood and part of his brief was to look after the school boys. I was at Pretoria Road School at the time and John was coaching in the evenings with Bill Lansdowne. John also coerced Frank Lampard into helping out, and that is how I met everyone.

I didn't know I was going to make my debut against Chelsea at Upton Park. It was in March, 1975 and, in the morning, I had taken the bus to Chadwell Heath to watch the Youth team. When I got there Ron Greenwood came over to me and asked me why I was there? He said I should get over to Upton Park straight away. Obviously, he knew that John had picked me so I dashed to the ground and, sure enough, John told me I was playing.

John learned a lot of his coaching from Ron. I can remember Ron saying something to me and a group of young lads which has stayed with me all my life. He called us in and said; "Everyone at West Ham is here to try and turn you into players. But not all of you will play for West Ham. But if we all work hard you will play somewhere."

As a kid I had to work at the Boleyn Ground on Friday to

1974-75 Youth team - front row, third from right

prepare it for match day. My job was to clean the brass and I used to polish all the door handles. All the other lads used to mess around leaving their finger prints everywhere and Ron Boyce, who was my youth team manager at the time used to tell me to do it last of all but I didn't want to be the last one to leave. We had such a great time it didn't really matter what chores we had to do. We used to finish training in the morning, go to Cassettaris for lunch and then go back to the ground to get it ready for Saturday's match. When I signed pro I was put on £50 a week and the most I earned was £150 per week.

The education every kid received when passing through West Ham would have been something worth remembering. We were taught about awareness, one-touch, two-touch, sideways on, how to receive the ball, how to keep an eye on the bigger picture, the list was endless and each discipline improved your game, especially some of the keep-ball sessions. During my managerial career, I tried to replicate a lot of these techniques but a lot of the players were just not interested and without player enthusiasm it makes it very difficult. Everyone at West Ham, under John, had training ground enthusiasm. Some of the sessions went on for ages and I remember times when keep-ball was so good, so intense and so enjoyable that we only played that for the whole training session.

Some of the training was very hard, especially the running. John would take us out to Hainault Forest and we would run around the lake. At the end of it he would say, "Okay,

now run back to Chadwell Heath." John Radford signed from Arsenal and he joined us for a 30-minute run around Mott Street near Loughton. John and Ron Boyce would try and arrange the run so that the players finished at roughly the same time. They would let the slow ones set off first – that would be the goalkeepers and defenders, people like Mervyn Day, Tommy Taylor and Keith Coleman. The next group would be a bit faster and would go off about five or ten minutes later – the likes of myself and Frank Lampard would be in that group. Finally, the really fast runners would be last to go. That would be Bonzo, Dev, Pat Holland, Alan Taylor, that crowd. Ron and John would follow us all in Boycey's car. Anyway, we turned a corner into Mott Street and there was Raddy laid out on someone's lawn being hosed down by this woman who was watering her garden! "I've never run like this before," he said, gasping for air! They ended up putting him in Boycey's car who wasn't best pleased because Raddy was soaking wet!

I was with John during his formative years as manager and, at the time, I felt he would have liked to have continued with Ron Greenwood involved. Of course, if I had stayed at West Ham for ten years and seen how he developed as a coach I may have a different point of view. I felt that John didn't like the contractual side of things, negotiations with the players - the buying and selling - and would much preferred to have left that with Ron so that he could get on with coaching. Having said that I've spoken to a lot of the players who came after me, who said that John was a really good man-manager and a tough negotiator. I was interested to hear that because after three or four years he had obviously changed and that was my experience when I was a manager. At the beginning, you work hard to be on the good side of everyone but as time goes by you learn to be a bit more ruthless. I was a very different manager at Charlton Athletic in 2005 than I was when I joined them ten years earlier. So, it wasn't until Ron Greenwood took the England job in 1978 that John became his own man. I probably got the softer side of John while I was at the club. On reflection, it seems as though he revelled in being responsible for every aspect of the running of a football club.

My disagreement with John was solely about team selection. He wasn't playing me enough. There was a lot of competition for midfield places with Trevor, Patsy, Bonzo, Dev, Graham Paddon and Pikey. Then he paid quite a bit of money for Anton Otulakowski from Barnsley. I was a ball playing midfielder whereas someone like Pikey was more of an all-rounder. He could sit in the midfield allowing Trevor a bit more freedom. Even though I was offered a contract I just had this feeling that I wasn't in John's plans. Jim Smith offered £225,000 for me so I went to Birmingham. I needed

to get out of London because I felt I had the combination of not playing and socialising a bit too much which was not sending me in the right direction.

Quite a few players also left West Ham at that time – Mervyn Day, Billy Jennings and Tommy Taylor went to Orient, John McDowell and Alan Taylor went to Norwich and Pop Robson went to Sunderland. It helped clear the decks and John recreated his own atmosphere. He brought in Ray Stewart, Stuart Pearson and Phil Parkes.

I think if John was here now he would look back on that time when eight or nine players left due to freedom of contract and maybe thought to himself; I didn't plan that but I'm pleased it happened. There were a lot of angry players at the club at that time but there were also some good players coming through like Paul Allen, Alvin Martin and Geoff Pike.

I think I massively underachieved at West Ham. If I had to compare myself to a more recent player I would say Michael Carrick. I had a good passing range, good vision and could make a goal. I wasn't quick but my England youth team generation included Glenn Hoddle, Ray Wilkins and Bryan Robson. We had won the Youth World Cup in Finland but for whatever reason, I didn't develop as quickly or to the same

The Whizz takes on Fulham

extent as those players did. It might have been my fault or it might have been John Lyall's. I was just coming through and we got relegated in 1977-78. I wasn't playing as many games as I wanted to and started arguing a lot with John. If he said two plus two equalled four I would contest it. I could see the progress being made by other players and felt angry most of the time. For the last six months I was at West Ham, John and I couldn't agree on anything. If he said something I would automatically take the opposite view. Of course, he would be right most of the time but my attitude was that I'd played almost 100 games and I was only 20 and should be in the team. On one occasion, he put Alan Taylor in midfield because I was so far out of his reckoning. I realised then that I would have to move on if I was going to play regularly and it just so happened that freedom of contract was coming into the game. It wasn't until I had my own time as a manager that I could fully understand John's position.

Ironically, when I was manager at Charlton I had a player who was going through a very similar experience to me - Scotty Parker. He was at Lilleshall with the likes of Michael Owen and others and they were all first team regulars and he thought he should be doing the same. At the time, we had just won promotion and I simply didn't have room for a 19-year-old newcomer in the Premier League. When he was coming back at me with anger and frustration it took me back to the exchanges I used to have with John at West Ham. Paul Konchesky was another who was frustrated at how his career was developing at Charlton and if I said two plus two equalled four he would disagree with me. Sound familiar?

Although I played my best football at Birmingham City, I was a young East End lad living in the Midlands so I wasn't really enjoying myself. In fact after one game against West Ham I remember asking Frank Lampard to ask John if I could come back but obviously nothing came of it. Then Birmingham won promotion and I was in the England B squad and playing really well. Ron Greenwood was England manager at the time and I was right on the fringes of the squad for the 1982 World Cup in Spain. That's when I fractured my other knee cap after going in for a tackle with Luton Town's, Brian Horton. I was out for the entire summer and never really recovered.

When I was manager at West Ham I remember Alex Ferguson coming down to Upton Park for a tribute evening to Ron Greenwood and John Lyall. We had a chat and he asked me where I lived and I replied: "Abridge." He said he knew it because he had visited John at his home there a few times. That's when I discovered that Alex had been helped by both John Lyall, and former Charlton manager, Lennie Lawrence when he had come down to Manchester United from Aberdeen.

It is quite a coincidence that both John and I lived in Abridge. I'm still there and I think John's brother is still

Young Curbs in action against Newcastle United

involved with the village cricket club. Imagine that, two West Ham managers living in little old Abridge? West Ham used to have a pre-season cricket match in Abridge every year so there was a strong Lyall connection.

John was ahead of his time and could have easily coached all around the world and been a success. Bobby Robson did it from that era and was massively successful and John could have achieved the same levels. In today's game John could have been a Mourinho-type, having great success at four or five different clubs all over Europe.

I don't regret my form after I left but I do regret the level of my performance while I was at West Ham. I really underachieved. When I returned to West Ham as manager I was returning not as an ex-player, but because of my record at Charlton.

I had 16 years as a player, 18 years as a manager and now six years as a pundit with Premier League TV. The power of television is colossal. The final match at the Boleyn Ground against Manchester United went to over 120 countries and was viewed by 750 million viewers.

It is a crying shame that the 'West Ham way' isn't really understood these days and that is largely because it was developed in the 60s, 70s and 80s and is and was understood by that generation of players and coaches. The people who ridicule the Academy don't understand it and weren't a part of it. Young players nowadays don't want to get it. They just want short-cuts instead of hard work and routine. Just thinking back to the sessions John ran at

Pretoria school and on the forecourt at West Ham, they were so full of enthusiasm and positive attitude. Ron Greenwood was exactly the same. I remember as a young kid watching Bobby Ferguson rolling the ball out to Bobby Moore and the crowd getting a bit frustrated with it, especially if we were behind. Afterwards, Ron would say that if Fergie kicked the ball out then it was a 50-50 or 60-40 chance that we would keep hold of it whereas if the ball was given to Bobby we were guaranteed possession. Another example from the Greenwood era, which John would have doubtless benefited from, came when Alvin Martin joined the club. He was a bit gangly and I remember playing in a South East Counties match and it was really windy. Their goalkeeper could barely reach the centre-circle such was the force of the wind. So Alvin moved up and was winning these goal kicks unopposed but they were either going back to the keeper or nowhere at all. I can still see Ron on the side of the pitch calling Alvin over and telling him to take a step back and bring the ball down on his chest, get it under control and lay it off to one of the midfielders. It became an Alvin trademark in the end. Just a simple piece of advice but how many players do you see today still thinking: 'I'm a centre-half, so I'll head it clear'?

At one stage there were so many coaches, managers and scouts who had played for West Ham it was simply incredible. It was all down to Ron and John and the education they gave to the young lads joining the club. We were so impressionable and were taught the right way so it is hardly surprising that so many of us developed a passion for coaching.

John always said that he expected me to go on to become a coach because, when the team travelled to away matches, I would always sit next to him at the front asking questions all the time.

Alan Curbishley

Following are some comments about Alan from former players and staff;

He was the most confident young kid I have ever met in my life. He totally believed he could do everything, even if he couldn't! I think it was due to his steely confidence that he became such a good manager.

Pat Holland

I thought he handled himself very well at West Ham because he was up against it with both Trevor Brooking and Graham Paddon in midfield. He produced some really excellent performances for West Ham. He could create, his passing was very good, he could organise, he scored goals, he wasn't afraid to tackle and his reading of the game was excellent.

Mick McGiven

A very good passer and never gave the ball away. He got into the first team very young and had a bit of devilment in him but his short, mid and long-range passing was spot on.

Ron Boyce

What talent he had! So much control and tremendous vision. He read the game so well and had the passing ability to match.

Alan Wooler

I followed Alan's managerial career, especially when he was at Charlton Athletic. When he left, that club went down the drain. I always tell my friends that he is one of the boys I played with at West Ham.

Yilmaz Orhan

We grew up and played in the street together so we have a special bond. I remember we played district football together and could find each other on the pitch without even looking. He got his first-team chance before me and had a lot of ability but he had less patience than me, which is why he moved on.

Paul Brush

Wally St Pier called me up one Sunday in the early 1970s and asked me to look at this kid who'd pick up an injury. It was 11:45 in the morning and I wanted to get to the pub for a pint - best drink of the week - because back then the pubs only opened between 12-2pm on Sunday, but I had to stay and look after this lad. It was 13-year-old Alan Curbishley who was playing for Senrab at the time. He was a very good footballer and had a great shot on him.

Rob Jenkins

Curbs back at the Boleyn Ground in 2016, flanked by fellow West Ham teammates and managers, Trevor Brooking and Billy Bonds.

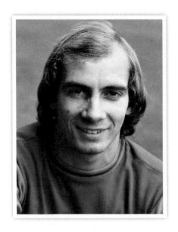

18 – ALAN WOOLER

"I can't speak about John without mention-ing Ron because I was signed by Ron and played under him in most of the handful of games I had at West Ham United. John's teams had a bit more steel and he probably received a bit more respect from the players, but I learned a lot from both men."

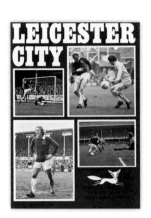

Born: Poole, Dorset, August 17, 1953 • **Position:** Defender/Midfielder • **Games played for John Lyall:** 2 (1975-1976)

Total games played for West Ham United: 5 (1973-76)

First game for John Lyall: April 1, 1975 v Leicester City (a) L 0-3 (Worthington, Garland 2) Att: 30,408

Leicester City: Wallington, Whitworth, Rofe, Lee, Blockley, Cross, Weller, Sammels, Worthington*, Birchenall, Garland. Sub: Glover.*

West Ham United: Day, Coleman, McDowell, Holland, Taylor T, Lock, Best, **Wooler**, Taylor A, Brooking, Gould.

Alan Thomas Wooler was born an only child to Thomas and Eileen Wooler. He grew up in Sandbanks Road, Poole and his football journey included Arborfield School near Reading, Preston secondary school, Yeovil district and county football with Somerset. In 1973, he was signed by Ron Greenwood on a free transfer from Reading, who had given him his first chance in professional football. Wooler ended up spending three years at Upton Park and wore the Number 6 shirt for his finest moment at the club - a 2-1 victory over Manchester United in January 1974.

During Wooler's time at West Ham United, there a few positions which were simply not available. If Bobby Moore had monopolised the Number 6 shirt from 1958 until 1974, then Frank Lampard, Billy Bonds and Trevor Brooking, ensured that the Numbers 3, 4 and 10 shirts were rarely available, too.

Alan made a name for himself playing for the Boston Minutemen in the United States and was one of the first English professional footballers to play in Finland where he lived for many years.

Nowadays, Alan is the special projects manager at Tindle Newspapers, where he has worked for 25-years. Sadly, a problem with his back and knee keep him away from the golf course for longer than desired. The interview was conducted in lush green Hampshire with a jolly nice glass of wine...or two, and an equally satisfying lunch. As the sun set on a marvellous day, Alan was in reflective mood and declared;

"I had a good career and a reasonable lifestyle, so I have no regrets really. I played in the United States and in Finland and have three wonderful kids – Jussi, Farran, and Andrina."

Here is Alan's story:

When I was a kid playing local and county football, I was called up by Matt Busby and invited up to Old Trafford. He asked me who I supported and I said Chelsea, because I liked their blue and white kit. "We'll have to change that," he said. I was then taken to the trophy room and the European Cup was sitting there, which Manchester United had just won in 1968. Obviously, it didn't work out for me there, so I was sent to Burnley, who had one of the best youth systems in the country. From there, I went to Tottenham Hotspur where I met Bill Nicholson. The Spurs' Youth Team trained with the first team back then and I had a run out on the left-wing. I ended up playing left-back most of the time, although I preferred centre-back, because of my height - six feet two inches. I was just under 12 stone and could run 400 meters in 49.9 seconds with my football boots on! That is not a wild boast but a timed fact from participating in Super Stars in Boston!

At West Ham United, I played left-midfield in most of the first team games, except away at Leicester City, where I played centre-back. My best match for West Ham was before John Lyall became manager. It was against Manchester United, and I played left-midfield. I didn't have much of a right foot.

Alan's finest moment at West Ham United, beating Manchester United 2-1, January 1974

I was signed by Mr Greenwood but Mr Lyall was coming through and eventually took over. John had come up through the ranks as a player and then as a coach under Ron. John knew how West Ham worked and developed a host of young players, and, alongside the great crop of talent already playing in the first team was in a very strong position. He had gained an education from Ron, knew everyone at the club and had a good squad of young players and senior pros to choose from.

When I joined West Ham from Reading there was a chasm between the standard of training. Ron and John put on a masterclass, whereas Reading just made you run around the park and practice a few set pieces. Understandably, the tempo at Chadwell Heath was greater and the football minds of the players were that bit quicker. It took quite a bit of time to match that pace and speed of thought. Ron and John definitely improved my standard, which is why I had a relatively successful time in the United States and Finland. I was playing in most reserve team games and then went off to the States in the close season to play for Boston Minutemen. I was easily playing 50 plus matches every season for a good ten-year period.

Little things can transform your fortunes and I remember on my debut against Stoke City I had a shot which was all set for the top corner but their keeper tipped it over. If that had gone in I'm sure it would have made me! Another time, I was close to playing against Chelsea, but Mick McGiven got the nod, probably because of his greater experience. West Ham won that game which was another set-back in my progression – I only played four more matches over the next two years. Even in the game when we beat Manchester United I had been responsible for their goal. It had nothing to do with the fact that I had been a schoolboy at United. Honest!

I didn't play first team football with Bobby Moore but was at the club at the same time and he was easily the best player I ever saw. For someone who couldn't run 400 metres in 49.9 seconds he wasn't too bad!

I wish that John had picked me to play a few more times. It would have helped me to get into the rhythm and pace of the game. I was a substitute in the Anglo-Italian cup final but I didn't get on. However, I did swap shirts with one of their players, which I still have today.

The simple fact is that I came into a West Ham team where the back four all had England Under-23 credentials, which proved to be an insurmountable situation for me.

Coupled with the fact that I wasn't selected to play in my favoured left-back position, the writing was on the wall. My football idol growing up was Giacinto Facchetti, a left-back at Inter Milan for about 20 years, who scored over 60 goals from that position and won 94 Italian caps.

If I'd stayed at West Ham, I am in no doubt that I would have developed so much more as a player. When I played in the States for the Boston Minutemen I held the record for appearing in the most consecutive number of games.

In 1976, I had the opportunity to sign another contract but John Lyall said to me: "Are you better to be a big fish in a small pond or a small fish in a big pond?" I received an

offer to go down to Aldershot Town and decided to take it. At Aldershot, I featured in every game which was a similar story at every club in Finland, too. It was really only at West Ham where I didn't establish myself as a regular first team player. In 1978, following relegation, John gave a lot of the young kids a chance to play in the old second division, so I would probably have got my opportunity, too.

I'm probably one of the only West Ham players, who has received a standing ovation at Millwall. In 1991, I managed their ladies team to a 1-0 victory over Doncaster Belles in the women's FA Cup final! I got the job because I put on my CV that I'd been coached by Ron Greenwood, John Lyall and

Alan and Mick McGiven in action against Willie Morgan of Manchester United, January 1974

Playing for Boston Minutemen in the North American Soccer League

Martti Kuusela, the famous national coach of Finland.

If you want to get on in the game you have to learn from the coach and, good or bad, I believe that anyone with the bottle to become a football manager will have something to offer. I certainly learned something from every coach I played for, whether it was Leatherhead, Boston or West Ham. Of course, it is important to be able to decipher the good from the bad! I was one of the best left-backs in the North American Soccer League and won Man-of-the-Match in a game against Pele's New York Cosmos. I also held the record for most assists in one half of football, all for the Boston Minutemen. I played with Eusebio, Antonio Simoes, Jorge Calado, Carlos Maneca and Fernando Nelson. As well as Pele, I played against Chinaglia, Jimmy Johnstone and George Best. I'm very happy with that.

The biggest influence on my career was my dad who worked for the Ministry of Defence I played for some truly great coaches but the best of all was my father. Some of my fondest football memories are kicking a ball about with him in our back garden in Yeovil.

I was brought up to respect the person I was working for so I had the same respect for both Ron and John. There is no comparison to make between Mr Greenwood and Mr Lyall. They are both equal. One was the teacher and the other the student. The main beneficiaries, of course, were the West Ham United fans who saw Ron's philosophy win trophies for both himself and John.

They had many fine attributes and a good man management technique was one of those. Man-management is something that has largely left the game nowadays but men like Ron Greenwood, John Lyall and Brian Clough had it in abundance.
Alan Wooler

Following are some comments from Alan's former teammates;

Alan was honest and hard working.
Mick McGiven

Alan was a good pro and a nice lad to have around the ground.
Pat Holland

We played together in the reserves and it was good to see him at Upton Park for a game during the final season at the old place.
Alan Taylor

A big, leggy, left-back, who I played with in the reserves.
Paul Brush

Two of the lesser known West Ham players, Alan Wooler and Bertie Lutton, both have a victory over Manchester United on their football CVs.
Billy Bonds

Alan in 2017 with the programme from his debut

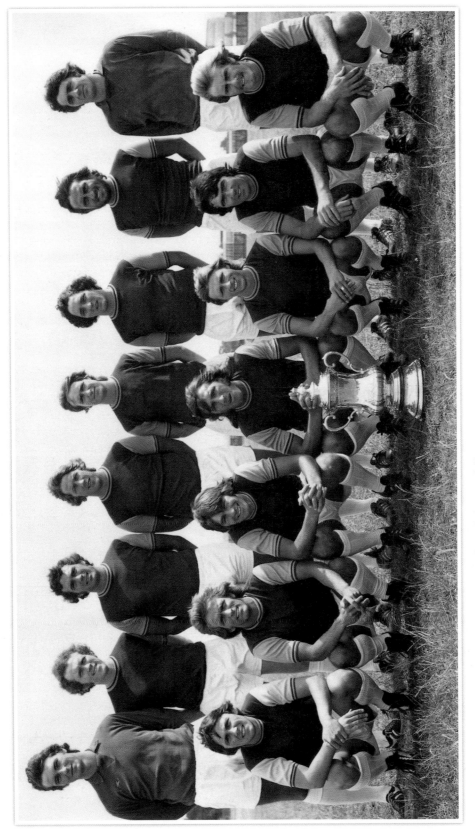

Back row: Day, McGiven, Brooking, T Taylor, Lock, McDowell, Lampard, Ferguson.

Front row: Coleman, Jennings, K Robsor, Bonds, A Taylor, Gould, Paddon

They Played For John Lyall – The West Ham Years

CHAPTER TWO
1975-76

"I don't think you could possibly see a better match than that. This is the greatest display in the club's history. Everything I hoped for when I took the job came true tonight."
John Lyall's Eintracht Frankfurt post match comments

John arranging a space for the FA Cup with club secrerary, Eddie Chapman

West Ham fans enjoying a knees up before the European Cup Winners' Cup final in Brussels.

West Ham United are back in Europe after a 10 year absence. John Lyall ensured his team did not rest on its FA Cup laurels by remaining unbeaten in the first nine league matches. After a point at home to Coventry City in November 1975, West Ham went top of the league for the first time since 1959. Trevor Brooking's goal against Derby County at the Baseball ground on November 15 won ITV's 'Goal of the Season.' Martin Peters was the only previous Hammer to achieve the honour.

Tottenham Hotspur's legendary manager and long-time friend of Ron Greenwood, Bill Nicholson, joined the West Ham staff. The 55-year-old won eight trophies in 15 years for the north London club, including the European Cup Winners Cup in 1963. It was hoped his experience would assist the Hammers during their own European campaign: *"West Ham have the ideal system,"* commented Nicholson: *"Ron Greenwood, with all his knowledge, is able to control the administrative side of the club, leaving John Lyall, an outstanding coach, to concentrate on preparing the players. Advice is available should he need it."*

The stability at the club was personified in the shape of Chairman Reg Pratt who celebrated 25 years in the role. After watching his side defeat Eintracht Frankfurt to make it to the European Cup Winners' Cup final, Mr Pratt made the following comment: *"I've had my proud moments at West Ham United, but this equals anything we have achieved before."*

John Lyall was in no doubt about the benefits of playing in European competition: "In the last couple of months in Europe we have gained the equivalent of six years maturity in the league."

The family traditions of the club are beautifully captured in an announcement made in the club's 'Hammer' programme: 'George Izatt, the man who has looked after the Upton Park pitch for almost three decades has retired. He was a fully qualified groundsman and horticultural expert. He had replaced form Hammer Dan Woodards after World War II.'

Four Hammers were selected by John Lyall for the very first time: Yilmaz Orhan, Mick McGiven, Geoff Pike and Bobby Ferguson.

Here is their story...

19 - Yilmaz Orhan

" I'm in my sixties now and a few of us old guys still have a kick about every Saturday and Sunday morning in Las Vegas. I pull on the West Ham United shirt and still try to play the John Lyall way! "

Born: Nicosia, Cyprus, March 13, 1955 • **Position:** Midfielder • **Games played for West Ham United:** 9 (1976)

Debut: January 24, 1976 v Queens Park Rangers (h) W 1-0 (Taylor A) Att: 26,677

West Ham United: Day, McDowell, Lampard, Holland, Taylor T, Coleman, Taylor A, Paddon, Brooking, Jennings, **Orhan.**

Chelsea: Parkes, Clement, Gillard, Hollins, McLintock*, Webb, Thomas, Beck, Masson, Leach, Given. Sub: Nutt.*

Yilmaz Orhan played nine times in West Ham United's first team. Contemporary press reports, after his debut against QPR, included an assessment from John Lyall: "He is strong, has pace and used the ball intelligently early on." It was an encouraging start for 'Yilly', who had travelled to London from Cyprus to study law but developed a talent for football.

He was signed from Aveley FC by Ron Greenwood, who was impressed by his pace and ability to score goals. Although his opportunities at West Ham were limited, Yilmaz did spend five years at the club. The vast majority of his playing career was spent in the United States of America where he became something of a journeyman, playing for no fewer than 14 clubs before finally retiring in 1989.

Orhan then settled in Las Vegas where he worked in the Riviera Hotel for 20 years. He still resides in Vegas today and is as effervescent as ever: "I have a 34-year-old daughter who has a ten-year-old boy and I have a 31-year-old boy who has a six-year-old daughter, so I am enjoying life as a grandpa in 'Sin City!' I still try to play football every weekend. It is more like walking football but still gives me great pleasure. I am registered disabled due to a heart condition. I have an irregular heartbeat and suffer with arthritis in my knees, hip and hands. But, I am happy and loving life!"

Yilmaz has a sister who lives in Hornchurch and plans to visit these shores in the not too distant future:

Whenever I think of John Lyall I think of a very nice gentleman. Sadly, I wasn't his type of player. Someone like Keith Robson was a better player for Mr Lyall. Keith was prepared to go through brick walls, he just didn't care. Robbo would put his head where others would not even put their feet and that is what John really liked.

I was born in Nicosia, Cyprus. My father was a hospital porter and my mother looked after my sisters and me. She also travelled to Beirut to buy gold jewellery which she sold at weddings in Cyprus. This brought in some extra money for the family which helped to bring better food and clothes into the house. Then I got the chance to live with my grandmother in London so everything changed for me.

The big influence in my football life was my sports coach at Clissold Park School in Arsenal where I was living. His name was Terry Matthews and he was the coach at Aveley Football Club, where I used to practice. I travelled there by train for a couple of hours and that was quite scary for a young kid but for football I would do anything. Most kids were like that back then.

One Thursday morning Terry took me to Loftus Road for a trial. I felt I had a decent game and the QPR manager - Gordon Jago - said he would discuss everything with Mr Matthews and get back to me. A few weeks went by and I didn't hear anything and then Terry said he was going to take me to West Ham for a trial. When I heard this I realised that QPR didn't want me and I was in tears. Why didn't they like me? What was wrong with my game? I had so many doubts but I was just a young kid.

Terry took me to Chadwell Heath and introduced me to Ron Greenwood and John Lyall. May both of them rest in peace. I practiced with the reserve team but not with the big boys. After one week, I played in a practice game between the reserves and the first team and after a couple of months Mr Greenwood called me to his office and said: "Yilly", we want to sign you." Ron always called me 'Yilly' but I didn't hear anything else he said because I was the happiest kid on earth! That was February 1972.

I lived in Stoke Newington, not far from Arsenal's stadium. There was a Turkish community and I stayed there with my grandma, my auntie and my uncle. That is where I stayed the whole time I played for West Ham United.

I think it is fair to say that Mr Greenwood liked me more as a footballer than Mr Lyall. Ron looked for speed, skill, dribbling and scoring goals. John, on the other hand, liked his footballers to be strong, aggressive and tough in the tackle and I certainly wasn't one of those boys. I didn't really like tackling for fear of getting injured or hurting people. I was always confident that I could get to the ball first by using my speed.

The number one player I remember at West Ham was Alan Curbishley, God bless him and his family. We played in the reserves together and his distribution to Ade Coker and myself ensured a lot of goals. I think we scored 20 goals each in the reserves during the season I made my first team debut. Ade was also a good friend to me. I always felt that he was like my brother. We also played in San Diego against each other and I would love to see him again one day.

I enjoyed running and every pre-season we ran around Epping Forest. I was up the front with Billy Bonds but not that close because Billy was the best runner at the club. Another thing I remember was training with a medicine ball. The physio, Rob Jenkins, threw it at our stomachs and if we said a word he would do another ten. Rob was such a big character. If I had a muscle pull he would put some kind of heat lamp on it and if I was cheeky or complained he would turn it up to 500! I would be begging for mercy: "Please, Rob!" I would say: "I will never speak again!" He called me Turkish Delight!

I had no complaints with any of the players at West Ham – the youngsters or the old boys – they all treated me very well and I thank them for that.

I was very lucky because I was never an apprentice and signed professional forms straight away, so I didn't have to clean the boots or wash the shirts and shorts. However, every morning I would ask Bobby Moore, Frank Lampard, Trevor Brooking and Billy Bonds if they would like a cup of tea. I did like to help out with that to show that I cared and had respect for them.

In 1977 a German coach called Hubert Vogelsinger came to West Ham and talked to us about playing in the North

'Yilly' on the ball

America Soccer League for a new franchise called Team Hawaii. Five of us took up the offer - Tommy Taylor, Pat Holland, Keith Coleman, Keith Robson and myself. When I came back, Ron Greenwood was on his way to the England job, which I felt was bad news for me. I had no idea what plans John had for me and it was disappointing that he didn't discuss anything. To be honest, I was a little bit hurt about it because I expected some kind of discussion about what is happening. I don't have any strong objections but I am curious to know how my contract was ended and what arrangements were made for me without my knowledge. In the end, a chap came from the United States and said he had my contract from Team Hawaii, and that he wanted me to play for Tulsa. From there I went to Houston Hurricanes because Tulsa had folded as well! Nevertheless, my journey through the outdoor and indoor soccer leagues had started. I decided to stay in the United States and have no complaints with that decision at all. I was a young kid and would go anywhere to play football. I played on the same pitch as all the great footballers – Pele, Beckenbauer, Eusebio, Chinaglia etc. They were all just normal guys. We went to the bar

In action on his debut against Ian Gillard of QPR, January 1976

afterwards and talked and signed autographs for the fans. They were just really nice people, very nice people, indeed.

It is funny because sometimes over dinner with my family we talk a lot about our childhood and I like to talk about my days at West Ham. I have three pictures in my mind from my debut against Queens Park Rangers. I can see myself in the tunnel on the way out, running onto the pitch at the back of the team. Then I remember, Graham Paddon finding me with a cross and I controlled the ball and had a shot which went over. That was my highlight in the West Ham shirt! My third picture is playing a couple of one-twos with Trevor Brooking. I must say that I didn't have that feeling of confidence which I had when playing for the reserves where I was comfortable and relaxed. I had Geoff Pike and Alan Curbishley around me and it just felt right. We were so confident that we would win those games and I think we had a very good record in the reserves at that time. Maybe I was young and didn't have confidence in myself and my ability to play in the first team. We still talk about it over dinner even now. But I have to thank John because he did give me enough chances. I played nine games but we only won once so it was difficult. However, I am grateful that the only victory came on my debut.

I don't remember much about John in the dressing room but I do remember where I sat. It was the same place where I sat when playing for the reserves, on the south side of the room. I remember the shower and the large bath where we warmed up our muscles. There was a board on the left hand side which had the team sheet pinned to it. As young boys, we sprinted to see if our names were on the list and which team we were in. John didn't tell me that I was going to play but when I went to check the lists, my name was there. I

was so shocked and so excited.

I think it is fair to say that I had a better relationship with Mr Greenwood than I did with Mr Lyall. Ron would always say: "Good morning, Yilly" He'd ask me how I was and what I'd been doing, whereas John would just say: "Good morning." Nothing else. There wasn't much talk. Ernie Gregory was always very good to me. He'd ruffle my hair and ask me if I was ready to go: "Yes, sir," I would reply. "I'm always ready." Bill Lansdowne was our reserve team coach and he was another really nice guy.

I retired from football in 1989, after I broke my big toe playing for Milwaukee. I moved to San Diego with my wife at the time but, on one occasion, I went to Las Vegas to visit a friend for a couple of weeks. Once you visit Las Vegas you cannot leave! There were plenty of job opportunities and I worked for 20 years in the Riviera hotel. I worked on the floor looking after the slot machine players. After a while, I got heavily involved on the slot machines and it took me many years to realise that there are no winners in gambling.

I was caught in the grip of Texas Hold 'em Poker. It's so easy to get hooked on those machines and I was working all week and then losing everything at the weekend. Sometimes I would win $5,000 but then, two weeks later, I was borrowing money from here, there and everywhere to fund my habit. It just wasn't a happy situation. I was caught in the grip of gambling for at least 10 years so it is not a pleasant thing to talk about. At the lowest point, I was only thinking about playing poker and nothing else. This was particularly bad because I was a single father bringing up two children. I know it did some damage to them and, although they had clothes on their backs, food in their stomachs and a roof over their heads,

Yilmaz-a Turkish Delight!

LEN WHALEY AT UPTON PARK

YILMAZ ORHAN made an impact in his first am debut at Upton Park on Saturday but nearly id not become a West Ham player in the first place — in fact the first pro club colours he wore were

it is not something I am proud about. It took a lot of help from my friends and family before I could release myself from the grip of gambling. I had to be honest and talk about the losses before I could get myself out of it. That is the only way.

Even though I have a heart condition, I remain active and I am a member of a health club. It is a good social outlet for me because I can swim and cycle and watch football with my friends. I still play football every Saturday and Sunday but I have to be careful because my heart can start racing and doesn't slow down. I then have to go to hospital where they regulate my heartbeat. They stop my heart for three seconds and reset it. Afterwards, I'm okay - until the next time! It is not life-threatening but it is not a good thing either. You don't want to mess around with your heart. If the engine stops, you can't go anywhere! I enjoy my football and I'm actually one of the younger players. There are several over 70, who are from Chile, Argentina and Peru. Some of them are ex-pros so they're in very good shape. We also have some youngsters to help us compete and enjoy our Sunday mornings.

A couple of years ago I visited my sister and brother-in-law in Hornchurch and bought a few things from the West Ham shop for my friends in Las Vegas.

I am a very emotional person so I cried when both Ron Greenwood and John Lyall died. I told my girlfriend, Jenny, that these were the people who made my life. Whatever I have done in my life and wherever I end up it is because of them. I am very grateful for that. It was a black moment when we lost those two great men.
Yilmaz Orhan

Yilmaz is still fondly remembered by his former teammates:

He was fast, good looking and well groomed.
Alan Taylor

A flying machine and a very good player, who could put the ball away. We were all expecting good things from him. He had pace and trickery but like a lot of young players didn't get the rub of the green.
Alan Wooler

He was a very good runner. I could run for fun but Yilmaz even edged me. He had a lot of good attributes.
Pat Holland

He was a pioneer in a way, because he was the first Cypriot to play for West Ham United. He deserves a lot more recognition for the journey he took and the standard he reached.
Alan Curbishley

He was a winger, a real Tricky Dicky who had plenty of ability but didn't seem to impose himself on a game which was a pity because he put everything into his training.
Mick McGiven

He should have been a model rather than a footballer!
Kevin Lock

Enjoying life in Las Vegas with partner, Jenny

20 – MICK McGIVEN

*"How can you sack a man
like John Lyall?"*

HAMMER

1975-76 OFFICIAL PROGRAMME
TENPENCE

Saturday 3 January 1976
KICK-OFF AT 3 p.m.
LIVERPOOL
Football Association Cup : Third Round

Born: Newcastle-upon-Tyne. February 7, 1951 • **Position:** Defender • **Games played for John Lyall:** 32 (1976-77)

Games played for West Ham United: 56 (1973-77) • **First game under John Lyall:** January 3, 1976 Liverpool FA Cup
3rd round (h) L 0-2 (Keegan, Toshack) Att: 32,363

West Ham United: Day, Coleman, Lampard, Holland, **McGiven,** Lock, Taylor A, Paddon, Brooking, Jennings, Curbishley.

Liverpool: Clemence, Smith, Neal, Thompson, Kennedy, Hughes, Keegan, Case, Heighway, Toshack, Callaghan.

Michael McGiven joined West Ham United from Sunderland in November 1973 for the princely sum of £20,000. 22-year-old 'Mick' could not have known that his spell with the Hammers would evolve into a coaching role which would keep him at the club for the entire duration of John Lyall's tenure as manager. Both he and Ron Boyce sat beside John throughout the highs and lows of domestic and European endeavour, which defined a generation of West Ham United fans. Relegation, promotion, cup successes and unprecedented league achievement, all revolved around the colossal effort and output of John's coaching machine, of which Mick was a vital cog. The experience has resulted in Mick being a dyed-in-the-wool Hammer from the Lyall school of West Ham United management and his knowledge of the era is unsurpassed.

Although Mick has one foot in retirement, he still supports the Chelsea management team with player assessments and scouting reports. He is another ex-Hammer whose knowledge and experience of the game has provided success to other clubs, an accidental by-product of John Lyall's sacking in 1989. The brain drain created as a consequence of that decision – arguably the worst in the club's history - is unfathomable.

Not only did Mick give several hours of his time to talk

about John Lyall, he also provided, what amounts to a scouting report on most of the 77 Hammers to have played for West Ham United between 1974-89:

John was very, very, similar to Ron. Educated, articulate and intelligent.

I had played under John, before joining him on the coaching side of things. I always did some extra training in the afternoons at Upton Park. There was a little gymnasium there and I'd get a ball out and practice a few things. I was just trying to improve my game. John would also come back to Upton Park and he'd see me in the gym and ask me what I was doing. I talked to him about what I was working on and he would offer up some advice and then suggest some different things to try out. He was just being John, just wanting to help. I was struggling with a few injuries and had a problem with my knee but in the evenings I did some coaching for the Under-14s and Under-15s at the club's Centre of Excellence.

When Eddie Baily joined the club John asked me if I wanted to get a bit more involved on the coaching side and I said I would think about it. My priority at the time, of course, was to get back to full fitness in order to play football again. However, at the end of the 1977-78 season, John asked me if I wanted to be player-coach for the reserves and, this time, I decided to accept. Bill Lansdowne was reserve team coach

1977 pre-season tour of Norway v Moss FK. Mick (6) slides in as teammates Curbishley, McDowell and Day are on hand

at the time and my job was to help Bill. Sometime later, after one particular game when the reserves got absolutely battered, John and Bill had a falling out and Bill lost his job. Soon after that I was asked to take over full responsibility for the reserves until the end of the season. Things developed further, when John asked both Ronnie Boyce and me to assist him with first team affairs. So, Boycey and me would split our time between looking after the reserves and helping John. Basically, it meant I worked a lot more with John which was a fantastic education for me.

John would usually be one of the first at Chadwell Heath in the morning. He'd ask for a roll-call of injuries and draw up a list of all those who were fit to train. Then he'd write down what was to be done that day. There were no computers back then so everything was set down, by hand, on paper.

At the start of pre-season training John would devise a six-week plan, which would include running around either Epping or Hainault Forest and a little bit of ball work in the afternoons. Nothing too intense because John was all about a gradual progressive build-up towards full-time training. After a few weeks, John would introduce more ball work, more speed work before taking the squad to Norway or

Sweden for a pre-season tournament. Towards the end of John's time at the club we went to Finland. John enjoyed those trips and the club was very well received.

On our return, both Eddie Baily and Ernie Gregory would furnish John with assessment reports on the teams West Ham were due to face in the first few weeks of the season. Ernie was the goalkeeping coach, of course, but he travelled absolutely everywhere in his white Hillman, gathering information on the opposition.

If there was a chance for John to watch a match during mid-week, he would invariably take Boycey along. The next day he'd discuss tactics and organise training around how the team could exploit the weaknesses of the opposition and negate their strengths. So, if the opposition was very physical, John made sure the training sessions were very physical. If our opponents relied on the long ball, John would set up plenty of heading practice and hard, physical aerial battles. Another time we might be playing Arsenal, who liked to set an offside trap and John would have the team in the grids working on how to spring it. He would also make sure that a good part of the session was focused on our game, the West Ham approach to the match - the one-touch, two-touch football with quick movements off the ball, combination play in wide areas and near post runs and precision around the timing of our crosses. Everything was very thorough, well thought through and it all had a purpose. The players understood it and felt part of something. John made everyone believe in it and we all had faith in his approach and enjoyed it.

Even before John was formally appointed team manager in August 1974, I remember benefitting from his knowledge of the game. We were playing Don Revie's Leeds United, who were a force back then. I was marking Allan Clarke and he was making lots of darting runs and I wasn't sure whether or not to go with him. I didn't want to leave a space for their other centre forward, Mick Jones to exploit. I was caught in two minds but I looked over to John and he was urging me to follow Clarke and man-mark him. That little bit of guidance gave me all I needed to feel confident in what I was doing and I shadowed Clarke and was snapping at his heels and he didn't like it one little bit. We beat a very good Leeds United side 3-1 that day. They eventually went on to win the league.

One thing that annoyed John was players not playing to their maximum potential. He'd say: "Don't confuse kindness with softness." If the team weren't performing he'd let them know. He was hard when he needed to be but usually preferred to improve his argument rather than raise his voice. He always knew where the team was falling short in

a game. Tactically, he was one of the best. Players know a good coach from a bad coach and they were spoilt at West Ham because John wasn't just a good coach, he was an outstanding coach. Exceptional!

John continued the coaching philosophy of Ron Greenwood. He worked tirelessly every day, week-in, week-out, month-in, month-out and year-on-year to produce a team that could play quick, attacking and entertaining football. That is why when Lou Macari joined the club I had a massive argument with him almost immediately. One of the first things Lou said was: "If you win, it doesn't matter how you play." I couldn't stomach such a comment because it flew in the face of everything we'd been working for at West Ham for as far back as you care to go.

It does matter how you play. It will always matter how you play and during that era West Ham fans had been raised on a very specific style of play which had garnered success for the club. When you move away from that, yes you might win games but you won't win the hearts of the West Ham United people. Some of the football we played in 1985-86, when we finished third in the league, was sensational. Absolutely outstanding! It lifted the supporters off their seats. It was quick, decisive and the fans loved it. Everyone connected to the club couldn't wait for the next game. We were scoring goals, Alan Devonshire was mercurial, our defence was tight and the whole team was completely synchronised with one

Mick (far right) tussles with Charlton Athletic's Derek Hales with Tommy Taylor on hand, September 1976

another. They all had faith in their ability, all wanted the ball and confidence was sky high throughout that amazing season.

I worked so closely to John and had a good sense of the players he really liked. I remember how he did not want to lose David Cross but, sadly, fought a losing battle on that occasion because David wanted to go back home to Lancashire. It is my opinion that John would put Crossy in his best eleven, alongside Pop Robson up front. He rated David very highly, largely because he possessed those three elements that John loved - honesty, endeavour and loyalty.

Between John, Ron and myself, we knew every boy at the club from the age of 13 upwards. One of the controversial decisions John made, which is often looked back on with incredulity by many, was the decision not to extend the contract of Ray Houghton. At that particular time, however, football was so different. You didn't have squads of 25 or 30. West Ham had a squad of about 18, maximum. It was our responsibility to improve every player we coached. John felt the best way that we could help Ray was to give him a free transfer. As fine a player as he was, there was quite a busy midfield at the club at that time - Trevor Brooking, Geoff Pike, Paul Allen and Alan Dickens. Where was Ray going to play? He was certainly an exceptional player, there is no doubt about that but, at the time, he was no more exceptional than those players I have already mentioned. In my opinion, Paul Allen and Alan Dickens were better players than Ray back then. They were different players, but better. John did the right thing by Ray because he went on and had a fantastic career for Fulham, Oxford United, Liverpool, Aston Villa, Crystal Palace and the Republic of Ireland. He was a terrific lad as well. The sad thing about football today is that a player like Ray Houghton will be put on good wages and never get a chance. Sure, he'll end up being very wealthy but he won't ever fulfil his potential. Far too many players prefer that set up because they are too worried about playing and being found out and losing everything.

John had a certain way of keeping on top of his players. Most of the time he wouldn't ask about a specific player. Instead he would say: "Who played well today? Who trained well today?" Then on certain occasions he may ask you a direct question about a certain player: "How did Ray Houghton play today?" or "How did Brushy train today?"

In terms of transfers and the recruitment of players, John usually discussed that with the chief scout. Initially, it was Wally St Pier but after he retired, John brought in Eddie Baily. Together they decided who would be coming into the club and who would be leaving. I can't vouch for Ronnie Boyce but John never discussed the signing of players with me, except on one occasion – the return of Frank McAvennie to West Ham. John asked the opinions of all his coaching staff and not everyone agreed to bring Frank back for a

Catching up with paperwork in his office

second spell. I think John understood it was a gamble and he probably knew Frank wasn't the player he had been, but felt that he could still bring a stimulus and a dynamic to lift the team. More so than the alternative of bringing in a new, untried player.

One thing about John was that he'd never have any truck with agents but nowadays they run football. John felt a player transfer was between club and club. These days, transfers are determined by the agent and that cannot be good for football. Where are we if a club can't sign a player because the agent doesn't want him to go there? It certainly isn't good for those pillars of strength which have always defined West Ham United – endeavour, honesty and loyalty. The really sad thing for me is that the past is so quickly forgotten. There is a new generation of West Ham United fans who hang their hat on a goal by a player such as Dimitri Payet, completely unaware that Alan Devonshire was ten times the player he will ever be. They herald the contribution of Chicarito Hernandez and countless other strikers, while being blissfully ignorant of the fact that Pop Robson scored many more spectacular goals. Many more!

I feel privileged to have known John, as a man, as a friend and perhaps most importantly of all, as a mentor. Without John Lyall - and to an extent Ron Greenwood - I wouldn't be in football today and wouldn't have had the career I've had working at some magnificent football clubs with so many magnificent people - people with whom I have shared good times and bad. What a ride!

My only wish is that there were more people like John Lyall in football today because our national side is crying out for them. If we had someone with the characteristics of John to take over the national team it would undoubtedly breathe life into something that is dying. It is painful to think about it, but at this moment in time there doesn't appear to be anyone.
Mick McGiven

Following are memories of Mick from his former colleagues:
A good defender, as brave as a lion. Mick is a very conscientious man and a talented coach. He was very loyal to John.
Pat Holland

Mick roomed with Keith Coleman but when we played Ararat Erevan the rooms were riddled with cockroaches, holes in the floors and filthy mattresses, so they slept head to toe on one of the single beds in the room I was sharing with Mervyn Day. Merv and I went head to toe in the other single, too!
Alan Taylor

West Ham put out a cricket team as part of Pat Pocock's Testimonial (Surrey and England). All the London club's played and West Ham won it. Mick was a good cricketer and played that day. It took place at the Oval in July 1977.
Bill Green

Mick didn't say much but he went about his business on the pitch very well. He was a quiet gentleman.
Yilmaz Orhan

Mick used to make us laugh when he was coaching the young lads. A couple of us would go for a ball and enter into a crunching tackle with blood and bruises everywhere and he'd say in his Geordie accent: "Well done the pair of you." My dad, Bobby, helped him to get the job at Chelsea.
Greg Campbell

Mick did a lot of the spade work for John and is a deep thinker about the game and very thorough in every detail. He is always pleased to see the West Ham boys from that era. He'd stay all day and night with a player if he thought he could help.
Paul Brush

We went on tour to Japan once and Mick had far too much Saki and was bilious. John told me to look after him so I went to his room and there was sick everywhere. "Don't tell the lads," he groaned, so the first thing I did was tell all the lads!
Rob Jenkins

John loved Mick. He'd go round to John's for dinner and loved to pick John's brains about coaching and football in general.
Kevin Lock

'Capper' we called him after Arnold Capper in General Hospital.
Tommy Taylor

L-R Kevin Lock, Mick McGiven, Alan Taylor and Bobby Gould. Paraded on the pitch for the last ever visit of Arsenal to the Boleyn Ground, April 2016

21 – GEOFF PIKE

"I'd put John right up there with the great coaches. He was progressive, modern in his outlook and was always looking for that small margin to make his team better. One of the best traits you can have as a leader is humility and John had that in abundance."

Born: Lower Clapton, London, September 28, 1956 • **Position:** Midfield • **Goals:** 41 (Joint 42nd with Harry Stapley and Jermain Defoe on the all-time list) • **Games played for West Ham United:** 368 (1976-1987). Joint 21st with Tony Gale on the all-time list • **Honours under John Lyall:** 1975 FA Youth Cup runner-up, 1980 FA Cup winner, 1980 Charity Shield runner-up, 1981 League Cup runner-up, 1981 Second Division Champion, 1985-86 Member of highest every league finish (Third)
Debut: March 6, 1976 Birmingham City (h) L 1-2 (Curbishley – Withe, Emmanuel) Att: 19,868
West Ham United: Day, Coleman, Lampard, Bonds, Taylor T, Wooler, Taylor A, Paddon, Curbishley, Orhan,* Robson K. Sub: **Pike.***
Birmingham City: Latchford, Martin, Styles*, Kendall, Gallagher, Burns, Emmanuel, Francis, Withe, Page, Hibbitt.* Sub: Calderwood.*

Geoff Pike was born to parents, Alan and Eileen. His father worked in insurance and his mother was his biggest fan. 'Pikey,' as he was affectionately known by the West Ham faithful is one of only 30-Hammers to have won an FA Cup winners medal.

It is not widely known that Pike had trained with the club in the mid-1960s and had over 100 first team appearances under his belt by the time he walked out at Wembley for that historic victory over Arsenal in 1980.

In 1976-77, 20-year-old Pike made a tremendous contribution to West Ham United's successful fight for survival. His young shoulders took on the mantle of penalty taker and his successful spot kicks against Derby County and Coventry City had given the Hammers a glimmer of hope. In the final match of the season - against Manchester United – Pike scored a goal which took the roof off at Upton Park: *"The atmosphere was electric. We ended up winning 4-2 and it was one of the great, great nights."*

After leaving Upton Park in 1985, Pike played out the remainder of his career with Notts County and Leyton Orient. John Lyall always felt dedicated professionals such as Geoff Pike and Pat Holland were perfect candidates to work for football's top organisations such as The FA and The PFA.

Geoff took that path and in 2004 gained his UEFA pro licence: *I've been working at The FA for the past 10 years and always stay in touch with the players from that Golden era in West Ham's history."*

In September 2017, Geoff caught up with former teammates Phil Parkes, Alan Devonshire, Steve Walford, Alan Dickens, John Ayris, Tony Cottee and Tony Gale, during a reunion at Dagenham and Redbridge's Victoria Road ground.

I first met John at Chadwell Heath as a 10-year-old in 1966, when he was youth team coach. His first words to me were: "How old are you?" I told him my age and he said I was a bit young but to train anyway. At the end of the session he told me to come back on Thursday.

By the time I made it to the first team in 1976, John was in charge of first team affairs. Ron Greenwood was largely a figure head. I didn't feel comfortable approaching Ron, but because I'd know John for 10 years I was much more relaxed talking with him.

I loved football but John made me love it even more. There was never any monotony in anything he did. Training was fresh, exciting and full of variety. I was a very committed player and John probably saw more in me than I did in myself. He was very good at recognising certain skills and ability. He worked tirelessly to help his players express that ability. Frank McAvennie is a good example of that. He hadn't been the star of the show up in Scotland and was relatively unknown when signing for West Ham. John recognised something in him and he became one of the great names in West Ham's history.

My debut came against Birmingham City, at home, in March 1976. I came on as a substitute for Yilmaz Orhan but it was later revealed that he was injured before kick-off so, actually, I should have made my first start in that match. I had to wait eight months for my first start but it was well worth it because we beat Tottenham Hotspur 5-3 at home.

The happiest I saw John was after winning the FA Cup in 1980. The angriest I saw him was the following season when he felt we should have won the League Cup against Liverpool. It was only David Cross who stopped him getting to the referee, Clive Thomas. He was disgusted that Liverpool's goal was allowed to stand even though Sammy Lee had been lying in an offside position. It's funny, because Sammy Lee worked for The FA for a while and we often discussed events from that final. I think he thought it should have been disallowed but he'd never admit to that.

My first full season came in 1976-77. Up until March, I was in and out of the team. The club was in the grip of a relegation

One of only 30 Hammers to win the FA Cup

Weaving a way through Arsenal at Wembley, May 1980

scrap and we went up to play Derby County at the Baseball Ground. In the dressing room beforehand, John asked if anyone fancied taking the penalties. At the time, Billy Bonds and Pop Robson had both missed penalties so I put my hand up and said I'd do it. We drew that match 1-1 and I scored from the spot. We then went on a run of seven matches without defeat and I scored another penalty in a 2-0 win at home to Coventry City.

The final match of the season was against Manchester United and we had to win to stay up. In the first half I missed a penalty and we went in at 1-1. John's half-time talk has stayed with me forever. He was convinced we were the better team and passionately implored the lads to win it... "For that young lad," and pointed at me. It made me feel a lot better and I managed to score in the second half and we ran out 4-2 winners, which meant survival and euphoria.

The following day I flew out to the United States of America to play in the North America Soccer League. I lined up for the Hartford Bicentennials against Pele and the New York Cosmos. As a 20-year-old it really doesn't get any better than that.

I scored 41 goals for West Ham and there are a few which stand out. I scored a volley against Norwich City at home during our relegation escape in 1977. The cross came over and Billy Bonds said he was going to shout for me to leave it but decided against it. I'm pleased he did because it was the only goal of the game.

I scored at West Bromwich Albion during the successful 1980 FA Cup run. John played me up front in that match and I beat their centre-half, John Wile, to side foot home. I scored against all the big clubs – Liverpool, Arsenal, Spurs and Manchester United. The goal everyone remembers is the header up at Old Trafford in the FA Cup. That is a very special memory for me.

One of the super charged conversations I had with John came before a match against Southampton at The Dell. My mum had suffered a brain haemorrhage and was in traction. A couple of days before the match I went to see John and told him that I wasn't in the right frame of mind to play. He was very understanding and we were having a conversation as friends rather than as manager and player. In passing he said: "What do you think you're mum would want?" That question made me think about the situation in a different way. My mum was my biggest fan and would have hated it if I hadn't played because of her. After some consideration I decided to play. It just so happened that Kevin Keegan was in the Southampton team that day. He was one of my mum's favourite. In the tunnel beforehand I had a chat with him and asked him if he'd sign the programme for my mum. Once the match was over we were sitting in the dressing room when Kevin walked in with the signed programme. I thought that was the mark of a very special person. I didn't have to remind him, he came and found me.

John had so much belief in me and on one occasion selected

The joy of scoring against Liverpool, October 1982

me to play at Highbury in a friendly between a London Select XI and the England team. He clearly wanted to showcase my talents on that type of stage. I played really well and felt that I'd controlled the midfield. Afterwards, all the talk was about Brian Talbot, and why he was playing for England and I wasn't. I was very grateful to John for that opportunity.

Just before Christmas, 1982, I was in the corridor at the ground when Ronnie Boyce called me into his office. John was down with flu but wanted me to captain the side against Notts County in a League Cup match. It was one of the greatest moments in my football career. To lead out the team I loved as captain, well, it still makes me shiver.

Ironically, I signed for Notts County when I left West Ham in 1987. I hadn't been having the best of times and had lost my form. I think the last six matches I played in all ended in defeat and I was under enormous pressure. John Barnwell came in for me and made an attractive offer – decent money and the captaincy - so I decided to drop down a couple of divisions. I spent two years at Meadow Lane before playing out my career at Leyton Orient and Hendon.

Even after I left West Ham John was a continued source of support. One of the last times I saw him was at a Charity Event which I help to organise each year. I have a group of friends that I have known for 40-odd years and we raise money for St Francis' Hospice. I invited John and Yvonne along to an event, at the Prince Regent in Chigwell. They were only too happy to oblige.

John was a mentor and a friend. He had a massive influence on my development, both as a footballer and as a person.

Geoff Pike

Captain of West Ham United, December 1982

Pikey was a bundle of fun, like Benny the Ball out of Top Cat. He was another typical West Ham recruit - a local lad with the raw talent waiting to be developed by the top coaches at the club.
Bill Green

He was one of the senior pros who took the time to help the youngsters. He knew the game really well and passed on his advice and experience. We got on well, and I felt he was a little under-appreciated at times. He deserved a lot more credit than he was given.
Ray Houghton

He was a busy, friendly, energetic, young kid and we became friends during my first training session. He was so responsible with the ball on the pitch and really good in tight situations with his touch and movement.
Paul Brush

He was a good player, Pikey. Very underrated. Alan Devonshire John Lyall loved him, that's for sure. We played a lot together in the reserves. He was hard working and could run all day and loved to tackle. He would run through walls for West Ham.
Yilmaz Orhan

Pikey was a few years younger than me and got into the team at an early age. Very similar to Ronnie Boyce as a player. A bit more athletic than Ronnie but a very good one and two-touch player. He didn't possess great pace but could see things and read the game well.
Pat Holland

A bit like Mark Noble. A real grafter with a great shot.
Alan Wooler

Mr Dependable. He'd always give you an 8 or 9 out of 10 performance. He rarely had an off day. Very rarely. He was the perfect foil for Trevor Brooking. Who could forget his header at Old Trafford to knock Manchester United out of the cup?
Mick McGiven

At a Hammers reunion in September, 2017- L-R Phil Parkes, Geoff, Rob Jenkins and Alan Devonshire

They Played For John Lyall – The West Ham Years

22 – BOBBY FERGUSON

"I had a good life at West Ham and absolutely loved the East End. I was in no great hurry to leave. John was happy to keep me at the club and I had a testimonial in 1981."

Born: Ardrossan, Ayrshire, March 1, 1945 • **Position:** Goalkeeper • **Games played for John Lyall:** 47 (1976-79)

Games played for West Ham United: 277 (1967-79) • **Testimonial:** 1981 v Southampton (h) W 4-3. Att: 8,831

First game under John Lyall: April 17, 1976 v Aston Villa (h) D 2-2 (Robson, Brooking – Deehan, Hunt)

West Ham United: Ferguson, Coleman, Lampard, Lock,* T Taylor, McDowell, Holland, Paddon, Jennings, Brooking, Robson. Sub: Ayris*

Aston Villa: Findlay, Gidman, Robson, Phillips, Nicholl, Mortimer, Deehan, McDonald, Gray, Hunt, Carrodus.

Robert Ferguson spent 15-years at West Ham United. Not a bad stint for a player whose transfer was deemed to be one of the most controversial in the club's history. Ron Greenwood paid Kilmarnock a record transfer fee of £65,000 for him, instead of £50,000 for World Cup winner, Gordon Banks: *"I had no idea about the decision Ron was making at the time. I discovered his dilemma years later. Ron Greenwood was clearly a man of integrity."*

Ferguson made only 47 appearances under John Lyall and was understudy to Mervyn Day for much of that time. He was very much a Greenwood boy and played 229 games behind Bobby Moore. No other West Ham 'keeper can boast such a record.

Ferguson is yet another player from the Greenwood and Lyall era to earn a testimonial. Almost 9,000 fans clicked the turnstiles to see a 4-3 thriller over a Kevin Keegan led Southampton in 1981. The £15,000 proceeds went to Ferguson's new life in Australia.

Fast forward 36 years and 'Fester,' as he was affectionately known, still resides in Adelaide with his wife, Greer. "I still play a lot of golf and drink a bit of wine. Maybe, it's the other way round!"

I shared a good relationship with John. I knew I wasn't uppermost in his first team plans, but I loved the East End and being part of West Ham United. John was happy to keep me on as second choice keeper.

From 1974 until 1976, Mervyn Day was untouchable, but, for some reason, he just lost all confidence. There were a few cracks beginning to show. He made a couple of errors in the 1975 FA Charity Shield against Derby County. John eventually took the decision to drop him and I had a good run in the side between 1977 and 1979. I was 34-years-old when John paid a new world record fee for Phil Parkes. It was the

Playing up front in the reserves

Golfing success. L-R Tommy Taylor, Mervyn Day, Fester, Pop Robson and Trevor Brooking

natural progression which all football clubs go through. I still had two years on my contract and stayed around the club throughout the historic 1980-81 achievements.

Throughout my 15-years with West Ham, I never wanted to leave. Not only would it have been hard for another club to match my wages, but my heart was firmly at Upton Park. I trained hard and John respected the position I was in. I didn't drive him mad about my lack of first team opportunities and conducted myself in a professional manner. I certainly trained as hard as anyone else.

I spent a lot of time in the reserves and not always in goal. I managed to play up front on quite a few occasions and scored half a dozen goals.

I played a lot of golf with Trevor Brooking and Pop Robson and lived around the corner from Jimmy Greaves in Upminster. We got on well together and played a few rounds and sunk a few rounds! He is godfather to our son, Glenn.

I roomed quite a bit with Pop Robson for away matches. He was into the physical and mental side of the game. As soon as he thought about doing something, he'd act on it immediately to sharpen his instincts. I woke up one morning and he was standing on his head! Apparently, it was good for his circulation.

John went on to sign quite a few Scottish players and I looked after fellow scot Ray Stewart when he first arrived.

I look back on my time with Ron more than I do with John but respected both men equally. They both built teams that could play the game the proper way. We played some brilliant football at times and could beat anyone on our day.
Bobby Ferguson

Following are comments about Bobby from his former teammates:

Fergy was an understudy for much of his time at West Ham but had a good lifestyle. He played a lot of golf and put in a good shift when he did play in the first team.
Mervyn Day

Whenever Fester comes over from Australia he always pops into my bar in Shenfield. He is still as good looking as ever!
Pat Holland

A few years back I was scouting for Sheffield Wednesday and I went to Australia to look at a few players. I had a bit of time on my hands and found out that Bobby was running a café in Adelaide so I popped in to see him. I was with my wife and ordered a couple of coffees. I was wearing dark glasses so he wasn't sure who I was but he kept looking at me and then said: "Jolly!"
Bill Green

He used to play centre-forward in the reserves!
Alan Wooler

Punching clear against Coventry City, April, 1978

Bobby was a very smartly dressed man who was at the club for a long time. He was reserve to Mervyn Day most of the time, but he had a lot of experience and knowledge of the game.
Alan Taylor

I roomed with Fergy. He was a good steady lad and we played a bit of golf together. We won a couple of golf tournaments with Tommy Taylor, Trevor Brooking and John McDowell. I was the better golfer!
Pop Robson

If you chipped him in training you'd get smacked!
Alan Devonshire

He could strike a ball really well but he will always be Mr Miserable to me because he never stopped moaning.

Tommy Taylor
He had a cannonball for a shot and scored a belter against Arsenal at Highbury.
Paul Brush

He was one of the top trainers at West Ham. I remember we won a pre-season tournament in Spain and Fergy scored the winning goal. I still laugh about that now!
Mick McGiven

I made my debut in the reserves against Leicester City and Bobby played up front. He loved to play outfield. We lost 2-5 but I scored from 30 yards. He was certainly a better goalkeeper than he was a striker!
Billy Lansdowne jnr

Enjoying family life in Adelaide

Back row: Lock, Bonds, Green, Day, T Taylor, Brooking, K Robson,

Middle row: Curbishley, Jennings, A Taylor, Fergusons, Lampard, McDowell, McGiven

Front row: Orhan, Ayris, Holland, Paddon, Coleman

CHAPTER THREE
1976-77

"Nothing dramatic can change at West Ham United because we're all brought up in the same way. All the staff we have now were players I coached when I first came here in 1961." Ron Greenwood

After two major finals in his first two seasons in charge, John Lyall faced up to a brush with relegation. The season was plagued with injuries on the pitch and wayward behaviour off it. Pat Holland, Billy Bonds, Frank Lampard, Alan Curbishley, John McDowell and Keith Robson, all had long spells out of the side due to injury.

Ron Greenwood shook hands on a deal to bring Plymouth Argyle's Paul Mariner to Upton Park. He actually sent someone to meet him at the train station, but Plymouth Argyle brokered an alternative deal, with Bobby Robson of Ipswich Town, involving cash and a player exchange. Greenwood was disgusted: "It is just not possible to do business with people who handle things the way this has been handled," he lamented. Mariner scored a hat-trick against the Hammers later in the season ahead of an England call-up.

John Radford is signed from Arsenal while club favourite, Pop Robson, returned for a second spell at Upton Park.

It was a fractious time at West Ham. European Cup Winners' Cup hero, Keith Robson pleaded guilty to driving while unfit through drink and was fined £600 and disqualified for three years.

Striker, Billy Jennings, gave the 'V' sign to the boo boys after a 1-1 draw at home to Sunderland: "I found it senseless when they started booing Trevor Brooking and Billy Bonds.," he explained in his defence.

Wally St Pier retired from scouting, ending 47 years at the club as player and scout. He was succeeded by Eddie Baily.

It was left to 20-year-old Geoff Pike to provide a beacon of light. He scored vital goals against Norwich City, Coventry City and Manchester United to help keep the Hammers up.

Bill Green, Bryan Robson, Alan Devonshire, Anton Otulakowski and John Radford play under John Lyall for the first time.

Here is their story...

Lord of the Manor

23 – BILL GREEN

"John's training quickly taught me that I had never been properly coached. No two sessions were ever the same. They were innovative, enjoyable and always had a purpose. He would show you how and tell you why."

Born: December 22, 1950, Newcastle-Upon-Tyne • **Position:** Centre-half • **Games played for West Ham United** 40 (1976-78)

Goals for West Ham United: 1 • **Debut:** August 21, 1976 v Aston Villa (a) L 0-4 (Gray 2, Graydon 2) Att: 39,012

Aston Villa: Burridge, Gidman, Smith, Phillips, Nicholl, Mortimer, Graydon, Little, Gray, Robson, Carrodus.

West Ham United: Day, Coleman, Lampard, Taylor T, **Green,** Bonds, Taylor A, Paddon, Holland, Brooking, Curbishley.

William "Bill" Green sadly passed away in early September 2017, just a short while after this interview was conducted. Mick McGiven, Bill's life-long friend, phoned to share the terrible news and was clearly choked at losing his good pal. They were fellow Geordies who went to St Mary's Roman Catholic Boys School together. "There must have been well over 500 people at Bill's funeral. People came from all over to pay their respects," recalls Mick.

Bill was so generous with his time, and shared some fine memories of John Lyall and West Ham United: *"I had 15 years as a player and my only regret is that I didn't play longer with full fitness at West Ham. It was a great club with terrific fans."*

I had initially chatted with Bill at the Boleyn Ground prior to the visit of Manchester United for the last ever match at the old place. He clearly enjoyed catching up with former teammates Keith Robson and Billy Jennings on that special evening: "That was quite a night and so many memories came flooding back. It was great to see quite a few of my old friends."

Bill had grown up on Monday Street in Newcastle-upon-Tyne during the 1950s – the heyday of Geordie dominance in the FA Cup. His father, William, worked for WD&HO Wills, the cigarette manufacturer, while his mother, Susannah, was a housewife.

Although his two years at West Ham were comparatively short, Bill had a playing career which spanned 15 years, during which time he played for Hartlepool United, Carlisle United, Peterborough United, Chesterfield and Doncaster Rovers.

Bill had a spell as manager of Scunthorpe United, 1991-1993, but primarily worked in a scouting capacity at clubs such as Wigan Athletic, Derby County, Burton Albion, Bolton Wanderers and Leicester City. Since 2011, Bill had been the chief scout at Southampton.

Following are his recollections of John Lyall:

I was heavily into football as a kid so I had heard of John Lyall when he was playing for West Ham United in the early 1960s, just before injury ended his career.

In 1970, John expressed an interest in signing me and invited me down to London. I pitched up at King's Cross, where I was quite surprised, to say the least, that John had come in person to meet me. West Ham had just won the FA Cup and had been narrowly beaten in the European Cup Winners Cup final against Anderlecht, which made it all the more impressive to me. Can you imagine that today? A Premier League manager turning up at a train station to meet and greet a potential new signing? So obviously, my first impression of John was an extremely good one, indeed.

I'm not sure if Mick McGiven had any influence on West Ham signing me. I think it was more to do with the fact that I'd played quite well for Carlisle United against West Ham during

Bill's one and only goal for the Hammers - against Chelsea, March 1978

their one and only season in the top division - 1974-75. I went to school with Mick and played for his dad's football team. We had also played cricket together so I suspect that if John did ask him about me, the feedback would have been positive. I think John was after a bit of northern grit. If you look at his record, he signed quite a few lads from up north and Scotland.

My time at West Ham wasn't really successful and it just didn't get going for me. Unfortunately, injuries played their part. In one game, against Manchester City, I broke my cheek bone in the first half and my leg in the second half!

John was always very supportive and offered me plenty of advice. I remember him saying that I was trying too hard to fit into the West Ham style rather than showing the steel I'd played with at Carlisle.

I was good pals with the other north-east boys. Obviously, I knew Mick and Keith Robson from our time up there and I became good friends with Keith Coleman, too. Pop Robson also joined us for his second spell while I was there. They were all good lads and Coley, Robbo and I were admonished once by John for breaking the curfew on a pre-season trip abroad. Maybe twice come to think of it!

There was a bit of a drinking culture at West Ham. A few of the lads, myself included, would frequent various establishments after training and we'd often end up in Frank Lampard's pub, The Britannia, in Plaistow, after a match.

John was not only an excellent coach but he was a terrific man-manager, too. He was close to his players and wanted to know what was going on and took a real interest in their lives both on-and-off the pitch. I remember him picking me and my wife up and driving us around Essex to look at houses. He even drove us to his house in Abridge for a cup of tea and a piece of cake that his wife, Yvonne, had prepared for us.

It was on the training pitch, where he really opened my eyes to coaching and the development of players. Pre-season was pretty tough with plenty of running around Epping Forest to lose any excess weight you'd piled on during the summer break. I just remember it going on for miles and miles and looking up to see a tiny Billy Bonds powering away in the distance!

John was quite a hard task-master but his sessions were so innovative. They were enjoyable and always had a purpose. I saw things at West Ham United that I had never previously encountered. I quickly realised that I had never been properly coached and that my formative years as a player before West Ham had been a case of me listening and learning from the older and more experienced players. John taught me the difference between training and coaching.

He had such a good understanding of space, positioning, how to mark and where to play the ball. He would show you how and tell you why. John would never tire of emphasising the importance of the final ball. Every day was an education and I cannot remember doing the same session twice. It was easy to see why so many West Ham players got into coaching, because they had all benefitted from John's methods, including myself. After my playing career I had a spell as manager at Scunthorpe United and phoned John when he was manager at Ipswich Town. Mick McGiven was there, too, and we'd discuss certain players and loan spells, that sort of thing. John was always approachable, always affable and always helpful.

I had a forgettable debut away at Aston Villa. We lost 0-4 and I was pleased to keep my place for the next game at home to a very strong Queens Park Rangers side, who had finished runners-up behind Liverpool the previous season.

We beat them 1-0 with a Graham Paddon goal.

I was competitive and combative and good in the air. I wouldn't say I was the greatest on the ball but no-one could ever say I didn't give 100%. I have the broken nose, broken leg and damaged knees to prove it!

Back then, the game was a lot tougher and the referee normally let you have the first bad tackle. I felt I could go through the back of someone and get away with it. I worked on the theory that an opposition striker would never be able to limp quickly! I seriously doubt whether I would last 90 minutes in this day and age.

John kept me on for a second season but it would have been easy to release me because I'd been out with a broken leg for five months and my wife was finding it difficult to settle in London. As it turned out, I left the following season but, even then, John said I didn't have to go. I was 27 at the time and Alvin Martin was coming through, so a fresh start seemed like a good idea. With hindsight, I would have been better off staying a bit longer at West Ham. Furthermore, I wish John had stayed longer at the club, too. Who knows, I might have become part of the backroom staff there?

Don't mess with the Jolly Green Giant!

I was pleased to score a goal during my time at the club. It came in March 1978 against Chelsea. We had a corner which I managed to head past Tommy Langley who was usually a striker but had to go in goal because their keeper, John Phillips, had been accidentally kicked in the head during a goal mouth scramble. It happened in the 88th minute and Patsy Holland scored a minute later to make the final score 3-1.

There was a funny story after a game against Ipswich Town on Good Friday. David Cross had signed and we were similar in size and build. Basically, we both had beards and big noses! In the dressing room afterwards the Chairman Reg Pratt came in, walked up to me and said; "Well, David, that was a very fine hat-trick indeed. Well done!" Crossy and I still laugh about that when we see each other. He was a lovely old boy, Mr Pratt, but that did make us laugh.

I played under some very good coaches in my time - John Barnwell at Peterborough and Arthur Cox at Chesterfield - but, respectfully, John Lyall was a notch or two above them. They talk about Martin Peters being ahead of his time but both Ron Greenwood and John Lyall were too. They played the game the way they wanted to play and not the game other people wanted them to play. They stuck by their principles through feast and famine.

I couldn't believe it when they sacked John. Why would you discard that amount of experience, that amount of knowledge? There should've always been a place for him at the club. We all knew at the time it was the wrong decision and history has borne that out. It was good to see him resurface at Ipswich Town and do well.

I don't think I saw John after his time at Ipswich but I was full of sadness when I heard that he'd passed away. Football had lost one of the good men - a loyal man and a gentleman.
Bill Green

Following are some teammates' memories of Bill;

Strong and aggressive both in the air and on the ground. Bill struggled a little with mobility when being turned by a player with pace but he was a good player. Honest as the day is long.
Mick McGiven

We called him 'Jolly' after the Jolly Green Giant which was an advert from that time. I was devastated to hear that he'd passed away.
Keith Robson

I really liked Bill. He was one of my mentors when I was at West Ham. I lived with Bill and his wife in Hornchurch along with another West Ham lad called Brian Thomson, who played in the reserves before going up to Mansfield.
Anton Otulakowski

We played quite a few games together in the reserves. Bill had a really good attitude because most first teamers, who played in the reserves didn't want to be there and didn't take it seriously. To Bill, a football match was a football match and he always tried his best, regardless of the level. He was also a really good cricketer.
Billy Lansdowne jnr

Bill was such a nice guy. A quiet, determined sort of bloke who was proud to play for West Ham United. I'm so glad he spent a long time working in the game because he was a proper football man.
Paul Brush

Bill was as hard as nails. I remember he broke both his jaw and his leg in a match against Manchester City.
Kevin Lock

At the last ever match at the Boleyn Ground - versus Manchester United, May 2016

24 – BRYAN ROBSON

"He was a genuine, honest guy, who totally believed in what he was trying to build and achieve at West Ham and he was very good at passing on that belief to everyone at the club. Not just the players but everyone. He had your best interests closest to his heart and was very loyal to his players and staff."

Born: Sunderland, County Durham, November 11, 1945 • **Position:** Striker • **Games played for John Lyall:** 116 (1976-1979)

Games played for West Ham United: 255 (1971-74/1976-79) • **West Ham career goals:** 104 (Ninth on the all-time goalscorers' list)

First game under John Lyall: October 16, 1976 v Ipswich Town (h) L 0-2 (Woods 2) Att: 24,534

West Ham United: Day, Coleman, Lock, Bonds, Green, Taylor T, Jennings, Paddon, Taylor A*, Brooking, **Robson B**. Sub: Ayris.*

Ipswich Town: Cooper, Burley, Mills, Talbot, Hunter, Beattie, Osborne, Wark, Bertschin*, Whymark, Woods. Sub: Lambert.*

Bryan Stanley 'Pop' Robson had two spells at West Ham United - the first while Ron Greenwood was at the helm (1971-74) and the second under John Lyall's management (1976-79). The experience left a legacy of goals, a Golden Boot and a popularity which endures to this day.

Pop is another big name from the John Lyall era, who stayed at the club following relegation in 1978. It is inconceivable in today's game that a top-quality striker would not leave a club when it is down on its fortunes. Or even when it is high on its fortunes for that matter! This simply wasn't a consideration for Pop whose instinct was to stay and play for John Lyall's West Ham United.

Pop is now in his seventies and is a joy to talk to. The knowledge he has accumulated from his time as a player at Newcastle United, Sunderland, Chelsea and Carlisle United, combined with his coaching roles at Manchester United, Leeds United and Sunderland, mark him out as one of the heavyweights in the game. Such experience cannot be learned at university and is a first-class advert for the School of Life.

Pop's irrepressible love for football is infectious, but he is philosophical about the future: "I think I have finally retired from the game. I had the chance to go back to Sunderland to coach the kids but I snapped an Achilles playing table tennis and now I'm reluctant to get back into it.

Look who's back in town! Pop signs for his second spell at West Ham United, October 1976

A little chuckle as Pop gives Fulham's Tony Gale the slip, September 1978

I spend a lot more time with my wife, Maureen, babysitting our five grandchildren and playing a bit of golf, not necessarily in that order! We pop over to Spain quite a bit and just try to enjoy life. We have a nice little spot near Malaga. Maureen and I haven't played much table tennis but we want to get back into it."

Pop also featured in the forerunner to this book: They Played with Bobby Moore – The West Ham Years. It is right and proper that the club's one and only top flight Golden Boot winner should have his place in West Ham United's history preserved for future generations.

His recollections of John Lyall resonate with the love his has for all things claret and blue:

My earliest memory of John Lyall is from the time when I first travelled down to Upton Park in 1971. I met Ron Greenwood and then John, who was assistant manager. He took me for

lunch and we spoke a lot and got on really well. He was on my wavelength and had an easy manner about him. He talked to me about the type of football West Ham United played and what they expected from me. Then he took me to an evening game to watch the reserves play Tottenham Hotspur, so I got very close to him very early and we remained very close from that time on.

John was always very positive in the way West Ham played. He would never suggest sitting back and defending. That wasn't his style at all. He liked to play football which would please the fans. He loved Dev and Trev running with the ball with plenty of movement and options around them. He liked overlapping defenders joining the attack and strikers who could finish a move. I remember we played Sheffield United in a League Cup match during our run to the 1972 semi-finals. We beat them 5-0 at home and I scored a hat-trick. One of the goals came from a little run I made before flicking the ball with the outside of my foot past the keeper. After the match John

Pop with John, celebrating an Evening Standard Player of the Month award

came up to me and said: "I loved that goal – that was class!"

John didn't want me to leave in 1974 but Sunderland had won the FA Cup and were looking to bring in some new players and I knew they were interested in me and had put a good deal on the table. I was 28-years-old at the time and I wasn't really sure how long I was going to carry on playing, so I was interested in what was being offered. I had won the Golden Boot, scoring 28 goals, so my value was probably at its peak. I'd had a really bad virus which had put me in hospital and both Ron and John came to see me. I ended up deciding to go back to Sunderland but John tried really hard to keep me at West Ham. He always stayed in touch and that was part of the reason it was so easy for me to return to West Ham in 1976. It was like coming home. Alan Devonshire joined the club about that time and then later John signed David Cross,

so he was starting to bring together a very useful side. I had a very good understanding with Crossy and we developed a great partnership.

John's training sessions were always hard but always enjoyable. He put us through our paces, running around Epping Forest and setting up some great sessions with the ball at Chadwell Heath. Lots of one-touch, two-touch passing and setting up mini-games of three-on-three. I was always with Billy Bonds and Trevor Brooking and we soon understood each other inside out. Instinctively, we knew how to make the right angle and fire really quick passes to one another. This was part of the reason why we worked so well together in matches. We practiced the near-post crossing and heading, over and over again. That was a West Ham trade mark but you never see it anymore. Harry Redknapp used to be really good at wrapping his foot around the ball and getting a good shape on his crosses and then Trevor started doing it and Graham Paddon got really good at it, too. They didn't even have to beat a defender and could just dink in a cross from the left or right. I would get criticised if I wasn't making the right run towards the near post to finish off their centres.

We also had some really talented defenders who could put in good crosses. We had wing backs before they were even called that and players like John McDowell were great at making those overlapping runs and whipping it over. I used to get seven or eight chances in a game and there was a time when I was scoring a couple of goals most weeks. John liked to work with me and David Cross in training to develop our partnership to the maximum. John would also set up some really great shooting sessions in the gym. We'd shoot with the inside of the foot, the outside of the foot and he would always try and be creative and keep us sharp. It wasn't surprising that West Ham went on to do really well in Europe because their style of play was suited to that arena.

We played entertaining football and scored plenty of goals but we conceded a lot as well. We almost went down in 1976-77 and had to beat Manchester United in the final home game. Thankfully, they were in the FA Cup final the following Saturday so Martin Buchan and Gordon McQueen didn't make a single tackle. I got a couple and it was one of those great nights under the lights at Upton Park.

The things I liked about John was that he pushed me hard in training. He had an easy manner about him and got his point of view across without having to raise his voice or be aggressive. He was never down on me and always believed in my ability and, through that, my confidence was high most of the time.

Sometimes, if I was going through a bad patch John and I would go to the little gym at Upton Park for an hour or so and practice bending the ball and shaping the ball. John would help to build my confidence again and that was very useful for getting me back on track. He wasn't just a manager and a coach, he was my friend, who I could confide in and turn to for pretty much anything. He was always interested in my opinion and had that type of dedication to most of the players at West Ham. It is quite unusual to be that close to a manager but with John it just felt right to share my thoughts and feelings.

During my second spell with West Ham, John really wanted to get me involved on the coaching side, but I wanted to carry on playing. He asked me to coach the kids on Tuesday and Thursday nights, but I felt it was taking away my fitness. Billy Bonds did some coaching for a while but, like me, he wanted to play for as long as he could. In the end John brought in Mick McGiven. When John eventually left the club and Billy took over from Lou Macari it was mentioned that I would return to West Ham in a coaching role. I was never formally approached but it would have been interesting.

Pop with one of his three hat-trick balls from his time at West Ham United

I remember going to Trevor Brooking's 30th Birthday party at his house in Brentwood and John came along and made a speech and said some really nice things about Trevor. John was a good talker and that helped him in all walks of life. He was very comfortable with the players, the press and the board. I can't remember him ever really losing his temper. He would get upset and annoyed and frustrated but he would never lose control. He used strong words when he felt they were needed.

John always stayed in touch and after I left the club for the second and final time in 1979, he called me up after West Ham had won the FA Cup in 1980. It was crazy really because I was back at Sunderland and we had to play West Ham in a rearranged fixture after the FA Cup final. That was a night to remember in Sunderland because we needed to win to get promotion. The queues to get into that game went on forever. Sunderland fans were locked out and the whole place was rammed. I don't think Billy Bonds put in a single tackle on me that night and we won comfortably. John came in to congratulate me after the game and I went into the West Ham *dressing room to see the lads.*

As a player, Ron and John were the best coaches I played for. Joe Harvey was good and successful at Newcastle, but his tactics were a bit too direct. The two styles were very different at each club.

The players were so loyal to both Ron and John. That kind of loyalty isn't around anymore. When we got relegated in 1978 it never even crossed my mind that Billy, Trevor or Frank would contemplate leaving. There was a time when I was thinking of going to play in the States and I mentioned it to John but he said: "No, no, I don't want you doing that." So I didn't. Then when Ken Knighton of Sunderland came back in for me I discussed it with John but he asked me to stay. He explained how he'd keep me at West Ham long enough to get a Testimonial. He tried so hard to make me stay and mentioned that I had a good chance of playing for England now that Ron was in charge. That is the closest I came to getting a full cap. I felt really guilty when I left that time, but it helped when West Ham won the FA Cup and Sunderland gained promotion. On reflection I could have had another four years at West Ham and earned that Testimonial. There would have been a greater likelihood of joining the coaching staff if I'd stayed that bit longer, too.

It was a real shock when I heard that West Ham had sacked John. Of course, it has to come to an end at some stage but it just wasn't the right time. John had been there a long time and had enjoyed great success. He was only 49 and, with that type of knowledge and experience in management, was just entering his prime. I was pleased that he did so well with Ipswich Town and enjoyed his latter years on his farm with Yvonne. They had a big fishing lake and John would have taken a lot of pleasure from that. He invited Maureen and me there a couple of times and it is one of my biggest regrets that we didn't get down to Suffolk to see them.

Even after I left West Ham we stayed in touch and John was instrumental in helping me to get a coaching job at Manchester United. He had a very good relationship with Alex Ferguson and recommended me for the role, so I went to Old Trafford in 1991 and spent five years there.

It was during that time at Manchester United when I last saw John. Alex Ferguson had a room for the manager and coaches and when John brought his Ipswich team up, we had a glass of wine after the match. I remember it so well because he walked into the room and saw me and reached over a table to shake my hand before pulling me over the table and chairs to give me a massive hug. He almost crushed me to death! It was just so nice to see him. John was just fantastic. He brought Chris Kiwomya into the room and said: "This is who you should be watching."

When I watch a match nowadays I find it so slow, so boring. The ball goes backwards and sideways. There isn't

Star Striker

any excitement and hardly any chances, maybe one shot in the first half. John picked up from where Ron had left off. Quick play from defence with the full backs bombing forward. Midfielders who could pick a pass to anywhere on the pitch and strikers having seven or eight chances in a game. Most matches had plenty of excitement, a thrill ride worth talking about. When people question the West Ham way it's easy to explain what it was - entertaining and exciting football.

Bryan 'Pop' Robson

There was no shortage of comments about Pop from his former West Ham colleagues:

A top player and a top man. What a team player! His work rate and running off the ball was unbelievable. Whether it was when we were attacking for goals or with our backs to the wall soaking up pressure, Pop would be there making a massive contribution. He loved scoring goals and could score poacher's goals, spectacular goals, headers, volleys, near-post headers, every type of goal conceivable. Prolific English goalscorers are a dying breed nowadays and it is a travesty that he didn't get a full England cap back then because he'd get 50 today, no problem.

Mick McGiven

Pop was a terrific player and a good friend. He could also play in midfield and sit off the front men. He scored a lot of his goals from outside the box, some of them were absolute screamers.

Billy Bonds

I only played with Jimmy Greaves once at West Ham and, in his prime, he had been the best finisher I've ever seen, but, to me Pop wasn't far behind.

John Ayris

One of the best two-footed players I ever played with. A real Mr Nice Guy as well. I only played with him during his second spell at West Ham so he must have been out of this world during his first visit.

Derek Hales

A top, top finisher and a great, great, fella. John would set up crossing and finishing sessions in training - I'd be putting the ball in at different angles and Pop would just finish them all. Fantastic technique.

Pat Holland

A busy, bubbly, intelligent footballer who had a great touch. A top technical player and a great bloke.

Paul Brush

Pop helped me quite a bit. We sometimes stayed behind for some extra shooting practice together.

Billy Lansdowne jnr

A top class player and a top class bloke. I've got a lot of time for Pop.

Keith Robson

He was prepared to do anything to get a goal for his team. He would put his head in where others wouldn't put their feet. Fearless, all for the team and a gentleman too.

Yilmaz Orhan

I used to bunk off school to watch him play for Newcastle. He was one of my boyhood heroes because Newcastle were my team. When we were playing up front together for West Ham I learned so much from him. He showed me how to play football the West Ham way. Playing with Pop at West Ham was a very special experience.

David Cross

Pop Robson and wife, Maureen, attend a West Ham legends evening at the London Bridge Hilton Hotel, December 2016

25 – ALAN DEVONSHIRE

"Before extra time against Everton in the FA Cup semi-final replay, John said to me: "You do know that if you score now, you'll play for England. I did and I did!" It is kind of difficult to find a man like that in football today."

Born: Park Royal, Middlesex, April 13, 1956 • **Position:** Midfield • **Games played for John Lyall:** 437 (1976-1989)

Games played for West Ham United: 448 (1976-1990) • **Goals scored for West Ham United:** 32

Honours won under John Lyall: 1979 Hammer of the Year, 1980 FA Cup winner, 1980 FA Charity Shield runner-up, 1980-81 Division 2 Champion, 1980-83, 8 England caps, 1981 League Cup runner-up, 1989 Testimonial v Crystal Palace. Att: 12,613

Debut: October 27 1976 v Queens Park Rangers - League Cup 4th round - (h) L 0-2 (Bowles, Clement) Att: 24,565

West Ham United: Day, Bonds, Lampard, Curbishley, Lock, Taylor T, Orhan, Paddon, **Devonshire,** Brooking, Robson K.

Queens Park Rangers: Parkes, Clement, Gillard, Hollins, McLintock, Webb, Thomas, Kelly, Masson, Bowles, Givens.

Alan Ernest Devonshire will live long in the memory of all who saw him play. He was a key player in both the highly regarded 1980-81 and 1985-86 teams. *"If I was pushed to say which team I preferred it would probably be the 80-81 side, given the skill level of the players at that time."*

Ian Ernest Devonshire will live long in the memory of all who saw him play. He was a key player in both the highly regarded 1980-81 and 1985-86 teams. *"If I was pushed to say which team I preferred it would probably be the 80-81 side, given the skill level of the players at that time."*

Devonshire was not an East End boy: "I grew up in Park Royal and QPR were my team as a kid. Rodney Marsh was one of my heroes. I wasn't a massive fan because I preferred to play rather than watch but I was taken to see a few matches."

He joined West Ham United from non-league Southall at 20 years of age. Mick McGiven, former player and coach at West Ham, recalls the £5,000 signing of Alan Devonshire in 1976 like it happened yesterday: "Eddie Baily said to John: "They want five grand for him. Five grand!" John replied: "Just get it done."" Mick continues: "It was easily one of the greatest

John Lyall presents an Evening Standard Player of the Month award to Dev

Dev's finest moment - scoring against Everton at Elland Road in the 1980 FA Cup semi-final replay

signings in the club's history. Five thousand pounds and he ended up an England international. Dev loved the fans at West Ham and they loved him, too. He left so many opponents on their backside it was laughable."

Winning trophies, being voted Hammer-of-the-Year, playing for England and earning a Testimonial is as good as it gets for any West Ham United player. It was a pity that after his 448 match contribution, the fans were not given the opportunity to give Dev the send-off he deserved and he left the club, unheralded, in 1990, to join Watford. His final match for the Hammers was the 'Valentine's Day Massacre' at Oldham Athletic in the 1990 League Cup semi-final first leg – a 0-6 drubbing.

Today, Devonshire continues his success in non-league management and, in 2017, won promotion with Maidenhead United, guiding them into the National League. It followed on from the success he enjoyed at both Hampton & Richmond and Braintree Town. Sadly, the fifth-tier of English football is the most Devonshire can expect, having not passed the requisite coaching badges to manage in the top four divisions.

Alan lives in Ealing with his wife, Christine, where he enjoys the lighter things in life; a restaurant meal and listening to his collection of Soul, R&B and Jazz music: "If I had to pick a favourite group, it would be The Whispers."

It is always a pleasure to talk with Dev and discussing all things John Lyall had an extra frisson of excitement:

We had some super-charged games under John which went to extra time – the semi-final replay against Everton of course, and, an FA Cup game against Wrexham, as well as one against West Bromwich Albion. Each time, John's pep talks were all about his total belief in the team. His words gave us the extra confidence to keep on doing what we were doing and most of the time it worked. Before extra time against Everton in the FA Cup semi-final replay, John said to me: "You do know that if you score now, you'll play for England?" I did and I did! In fact I ended up with eight caps which I gave to my mum and dad and three kids.

Charlie Faulkner, a scout at West Ham, had watched me in half dozen games and, after one match against Slough Town on a Tuesday night, the manager, Geoff Taylor, told me there were a couple of people from West Ham United to see me - Charlie and Eddie Baily. A few clubs had been watching me but that was the first concrete offer and Southall accepted it.

John's training sessions were brilliant. Always with the ball, always with energy and always with a purpose. Above all it was enjoyable. I got a buzz training and playing for West Ham and that never deserted me until about a year before I left.

Adored by the fans

John was naturally positive, but, he was serious whenever he needed to be. If things were going well you didn't have to worry about anything but if something had upset him during a match then the training would be noticeably harder. One time, after our run at Hainault Forest, we were waiting to get on the coach back to Chadwell Heath when John just drove off and left us to make our own way back to the training ground.

My debut against QPR took me by surprise. It was a League Cup tie and John called me to one side about an hour before kick-off. He asked me if I was alright to play. I'd been at the club a few weeks and had played in the reserves but I wasn't expecting to be playing in a London derby under the lights at Upton Park so soon. I've heard that John spoke with Billy, Trevor and Frank and they all said to put me in. John played me on the right side and told me to just go out there and play my game. They had John Hollins and Eddie Kelly playing and I didn't touch the ball for ten minutes. When I did eventually get the ball, Kelly put his studs straight down my thigh which was a very painful introduction to top flight football. I was lucky in that John didn't drop me and I pretty much remained a first team regular from that point on.

John always treated me in the same way. He was very straightforward and he loved me to go out and play the way I enjoyed playing. He would never dictate to me to do things this way, or that way, and preferred me to do the things that came naturally. It was great for me to have a manager who was happy to let me go out and play in the same way as I would if I was playing in the local park. That was perfect for me, and exactly the right way in which to get the best performances out of me.

I usually sat down with John on Monday morning and discussed the match and analyse my own performance. He was very straightforward with his opinions and helped me when I was down and helped me when I was flying. He was true a friend and we'd often see the lighter side of things. John had a great sense of humour and I had the type of respect that a son has for his dad.

I tried not to get called into his office too much because John and Boycey both loved a cigarette and sometimes I'd come out of there gasping for some fresh air!

I've always lived in Ealing and, in the early days, used to take the 7am train to get to training. John wanted me to live a bit closer but I was lucky in that Phil Parkes, Tony Gale and Paul Goddard all lived out west and picked me up in the morning. We'd stop off at a Wimpey bar for breakfast or have egg, chips and beans in a café on the way in. It was the perfect start to training really!

If I had to assess myself as a player I would say I was different, quick, could go past players easily and I was quite decent. I could change pace and would slow up as the defender closed me down and then pick up the pace and go by him. Don't ask me how I did it, but it just felt so easy. Viv Anderson at Nottingham Forest was one defender I struggled with. He was a good player. There were certain full-backs I knew I could terrorise and Pat Rice of Arsenal was one of them.

It is a crying shame that nowadays you don't see a player get to the byline and cross the ball. I used to do that as did Trevor Brooking and Mark Ward later on, but today, players prefer to simply cross it in from 20-yards out. It saddens me. John liked me to get to the by-line before sending it into the box.

John had a clear-out after West Ham were relegated in 1978 and I was lucky enough to be part of the great teams he built in 1980-81 and, again, in 1985-86. If I was pushed to say which team I preferred it would probably be the 1980-81 side, given the skill levels of the players at that time. I certainly played better that season because it was before my injury. I was only 27 when, in 1984, I smashed my knee to pieces against Wigan Athletic in the FA Cup. At the time, I was playing the best football of my career.

John knew everything about his players and worked hard to nurture strong relationships. When I damaged my knee, John followed the ambulance and made sure my wife and mum came along. He even dropped them back home in his Jag at about five o'clock in the morning. That journey took him to the other side of London, after which he had to head back across London again to get home. That was the type of person he was. John was such an exceptional man and I was so close to him that I still miss him now.

The FA Cup semi-final replay against Everton was my best game for West Ham United, especially after I had given the penalty away in the first game. That was never a penalty by the way! How the referee gave that I do not know, but I feel that I made up for it in the replay. From a personal point of view, I enjoyed the semi-final replay more than the final. I will remember that game until the day I die.

The European Cup Winners Cup match at home to Real Castilla, behind closed doors, was an eerie experience - just the two clubs, a load of ball boys and 262 observers. It was one of those occasions when you had to get geared up to get the adrenalin flowing without the help of the crowd. It was like a training session, but we were super-pumped up because of the importance of the tie. You could hear everything echoing around the stadium and we certainly found out who the club's big swearers were that night!

The senior pros were brilliant to me. Bonzo, Trevor and Parkesy - to name a few - were terrific. They really looked after me and, in turn, I tried to pass it on to the young kids coming through like Tony Cottee, Kevin Keen and Steve Potts. During my career, I found that the better the player the better the person and that was definitely the case with those guys. They were modest and humble, dependable and honest. The guys below that level could have tried harder with their personalities and it was understandable that they didn't do quite as well.

John knew how I ticked. He knew when to give me a bollocking and when not to. He'd let me know if I'd let the team down or hadn't played that well, but he'd never embarrass me in front of others and would usually take me into his office and discuss it there one-on-one. I'd get my point across without ever losing my temper because I respected him too much for that.

John liked me to play out on the right but I preferred to play in the middle, so we discussed that quite a bit. In fact, the last time I saw John, at a reunion in the Docklands, we bumped into each other and the first thing he said was: "I don't want to play out on the right, I want to play in the middle." He put on a whining voice, mocking me, and we had a good laugh about that. In fact, when I look back, I can see us laughing a lot and sharing a fantastic relationship. One time, when I was voted the match-day sponsor's Man-of-the-Match for 15 games on the spin, John said he was withdrawing me from selection to give others a chance: "How much cut glass crystal does one man need?" he joked. I'm very happy with those memories.

I learned a lot from John and have adopted quite a bit from his training methods. At Maidenhead United, for instance, I always try and train with the ball and make it enjoyable. You work harder with the ball than if you are running. The big thing I took from John - and the thing I hope the players I've coached remember about me, too - was his man management skills.

Eight England caps

Honesty is always the best policy and John was as straight as they come. There were so many positives in John's approach it simply made sense to adopt them. I use techniques from all the good coaches I played under, like John at West Ham, Ron Greenwood at England and Steve Perryman at Watford. I don't use anything from the bad ones, like Lou Macari.

I was stunned when they sacked John. I really hadn't seen it coming. They couldn't have replaced him with anyone worse, either. Macari's philosophy was a million miles away from everything John had worked so hard, over so many years, to perfect. During the short time I stayed at the club under Macari all we did was running, running and more running. We only saw a ball on match day.

I was at home when Parkesy called me up to say that John had died. I can't really explain how bad I felt. Totally gutted doesn't really come close.

John Lyall was an exceptional man. I've never respected anyone more than John. He was the best manager West Ham will ever have in their entire history. He should have managed England. A lot of people believe Alex Ferguson is the best-ever manager in this country but, remember, he used to ask John for advice and that says it all really.

At the end of the day it was just a great time at West Ham and I'm just happy I was a part of it because there are so many great times for the players and fans and everyone involved with the club to look back on.

Alan Devonshire.

With John Lyall in 2005 for a West Ham United reunion, Britannia International Hotel, Isle of Dogs

There was no shortage of comments about one of West Ham United's all-time greats:

When Dev passed out and was vomiting during his first training session at West Ham we all thought: "Here we go, we've got a right one here." But later that week we played five-a-side out at Redbridge and Dev was running with the ball and caressing it with the inside and outside of his right foot. Nobody could take it from him. They were all trying to ram him against the wall but he just kept gliding past them with total control of the ball. Then we were all thinking: "We've got a canny little player here." In 1978-79 I scored 26 goals but they gave the Hammer-of-the-Year to Dev! I couldn't believe it, but was also very pleased for him and proud of his achievement and what he'd become.

Pop Robson

When Dev arrived from non-league football he was a breath of fresh air. He made my job so much easier, because I'd pass it to him and sit back and watch him run the full length of the pitch and take on everyone. He was much younger than me at the time but I was at a reunion with him recently and now I'm not so sure! In all seriousness Dev was a terrific player and should have played for England a lot more than he did.

Frank Lampard snr

Make sure you put down that he should have scored more goals! I scored just as many goals as him! Dev was an exceptional player and no Hammer has ever had his change of pace over five yards. His balance and ability to glide past players created so many great memories.

Pat Holland

Dev was the second best player at West Ham, after me! He has been my best pal since West Ham and is just pure quality.

Tony Gale

I get a bit frustrated with the modern game. When they go on about Raheem Sterling and Theo Walcott, I actually think we've gone backwards a bit. I only have to think about how Dev used to play to realise that we haven't got any good wide players and haven't had any for some time.

Alan Dickens

I was fortunate enough to play with the greats - Trevor Brooking, Billy Bonds and Frank Lampard, but in terms of the player who I enjoyed playing with the most and who created the most chances for me, that would have to be Dev. Before my debut, he came up to me and said: "TC, when I get the ball I'll have three players around me, but what I'll do is pass it to you and all I want you to do is pass it back to me, spin, and I'll put you in on goal!" He came back from a terrible injury and was still our best player in 1985-86. He is a special friend.

Tony Cottee

Dev was a top-class player and perfect for me because I didn't really enjoy playing left-back but he always wanted the ball. The porfect player to have ahead of me on that left side.

Steve Walford

He reminded me of a player we had at Charlton Athletic named Colin Powell. Dev was also a schemer, who could run all day and he was a great dribbler of the ball. He was a really good guy with it but he loved his racing and it skinted him a lot of the time.

Derek Hales

Dev was very down to earth and was another of the senior pros who had so much time for the younger lads. He'd just come over and have a chat. A really nice guy. It was a pleasure to

watch Dev on the ball. He just seemed to drift past players and you don't see it so much in today's game. A proper entertainer.
Keith McPherson

Dev would eat a cheeseburger for breakfast before training and still be the best player at Chadwell Heath.
Ray Houghton

I got on well with Dev. I can still picture him in the dressing room before kick-off with his head in the Racing Post.
Dale Banton

Dev was so laid back and had so much natural ability. It was a shame he picked up that serious knee injury because he would have won many more caps and been remembered as an England International player of high renown. He never learned to drive but was given a sponsored car which Phil Parkes called a milk float! I picked him up from the Wimpey at Barking Station, where he'd have a mixed grill for breakfast because he thought it was better for him! I went to Wembley Dogs with Dev on the Friday night before the 1980 Cup final.
Paul Brush

I roomed with Dev. I remember we lost a pre-season tournament in Malaga on penalties and Dev missed the all-important one. Straight away he just said: "Okay, where are we going out tonight?" That made me realise just how laid back and carefree he was, which is why he played so well. Missing a penalty like that would have crushed me and I would have been crying back at the hotel.
Anton Otulaksowski

I tried to push the ball and run past defenders but Alan could go left or right with the ball at his feet.
Alan Taylor

Dev didn't have a driver's licence and instead paid an Italian fella named 'Carlo' to drive him everywhere.
Bobby Barnes

I played in his first few games at West Ham, when I was in midfield and he was out on the left-wing. He was just a young boy but played like he had been in the team his whole life. I rated him very highly.
Yilmaz Orhan

I think he was John's best ever buy.
Alvin Martin

He was a thoroughbred who ate like a mongrel!
Greg Campbell

Dev - one of West Ham United's greatest ever players

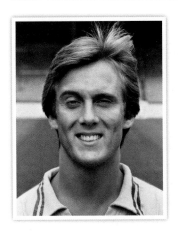

26 – ANTON OTULAKOWSKI

"John had so much time for me and was very encouraging. I ended up going to Southend United but if he'd asked me to return I would have ran back up the A13 to be with him!"

Born: Dewsbury, West Yorkshire, January 29, 1956 • Position: Midfield • Games played for West Ham United: 17 (1976-78)

Debut: November 27, 1976 v Manchester United (a) W 2-0 (Brooking, Jennings) Att: 55,366

Manchester United: Stepney, Forsyth, Albiston, Daly, Greenhoff B, Houston, Coppell, McIroy, Pearson, Greenhoff J, Hill.

West Ham United: Day, Lock, Lampard, **Otulakowski,** Taylor T, Bonds, Devonshire, Pike, Jennings, Brooking, Robson B

Anton Otulakowski enjoyed a dream debut for West Ham United, beating Manchester United at Old Trafford: *"It was an amazing debut and not only did we win 2-0 but I was given Man-of-the-Match in a couple of newspapers."*

Born to parents, John and Winnie, Anton was raised at Ings Crescent housing estate in Thornhill, Dewsbury and, from the age of 10, in the new family home in nearby Frank Lane. Anton's father, was a manager of some 200 employees in a textile mill while his mother dedicated her time to Anton and his three siblings. A schoolboy gymnast, Otulakowski continued his football journey with Barnsley, after being spotted playing for Ossett Town in 1975. He was also working as a surveyor for the National Gas Board. One year later, Anton - who had thrilled The Tykes in front of an average crowd of 3,500 - was playing in front of 55,000 in The Theatre of Dreams.

Despite Anton's successful start in the Claret and Blue, he struggled to hold down a regular first team spot and, after two years, continued his footballing journey, firstly at Southend United, where he regaled the Shrimpers with his forward somersault throw-ins and, subsequently, at both Millwall and Charlton Athletic. Otulakowski struck up a good understanding with manager, George Graham, at Millwall and would later undertake some scouting for him at Tottenham Hotspur.

After his playing career was brought to a premature end due to a persistent knee injury, Anton became one of the pioneering influences on Soccer Schools and set up several in the Southend-on-Sea area, before taking his life journey full circle with a move back to Yorkshire.

Nowadays, Otulakowski lives in the Yorkshire Dales and manages about 40 rental properties scattered across the north. *"I'd love to meet up with a lot of those players from the seventies but I just don't feel that I'm worthy. I cherish my time at West Ham United and am very humbled when people send up photos and programmes for me to sign. I was disappointed that I couldn't get to the final game at Upton Park but I had some major ankle surgery which has affected my mobility."*

It should be recognised that Anton has contributed a great deal to various charities down the years and the experience of playing for John Lyall has played a part in journey: *"For the past 13 years I have volunteered my time and energy to Cruse Bereavement Care as a counsellor and, for six years prior to that, I worked as a Samaritan. I often think about John and how he guided me and taught me the importance of help, support, advice and selflessness."*

Following are Anton's recollections of John:

My earliest memory of John came when I was playing for Barnsley. We had a game at Southport, who were in the old fourth division at the time, and I went to the game, even though I wasn't fit to play. Jim Iley, the manager, asked me to travel with the team. I watched the game from the stands and heard that John Lyall was in the ground. He had a big reputation at the time because West Ham United were flying high having won the FA Cup a year earlier. That was my first ever glimpse of John. After the match, in the Players' Bar, Jim called me over to say that Newcastle United had put in a bid for me. I told him I would think about it but things were happening a bit quicker than I was expecting. The Newcastle entourage were in a nearby hotel so I went along to see them with my teammate Martin Gorry. Gordon Lee, their manager, wanted to sign us both and Martin agreed there and then. But I held out. I wanted to hear what John Lyall had to say and, after speaking with him over the phone, I agreed, in principal, to a contract. John invited me down to London and picked me up at King's Cross station in his Jaguar. He was such a lovely man and the opposite of what I had been used to with Jim Iley, who could be quite aggressive and had a short fuse.

At Barnsley, I felt I was very skilful, tenacious and could use both feet. I was very industrious, especially on the left-side, and put in plenty of crosses. I think that's what John saw in me and why he wanted to bring me to West Ham United. I was also lucky because Barnsley had played West Ham in the League Cup at Upton Park and, even though we'd lost 0-3, I was Man-of-the-Match. Having said that, John did say that he'd already watched me quite a few times prior to that encounter.

John had a mild mannered, easy going, temperament and possessed gentlemanly qualities. He took the time to show me around the East End, including the houses of both Bobby Moore and Geoff Hurst as well as the West Ham United ground with all its history. I was hooked immediately and was put up in a hotel and started training with my new teammates.

John was very supportive and gave me a lot of advice. Something he said has always stayed with me: "Anton, you need to look at football like this: We're on a deck of a ship that's starting to sink. At the far end of the boat is one life jacket. I am going to get to that jacket before you do and that is how you should view football."

John always seemed to be there to offer advice or hands-on coaching. I remember kicking a ball up against a wall in the old West Stand with a few apprentices and young pros, when John turned up and ran an impromptu coaching session. I've got nothing but admiration for the man.

It was noticeable that John took a stronger interest in training, the nearer we got to match day on Saturday. He wanted us to be clear about shape and pattern. Most of the time I was looked after by Ronnie Boyce and Billy Lansdowne with Ernie Gregory shouting abuse in the background!

My first game was in the reserves against Arsenal and I felt I did alright. Next up, I played in Les Barrett's testimonial at Fulham, which was a very special occasion because I

On the hallowed turf at the Boleyn Ground

'A HARD DECISION'

says Anton

ANTON OTULAKOW-SKI, Hammers' £50,000 signing from Barnsley, is already an English international—at gymnastics!

The Yorkshire-born youngster with the foreign name earned English Schools honours against Wales as a gymnast and, if football had not intervened, might have gone on to the top level in that fast-growing sport.

"I was playing football with a local side, Ossett Trinitarians when I was invited for a trial with Barnsley. After that, I concentrated upon football, although I kept in gymnastics as a coach," reveals Anton.

The years of exacting gymnastic routines have had a useful spin-off in Anton's soccer career, however. "It has done a lot to improve my balance and also has taught me how to fall properly without hurting myself," he says.

Anton's mouthful of a surname is derived from his father, who came to Britain as a Polish soldier during the war and settled down to marry a Yorkshire wife and make his home here.

At school, Anton played for home town of Dewsbury

debut the season before last. He became a part-time pro with the Yorkshire outfit only this season, training largely on his own after finishing work as a Gas Board draughtsman in Tingley.

He hopes to continue working for his full qualifications as a draughtsman by going to college in the afternoons.

"I want to do this because it means I'll have something to go back to if I don't make it in football. I also want to continue with my gymnastic coach-

Hammers' newcomer Anton Otulakowski sits alongside team chief John Lyall as they watch last Saturday's game at Hawthorn Road.

The same down-to-earth thinking applied when he decided to join Hammers. "I had a lot going for me up home a good job, my gymnastic coaching, and football. It was a very hard decision to make but, in the end, I worked out that if I did not take this opportunity I might well spend the rest of my life regretting it," he explains.

Did Hammers' present troubles affect his decision? "No, not at all. They've too many good players to go down. I found that out when Barnsley came down here in the League Cup earlier this season. West Ham just did not let us have the ball in that game. I felt I did not play very well that night

News of Anton's transfer

was playing against Bobby Moore, George Best and Rodney Marsh. I managed to score and we won quite easily, 5-2. Then, quite incredibly, the next day John came to me and said: "I saw you turn Bobby Moore and that is what I want to see you do at Old Trafford on Saturday." Just like that I was in the line-up to make my first team debut against Manchester United.

John was very community minded, too, and at Christmas he would make sure the team visited the local hospitals, schools and community centres. I visited a school for disabled children, where I had my first ever dance with someone in a wheelchair. I felt a bit awkward at first but it was so amazing and incredible. I could see the person in the wheelchair was having such good fun. I soon lost my inhibitions being in a special moment like that. We handed out Christmas presents and made a real, positive difference.

John had a lovely way about him. Apart from being an absolute gentleman, I would highlight his expert eye for the technical side of the game. He was always talking about skill and how to receive the ball and then play it. How to perfect the basic skills. That was great for me because I hadn't come up through the ranks at West Ham. I'd been playing with my mates in the local park during the week and then for Barnsley's first team at the weekend. I had a lot to learn and John set me on the right track.

There were a couple of very influential personalities at West Ham and Billy Bonds topped them all. Once, we were training at the stadium which meant hard running up and down the steps on the Chicken Run and then sprinting the length of the pitch. Sometimes I just didn't fancy it at all and, on one occasion, Bill came over to me and said: "Anton, you played well on Saturday but you're not going to get any fitter training like you did today. Pull your finger out, son!"

I must say that the atmosphere in the West Ham dressing room wasn't particularly impressive. The only frame of reference I had at that time was my experience with Barnsley, which was electric and super-charged. Admittedly, it was the fourth division but, my god, we were so fired up we couldn't wait to get out on that pitch. We all tried to boost each other's confidence and felt ten feet tall when we played. It was nothing like that at West Ham which was very noticeable to me. The bell used to ring in the dressing room and a few of the lads would say: "Good Luck!" but that was it. It was also noticeable how the team announcer at West Ham just couldn't be bothered to even try and pronounce my name. I am of Polish descent and Otulakowski is an unusual name but quite easy to say once you give it a try. He would just say: "And at number 11, Anton."

I didn't score a goal for West Ham but I did hit the crossbar

On tour in Norway. L-R Anton, John Radford, John Lyall, Ernie Gregory, unknown, Frank Lampard

Taking a shot against Manchester City, March 1977

against Bristol City in what was one of my best games for the club. John said to me afterwards: "That was so close, Anton, but hopefully next time."

I struggled to play consistently well and, in 1978, John told me that Southend United had come in for me. I said I would talk to them and he told me he didn't want me to go but he would understand it if I decided to leave. In the end, I did go and it was the worst football decision in my life. It was a naïve decision and I should have been more loyal to West Ham. I teach my kids the importance of loyalty and that is a direct consequence of the regret I have from leaving West Ham. I was petulant and believed that regular first team football would be the new springboard I needed. Leaving John Lyall, who had stayed loyal to me, and going to Dave Smith at Southend United was as big a mistake as I could have made at that time.

I did keep in touch with John after I left and we had a few telephone conversations. I think he knew that I wasn't really enjoying my football but, when I had a good run of form, he'd bolster my confidence further. "We need your left foot here," he'd say. That was typical of the belief he always tried to instil in his players.

I wish I'd gone to West Ham later in my career. When I went to Millwall, I played without a care in the world and was voted Player of Year in 1984. At West Ham, I was so conscious of the £60,000 transfer fee that I felt under a lot of pressure to repay their faith in me. There wasn't any such thing as sports psychology at the time but I think that I would have certainly benefited from it. It might have given me the mental freedom I needed to play my best football. It was George Graham, who really transformed me as a player. He instructed me not to track back because I was too valuable to the team going forward and that gave me the licence to express myself. In his book, George mentioned that he almost took me to Arsenal but felt I was maybe too old – at 30.

Even now, I still think about John quite a lot. The business

world can be quite ruthless – like John's analogy about the sinking ship and life jacket – so I am ever-mindful of his advice. He was a big influence on my life, through the way he managed, the things he said to me and the way he showed respect. John Lyall treated me like a man and I have the very highest thoughts for him.
Anton Otulakowski

Anton is well remembered by several of his former teammates;

I liked Anton but I don't think he ever really won over the supporters. He didn't manage to fulfil what they hoped he was going to be, but as a person he is a terrific lad.
Pat Holland

He came to the club from Barnsley shortly after I arrived. He got through a lot of work on the pitch and put himself about a bit but didn't really stamp his authority on a permanent position.
Alan Taylor

I made my debut against Southend United in the League Cup at Upton Park and Anton was in their line-up that evening.
Paul Allen

A good player, a good gymnast and a good man.
Mick McGiven

Anton today

27 – JOHN RADFORD

" It still hurts today that I didn't score for West Ham United. The big irony of course was that I failed to score a goal in 30 outings for West Ham but I scored on my debut for Blackburn Rovers! "

Born: Hemsworth, Yorkshire, February 22, 1947 • **Position:** Centre-forward, right-wing

Games played for West Ham United: 30 (Dec 1976- Nov 1977) • Debut: December 18, 1976 v Liverpool (h) W 2-0 (Brooking, Jennings) Att: 24,175

West Ham United: Day, Lock, Lampard, Green, Taylor T, Bonds, Robson K, **Radford,** Jennings, Brooking, Robson B.

Liverpool: Clemence, Neal, Jones, Thompson, Kennedy, Hughes, Keegan, Mcdermott, Heighway, Toshack*, Callaghan. Sub: Case.*

John Radford lives in Bishop's Stortford with his Dutch wife, Engel. He came from a winning culture at Arsenal, where he still holds scoring records today. Sadly, in 30 outings for the Hammers he did not register a single goal, but his work rate and assists helped the club survive relegation at the end of the 1976-77 season.

Radford's International career was behind him when he joined West Ham but he had made two England appearances with Bobby Moore, the first against Romania in January, 1969 and the second, against Switzerland, in October 1971: *"I should've won a few more caps, but I believe Alf Ramsey didn't like picking Arsenal players. When we won the double at Arsenal in 1971, both me and Charlie George were scoring for fun but we didn't get selected for England."*

After his playing days, 'Raddy' ran The Greyhound pub in Thaxted: *"It was the thing to do at the time. Charlie George ran a pub and so did Ray Kennedy."*

"Nowadays, I try and do as little as possible to be honest! My memory isn't what it was so I don't organise the tours at Arsenal anymore. I sometimes tend to the garden, usually when the missus gets her whip out! I still like the horses but I've never been a heavy gambler. You have to be sensible to keep it fun."

John and Engel were very welcoming and Raddy had the following recollections of John Lyall and his time at West Ham:

Debut against Liverpool with Pop Robson, December 1976

Clashing with Everton's Bob Latchford, April 1977

It still hurts me today that I never scored for West Ham United. You are taking me back to a disappointing time in my career. It was heartache for me to leave Arsenal, because I'd been there for 14-years, having joined the club as a kid. I'd won the Inter-Cities Fairs Cup with them in 1970 and The Double the following season. Obviously, none of this was John Lyall's fault because it came about when Terry Neil returned to manage Arsenal. I had played with Terry at Arsenal. In fact he played in my debut against West Ham at Upton Park in 1964, but he preferred to play Malcolm MacDonald and Frank Stapleton up front. I can half understand that he didn't want people around him who knew him inside out, but it was a bitter blow at the time. I was only 29.

John Lyall was a gentleman who didn't know how to tell a lie. I was training on my own at Arsenal one Friday morning when I was told to go to the manager's office. When I got there both Ron Greenwood and John Lyall greeted me. At the time, I was so fed up with my situation that I immediately

asked them how quickly they could register me as a West Ham player. They asked why and I replied: "Well, process the forms and I'll play tomorrow." They ended up paying £80,000 for me and that was the end of my time at Arsenal.

To be honest, I didn't even know how to get to West Ham. All I knew was that my time at Arsenal was over and that Ron and John were the first to show any interest in me. It wasn't until I signed that someone told me to look at the league table and that is when I noticed West Ham were rock bottom - 22nd out of 22 teams. It was a week before Christmas so obviously John was putting his faith in me to get the club out of the mess which we ended up doing on the final day of the season when we beat Manchester United, 4-2. That was a terrific night at Upton Park, probably the best I had there.

The reason West Ham were struggling was partly because they didn't have a big target man up front. They had Pop Robson, Alan Taylor and Billy Jennings but none of them were the tallest so I was brought in to play that role.

Scaling the heights against Birmingham City, April 1977

I was living in Enfield and assumed the drive to Chadwell Heath would only take 40 minutes, but the traffic was that bad it ended up taking me two and half hours! I had little choice but to leave my house really early each morning, which meant I was the first one at the training ground by a good hour or two. It was little things like that which made my experience that bit worse. It had nothing to do with the club or the players or John, all that side of it was really good and I enjoyed playing with them all. That bit I really loved.

Even though I was laying on a few goals for Pop Robson, Alan Taylor and Derek Hales, the press were getting on at me about not scoring. Five games became ten games became 15 and it went on and on. I must admit, it got to me in the end. It was hurting so much and it just kept playing on my mind, over and over again, before every game. All I kept thinking was: "I've got to get a goal, I've got to get a goal." I was totally consumed by it because it had never happened to me throughout my career. Then, in one game, I rose at the far post and headed one in. Well, the relief was unbelievable but, as I wheeled away to celebrate, I saw that the ref had disallowed it. He said I had fouled the 'keeper which was nonsense. It was a perfectly good goal but typical of the way things weren't

running for me at the time.

John was as good as gold about the situation. He kept telling me not to worry about it: "We were bottom before you arrived and both Pop Robson and Billy Jennings weren't scoring, but you've helped turn things around and kept us up." All that was good to hear, but it was only going to be scoring a goal that would to help. Sadly, it never came so it was agonising for me.

The 1977-78 season was a shocker for West Ham and there was a growing pressure on the club right from the off. I'd left for Blackburn Rovers by Christmas and we'd only won a couple of games by that time. On one occasion I was sitting in the dressing room, after another defeat, and heard John criticising the performance. I noticed he was addressing his anger at some players but not others. There were quite a few kids coming through at the time like Geoff Pike, Alan Devonshire, Paul Brush and Alan Curbishley. I didn't think it was right the way John seemed to pointing the finger at them so I stood up and pointed at them myself: "Youngsters, youngsters, youngsters!" I said. "What about that lazy sod over there? – and I pointed at Trevor Brooking!" Well, you could've heard a pin drop. Trevor was god but I didn't care. He wasn't pulling his weight and nobody else would say it, so I did.

The last match I played for West Ham was a total disaster. It was against Leeds United and the game was only 10 minutes old when I clashed with Tony Currie and ended up breaking my jaw in two places. It was the worst injury I ever had and is something I wouldn't wish on anybody. When I got to my feet I noticed something didn't feel right. My bottom teeth were sprung apart in a V-shape and I put my hand where I thought my chin was but it wasn't there! My chin was on my chest so I had to hold my face together and make my way to the tunnel. The physio, Rob Jenkins, ran over to help. He was a lovely bloke who loved a drink and his eyes weren't all that clever. They were looking all over the place while was gargling a few sentences trying to tell him that my jaw was broken. I don't think Rob was convinced and put his sponge in a bag of water and forced it in my mouth! That's when my jaw dropped again and blood started gushing out of my mouth. Rob arranged for me to go straight to London hospital for treatment. I was sitting in A&E at about four o'clock, still wearing my Number 9 shirt and shorts when some old drunk came over and stared at me: "Shouldn't you be playing for West Ham?" he said!

John came to see me in the hospital straight after the game. I was in a right mess. It was ironic really because years before I had seen Ian Ure break his jaw at Arsenal, and when I saw him wired up I remember thinking that I hoped it would never happen to me. Now, here I was wired up, feeling sick from the anaesthetic and my head thumping with pain. John told me not to worry and that he would keep my place in the first team open, once I got back to full fitness. That's when I told him that he needed to go out and buy a big centre-forward to replace me because I was going to be out for some time and West Ham needed a target man. I was being very honest about it because that was the reality of the situation. That's when he went out and bought David Cross who went on to have a fantastic career at the club.

After a few months, when I started training again, Jim Smith at Blackburn Rovers came in for me. 'The Bald Eagle' they called him, but I didn't know too much about him. I went up to see him and he showed me a lovely Bungalow and it sounded like a club on the rise, so I decided to sign for them. What I didn't know was that Jim liked to move around and he left for Birmingham City soon after I joined. The big irony of course was that I couldn't score a goal in 30 outings for West Ham but I scored on my debut up at Blackburn!

If I had to draw a comparison between Bertie Mee of Arsenal and John Lyall of West Ham, I would say they both had very high standards, wouldn't put up with any crap and always told the truth. A lot of players hated Bertie Mee and quite a few of the rest were frightened of him, whereas you'd be hard pressed to find anyone who didn't like John Lyall. John was a very good coach. Probably a better coach than a manager. Some of the things he did in training I hadn't seen before and I had been a pro for 12 years and thought I knew it all.

John Radford

Trade card immortality!

Raddy was a great foil for me. Every time he played, I seemed to score. I would love to have played with him when he was a bit younger and free from injury.

Derek Hales

I remember seeing John at the club one Sunday. He was in one bath and Rob Jenkins, the club physio, was in the other. They were both reading the Sunday newspapers. Then someone said to Raddy: "I've just noticed you've played 15 games for us and haven't scored yet." He looked up and said; "Don't worry, it's gonna happen." Sadly, for John it never did.

Tommy Taylor

I had a lot of sympathy for John. He had tremendous pedigree at Arsenal but just couldn't hit it off at West Ham. He tried so hard but it just didn't happen for him.

Alan Taylor

I liked Raddy. He spent a lot of time on my treatment table. There wasn't much wrong with him but it was comfortable and he liked to read the Racing Post on it! We'd pick him up for away games and he'd get on the coach with nothing but his toothbrush in his top pocket.

Rob Jenkins

Raddy relaxing at home in Bishop Stortford

Back row: McGiven, Brush, Martin, Cross, Day, Bonds, Ferguson, T Taylor, Brooking, Lampard, McDowell.

Front row: Hales, Pike, A Taylor, Devonshire, Otulakowski, Holland, Jennings, Robson, Curbishley

They Played For John Lyall – The West Ham Years

CHAPTER FOUR
1977-78

"The heritage of West Ham football can be found in the search for attractive styles and players. The willingness of the staff to go out into the schools, teaching football, the Hammers' way, for the next generation." **John Lyall**

Ron Greenwood replaced Don Revie as England manager. John Lyall finally became manager of the whole club, not just the first team. He had carte blanche on all transfer activity. David Cross was his first signing. He joined from West Bromwich Albion for £180,000. Derek Hales arrived from Derby County for £110,000. Season Tickets soared from £33 to £45 and expectations were high

West Ham lost 0-2 at home to Liverpool in their final game of the season and were relegated. It was a calamitous end to John's first full season in total charge. Trevor Brooking was quick to quash any rumours by committing his future to West Ham: "I owe it to the fans," he was widely reported as saying. John had already made his thoughts about Brooking well known: *"I wouldn't swap Trevor for any other player in Europe."*

Mervyn Day made one error too many and Bobby Ferguson was recalled to first team action. The shock news was revealed that FA Cup winner, Day, was on the transfer list for £200,000.

Trevor Smith, a well-respected journalist at the Newham Recorder, blamed Ron Greenwood for the demise of the club: *"Since 1975, he failed to sign the right players at the right time and that is the single biggest factor behind the club's relegation."*

Bobby Moore once again played at Upton Park in a West Ham United shirt. He lined up in a memorial match for journalist, Victor Railton. Such a show of respect for a man in the media has not been shown by West Ham before or since.

A much needed lift was given by the reserve team who clinched the Football Combination Championship.

Trevor Brooking picked up £30,000 for his testimonial which resulted in a 6-2 victory over an England XI.

John Lyall gave debuts to the following Hammers: Paul Brush, Derek Hales, David Cross and Alvin Martin.

Here is their story...

David Cross became a Hammer for a club record fee of £180,000

Ron Greenwood left West Ham for England after 16-years at the club

28 – PAUL BRUSH

*"I've never forgotten the help and support
John Lyall gave me during a very difficult
period in my life."*

Born: Plaistow, London, February 22, 1958 • **Position:** Left-back • **Games played for West Ham United:** 186 (1977-85)

Goals for West Ham United: 1 • **Honours under John Lyall:** 1980 FA Cup final (unused substitute), 1980 FA Charity Shield runner-up, 1980-81 Division 2 Champion • **Debut:** August 20, 1977 v Norwich City (h) L 1-3 (Robson B – Ryan, Jones 2) Att: 28,178

West Ham United: Day, Lampard, **Brush**, Pike, Taylor T, Lock, Taylor A, Robson, Radford, Brooking, Devonshire.

Norwich City: Keelan, Ryan, Sullivan, Evans, Jones, Powell, Neighbour, Busby, Reeves, Suggett, Gibbins.

Paul Brush was born to parents, Peter and Joan, and lived just a gentle jog away from the Boleyn Ground: *"I grew up at 33, Mafeking Road, Canning Town,"* he recalls: *"My uncle took me to West Ham in 1964 for the visit of Leyton Orient in an FA Cup replay. It was my first match and I was only six-years-old."* Paul's father was an expediter for a BP subsidiary in Africa, but took Paul, complete with a fold-up stall, to watch the Hammers from the South Bank: *"I'd set it up next to the wall, which was a safe place to be, because I didn't get knocked about by the swaying crowd. The downside was that I couldn't see the bottom of the goal at that end, so when Brian Dear scored five goals against West Bromwich Albion in 1965, I didn't see all of them go into the net!"*

Paul is one of 10 players from the John Lyall era to have been ever-present during a single league season. It came in 1978-79 when he established the left-back position as his own, moving Frank Lampard over to right-back. Unfortunately, 'Brushy' was unable to sustain such consistency and was in and out of the team until he left the club in 1985.

Following spells at both Crystal Palace and Southend United, Paul entered the world of management when, in 2001, Barry Hearn appointed him to replace ex-Hammer Tommy Taylor at Leyton Orient. Subsequently, he held several coaching positions, the most successful being with Steve Tilson at Southend United between 2003-2010.

Nowadays, Paul is an Academy Development Coach at Tottenham Hotspur. In 2015 he attended a reunion of West Ham United's 1980 FA Cup winning team at the London Bridge Hilton Hotel and remains in touch with many of his former teammates. His heart will always be with the Hammers: *"I was a young kid growing up in the East End and playing for West Ham United. How can I have any regrets?"*

In some ways, when I think about John, I feel he was hard done by. For someone to put as much into a football club as he did and then find himself asked to leave it in the way that he was, just seemed inappropriate. John Lyall had built something there, something special, something with strong family values and a powerful togetherness at its core and the way it all ended was very, very, harsh, indeed.

Wally St Pier came to see my parents during my first year at senior school and I started training on Tuesday and Thursday evenings on the forecourt at the ground. We played under the main stand and kicked the ball up against the wall near the toilets.

I think the first training session I went to was with Alan Curbishley at Pretoria Road School in Canning Town. It's now called Eastlea Community School. I remember the great West Ham striker, John Dick, coached the kids there.

I signed as a first-year apprentice in 1974, on £6-per-week. That was increased to £8-per-week in my second year. This went up to £30 when I turned pro at the age of 19.

Coming from Canning Town, I'd watched Bobby Moore, Ken Brown, Jack Burkett and all those boys win the Cup in

Scoring against Chelsea in FA Youth Cup 5th round, 1975

1964. When they brought home the European Cup Winners Cup the following year, I watched them from the bridge at Plaistow Station.

I joined West Ham as a midfielder but played up front in the 1975 FA Youth Cup final. I then moved back into midfield but, one day, I was picked as a substitute for the reserves. Our left-back got injured, so Bill Lansdowne, who was in charge of the team, told me to play there until half-time. I ended up playing in that position for the next ten years. Secretly, I wish I'd played at centre-back, alongside Alvin Martin, but Bonzo and others had that position sewn up.

I think John liked me because I was a local, whole-hearted, lad, who felt a lot for the club. I didn't complain and got on with stuff and gave my all. Personally, I'd say I was more defensive minded, had a bit of pace and liked to tackle.

My debut came about after a pre-season trip to Majorca in 1977. I was taken along by John and it was the first time I had been that close to the first team. Both John McDowell and Tommy Taylor were injured so I played in the final game.

When we came home, there was only one week to go before the season started. Training was quite light in the run up, we did a bit of running on the gravel track, that sort of thing. Then, on the Friday, the team sheet went up in the changing room and I had been selected. John was very low-key with the news because he didn't want to cause any panic or worry.

He just told me I was playing and that he thought I'd be fine.

We were at home to Norwich City and I marked Jimmy Neighbour. We lost that game 1-3 but I kept my place for the next match against Leicester City. It was on a Tuesday night and there was a heavy thunderstorm. I was marking Keith Weller and we lost 0-1. It was a difficult time because we lost our first four matches that season before coming from 0-2 down to win at Newcastle 3-2. I can still picture the relief and enjoyment I felt on the journey home after that victory. Being part of a winning team was pretty special.

John's training was fantastic. No two days were ever the same and that made it exciting. I was around good people, in a good atmosphere and learning something different every day. Each session was relevant and well thought through. John made the whole experience a nice blend of hard work and enjoyment. He taught his players so much about themselves and also about the wider world of football. Towards the end of my time at West Ham, quite a few coaches from other countries came to watch John Lyall at work on the training ground. His reputation as a top-quality coach had spread to many clubs and many countries. It was quite remarkable given the absence of the mass media which exists in today's game. It is no surprise to me that so many West Ham players from that era went on to pursue a post-playing career in coaching.

In the dressing room John was very clear with his

With Phil Parkes, Alan Devonshire, The FA Cup and a brand new Lacey's coach!

rounds. We've always been a respected part of that group but it is still a bit strange to be known, more for a game I didn't play in, rather than the 186 games in which I did!

John did select me for the FA Charity Shield, against Liverpool, so I did have the Wembley playing experience. If I'd blown my top, and stormed out of the club I would have also missed the European Cup Winners Cup campaign the following season. The match in Georgia against Dinamo Tbilisi was the best experience I had away from home. Paul Allen fell ill in the warm up and John told me I was playing just five minutes before kick off. Tbilisi were the best team I had ever seen and deserved to go on and win the trophy. We had lost 1-4 at home in the first leg, but beat them away 1-0. For me to play well out there against a top quality side is a special memory.

I also played in the Bernabeu Stadium against Real Castilla in an earlier round. The 'Ghost Match' in the second leg was very strange. We needed proof of ID to get into the ground and could actually hear the radio commentators reporting on the match. It was eerie and the old terraces were so bare. I did actually experience something similar when I was 36. I played for Enfield against Wembley in front of about 80 fans, but that's a different story!

I had a lot of self-belief and even though the club had an

instructions. He was never too emotional that he couldn't get his point across. The players had so much trust in what he said that you could hear a pin drop when he was talking. They totally believed that what he was saying about the match is what would happen. He usually stopped talking at about 2pm, so the players had a bit of time for their own preparation. Bonzo would run and jump around the dressing room, while others went for a kick-about in the little indoor court near the bathroom. Alan Devonshire would have a sleep!

The biggest disappointment of my playing career was missing out on the FA Cup final in 1980. I'd played in every round, so not seeing my name up on the team sheet for Wembley was a jolt to the system. The journalist Trevor Smith, who wrote for the Newham Recorder, penned an article titled: 'The Seven Certs for the Final,' and I was in it.

Not much was said beforehand, but I did ask to talk with John after the final. I told him that even if I'd played for just a couple of minutes, it would have softened the blow a bit. Nevertheless, I had played more matches in that FA Cup run than most of the guys who played in the final, so I did make a big contribution. I did get a medal, which is in a plastic Tupperware dish up in the loft! It hurts a little less each year.

It was a difficult day but more people have asked me if I played in the final than would have done if I had actually played! I wish I had a pound for every time someone asked me: "Did you play in the FA Cup final?" It was just one of those things, but I was a part of that group of players and had pulled on the Number 3 shirt in the fifth round, sixth round and both semi-final matches. It was the same for Pat Holland and Jimmy Neighbour, both of whom played their part in the earlier

Riding a challenge from Grimsby Town's Joe Waters, November, 1980

established left-back in Frank Lampard with others coming through like Mark Smith and Everald La Ronde, I always felt that I could hold my position and that I could play and should play. It was difficult at times because on Thursdays Mick McGiven would run a defenders session in training. There were five of us and I'd look at Billy Bonds, Frank Lampard, Alvin Martin and Ray Stewart and think: "I've got to replace one of you lads." They were all International players at the time, or should have been if Bonds had got what he deserved. I played a lot of times when I was 19, 20 and 21 but then had a quiet couple of years. It was very frustrating but I stayed because I wanted to play for West Ham United.

I benefited first hand from John's decency and dedication to his players and staff. When my first wife – Marilyn - died from leukaemia. John gave me a huge amount of help and support. I remember going to the training ground and John spending all day with me helping me through that very difficult time. He called doctors and hospitals and arranged a nanny for our son, Peter. I've never forgotten the help and support he gave me. The way he helped me and my family was just very special. My wife had just passed away and we had a six-month old baby. John sat with me in his office at Chadwell Heath and made all the calls until I had a plan. Like me, he didn't know the answers but he spent all day finding them out for me. He treated me like one of his own family. Given the responsibilities he had as a manager he could have easily passed on the task to somebody else but his nature was such that he wanted to take a central role in helping me with Marilyn before and after she died. John did everything he could and found me a way forward.

When Marilyn was diagnosed with Leukaemia, John told me to train when I wanted, to play when I wanted and spend the time I needed to help my family. Marilyn died a week before the 1985-86 campaign. I'd played 23 games the previous season but obviously missed the start. When I did eventually decide to get back into training, the team had gelled. Steve Coppell at Crystal Palace came in for me and I asked John what he thought I should do? As always, he was very straight forward with me and said: "You can go and play five first team matches for Palace or play three games in the reserves here." So I decided to go and I enjoyed it. I was a senior player there and the 90-minute drive each morning helped me to clear my mind so that I could concentrate on my game. Football became more like a job then. I went to work and then came home to my son. It had never felt like a job at West Ham. I would have turned up and played for nothing. Unfortunately, my time was beset by injuries at Palace, so it became very frustrating.

Even after I finished my playing career and got into coaching, John always remained a parental-like figure. If we were at a function together he would always say how he was following my career.

I went to John's funeral and, after the Church service, we sat behind the goal at Ipswich Town. There were so many ex-players who just simply had to be at Portman Road that day. The mood was not of deep mourning and not brilliant reminiscing either. It was something in-between because everyone who came into contact with John had a worthwhile experience with which they could remember him by.

Everyone knows the two worst days in my life, one off the pitch and one on the pitch. Life has taught me never to be too certain of anything.

Paul Brush

Following are a few players' comments on Paul:

We didn't know what line-up John was going to pick for the 1980 FA Cup final until 12 noon on the Friday. I was not a full-time member of the team at that particular time but it was a big surprise to me to be included and Brushy to be left out. We've always been best of mates and enjoy each other's company.

Geoff Pike

Football can be a harsh game. Very harsh. Paul Brush felt the full force of that. He was a good lad and a good player. To be fair to John he always made decisions, which he thought were right and in the best interests of the club.

Mick McGiven

Grandad Brushy with six month old Olly and Harry the dog

29 – DEREK HALES

"I did as well as I could at West Ham United, under difficult circumstances. I liked John Lyall but West Ham never saw the best of me."

Born: Lower Halstow, Kent, December 15, 1951 • **Position:** Striker • **Games played for West Ham United:** 27 (1977-78)

Goals for West Ham United: 10 • **Debut:** October 3, 1977 v Middlesbrough (h) L 0-2 (Mills 2) Att: 26,508

West Ham United: Day, Lampard, Brush, Holland, Taylor T, McGiven, Taylor A, Robson B, **Hales***, Brooking, Pike. Sub: Devonshire.*

Middlesbrough: Platt, Craggs, Cooper, Souness, Boam, Ramage, Mahoney, Mills, Ashcroft, McAndrew, Armstrong.

Derek David Hales spent just a single season at West Ham United but left an enduring legacy. He was born and raised in Lower Halstow to parents Richard ('Dick') and Mary who ran a couple of Kent butcher's shops in both Rainham and Upchurch. *"I was brought up on a farm around knives and guns because my dad and his brother, William, killed animals for a living. As a kid, my dad bought me a gun for my birthday and encouraged me to use it on birds and rabbits. It was only a shot-gun or a twenty bore! That's why I got the nickname 'Killer' at Charlton. We were country lads and that's what we did. My dad and uncle also played football and were very decent footballers in the old Kent league. We were all football nuts."*

Although Derek's goals-to-games ratio at Upton Park was impressive – 10 strikes from 27 matches - he only stayed for one season, returning to Charlton Athletic in 1978, where he went on to become their all-time leading goalscorer. His 168 goals from 368 matches for the Addicks is unlikely to be bettered at The Valley for some considerable time to come.

Nowadays, Derek works at the Howard School in Gillingham, having been a publican in Lower Halstow for a number of years. He returned to Upton Park for a 3-3 thriller against Arsenal in April 2016, during the last ever season at the Boleyn Ground. He was warmly received by the Hammers faithful.

I first met John Lyall in 1977, off the M1, when I was playing for Derby County. He was with Ernie Gregory, the old goalkeeper. John took Ernie along on most scouting missions or for little chats with those players he had an interest in.

At Derby, Tommy Docherty had been brought in as manager and I wasn't having the best of times. Not many people know the full story but, when I moved from Charlton Athletic to Derby County, my mother-in-law was diagnosed with breast cancer. I was recently married and my wife was, understandably, by her mother's side and trying to flit between Kent and Derby. I was living in a hotel, so the whole experience was unsettling and I felt distracted most of the time. Having said that I didn't do too badly, scoring seven goals from 20-odd appearances living out of a suitcase!

I told John that my mind was here, there and everywhere and that I had to get back down to Kent, closer to my family. Tommy Doc' had set a fee for me, which West Ham seemed happy to pay but I said to John that I needed a few extra quid as part of the deal so he said he would sort me out with a signing-on fee. The bottom line was that I wouldn't go anywhere without a brown envelope. Back then you had to look after yourself and I always enjoyed a good pay day, when joining a club. In fact, I had a double pay out at West Ham because after we got relegated at the end of my first season, John had to reduce the wages bill and he told me that he needed to move me on. He knew he was reneging on our agreement which had been for a longer stay at West Ham so I received another brown envelope as a form of compensation, let's say. I also picked up a pay-out for signing-on at Charlton Athletic again so

Beating Paul Cooper of Ipswich Town, October 1978

that was a really good pay day all round!

Back at that hotel, we agreed to meet a second time near Purfleet and that was another memorable occasion. I was asking for a few bits and bobs like a car and a good salary but John just looked at me and said he wouldn't be able to give me a car and that the wages I was asking for were far too high: "Even Trevor isn't on that!" he explained, so I backed down a bit and we met in the middle and shook hands there and then.

The whole time I was playing for West Ham I was living with my mum and dad in Lower Halstow, which was okay, but not okay, if you see what I mean. Sadly, my mother-in-law died so West Ham didn't see the best of me to be fair. I still scored 10 goals in 27 appearances which would be more than enough nowadays to get you a King's ransom, an England cap and a silly amount of media plaudits.

It took me a couple of games to settle in and I was carrying a bit of an injury on my debut at home to Middlesbrough but John wanted to play me so I had a run at it.

John's training sessions had quite a bit of running which was alright I suppose. The worst day was always Monday because we had cross country running regardless of how we had done on the previous Saturday. Pre-season training usually saw us running around Epping Forest and I always sat in at the back with Trevor Brooking and Bobby Ferguson. I wasn't a cross-country runner and it wasn't important to me. As a striker, sprinting was far more important. Bonds and Pikey and all that crowd won all the cross country races but they couldn't beat me over a short sprint so it made no difference to me. Sprinting was my game and I was always the fastest

over short distances at every club I played for. If Bonds was marking me in training and we had a ten yard sprint for the ball I would get there a yard ahead of him, which is plenty enough for me to score a goal, I can assure you of that!

If I'd settled down a bit quicker things may well have been different but I had no luck in the housing market. That was back in the day when gazumping was happening which caught me out a couple of times.

We ended up getting relegated and John knew that I was one of the few at West Ham who could actually command a transfer fee, so we had a chat and he asked me what I thought. I said it didn't really matter to me. Football was football. I'd happily play for Bogoff Lamplighters for 260 quid a week or West Ham. In those days, a player's career didn't last very long so I always found it good to move around a bit to keep those brown envelopes coming.

When I look back on that 1977-78 season I didn't stand a chance really. I think we conceded, on average, about two goals per game so we had to score three goals to get all the points and, back then, it just didn't happen. It certainly didn't happen at West Ham because, along with Derby, they had the worst pitch in the league. Unfortunately, I had to play on both of those f******! It was nigh on impossible to perform at any sort of level on pitches like those, let alone getting any kind of winning streak going with defences like the one we had at West Ham during that 1977-78 season.

John was a very good talker and he made a lot of sense, but we still got relegated and it took three seasons for West Ham to get back to the top division. I think if John had kept me at

Going head-to-head with Dennis Tueart of Manchester City, January 1978

the club I would have got them up a bit sharper than that.

There was a terrific camaraderie at the West Ham. It was a proper family club right from the tea ladies through to the chairman. Quite a few of the players sat in the groundsman's hut and had a beer! I can't remember the groundsman's name, but boy could he tell a tale. He told me he'd worked at Highgate crematorium putting the coffins into the furnace. They earned a fortune by keeping back half the coffins and just disposing of the bodies. The coffins were so well made with mahogany and brass fittings and leopard skins that they made a pretty penny from recycling them. He also said that some of the guys used to have a few gold teeth away when they could!

I got on well with Frank Lampard and sat with him at the back of the team coach. I liked Bondsy and Brooking, both great talents in their own right. John Radford was good for me at West Ham, too. He set up quite a few of my goals and he liked a drink and a bet which was always a good thing.

In the short time I knew John Lyall, I can say that he was a nice man, who was surrounded by good people. Eddie Baily, Ernie Gregory and Rob Jenkins were all really nice people. I wasn't at West Ham long enough to say that he was the best coach I played under but he had something about him and was a very good talker. It was just unfortunate that my circumstances weren't great when I signed for him and I'm sure he would be the first to admit that 1977-78 wasn't one of his best seasons.

When I think about it, John had been a defender at West Ham so it follows that he would have been expected to get that bit right. But that season the team had one of the worst defensive records in the league. If I'm brutally honest, both Mervyn Day and Bobby Ferguson weren't as good as they thought they were. They were decent keepers but not anything great. If you ask Tommy Taylor, Kevin Lock, John McDowell, Paul Brush and Frank Lampard about that season, I think they would admit they played more bad games than good ones. Don't get me wrong, they were all nice chaps but apart from Trevor, Bondsy and Pop, we just lacked a little bit of class. Nowadays, the manager would be out on his ear with a defensive record like that. Ironically, John kept his job and most of those defenders were moved on. A friend of our family is Tony Pulis and wherever he has coached he has always been very effective at shoring up the defence. It is always very difficult to sack a man with a good record in that particular area.

John tried to fine me once and we had a bit of a run-in. I didn't mind speaking my mind. He was only a manager after all! It all happened after I had been sent off in a game against Wolves. John called me into his office on the Monday and told me I was going to be fined two-weeks' wages. I told him he couldn't do that because there wasn't anything in my contract. He was adamant and said it was club policy, so I told him that if he was going to fine me two-weeks' wages, he wouldn't see me for a couple of weeks. I've never been the type to work for nothing. I was sorry for being sent off but their left back, Derek Parkin, had caught hold of me and pulled my shirt so I just gave him a little back-hander, nothing sinister, and he went down like a sack of potatoes.

I enjoyed the club, I enjoyed the players, I enjoyed the supporters and John was good to me. Sadly, it was just unfortunate that it was a case of the right club at the wrong time. I tried my best under difficult circumstances. I used to love going back to Upton Park and returned during the final season and got a terrific reception on the pitch at half-time. I thought to myself: "Why would they remember a bald old bugger like me?" But they did. They are great football fans at West Ham and remember their history.
Derek Hales

Players' comments:

I remember we were playing Wolves. They had a defender named Derek Parkin, who I could never get past. There was a clash and I could see the red mist descending on Halesy and he smacked Parkin flush on the chin and he went down. As the ref was fumbling for his note-book, Halesy just took off his shirt, shouted 'Hales!' and walked off the pitch. I'll never forget it. Wallop. 'Hales!' And off he went!
Pat Holland

He worked his socks off and scored goals but he couldn't win over the crowd at West Ham.
Mick McGiven

He was a straight-talking gangster from south of the river.
Paul Brush

I played with Derek for half-a-season and he was a really good finisher. He was a good lad and I enjoyed partnering him up front. He had a very useful knack of scoring goals from all angles and putting the ball where the 'keeper couldn't get it.
David Cross

I know Halesy well because we played at Charlton together. Unfortunately, all the stories I know about him can't be printed!
Billy Lansdowne jnr

Loving the game!

Back at The Boleyn Ground one last time, April 2016

30 – DAVID CROSS

"For most of my career I had a lot of self-doubt and wondered if I was good enough. Then I met John Lyall and he gave me the confidence to improve my game."

Born: December 8, 1950, Heywood, Lancashire • **Position:** Striker • **Games played for West Ham United:** 224 (1977-1982)

Goals scored for West Ham United: 97 (13th on the all-time scorers' list) • **Honours:** 1980 FA Cup winner, 1980 Charity Shield runner-up, 1980-81 Division 2 Champion and Golden Boot winner (22 league goals), 1981 League Cup runner-up.

Debut: December 17, 1977 v West Bromwich Albion (a) L 0-1 (Brown A) Att: 18,868

West Bromwich Albion: *Godden, Mulligan, Statham, Brown T, Wile, Robertson, Martin, Regis, Brown A, Robson, Johnston.*

West Ham United: *Day, McDowell, Brush, Bonds, Taylor T, Pike, Devonshire, Robson, Cross, Brooking, Hales.*

David Cross scored four goals against Tottenham Hotspur at White Hart Lane. The achievement is unique and deserving of the widest possible recognition amongst the claret and blue faithful. Interestingly, prior to David's heroics in September 1981, his previous goals in the West Ham shirt had also included a four-goal haul - at Grimsby Town the previous April.

David grew up on Bury Old Road in Heywood, Lancashire. His parents, Tom and Mary, were from Newcastle-upon-Tyne, so supporting the Magpies was handed down to the youngster and his three brothers. Their father worked in the Air Ministry but died when David was just four-years-old. "I was the youngest and there wasn't any Widow's Pension back then so my mum had worked hard to bring some money into the house."

David had a long and varied football career which saw him play for Rochdale, Norwich City, Coventry City, West Bromwich Albion, Manchester City, Vancouver Whitecaps, Oldham Athletic and Bolton Wanders, as well as the five years he spent at Upton Park. He is fondly remembered as 'Psycho!' by the fans.

David's six goals in the 1981 European Cup Winners Cup campaign remains a club record. His antics and wisecracks in the dressing room established him as a firm favourite

amongst the players and he will always be remembered with high regard amongst the fans.

"My wife, Christine, and I have two daughters and a son. Bobby is a decent cricketer, while Jennifer plays netball and my youngest, Kathryn, also plays cricket for Lancashire ladies and England. Everyone pulled my leg when I got married because it was typical of me to find a wife called Chris! I have retired now, but I did have six years at Blackburn Rovers, working on opposition analysis. I am a grandfather so have a different set of responsibilities, these days. I find it flattering that even today people still contact me on Twitter and remember my time at West Ham United with real appreciation and affection. I love to catch up with the lads at various reunions which are held from time to time."

David's recollections of John Lyall resonate with the very highest regard and affection for the man:

He always called me Dave. When I think of John I think of the confidence and belief he gave me. For most of my career, I had a lot of self-doubt and wondered if I was good enough, especially when I joined West Ham, because they had star players like Trevor Brooking and Billy Bonds. I was expected to fit in with them and score the goals to try and keep the club up during the 1977-78 season. John gave me the boost I needed. He really believed in me. I wasn't a player in the typical West Ham mould. I was brave and honest and could

Lyall finally gets his man

could talk to about all manner of things outside of football. At his home, he asked me what I thought about signing for West Ham United and I looked around at this lovely family man and could see that he genuinely cared for who I was. I wasn't about to say no to that. I ended up signing for him on my 27th birthday. When I saw him at work as a coach, I knew that I'd made the right decision. In the five years I was with West Ham, John improved my game no end.

One of the first things John told me was that if we played well at home the fans would stick with us forever, even when we lost I found that to be the case. It hadn't been like that at other clubs. John used to say that if we kept Manchester United quiet at Old Trafford for 25 minutes their fans would start getting frustrated and be on the player's backs. It wasn't like that at West Ham. I loved playing at Upton Park because the fans really took to me. I was fortunate in that the fans hadn't seen the best of John Radford and Derek Hales so I knew they would probably cut me some slack.

The 4-0 win at Tottenham is what most fans remember me for. We had drawn our opening match against Brighton, so facing Spurs away in our second match wasn't ideal. They had just signed Ray Clemence who was England's goalkeeper at the time and were the FA Cup holders, so it was a bit of a daunting experience.

I liked to play on the left-side of the front two, because I always felt that it was part of my job in a 4-4-2 formation. It took a bit of pressure off of our left-back and left-sided midfielder by closing down the opposition's right-back and preventing him getting down the line. Unfortunately, Steve Perryman just kept going forward relentlessly so it was quite difficult. It was a hot, muggy, September night and all of a sudden Jimmy Neighbour went down the right and crossed one over, which rebounded to me and I volleyed it in.

We went in at half-time 1-0 up and the second goal also came about from a cross from the right. This time, I had two bites at the cherry before it ended up in the net.

The third was the best of the night and a real West Ham goal. Frank Lampard took a throw-in and then it was like the one-touch football John liked us to play in training. Dev back to Lampard to Paul Goddard to Geoff Pike to me and I really fancied it and hit it as sweet as a nut. Some say it came off my shin which isn't right. I hit it in that area above my laces where your leg meets your foot. It flew into the top right corner. Technically, it was a very good goal.

The fourth was a scrappy affair and I put it away after it looked like others might score. I tried not to get too high when I scored, like I tried not to get too low when I didn't score. It is something I've tried to pass on to my daughter, who plays cricket. Sometimes she is the star when she takes five wickets but then she may not take any in the next game so it is important to keep everything in perspective.

score goals but I didn't know if that was enough for me to make it at West Ham. The fans were reared on stylish and entertaining football. In fact, we used to say that West Ham were a bunch of pretty boys and if you knocked them about a bit you'd get something out of the game.

In 1976, I had been at Coventry City for a few years and it was obvious that I was going to leave. Ron Greenwood came in for me but I turned the club down. Ron said he was really keen to sign me but I told him I was only 25-years-old and single and a bit wary of coming to the bright lights of London and all the temptation it held. I knew what I was like! I ended up going to West Brom instead and I had a great year there before John Lyall came back in for me.

John had remembered that I was very concerned about coming to London as a single man because I thought I'd get washed away by it all. John showed me a lot more to London. He took me to the countryside and I remember going to his house in Abridge and his wife, Yvonne, baking cakes and preparing a lovely tea for us all. I couldn't believe I was in a football manager's house enjoying tea and cake!

I immediately liked John as a man, he was someone I

Crossy holds the FA Cup aloft at East Ham Town Hall in 1980

I gave the match ball to Phil Parkes because after the four I'd scored at Grimsby Town, he had said he would never be in a position to get one. I promised him that I would give him mine the next time I got a hat-trick.

John's training sessions were very hard but very fulfilling. I had this image of West Ham as being easy-osey, playing nice football with little passes using the outside of the foot, little curves and twists and nice skill. But it was exactly the opposite. We did a lot of running and played a lot football. I didn't realise that John was such a hard task-master.

On Mondays, we usually did nothing with the ball. John wasn't daft, he knew the players had been drinking over the weekend and started the week with a running session. Then, as the week progressed, he would set up training in line with who we were playing at the weekend. I'd be involved in a lot of crossing and finishing sessions. On Friday, we would have a short, sharp session of eight-a-side in the new gym at Chadwell Heath. This was a high energy work-out so we were sharp and ready for Saturday's match.

John improved my game in several ways. My touch had always been good, even when I was a young kid starting out at Rochdale, but John improved my awareness. A good example to illustrate this came when we won promotion in 1981 and had a very tough match against Swansea City at Vetch Field. They had a good side at the time but we beat them 3-1 and I managed to get one. The following week during training, John set up a session where he rolled the ball to me 30 or 40-yards out from goal, to set up a one-on-one between me and Phil Parkes. I was more of an instinctive player and didn't benefit from having too much time to think about things so it was a good session for me to learn. Anyway, John played it into me on my left side and I closed in on Parkes and shot with my left and put it into the side netting. "Why did you do that, Dave?" asked John. "What, put it into the side netting?" I replied. "No, kick it with your left foot?" continued John. "What did you do at Swansea on Saturday?" Then I realised what he was getting at because I had been in exactly the same situation, closing in from the left and dinking it over Dai Davies with my right foot. "Stick with what you're good at," he insisted.

That was typical of John. He simplified things and made me aware of my strengths. I was the type of character who needed that and I improved as a result. Some coaches worked on a player's weaknesses and I'm sure John took that approach with other players, but with me he worked on what I was good at. John knew I was quick and brave and that I worked hard and chased things over the top. He knew that I was mobile and that I'd pressure defenders as our first line of defence, which is why he played me up front on my own against Arsenal in the 1980 FA Cup final.

My 'Psycho' tag was given to me, not by the players, but by the fans. We were playing at Cardiff City and I had got involved in some altercation on the half-way line. I was probably looking for it because I liked to look for an argument on the pitch. It helped to fire me up. The referee blew for half-time and as I went down the tunnel one of our fans just looked at me and shouted: "You're a psycho aren't you?" I just laughed but from that moment it became my nickname amongst the fans. It's funny because that was never my nickname with the players. They used to call me Norman. When I signed for West Ham, Ernie Gregory introduced me to all the players as Norman Cross! From that day on I was known as 'Norman' to the lads and Billy Bonds and Trevor Brooking still call me that today. When I got to know Ernie I asked him one day where 'Norman Cross' came from but he said he had no idea and put it down to being nervous. Sometime later, I was driving up north and I passed through Peterborough and there was this big junction on the A1 called 'Norman Cross'. It turned out that Ernie had a sister living in Peterborough and would drive to see her three or four times each year! Everything finally made sense!

It seems weird to say, given how football clubs approach the game today, but we didn't really have a game-plan. There wasn't any great insight into how the opposition were going to play or how we were going to nullify that and counter it with something else. We just knew how we wanted to play and what we wanted to do. We were positive in our approach and wanted to get the ball into the strikers playing passing football. John made us work on that week-in, week-out. He was always calm and assured and we worked our socks off playing the West Ham way. He used to say: "You know what we are, you know what we do, just go out there and play our way."

As a teaching and tactical coach, John was the best I played for. I played under some very good coaches and must mention Johnny Giles because he signed me three times during my career. I remember Giles playing in the 1963 FA Cup final with Manchester United and later on with the great Leeds United team under Don Revie. For him to sign me three times – for West Brom, Vancouver Whitecaps and then West Brom a second time – left me in no doubt about how he rated me. Ron Saunders was very good as well. He signed me at Norwich City. The main difference between the three

First goal v Tottenham Hotspur, September 1981

Second goal...

Third goal...

Fourth goal - Dreamland!

men was that John Lyall was a qualified FA Coach, whereas Ron and Johnny Giles didn't have coaching badges, they just knew the game inside out. John always urged me to take my coaching badges but I needed those seven weeks during the close season to get away from football, altogether. I didn't get my badges until after I had finished playing. Those three managers were not just great managers, they were also very good men. I wanted to be associated with them because of the standards they set and the type of people they were.

John never fined me, but he did give me a good talking to sometimes because I liked to joke around. It was my outlet really, particularly in the dressing room before a game. I liked to have a laugh, it helped to lighten the mood. On a couple of occasions I overstepped the mark and John let me know about it. I could impersonate a few of the players which always raised a laugh. Bobby Ferguson was easy to do and I'd even take off John from time to time. I could do his mannerisms quite well but his voice was harder to mimic. I never let him know about it because he was the manager and I wanted my name on the team sheet when it went up

The only Hammer to score a hat-trick in European competition, against Real Castilla, October 1980

each Friday!

John was very kind to me in his book – 'Just Like My Dreams.' He highlighted my work-rate and prowess as a top scorer. Personally, I am very proud of the fact that over 40 of the 97 goals I scored for West Ham were away from home. There were a lot of strikers who were very good scoring at home in front of their own crowd, but couldn't deliver on the road.

I was lucky to have played with some very good strikers at West Ham - Pop Robson, Derek Hales, Stuart Pearson and Paul Goddard. They all had attributes that I didn't have, which is important, and I had elements to my game that they didn't have, so we complemented each other.

John knew that I had lost my father at a young age and I think he took on the persona of a father-figure because it felt like we had that type of relationship. He gave me plenty of advice and we used to talk a lot and had some good conversations. I wasn't part of the card school on the coach like Bill, Trevor and Parkesy. I preferred to sit at the front talking to John or reading. John liked to read biographies and I remember him reading one about Stirling Moss. He was really impressed by the man and I he mentioned that if Moss hadn't been a top racing driver, he would have been top at something else because of his attitude, dedication and will to win. I liked to read about the city we were travelling to so we had some really good conversations on those trips.

John liked his players to think for themselves. In one game we were being over-run in midfield. Bill was concerned and said to Trevor that they were slicing through us too easily. Trev asked me to drop back to pick up one of their main threats and add a bit of support to our midfield. At half-time, John asked me why I did that so I explained to him what had happened and he liked that a lot. He liked his players to solve problems, to think for themselves and talk to each other to work things through. Nowadays, you can see players looking to the bench with their hands out wide, shrugging their shoulders, not knowing what to do and waiting for advice from their manager. A lot of players are too scared to think for themselves these days and I think the game has lost something as a consequence.

I was a notoriously poor sleeper but John helped me a lot. Friday night was particularly bad because I would be thinking about the game. John had a chat with me about it and I told him that it was actually Thursday night, which I found the hardest. The club had a no-drinking policy after Wednesday so I got anxious from Thursday onward. I remember John saying that Thursday night was his best night of the week because on Friday and Saturday he was wrapped up in that week's match, while Sunday was spent planning Monday's training session and analysing the previous days' game. On Monday, Tuesday and Wednesday, he would invariably be watching a

The last encounter with John, Britannia International Hotel, Isle of Dogs, 2005

game somewhere, so Thursday was the night when he could relax at home with Yvonne. John recommended that I went out for a beer on that night as he thought it would do more good than harm. He was the first and only manager to urge me to go out for a drink! I didn't abuse his trust, of course, and I'd find a quiet pub in the country somewhere and have a couple of beers. It worked a treat because that was the season I scored 33 goals in all competitions and won the Golden Boot in the second division.

Just before the 1980 FA Cup final, John told me of his intention to play 4-5-1 and leave me up front on my own. The main thing was that John believed I could do the extra running, on a very hot day, and hold the front line, which really helped boost my confidence. I had to give a good return on the unwavering faith he had in me. I was quite good at running about - it was only a problem when the ball came near me! He didn't tell me about his tactical change until ten minutes before kick-off. Stuart Pearson seemed to be hearing it all for the first time, too, but fast forward 25-years, to a West Ham reunion at the Britannia Hotel in Canary Wharf, and John told me that he'd already told Pancho on the Thursday prior to the

game. He said he knew that I would've worried about it, and he was right.

It was an innovative tactical move from John and Arsenal's manager, Terry Neil never countered it with any changes of his own. When you think they had Liam Brady feeding both Frank Stapleton and Alan Sunderland it just goes to show how well Billy, Alvin and Phil played in our defence. We soaked up their pressure in the second-half and, with about 15 minutes to go, I thought to myself: "We might win this."

The European Cup Winners Cup campaign the following season was really exciting. The game against Real Castilla behind closed doors was a weird experience. We went in at half-time 3-0 up and looked like we would cruise through, but they evened it up on aggregate with the only goal in the second half. Fortunately, we got a couple in extra-time to ease through. It's funny because a few years ago, Sam Allardyce who was managing Blackburn Rovers at the time, brought in a Spanish player called Michel Salgado, who had won over 50 caps for Spain. One day we had a chat about Real Castilla and I told him about the game and I brought in the programme which I'd got signed by all the players that night. Michel took a look at their line up and pointed out four players who went on to become Spanish internationals. It made me reflect on just how good a result that was for West Ham that evening.

Playing in the Bernabeu was also a special experience and the one thing I remember about the first-leg was how lush the grass was. It was thick stemmed and the ball didn't run smoothly. Instead, you had to go to it to receive it. Thankfully, the regulation at the time was that we could train on the pitch the day before so we knew what we were up against. Sadly, the trouble in and around the stadium had affected us and I think we all thought we were going to get thrown out of the competition. The three likely outcomes John was expecting were to be ejected, forced to play at a neutral venue or play behind closed doors. Our run came to an end when we lost heavily at home to Dinamo Tbilisi. I've still got Shevadze's shirt from that game.

I've talked to a lot of West Ham fans over the years and most of them feel that I left West Ham prematurely. I was about to marry my fiancée, Christine, but that wasn't the main factor behind heading back to Manchester. She was a trainee lawyer at the time but knew I was West Ham's Number 9 and was prepared to live in London. I had always felt throughout my career, however, that I wanted to move back home and it felt like the right time. Christine was from the same village as me even though I didn't meet her until I was 31. Another key factor was that I felt I may have peaked during that 1980-81 season. I was top-scorer again in the top-flight the following campaign, but maybe I was just leaving my best behind me? Not quite over the hill but on the peak looking down. I'd had five great years at West Ham and didn't want to leave on the back of a bad season. I wanted to depart on my own terms, which I had never done at any time during my career. John had offered me another two years on a very good deal. He was shocked when I said I was having deep thoughts about leaving. In the end, I turned down the contract. Michael Hart of the Evening Standard put something in the newspaper about it and straight away the phone started ringing. Eventually, I moved to Manchester City on a three-year deal under John Bond.

The transfer was a bit of a drama because the clubs couldn't agree on the fee. In the end it went to a tribunal. It took place at Old Trafford and John came up with Martin Cearns and Brian Cearns. West Ham wanted £600,000 for me but City only wanted to pay £50,000. In the end, the fee was set at £150,000. West Ham were so professional with their pitch and had clearly done a lot of research. Basically, they said that for the past two seasons Trevor Francis had been the top-scorer in the top division and Man City had just sold him for £1 million. The next best scorer behind Francis was me, and my goals-to-games scoring ratio was just below his. So West Ham concluded that £1m for Trevor and

£50,000 for me just didn't stack up. It soon became clear that City hadn't done any preparation at all. John Bond didn't even attend and sent John Benson instead and they simply didn't have any idea. Totally clueless, they looked so second rate. As we left the tribunal and walked out on the concourse at Old Trafford, I saw John, Martin and Brian walking one way and me walking the other way with John Benson and Bernard Halford. I really wanted to be walking the other way with John and I remember thinking: "F*** it!"

It didn't work out for me at Man City, which was a very strange club at the time. Whenever I walked into a room I got the impression that everyone stopped talking, which was completely different to West Ham, where it was always so open, welcoming and supportive. I left City after one year and went to play in Canada for Vancouver Whitecaps. I did feel like I'd let John Lyall down. He'd done so much for me, looked after me and improved me as a player so I really felt like I'd failed him by not signing that third contract. In fact, I still feel that now.

I always stayed in touch with John and still keep in touch with his wife, Yvonne, today. Every April 18th I phone her because that's the anniversary of John's death. John taught me that there was a life outside of football. I have a similar conversation with my daughter, Kate. She is totally dedicated to cricket and doesn't have much of a life outside of that. She is always training or playing on tour.

In 1988, I went back to West Ham to play in Geoff Pike's testimonial. I spoke to John and was surprised to hear him say that he didn't enjoy the game anymore and that the only thing he looked forward to was his wages at the end of the month. Now that didn't sound like John and when I asked him why he explained how agents were ruining the game: "They call me up offering players from other clubs, which means they are offering my players to other clubs," he sighed. He also said that the players didn't love West Ham as much as the players in my day. He said they were more interested in getting more money than entertaining the fans and that would have been tough for John to understand. That was why he enjoyed his time at Ipswich Town because they were another proper family club. It was run by the Cobbold family and John used to tell the story about when he was called in to see the chairman John Cobbold, who looked at him and announced there had been a disaster at the club. John showed great concern and asked what it was and how he could help, to which the chairman replied: "We've run out of red wine in the boardroom!" John would have liked that because it was so old school.

The last time I saw him was in 2005, at a reunion in Canary Wharf. My son Bobby was about to play cricket in Australia but he came along with me that night. John told him how I used to do the Daily Telegraph crossword on the coach and when my son asked him what type of player I was, John thought for a bit before looking him in the eye and saying: "Your dad was a good player."

I got a phone call the following year from Ray Stewart. He said: "I've got some bad news for you. John Lyall passed away last night." He was only 66-years-old, which is my age now. He always looked pale, did John. Even in the summer he had this pallid complexion, but he was a heavy smoker, which would have contributed to that. The players told him to stop smoking but he responded by saying: "You like a drink and I like a smoke."

When I sent a card to Yvonne and Murray after John had died I wrote inside; "John Lyall was the best man I've ever met in football."

David Cross

Following are some player recollections of David:

If ever there was a player who bore testament to the quality of training, coaching and man-management of John Lyall, it was David Cross. When he first arrived, his touch was heavy and erratic but when he left, almost 100 goals later, Crossy was a very accomplished striker with a very good touch. It was a crushing blow when he went to Manchester City. I was devastated because he was one of the best centre-forwards at West Ham and was terrific in the dressing room.
Mick McGiven

Crossy was great to have around the dressing room, very intelligent with a terrific sense of humour. He will tell you himself that John improved him 50% as a player.
Pat Holland

Crossy wears the battle scars from his endeavours as a player. An old fashioned centre-forward who earned the respect of his teammates and the fans at West Ham United.
Bill Green

He could dish it out as much as a centre-half. A very good player and a very, very under-rated striker.
Alan Devonshire

The joker in the pack.
Everald La Ronde

David came into my surgery one day and the phone started ringing. He picked it up and mimicked the voice of Dr Brill, the club's chief medical officer, who had a thick Scottish brogue. Eddie Chapman was on the other end asking for John Lyall. Crossy put him on hold before assuming the voice of John Lyall and carrying on the conversation!
Rob Jenkins

Tony Cottee and I were smuggled in to White Hart Lane as two 16-years-olds and saw Crossy bang in those four goals against England's Ray Clemence. That was a legendary performance.
Greg Campbell

He had great banter in the dressing room and a strong desire to win. He didn't over-respect the opposition. A special guy who left everyone laughing.
Alvin Martin

Pancho and Psycho at a reunion of the 1980 FA Cup winning side

31 – ALVIN MARTIN

"If you had to pick out a song to describe John it would have to be: "Simply the best."

Born: July 29, 1958 Walton, Liverpool • **Position:** Centre-half • **Games played for John Lyall:** 435 (1978-89)

Games played for West Ham United: 596 (1978-96) 5th on the all-time list • **Goals for West Ham United:** 34

Honours under John Lyall: 1976 FA Youth Cup runner-up, 1980 FA Cup winner, 1980 FA Charity Shield runner-up, 1981 Second Division champion, 1981-88 - 17 England Caps, Hammer of the Year (1980, 1982 and 1983) 1985-86 Member of highest finishing league team. (Third)

1st Testimonial August 21, 1988 v Tottenham Hotspur • 2nd Testimonial v November 11, 1996 v Chelsea

Debut: March 18, 1978 v Aston Villa (a) L 1-4 (Brooking – Gregory 2, Deehan, Mortimer)

Aston Villa: Rimmer, Gidman, Smith, Phillips, McNaught, Mortimer, Gregory, Little, Deehan, Cowans, Carrodus.

West Ham United: Ferguson, McDowell, Lampard, Curbishley, Taylor T, Bonds, Devonshire,* Holland, Cross, Brooking, Hales. Sub: **Martin.***

Alvin Edward Martin spent 21 years as a player at West Ham United. He was a worthy successor to Billy Bonds as club captain. Alvin enjoyed the highs of FA Cup success in 1980 and promotion to the top flight the following season. He missed only two matches during the famed 'Boys of 86' season when the club registered its highest ever league finish – third. He gained 17 England caps and remained with the club until 1996 despite suffering relegation on two occasions in 1989 and 1992.

Today, Alvin is a highly respected football pundit for talkSPORT and Sky Sports. His two sons, David and Joe, continue the line of professional footballers in the family.

I first met John Lyall in the Adelphi hotel in Liverpool when I was 15. The meeting had been set up by a contact of Wally St Pier called John McBride. He was a school teacher in Liverpool. My dad, Albert, was there with me. We sat in the foyer and listened to Ron Greenwood and his assistant, John Lyall, sharing their vision of me as a West Ham United player. Afterwards, my dad told me how impressed he was by both men. I'd been training with Everton as a kid and Ron suggested that if it didn't work out at Goodison Park,

I was welcome to come down and train with West Ham for a couple of weeks. That is exactly what I ended up doing. Those two weeks turned into 20 years.

John's training sessions were always inventive, creative and with a purpose. He was very well organised, a great motivator, an even better communicator, exhibited tactical nous, showed great strength of character, had a cultured eye when buying players and was a very good man-manager. These are the traits which differentiate one manager from another and John was at least 9 out of 10 in all of them, which is why I didn't play under anyone better than him. We enjoyed everything we did but John could also dish out a rollicking when he needed to.

If we had been on the receiving end of a bad defeat, John would keep us locked in the dressing room for as long as it took to communicate everything that he deemed to be wrong in our approach and application. Sometimes, it could be very unpleasant and he would let you feel the blunt end of his tongue. He always did it in a respectful way. The following day, he would be back to his normal self. He didn't hold grudges.

I played in a very good youth team which made it to the FA Youth Cup final in 1975. It was Ronnie Boyce's first season as youth team coach and we had Alan Curbishley, Paul Brush

Alvin's youth team, 1975-76

One of three Hammer of the Year awards - 1980, 1982, and 1983

and Terry Hurlock in that side. We ended up losing to a very good Ipswich Town team. John was heavily involved in all the youth team games and he came along to watch us on a regular basis. He oversaw everything at all levels of the club.

I made my debut as a substitute, away at Aston Villa, but my breakthrough game, which established me, came against Coventry City in April 1978. I came on as a substitute for Geoff Pike and we ended up winning 2-1. John asked me where I wanted to play because I could play in central defence and up front - not very well I should add! I told him I wanted to play at the back and I had a really good game and kept my place for the final six matches of the season. We won four of the six but it wasn't enough to keep us up.

Some of the more humorous memories I have of John relate to my contract talks. As I got older and started playing for England I felt I should be getting a better deal. He'd write down the amount he thought he could ask the board for and I would write down what I thought I was worth. On comparing the amounts, John would pull this face, like a grimace, as though the money was coming out of his own pocket! After time I just signed a blank contract because I trusted him so much.

Ron Greenwood was in charge when I gained my first England cap – against Brazil at Wembley in 1981. I'm sure he would have discussed my form with John so I was in a good position. There were a lot of very good players who were overlooked at International level, so I was lucky that my ability was well known by Ron and John.

John built two teams while I was at the club. The first won the FA Cup in 1980, promotion the following year and made it to a League Cup final. I really enjoyed that time as we gained a record points total and won a major trophy. John then built a team which challenged for the league title in 1985-86. It

was a magnificent time for the club and I have tremendously fond memories from both of those teams. If pressed, I'd lean towards the 1980-81 team as the one I preferred the most.

There were certainly times when the board needed to invest more to strengthen the team. We had the nucleus of a very capable side and a top class manager, but always seemed to be two or three players short. With the right investment we could have challenged for honours every season, but the board were not risk takers. We should have been playing in Europe every year but John's wants and desires were always secondary to those of the club.

Dinamo Tbilisi were the best side I played against at Upton Park. We were all surprised at just how good they were. They had knocked Liverpool out of the European Cup the previous season, but we had been told they were rusty and hadn't played throughout the winter.

After Billy Bonds finally retired from playing in 1988, John needed to find a new club captain to succeed him. It came down to a decision between Ray Stewart and me. I think Ray wanted it more than me. I wasn't too bothered about it because I thought it could potentially affect my focus. But when John started talking to me about the role and responsibility, I really wanted it. I must say that it brought us even closer.

If I had a problem related to football or a personal problem away from football, the first door I would knock on would be John's. He'd sit me down for twenty minutes, dissect the problem and find a solution. I'd walk out of his office thinking: "Why didn't I think of that?" Some of his help went above and beyond what was needed. I used to write a football

Learning from the best at Chadwell Heath

column in the Newham Recorder and I casually asked John about something. Just like that, John sat down and wrote the whole article for me!

I got sent off three times in 22 years but I didn't get fined once. John would take me to one side and say: "Tell everyone I fined you," but he never actually did. I never understood why we had a reputation of being too soft because Ray Stewart, Billy Bonds and Frank Lampard were anything but soft.

Only John would have known the exact reasons behind his sacking. Ultimately, I believe it was the players who let him down and I include myself in that. It was a very frustrating time and I always feel a certain amount of responsibility for what happened to John. I had a few injuries and probably played in games that, with hindsight, I shouldn't have done. I look back now and believe the board should have stuck by John, like he had stuck by them on several occasions. It was the start of a time in football when loyalty lost its way and, sadly, it has worsened ever since.

I always stayed in touch with John after his time at West Ham. I spoke to him when I got the manager's job at Southend United and we met up on a couple of occasions. One of the best memories I have is from a reunion of John's players at the Britannia Hotel on the Isle of Dogs. Everyone turned up that evening but the biggest cheer was reserved for John. There was a pouring out of love and affection for

him and deservedly so. It was an uplifting moment for all the players and John was left in no doubt about how much he was loved by those fans who had been part of his journey in the 1970s and 80s.

Ray Stewart called me with the news that John had died. I was in my car and pulled over and sat there in disbelief. I was very upset and realised that I hadn't really thanked him properly for everything that he'd done for me in my career.

John was a great manager to work under. So many happy memories and one big sad one – I still can't believe he's not around.
Alvin Martin

Following are some recollections of Alvin from his teammates:

Top quality as a bloke and as a player. Real top quality.
Steve Walford

He was one of the most underrated centre-halves I have ever come across. He was a lot better than people gave him credit for.
Derek Hales

We broke into the first team at roughly the same time so we enjoyed all the good times together.
Alan Devonshire

John presenting Alvin with an Evening Standard Player of the Month award, Februrary 1980

few days every week. Sometimes we wondered if he would come back because he was so homesick.
Paul Brush

The best tennis player I ever played against. We both loved playing tennis and we had a cracking five setter once at Redbridge sports centre.
Everald La Ronde

Alvin came down from Everton for a trial. After half an hour Ron Greenwood shouted: "Ok, I've seen enough!" Alvin, with his socks round his ankles, had been bringing the ball down on his chest, playing it out of defence and hitting 20-30 yard passes to feet. Ron knew he had a real talent on his hands and Alvin went on to become a key player for West Ham. A cup winner, England international and club captain. Fantastic!
Mick McGiven

Being a central defender, Alvin had Tommy Taylor, Billy Bonds, Bill Green and Mick McGiven all vying for those central defensive positions. He'd pick me up at Barking station in his mustard coloured Mazda. He was over six feet tall in a tiny car wearing tight jeans, a brown leather jacket and pointy shoes!
Dale Banton

Alvin was my room-mate and we understood each other's game. He's always been a good pal.
Tony Gale

I sometimes bump into Alvin at MK Dons when I'm scouting. He goes over there to watch his son, David, play in goal.
Warren Donald

I was in digs in Canning Town with Alvin for a couple of years. When he was playing for England and trying to get selected for World Cup Spain in 1982 they played a match in Finland where I was living at the time. We went out together after the game and he gave me an England shirt.
Alan Wooler

I always felt jealous of Alvin because he kept me out of the side and had the career at West Ham I would have loved.
Phil Brignull

He made the most of the many talents he had. To play centre-half, a tough position, for as long as he did deserves credit. When he first arrived he'd go back home to Liverpool for a

Back at the Boleyn Ground (far right) during the final season, April 9, 2016

Back row: Brignull, Brush, Lansdowne, Morgan, McGiven, McDowell.

Middle row: Brooking, Martin, Parkes, Bonds, Cross.

Front row: Lampard, Jennings, Pike, Holland, A Taylor, Devonshire.

CHAPTER FIVE
1978-79

"The spirit here is best typified by Billy Bonds. He can be running about all over the pitch playing brilliantly and then come in to say he thought so and so did well." **John Lyall**

West Ham United started a campaign in the second tier of English football for the first time since 1957-58. Kevin Lock, Bill Green, and Derek Hales all left the club for a combined transfer total of £210,000.

West Ham tried to sign Dutchman Bert Van Marwijk, a £100,000 rated midfielder, who actually played for West Ham in a friendly. The deal never happened, of course, but it is interesting to note that Van Marwijk went on to enjoy an illustrious career in management, winning the UEFA Cup with Feyenoord in 2002 and taking the Dutch national side to the World Cup final in 2010 – losing 0-1 to Spain.

Mervyn Day, once described in the press as the 'Super kid keeper,' was replaced by QPR's Phil Parkes, for a world record fee of £565,000. The previous record occurred in 1974, when Stoke City paid Leicester City £340,000 for Peter Shilton. Parkes got off to a flyer, keeping a clean sheet in a 3-0 victory over Oldham Athletic. Confidence returned to the team.

An injury to Trevor Brooking, during a 5-0 win at home to Newcastle United, proved to be a massive blow to the Hammers' chance of promotion. A failure to beat 10-man Wrexham meant a second season in Division Two.

Frustration and dissatisfaction were rife. Alan Curbishley slammed the club in the press and was fined two weeks wages: "If I stay here I'll be wasting away," he is alleged to have said. "I could be at West Ham for the next ten years and not make any progress. It's keep ball and give it to Trevor Brooking. I am so concerned about my future I would even take a wage cut to find a club where I was appreciated." John Lyall promptly sold him to Birmingham City for £225,000.

Reg Pratt decided to step down as Chairman. The 74-year-old was the longest serving Chairman, having been on the West Ham board for 38 years and Chairman for 29 of those: "It's time to settle down a bit," declared the East Ham timber merchant.

John Lyall gave debuts to three young players from the Academy – Nicky Morgan, Billy Lansdowne and Phil Brignull – as well as record signing, Phil Parkes.

Here is their story...

Chairman Reg Pratt retired after 38 years on West Ham United's board

Phil Parkes signed for £565,000, a world record for a goalkeeper

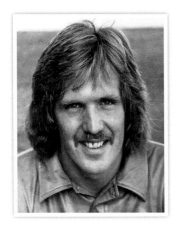

32 – PHIL PARKES

"There isn't really anyone in the modern game to compare with John Lyall. Perhaps Arsene Wenger has a similar manner, but I don't think he is anywhere near as good as John. The thing that struck me more than anything else was just how passionate John was about West Ham United."

Born: Sedgley, West Midlands, August 8, 1950 • **Position:** Goalkeeper • **Games played for John Lyall:** 405 (1979-89)

Games played for West Ham United: 400 (1979-1990) • **Honours under John Lyall:** 1980 FA Cup winner, 1980-81 Division Two champion, 1980-81 Hammer of the Year, 1981 League Cup runner-up, 1985-86 ever present in West Ham United's highest ever league placing – 3rd, 1990 Testimonial v Ipswich Town. Att: 8,733

Debut: February 24, 1979 v Oldham Athletic (h) W 3-0 (Holland, Martin, Robson) Att: 26,052

West Ham United: Parkes, McDowell, Brush, Curbishley, Martin, Bonds, Holland, Devonshire, Cross, Brooking, Robson.

Oldham Athletic: McDonnell, Wood, Blair, Bell, Hicks*, Hurst, Keegan, Halom, Young, Chapman, Gardner. Sub: Heaton.*

Philip Benjamin Neil Frederick Parkes is widely regarded as West Ham United's all-time greatest goalkeeper and there have been some outstanding stoppers in the club's history: Ted Hufton, Ernie Gregory, Jim Standen and Ludek Miklosko, respectively. All have ensured fierce competition for the prime position in Hammers folklore. Hufton won six England caps in the 1920s, compared to Phil's solitary cap, which was gained in 1974 whilst at Queens Park Rangers. Standen won both the FA Cup and the European Cup Winners' Cup, while Gregory was part of the famed Hammers of 1958 that won promotion to the top-flight after a 25-year absence. Last but not least, 'Ludo' had close encounters with both the FA Cup and League Cup and formed part of two successful promotion teams in the early 1990s. However, Phil's claim to the title of 'Best ever 'keeper' is bolstered by an FA Cup winner's medal, a second division championship medal, a League Cup runners-up medal and an ever-present season during the club's highest league finish in 1985-86.

In 2017, Manchester City set a new world record for a goalkeeper, when paying £34.7m for Ederson of Benfica. It was some 38 years on from the world record transfer fee of £565,000 that West Ham United paid QPR for a 29-year-old

with suspect knees. That amounts to a 70-fold increase in price and, one would suspect, not a 70-fold increase in talent. Ahh, the modern game!

Phil played for John Lyall at both West Ham United and Ipswich Town and the experience has left a bank of first-class memories. Such memories were shared by Phil during his long-standing role as Match-Day host at Upton Park. I was fortunate enough to sit with the great man during the last ever game at the Boleyn Ground, a 3-2 win over Manchester United in May 2016. That experience definitely topped the result.

Nowadays, Phil is finally easing himself into retirement and both he and his wife Lavinia divide their time between their homes in Wokingham and Florida. A bowel cancer scare in 2014 was thankfully averted and Phil continues to attend various West Ham reunions.

His popularity never wanes, just like his high regard for John Lyall:

My earliest memory of John was talking to him on the phone after a training session with QPR. Steve Burtenshaw, the manager, had told me a few days before that a club had come in for me. He couldn't tell me who it was but he did say it was a lot of money. I thought it must have been Dave Sexton at

With John after signing for the Hammers

Manchester United because he had made six bids for me but had been turned down every time. Dave had managed me at QPR before his move to Old Trafford in 1977. However, when I went to see Jim Gregory, the QPR Chairman, he told me that the interest was shown by West Ham United. I must admit, the news didn't excite me very much at all and I told him that I wasn't interested. But, Jim told me they had offered a world record fee - £565,000 - and that he had already given John Lyall permission to talk to me. I was given John's phone number. We'd never spoken before so we had a chat and agreed to meet. I was a bit sceptical because I'd played under a lot of managers; some spivs, some really good – Dave Sexton was a fabulous manager and obviously had a West Ham connection - some I could trust and some I wouldn't even shake hands with for fear of losing my rings!

I agreed to meet John and he drove out to Wokingham, where I still live today. Within an hour of meeting him, I agreed to drop down a division and sign. I had never met anyone quite like him. John was so different, he was like a breath of fresh air. The thing that struck me more than anything else was that he was so passionate about West Ham United. He could see exactly where he wanted the club to go and why progress had been slow: "For far too long, we have been giving goals away," He said. "We are great entertainers but we're never going to win anything if we keep shipping goals. Losing 3-4 or drawing 3-3 is not good enough and I want to bring you in to help us get to the next stage." He told me he had been after me for a long time. We couldn't find Jim Gregory that night to seal the deal - he had gone out for the evening - but rather than wait until the following day, John asked me to sign and gave me his word that if I changed my mind in the morning he would rip up the contract and never tell a soul that he'd been to my house. That level of honesty was impressive to me and got our relationship off to the best possible start. The ideal

he had for West Ham was exciting and that is exactly how it turned out to be. It was one of the most successful times in the club's history. Jim Gregory had said that I'd been at QPR for nine years and wasn't going to get any better, but for the next three or so years at West Ham I got a lot better.

I had a concern about travelling to Chadwell Heath for training. I didn't fancy driving on the M25 every day and was worried that the train wouldn't get me there on time, either. John told me not to worry about it. He just pushed back the start time by 30 minutes to 10:30am which made a big difference to me. It was about 70 miles so I took the train from Wokingham to Waterloo and then got the underground to Barking where I'd jump into a cab to Chadwell Heath. I did that throughout my 12 years at West Ham.

When I arrived I asked if he might consider bringing Bob Wilson in as a goalkeeping coach. I had worked with Bob at QPR. He had won the double with Arsenal and had been really good for me. John was very diplomatic with the situation and explained to me that Ernie Gregory had been at the club for over 40-years and that it would not be fair to bring in someone over him. That was John all over. His primary instinct was to be fair to people. So John made me Ernie's responsibility. I trained with Ernie. He didn't really coach me but he looked after me. We developed a really strong friendship and it was because of Ernie that I stayed at the club for as long as I did. There were times in my late-30s, when I just didn't fancy it anymore and Ernie noticed that and would take me out of training and we'd go for a walk and a chat around Chadwell Heath.

John was very good with encouragement. I was very confident in my own ability so didn't need to be showered with praise but John would rarely single out individuals for praise anyway because, to him, it was all about the team. That said, when John did praise individuals, he would do it on a one-on-one basis. He would come over to me sometimes and just very quietly say: "Well done today." John didn't show extremes of emotion. He never got over-excited and he never got too depressed. I thought that was really good because you don't need a manager who gets over-excitable which might affect his judgement. John was always striving to improve. When we won away from home he'd praise the whole group but would always highlight something that could have been done even better.

John knew his players inside out. He knew who liked a drink, who liked to gamble and who liked the women. He used to say that if your home life was happy and your family were happy then your time at work and playing football would be happy also. He was a great family man and he believed in the family ethic.

I got very close to John and we became great friends. We shared a common love of DIY and carpentry. John's son Murray went on to become a carpenter. On Friday, before a game, we would sit in the cafeteria and chat about what we were working on at home. We'd never talk about the game and I think we both benefited from switching off from football for a while to chat about something we were both very passionate about. For my 40th and 50th Birthday celebrations my wife Lavinia organised surprise parties and John never missed. Those memories are very special to me.

John was very good in the dressing room, too, where he was a very good communicator. If we'd had a bad first half, you'd be hard pressed to get up and grab a cup of tea or go to the toilet because he'd keep you sat there while he explained what was going wrong and how we needed to change things. One occasion which springs to mind was up at Leicester when we got badly beaten, 0-3, and were pretty woeful. We all laid into Tony Cottee because we were all covered in so much mud, but he came off and his kit didn't even need washing. John kept us in for over an hour while he tore into us. It was freezing cold but once he went into one you had no choice but to sit and listen. I think he felt that we'd worked so hard in training all week so to lose a game like that was just unacceptable. He certainly made sure we knew about it.

The worst time I saw John completely lose the plot was after the League Cup final against Liverpool in 1981. Referee, Clive Thomas, had overruled the linesman and allowed Alan Kennedy's goal to stand, even though Sammy Lee was lying in an offside position. We earned a late draw and a replay but I think John felt that West Ham had just been denied a

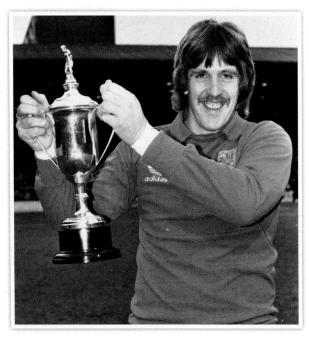

Hammer of the Year 1980-81

trophy. We were all angry and I remember volleying the ball at Clive, which just missed him. If it had hit him it would have knocked him down and I would have been in serious trouble. I had some bad history with Clive anyway and always felt he had it in for me personally and West Ham in general. John was fuming that day. We were unlucky in the replay because Kenny Dalglish scored one of the best goals I've ever seen. Any other player would have taken that ball down first but he just hit it on the turn. Only Dalglish could do that.

People always remind me of the FA Cup third round match at West Bromwich Albion in 1980 and I would certainly hold that up as my best-ever game for West Ham. The Baggies were a strong side under Ron Atkinson with the likes of Cyrille Regis, Ally Brown and John Wile, all good players. We could have been six down at half-time but we actually went in a goal to the good thanks to Stuart Pearson. I had made quite a few saves and Ray Stewart always reminds me of one, where Gary Owen took a free-kick and I was going one way but the ball took a deflection. I had to change my direction, mid-air, to push it away. At half-time I said to Bonzo: "How on earth are we winning 1-0?" He replied: "You never know, our name might be on the cup." That was at half-time in the third round. It ended 1-1 and they clapped me off the pitch at full-time and Big Ron gave me 11 out of 10!

I personally think the 1980-81 side was the best West Ham team I played in. The 1985-86 squad was an exceptional side, too, so it is very, very difficult to differentiate between them. But I preferred playing in the 1980 side, when we lifted the FA Cup and went on to win the old second division. We played some very good football that year and eight of us were selected for the PFA team of the season. It just shows you how good that side was when your fellow professionals vote for you in that way. I think if West Ham had strengthened that squad we would have had a real go at winning the league. It was strange because the West Ham board wasn't afraid of laying out big money. They did it for me with that record transfer fee and they did it again with Ray Stewart, making him the most expensive teenager, but for some reason they stopped when we needed to build on the success of that 1980-81 team.

I loved playing at Upton Park because it was similar to QPR, where the fans were also very close to the pitch. They could pat me on the back when I was taking a goal kick. I was in amongst the fans. I thrived on that. I roomed with Alan Devonshire at first but when he got injured I roomed with Tony Gale. Dev used to like a flutter but I've only ever had a couple of bets in my life. I won a few quid on Sea Pigeon when I was at QPR and, on the night before the FA Cup final, I gave Dev £20 because he was going to Wembley dogs. In the morning he gave me £60 so that was an early sign that it was going to be a good day.

John Lyall 's personal secretary, Pauline Moss, receiving leaving presents from Phil, Chairman Len Cearns and Bob Fixter

People remember the goal Johnny Metgod of Nottingham Forest scored against me from a free-kick up at the City Ground. We were talking about it at a reunion recently and both Mark Ward and Tony Cottee said they were in the wall that day. I couldn't believe that we had such a short wall in place so I took a look at the old footage and, sure enough, it was a dwarf wall...and they ducked!

Dinamo Tblisi were the best side I played against. It was a pity we played them at home first because it would have been a lot closer.

They go on about how intensive training is in today's game, but we trained really hard at West Ham, too. John even employed the services of Ron Jones - the old Welsh sprinter - to put us through our paces on the track. Nobody could be fitter than Bonzo or Dev, not even in the modern game.

There was a time when John was approached by QPR to become their manager. It was around 1987-88. Jim Gregory was still Chairman and wanted to give John a transfer kitty of ten million pounds to rebuild the club. That was an enormous amount of money back then and John wanted to do it. He saw it as a new challenge and he asked me if I would go with him as a player. He'd already asked Mick McGiven to join him on the coaching side. I would follow John anywhere and it looked like it was going to happen but then the West Ham chairman, Len Cearns, intervened and played hard ball with John and made him see out the rest of his contract. That was a big blow

to John and a little bit of West Ham died in him. He was never the same after that and it was noticeable how he would do the minimum of what was expected of him before going straight home to Yvonne and Murray. Before that, he would have gone from the training ground to the stadium and then on to watch a match somewhere but all that stopped once Mr Len refused him a chance to build a team somewhere else. Basically, that took all the fight and passion out of John Lyall.

When they sacked John a couple of years later it just left a really bad feeling at the club. It was a real sickener. He had been there for over 30 years and was a massive part of everyone's life. It was the worst day's business the Board ever did. It just wasn't the way West Ham went about things, and it was handled atrociously, too. They should have brought Bonzo through to replace John, who could have stayed at the club and eased Bill into the role, in much the same way Ron Greenwood had introduced John to management. The system was proven to work but it got smashed to smithereens by sacking John and I don't think they have ever got it back. The 'West Ham Way' died that day and the decision to bring in Lou Macari just ruined everything.

Lou took over but left during his first season leaving Billy in charge. Bonzo asked me to stay and help out as a goalkeeping coach. He knew John had made me an offer to join him at Ipswich Town and, when I told Bill about the deal - £10k signing on fee and only working a three-day week which included Match day - he jokingly asked if I could persuade John to make him an offer!

The last time I saw John was at his house. It wasn't long before he died. My wife, Lavinia, and I went out to Wallers Farm and had dinner with John and Yvonne. I'm so pleased we did that.

It wasn't too long afterwards that I took a call from Ray Stewart, who was in tears telling me the news that John had died. I was in tears, too, soon after, when I was telling Lavinia.

I was very lucky to be invited to the private family gathering at the funeral. I was there with Alex Ferguson, Trevor Brooking, Mick McGiven, Pat Holland and both Chris Kiwomya and Charlie Woods from Ipswich. That took place in the morning and then we went on to Ipswich Cathedral, which was packed with people wanting to show their respects to the great man.

Phil Parkes

There is never any shortage of glowing comments about Phil: Parkesy was my great mate at West Ham. We were big pals. His nickname was Eric and mine was Norm. Phil liked a glass of whisky and there was a funny joke at the time about a white horse, who went into a bar and asked the landlord about the whiskies he sold. "We have all sorts," he answered. "We've got Haig, Famous Grouse, Bells, in fact, we've even got one named after you." To which the horse replied: "What, Eric?" Because Phil liked White Horse whisky, he became known as Eric.

David Cross

In my opinion, West Ham's greatest-ever goalkeeper. Ernie Gregory may take a different view, god rest his soul, but Phil was an outstanding 'keeper.

Mick McGiven

I've never seen a 'keeper control a penalty area as well as Parkesy and I've never seen a better performance than the shift Parkesy put in at West Brom in the FA Cup 3rd round in 1980. But for Phil's heroics, we would have easily lost three or four nil.

Paul Brush

One of my finest memories from my 25 years at West Ham United was sharing a bottle of champagne with Phil Parkes on the eve of the 1980 FA Cup final.

Rob Jenkins

If Parkesy was on his game in training, you would never score.

Alan Dickens

Phil 'I like a cigar' Parkes. I used to call him Champagne Charlie.

Everald La Ronde

What a great servant to West Ham United! I only played a few games with Phil but we've become good friends in recent years through our work in the hospitality lounges at Upton Park. We must have done that for at least eight seasons and we were also involved in the stadium tours which took place during the final season at the Boleyn Ground.

Alan Taylor

He sat next to me on the coach for away games a couple of times. He could talk about anything and everything and was a genuinely nice person.

Billy Lansdowne jnr

I was six-years-old and on holiday in Minorca with my mum and dad. I was sitting on the beach crying because sand was in my eyes. Phil Parkes, who was at QPR at the time, helped me and took me to my mum. Fast forward 10 years and I'm playing with him at West Ham United.

Greg Campbell

Phil would be number one in any West Ham fan's greatest side and that says it all. A gentle giant and a really good friend.

Tony Cottee

I just couldn't believe some of the saves he made.

Alvin Martin

Phil with two programmes from his most memorable matches as a Hammer

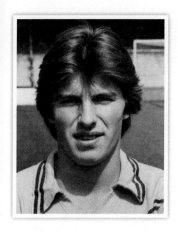

33 – NICKY MORGAN

"I have the utmost respect for John Lyall but found him difficult to get to know. He kept his cards close to his chest."

Born: East Ham, London, October 30, 1959 • **Position:** Striker • **Games played for West Ham United:** 26 (1979-1983)

Goals: 2 • **Honours:** 1980 Charity Shield Runner-up, 1980-81 Second Division champion

Debut: April 9, 1979 v Luton Town (h) W 1-0 (Carr og) Att: 25,498

West Ham United: Parkes, McDowell, Brush, Bonds, Martin, Taylor T, Holland, Devonshire, **Morgan,** Pike, Robson.

Luton Town: Findlay, Stephens, Aizlewood, Donaghy, P Masters, Carr, Hill, West, Stein, Hatton, Moss.* Sub: Taylor.*

Nicholas 'Nicky' Morgan was born to parents Terry and Betty: *"My whole family supported West Ham. My dad was a Lighterman on the river Thames and took over Cassettaris, the famous café along from the Boleyn Pub. He called it 'Bubbles.'"*

Morgan is another example of a local lad playing for his local club: "I grew up in Camel Road, Silvertown and went to East Ham Grammar School just before it changed to Langdon Comprehensive. I captained Newham district, which produced a few good players – Peter Hucker and Vince Hilaire. I played in midfield at that time."

Nicky played 26 times for West Ham United - 10 as substitute – and is remembered for his goal against Sheffield Wednesday in the final match of the 1980-81 promotion season. It ensured a record haul of 66 points for the club, under the old two point system: "To be honest, I can't remember the goal," laughs Nicky.

He is also one of only 13 Hammers to have played in a competitive match in the Bernabéu Stadium – against Real Castilla in 1980.

After retiring from the game, aged 34, Nicky ran a personal training gym near his home in Bristol: "I played for Bristol City and decided to settle down there in 1990. I blew up like a balloon but then took a course on the human body and got heavily into that for quite a few years. Nowadays, I run a

taxi service to and from Bristol airport and spend quite a bit of time on Betfair. I still maintain my fitness every day but sometimes it only amounts to taking the dogs for a walk!"

"I went to the final game at Upton Park. When I got out of the station it was like a war zone. There were barricades and broken bottles everywhere. I almost turned back because it was a really ugly atmosphere. I bumped into Ray Stewart that night. He looks super fit and hasn't changed a bit."

When researching this book, Nicky was something of a Scarlet Pimpernel to find and I had to employ the services of a genealogist to track him down. "You did well, because I like to keep myself to myself."

Following are his recollections:

I was training with QPR as a schoolboy but it was 27 stops on the train so I was pleased when West Ham took an interest in me. My dad, Terry, knew Wally St Pier so he managed to get me a trial and they kept me on. I signed professional forms in October, 1977.

I became good friends with Alan Curbishley and his brother, Paul. I think John liked me because I was a team player, with a good touch and someone who could bring others into the game. I was a good header of the ball and liked to score goals. I loved playing with wingers. That was my forte. The 4-4-2 system was brilliant for me.

Pre season match in Den Haag, August 1981. (Back row - 3rd from left)

I made my debut against Luton Town. We won 1-0 and I missed a sitter. I should have side-footed it into the net but it hit my ankle and went over the bar. Nevertheless, the crowd got behind me because I was a local boy. It was a special atmosphere at Upton Park.

Even though I have a very good overall impression of John, I felt that I should've been in the first team a lot sooner. That's my main gripe against him. He didn't play me until I was 19-years-old and even then he kept fiddling around with

Final appearance for the Hammers. Morgan outjumps George Berry of Stoke City, March, 1983

the team, putting me in and then dropping me. He never gave me a good run in the side. If I'd stayed at QPR I would have got into the first team at 17.

I only scored two goals for West Ham so John never got the best out of me. I had much better spells at Portsmouth, Stoke City and Bristol City. To be fair to John, he had a couple of good strikers at the club in David Cross and Stuart Pearson. I was just the little upstart trying to come through. Then he bought Paul Goddard and Sandy Clark and I realised it was time to move on.

West Ham got my career off the ground. I managed to buy a flat in Queenswood Gardens in Wanstead and drove to Chadwell Heath in a blue Ford Capri. Later, I bought a red Triumph Stag from Dave Webb, the old Chelsea boy. He ran a car dealership somewhere in Ilford.

I don't want to give the impression that I was earning loads of money at West Ham, because that certainly wasn't the case. John was very careful with the club's money. I was only earning a tenner a week as an apprentice.

The reason I was able to buy the Triumph is quite a story - I actually won the club's Matchday lottery! The story goes that I'd arrived at the ground before a game and a couple of girls were selling tickets outside, so I bought a few and ended up winning it. You may remember that all lottery winners were presented with a big cheque on the pitch at half-time but they decided not to do that with me because it probably wouldn't have gone down to well! They just gave me the money and a few days later I was driving around in that Triumph Stag. I can still remember the look on John's face when I parked alongside him at Chadwell Heath. He must have been thinking: "Where on earth has he got that from?"

The best time I had at West Ham was playing in the Charity Shield against Liverpool at Wembley. There were 90,000 there that day and even though I can't remember a great deal from my time at West Ham, I'll always remember that experience. I also played in The Bernabeu against Real Castilla in the European Cup Winners' Cup. John played me on the right-wing in that one.

The best players at the club were Trevor Brooking, who made everything look very easy, and Billy Bonds who played with heart and soul.

John had a good temperament and I don't recall seeing him angry. Joe Jordan was my manager at Bristol City and he could lose his cool quite quickly. I liked playing for Bobby Campbell at Portsmouth. He was a get up and go type of character and had the gift of the gab. Similar to John, he could motivate his players, which is a fine attribute in any good manager.
Nicky Morgan

A lovely, educated footballer. Not pacey but could hold the ball up really well and had a good eye for goal. It's surprising he didn't go further in his career given all the attributes he had. Perhaps he was too good looking to be a striker!
Ray Houghton

He had everything to make a name for himself at West Ham but lacked the determination to burst onto the scene. He could score goals, had two good feet, showed good awareness, but for one reason or another just couldn't bring it all together in matches over a sustained period.
Mick McGiven

Nicky went to Portsmouth and he broke my nose in a reserve team match!
Paul Hilton

We were good friends but he was very quiet. He has been very elusive down the years so you will do well to find him. I haven't seen him since our West Ham days.
Billy Lansdowne

I'd love to see Nicky again. He was one of my good mates at West Ham. We played in the reserves and went out drinking together. I visit the UK from Australia twice a year so ask him to get in touch.
George Cowie

Nicky was a big fan of Rod Stewart. He would go anywhere and everywhere to see him.
Everald La Ronde

My dad signed him at Portsmouth.
Greg Campbell

Tell Nicky to get in touch.
Terry Creasey

He was a strong player, a man's man, who liked a drink and socialising. He was a good lad and I saw him briefly at the final match at Upton Park, against Manchester United.
Dale Banton

Nicky was a good friend of mine and we played football together when we were nine-years-old. We played for Tate & Lyle on Sunday mornings and later for Newham Boys. I also played for Poplar Boys and from those teams quite a few went on to play professional football like Mark Falco at Spurs and Peter Hucker at Queens Park Rangers.
Phil Brignull

Walking the dogs with wife Liz, November 2017

34 – BILLY LANSDOWNE

"I have mixed emotions about my hat-trick against Southend United because John had sacked my dad only a few days earlier. To this day I haven't got a clue why he did that and my dad never talks about it."

Born: Epping, Essex April 28, 1959 • **Position:** Striker • **Games played for West Ham United:** 14 (1979)

Goals scored for West Ham United: 4 (1979) • **Debut:** April 28, 1979 Wrexham (h) D 1-1 (Bonds – Shinton) Att: 28,865

West Ham United: Parkes, McDowell, Brush, Bonds, Martin, Taylor T, Holland, Devonshire, Cross, Pike*, Robson. Sub: **Lansdowne.***

Wrexham: Davies, Cegielski, Dwyer, Jones J, Roberts J, Giles, Shinton, Sutton, McNeil, Lyons,* Fox. Sub: Buxton.*

William "Billy" Lansdowne jnr will always have a place in West Ham United's history. He and his father, Bill, are one of only seven father and son pairings to have played for the club. The other six are the Barrett's (Jim and Jim jnr), the Browns (Ken and Ken jnr), the Lampards (Frank and Frank jnr), the Potts, (Steve and Danny), the Moncurs (John and George) and the Lees (Rob and Elliot). Interestingly, the Lansdownes are the only father and son to have played both with, and for, John Lyall.

Up to 2017, Billy was also one of only 73 Hammers to have scored a hat-trick for the club since 1900. It is a figure which doesn't increase quickly given that only eight hat-tricks have been scored for West Ham this century.

Billy went on to play for both Charlton Athletic and Gillingham before making a name for himself in Sweden with Kalmar FF where he still resides today.

"I've been living out in Sweden since 1983. I'm involved in a couple of businesses out here; one produces corporate gifts, while the other sells RUIA socks. You probably know them as Sock Shop. The Swedish lifestyle is so very laid back and nothing is ever a problem. I play a lot of golf and actually coach a local football club. My son plays football and he's another Billy so we're keeping the tradition going!"

Billy flew over to attend the last-ever match at Upton Park:

"It was special being there with my dad and I caught up with Paul Allen, Geoff Pike, Everald La Ronde and Dale Banton. I would have loved to have seen both Phil Brignull and Nicky Morgan but we missed each other which was a real pity."

Billy had the following memories of his time at West Ham:

To be honest, I didn't have a lot to do with John. I played in the reserves most of the time and that was my dad's responsibility, until he got sacked and Mick McGiven took over looking after us. John left it largely up to his coaches to develop us so there wasn't a great deal of interaction with him.

My dad introduced me to the club in the early 1970s. As a junior I trained on the forecourt every Tuesday and Thursday evening. I just went along when I was about 13 to watch the training and, when I started playing for the youth team a year later, Tony Carr was in charge. Tony had taken over from John Dick and it was his first year in the role. I think I was one of Tony Carr's first ever Youth captains at West Ham.

All the Youth team players were given Wembley tickets for the 1975 FA Cup final against Fulham. I also went to the semi-final replay at Stamford Bridge against Ipswich Town. That was a special night.

I was an amateur when Alan Devonshire played his first-ever game for West Ham. It was for the reserves away at Oxford United on a Saturday afternoon at 3pm. My dad was

Dad, Bill in action. The Lansdownes enjoy a lofty history with the Hammers

in charge and wasn't sure where to play him. We'd heard he liked to play in midfield but didn't know if he could play out wide, in an attacking role or more of a defensive holding role. Anyway, Dev didn't turn up until half-past-two. Obviously, at Southall, he'd probably turned up just before kick-off, warmed up for a couple of minutes and played. He had long hair and a little moustache and turned up with his boots in a Sainsbury's carrier bag. Dev didn't realise it was a bit different at West Ham. In the end, he played central-midfield alongside me and I asked him which role he preferred and he just said: "A little bit of everything." After five or six minutes he wasn't really involved, but all of a sudden the ball came to him and he went gliding down the right-wing, took on three or four players and put in a cross for Nicky Morgan to score. A few minutes later, he did the same thing and I scored. We ended up winning comfortably. What a terrific signing he was for John!

I never signed apprentice forms for West Ham because I worked for Lloyds' insurance throughout my late teens, so I remained an amateur. I was an unused sub in an FA Cup match at Newport County in 1979 and would have set some kind of record had I played. During my first year in the reserves, I scored over 20 goals, and we won the Football Combination. I played in every game as an amateur. They obviously thought I had some ability and I agreed to sign professional terms.

I think John assumed that because my dad was part of the coaching staff, I would be receiving all the advice and direction that I needed, directly from him. John probably felt that he didn't need to man-manage me as much as some of the other players. In some respects I knew Ron Greenwood better than John because he often came and watch the Youth team play. I was a bit feisty and argumentative. I had a hot temper in those days and couldn't be quiet so I questioned some of the things Ron said.

I could play in most positions. I played quite a lot of games as a central-defender for the reserves and also up front, where I was top-scorer for a couple of seasons. I also played in midfield. Unfortunately, football didn't have seven subs on the bench in those days, so it wasn't possible to make three changes in a match. A pity really, because I would have had a few more outings. I should have focussed on playing as a forward, really, but I only preferred playing up front when

Billy (left) after scoring the winner against Burnley, September 1979

the supply to the forwards was good. Otherwise, I wanted to play where the action was so I was trying to be a Jack of all trades.

My debut was at home to Wrexham, in April 1979. We fielded quite an experienced team. Paul Brush, Geoff Pike and Alvin Martin were the youngest and I came on as a substitute for Pikey. We should have won 1-0 against 10 men because their keeper, Dai Davies took an early bath, but we shipped a late equaliser which took the gloss off it a bit.

My highlight at West Ham was scoring a hat-trick against Southend United in a League Cup third round, second replay. I remember the goals quite clearly; one was a tap-in from two-yards, one was from ten-yards, following a cross from Jimmy Neighbour and the third I lobbed over the 'keeper after Phil Parkes had punted it up-field. I have mixed emotions about that hat-trick because John had sacked my dad only a few days earlier. To this day, I haven't got a clue why he did that and my dad never talks about it. In truth, I don't think he has ever got over it. The only coaching he did after that was with ex-Hammer, Eddie Presland, at Dagenham. It was a really strange time because I'd been at the club since I was 13 and my dad had always been there since way back in the 1950s.

He'd actually played with John. The feeling I had for the club just evaporated really.

After my hat-trick I scored another goal, a match winner, against Burnley in the league and had a good run in the side where I played well in six or seven matches. Stuart Pearson had been out, which had given me my chance, but he was coming back to full fitness so I lost my place. Obviously, David Cross was there and then they signed Paul Goddard, so I was slipping down the pecking order. From that point, I didn't really enjoy it and my attitude worsened. I didn't really want to train and it was frustrating to be playing in the reserves with 15 and 16-year-olds when I was 20. Within a year, I had moved to Charlton Athletic under Alan Mullery.

It's funny because when I think of John Lyall I think of Terry Hurlock, who I got on well with at West Ham. Terry didn't play in the first team but I recall we were playing against South Woodford in a Youth tournament and John came along to watch. The match kicked off and Terry just ran and punched their captain. The pair of them got sent off and my dad even had to keep them apart in the dressing room. They were from the same area and absolutely hated each other. About a month later, John came along to watch the reserves and both Terry and I were in the team to play Leyton Orient. Terry got sent off after twenty minutes in that one! Not surprisingly, he left the club shortly afterwards. He did go on to play for Brentford, Millwall, Rangers, Southampton and Fulham, where he did very well. How a player conducted himself at West Ham United was just as important to John as how skilful and intelligent that player was on the pitch.

Billy Lansdowne

A few players' comments about Billy:

I got on famously with Billy. My brothers came and watched me play and Billy was one of their favourites. He had a great attitude. He knew he wasn't the best but he was brave and put his head in where most others wouldn't. Nothing but high praise for both Billy and his dad, Bill, who was a very good coach at West Ham.

Ray Houghton

Billy had ability but he wasn't the quickest. He had good football intelligence and knew when to come short and when to go long. He was opinionated but he was normally right. I really like Billy, he's a good guy. I can't believe I didn't see him and his dad at the final ever match at Upton Park. I would have loved to have met them again.

Mick McGiven

Billy scored a hat-trick against Southend United in the League Cup. I'll never forget it because it was my debut!

Mark Smith

A very good mate and someone I've got a lot of time for. We played and lived together in Sweden after our time at West Ham.

Everald La Ronde

Scoring at Upton Park

With dad, Bill, at West Ham's final match at Upton Park, May 2016

35 – PHIL BRIGNULL

"John was a big smoker, probably the big-gest at the club and usually had a fag on the go before, during and after the game. Then again, so did some of the players! I always found him to be an honest, but tough, uncompromising man."

Born: October 2, 1960 Stratford, London • **Position:** Defender • **Games played for West Ham United:** 1 (1979)

Debut: May 11, 1979 v Cardiff City (a) D 0-0. Att: 13,140

Cardiff City: Healey, Jones, Campbell, Sullivan, Roberts, Dwyer, Grapes, Evans, Moore, Stevens, Buchanan.

West Ham United: Parkes, Lampard, Brush, Bonds, Martin, Taylor T, Holland, Devonshire, Cross, McDowell* Morgan. Sub: **Brignull.***

Philip Arthur Brignull literally had 15 minutes of fame at West Ham United. It came at Cardiff City at the end of the 1978-79 season. That was the only first team action he experienced during his time at the club. As a defender, he will be pleased with the clean sheet he helped to secure at Ninian Park in a goalless draw. Sadly, the night will be remembered for the drama surrounding Patsy Holland, who, unknowingly gulped down a bottle of industrial fluid and was rushed to hospital.

Brignull continued the long line of West Ham United players who had grown up in the area and supported West Ham with a passion: *"I was born in Stratford but brought up in Sherrard Road, Forest Gate. My father was a French polisher and carpenter. He made me a wooden stand which I used in the Chicken Run to get a better view of the match."*

After almost eight years with the Hammers, Phil established himself as a first team regular at Bournemouth under both Dave Webb and Harry Redknapp. Subsequently, he linked up with Alan Durban, back at Cardiff City. After retiring, Phil then entered a long and successful career in financial services: "Nowadays I live in Cheltenham. My wife, Dawn, and I are still going strong. We are approaching 40-years of marriage. We went to the same school together and met when we were 15. We have two sons - Brian is the eldest and works in the City of London - while Liam plays international hockey for Wales. He was born in Cardiff, when I was playing there."

Phil visited Upton Park, during the final season, for the visit of Aston Villa and witnessed the 1-0 victory over Swansea City with his sons during the inaugural season at the London Stadium.

His experiences with John Lyall and West Ham United live long in the memory:

As a kid I supported West Ham United and often queued up at the ground to collect autographs. I had scrapbooks and photos and knew all the Youth Team players. I loved all that, absolutely loved it. My dad took me to my first game, in 1968 against West Bromwich Albion, and we won 4-0. Peters got a hat-trick that day and Harry Redknapp scored, little did I know that I'd be playing for Harry some 25 years on! It's funny because fast forward 30 years and I called West Ham to try and get tickets to take my two sons to a game. Harry was in charge at the time and the woman must have told him my name because he called me up and told us to get to the ground at about 1pm. When we got there Harry took us to meet all the players in the dressing room – Joe Cole, Paolo DiCanio, young Frank Lampard and, an even younger, Rio Ferdinand. To cap it all, the match was a thriller - against Bradford City - which West Ham ended up winning 5-4.

I went regularly with my dad for a few years and then went on my own from the age of 11 or 12, around about 1972. Bobby Moore was my hero because he was an absolute god

1977-78 Youth Team - Phil is in the back row, fourth from the left

and, when I joined the club, Billy Bonds became my hero. When we won the FA Cup in 1975, I went to the final as a fan and can remember the following day, when the open top coach took the players to East Ham town hall. I jogged behind it from Stratford to East Ham!

When I first started training at West Ham, I took the No.58 bus from outside my house to the ground. West Ham paid me sixpence expenses! Ronnie Boyce was my coach from the age of 13 right through to 20. Boycey was a really good guy and had a big influence on me.

Tony Carr was there and Jimmy Frith was always around as well. Even though you could train at 13, you could only play a match for West Ham when you turned 14. There were no pre-14-year-old teams, which is very different from football today. My son Liam had six years on the books at Aston Villa and was playing games at nine years of age. I remember the first game I played at 14 - against a touring Dutch team at Chadwell Heath - and even at that level I felt like a king!

I played for England Schoolboys at age 15 and was probably a better player then than I was at 19 or 20. I was an early developer and had offers to train with Manchester United and also Ipswich Town, when Bobby Robson was in charge. Offers were flying in from all over the place but one of the guys at Ipswich said to me that if he cut me in half I'd be claret and blue and he was right. I just wanted to play for West Ham United.

My dad was very ill when I was deciding my future and Spurs came round and offered to put him in a private home if I signed for them. My mum kicked them out of the house! Another club offered me a chunk of money to sign, so there was a lot of competition. I ended up talking to Wally St Pier and signed schoolboy forms for West Ham. I believe I was Wally's last-ever signing because he retired soon after. Funnily enough, I think I was also Ron Greenwood's last apprentice signing before he took the England job. I still have the letters he wrote to me on claret and blue embossed paper. He wrote them himself and they are full of typos! I was originally spotted by a chap called Arthur Lamb when I was 13 and playing for my school team - Stratford Comprehensive near the Spotted Dog ground.

John was very good at keeping his players level headed and on the right path. When I got selected to play for England Youth, I was expected to buy a blazer and trousers, but because my dad had just passed away in June 1975, money was quite scarce. The club kindly paid to get me the right clothes and I went to see both John and Ron Greenwood to

High flying Phil

of mine, as was Nicky Morgan. Jason Wright was another really good friend, along with Tony La Ronde, Everald's brother.

I was head apprentice at West Ham which brought me into contact with Albert Walker quite a bit. He looked after the kit and that sort of thing. Albert was very correct and proper and I remember he forgot Trevor Brooking's boots once for an away game. Albert was a very proud Bolton man and had played for West Ham in the 1930s. He was absolutely devastated by that oversight. Trevor ended up wearing someone else's boots.

Ernie Gregory was another big character at the club. The most unpolitically correct man in the history of life! He was a star and I got on well with him because he lived near me in Forest Gate and would often drop me off at home. On my first day as an apprentice, I turned up at the training ground and, aged 16, I had a full-on beard. Ernie looked at me and said: "I want that shaved off by tomorrow." I thought he was joking so did nothing and when I turned up the next day he stormed over to me and pinned me up against the wall with him arm pressed against my neck and my legs dangling off the floor shouting: "I effing told you to have a shave!"

The training at the stadium on Tuesdays and Thursdays was far from salubrious. It was on that stretch between the main gates and the long walk to the old West Stand. We'd be playing in and around the programme stalls. This was 1973. I signed apprentice forms in the summer of 1977 and professional forms on my 18th birthday in October 1978. At the end of the 1978-79 season I played my one and only game in the first team, at Cardiff City. It was an end of season affair on a Friday evening. We had just failed in our promotion bid so there was nothing on the game at all. John put me on the bench but told me before kick-off that I was definitely coming on so I was on tenterhooks all the time. Towards the end of the game, John took off John McDowell and actually played me in central midfield, alongside Trevor Brooking. I touched the ball a few times but didn't have to do too much but I didn't give it away. The best memory I have was warming up in front of the West Ham fans. There were a lot of them inside Ninian Park that night even though the game wasn't important. That was a real buzz for me. It was all too fleeting, but when you think that Billy Bonds and Alvin Martin were the central defensive partnership that night and still the central defensive partnership almost 10 years later, it was the right decision to move on.

At that time, there was only one substitute and John Lyall would never put a defender on the bench. He usually chose a midfielder or striker as his Number 12. I must have been in the squad 15 times but I never actually got a game or even on the bench. There were three or four times, when I was actually told on the Friday that I would be playing, but, come

thank them. They then spent the next 20 minutes telling me that this wasn't a destination but a starting point and that I shouldn't think I had made it. Instead, I should view it as the start of a lot of hard work. A lot of hard work. They were absolutely right, of course, and that was very sound advice, indeed. In fact, I have worked in financial services for 30-odd years now and I have lived my life with that view, which I've tried to pass on to the sales teams I have managed down the years. I would definitely say there is a little bit of Ron Greenwood and John Lyall in my own business management style!

I was quite a big lad for my age so I used to get on well with the older kids. Paul Curbishley was a really good friend

Saturday, there had been a change of heart and I didn't get a game. Ray Stewart was right-back, Billy and Alvin were in the centre and Frank Lampard or Paul Brush were vying for left-back. If one of them was injured, then John would just shuffle it around a bit. Frank could cover for Ray and Brushy would slot into the left-back position. Ray cold also play centre-half which gave John another option. The upshot of it all was that I would be the one to miss out. My preferred position was centre-half which also didn't help! The reality was that if I had been good enough, I would have got more games. I always felt that if I had got a chance to play a few games I would have taken it and developed into a decent player, but that opportunity just never came.

When I started training with the first team at Chadwell Heath, they had just finished building the indoor gym. It had Astroturf in there and we used that quite a bit. It was a massive step up from the reserves and a big, big challenge. I loved playing with the likes of Devonshire, Bonds and Brooking but, ultimately, I just wasn't quite good enough. I may only have been in a couple of team photos but one of them is in the 1980 FA Cup final programme against Arsenal so I'm chuffed to have that little bit of immortality!

John's training sessions were very clear and straight forward. Nothing was too intricate or complicated. He had a precise way that he wanted his teams to play and that was drilled into you at a young age. He wanted the Youth Team to play like the reserves and the reserves to play like the first team. Everyone knew what they were expected to do and attractive, attacking, football was central to that. He would never lose sight of the basics and we would practice how to receive the ball, that all important first touch and quick, accurate passing. The basics were drilled into us over and over again in every session. Even at the top level today you still hear the commentator say: "His first touch let him down." That would have been a personal affront to John, and, as far as he was concerned, you could never practice that basic skill too much.

I worked really hard on my left foot because, aged 14, I could barely use it for standing, let alone football. After a lot of practice, I would say that I had developed a competent left peg. After training, all the apprentices would go back to the ground and practice with a ball underneath the main stand, just passing it against the wall with the inside of each foot and then the outside of each foot, before volleying it and passing it with pace for about an hour each day.

At the end of the 1978-79 season, I was only offered only a one year contract, whereas Dale Banton and George Cowie were each offered three years. Obviously, I wasn't happy and I told John that I wanted to leave. I think he saw it as a bit of a challenge to his authority and didn't like it. I refused to sign but there wasn't any freedom of contract at that time so I was on a week-to-week contract for a whole season before I could leave.

John was a very strong character and was not the type to back down on what he had decided, so I just had to get on with it. It felt like a wasted year and, at the end of it, John called me in and said I could leave on a free. I was only 20 and had got married the year before and I remember calling my wife and telling her we were moving. When I got home I cried for about an hour. It completely broke me. If my dad had been alive he might have advised me to sign and keep in John's good books and maybe an opportunity might have arisen. It absolutely broke my heart to leave West Ham United because I had always been convinced I would make a name for myself there. I was good in the air but I wasn't the quickest, although I would say I was a decent footballer.

Sadly, I have a bit of a tarnished view of John because he didn't help me in any shape or form in that final year. He held me to my contract even though he had no intention of playing me. But, having said that, his priority was the football club and not me. To me, he was a tough, uncompromising guy. It should be remembered that most of my time at West Ham was spent with Ronnie Boyce, Bill Lansdowne snr and Mick McGiven, because I wasn't involved with the first team that much.

I ended up going to Bournemouth in the lower divisions and helped them win promotion under Dave Webb. I played for them for over five years and was named Player-of-the-Year twice on the trot. We had some good times and I played under Harry Redknapp in the team that famously beat Manchester United in the FA Cup. We all played well that day against a United team with Bryan Robson, Arnold Muhren and Frank Stapleton. I picked up a bad injury when I was 24 and ended up with 77 stitches in my knee. I struggled on for a few years and said that if it ever went again I would call it a day. When I was 27, that is exactly what happened. I thought I would seek some expert advice so I called up Rob Jenkins, the West Ham physio, and arranged to see him one Sunday morning. It was the only time I ever went back to West Ham as a player. Rob took one look at it and said: "You're f****!" So that was that. I retired at just 27-years-of-age. That's when I entered the insurance business and worked for Allied Dunbar, which later became Zurich Assurance. Latterly, I became an Independent Financial Adviser with Positive Solutions and today I work with Intrinsic, who are a major player in the financial services sector. I deal solely with mortgage and property finance.

I did see John Lyall on a couple of occasions after I left West Ham. Once, he came to watch Bournemouth play because Harry liked John and invited him along to take a look at what he was doing at Bournemouth. We said: "Hello!" It was all very friendly.

The best man-manager I ever played for is probably Dave Webb but I'm being a little biased because his mum and my nan were sisters! There is no doubt that John Lyall was a top-quality coach and I wished our relationship had been just that bit more harmonious.

John was a big smoker, probably the biggest at the club and would have a fag on before, during and after the game. Then again, so did some of the players. I remember John McDowell having a fag in the dressing room after a game. It was no big deal at the time. A different world altogether.

I love West Ham and would have played for nothing. Come to think of it, I did! I earned more during my first year in financial services than I did throughout my whole career as a footballer.

Phil Brignull

Following are some of the player memories of Phil:

I came through the youth team with Phil. He was one of the first apprentices to get a car and often gave me a lift to the station in his Austin Metro. We hung out together for a good few years until he moved on to Bournemouth.

Dale Banton

Briggers wasn't the quickest! He looked a lot older than he was and had grown a beard when he was 16. Ray Houghton Phil was really good at copying the autographs of every player at West Ham. He didn't play many games but I was pleased that he went on to have a good career at Bournemouth.

Paul Brush

We played quite a bit together in the reserves. He got married quite young so didn't really go out drinking or anything like that. He was a bit younger than me so was part of that generation which included Mark Smith, Jason Wright and Tony La Ronde.

Billy Lansdowne

We lived a few streets apart so we were close friends and grew up together.

Everald La Ronde

Phil was a local boy and a good athlete. Strong and competitive, but, for a centre-half, he lacked a little bit of pace and height although he certainly didn't lack determination or aggression.

Mick McGiven

Phil with his sons at the London Stadium, April 2017

Next up... glory awaits!

Back row: Lampard, Stewart, Parkes, Ferguson, Brush, Bonds.

Middle row: Allen, Neighbour, Pike.

Front row: Holland, Pearson, Cross, Brooking, Devonshire, Martin.

They Played For John Lyall – The West Ham Years

CHAPTER SIX
1979-80

"It is job satisfaction not praise or money that I appreciate. That feeling of going home on Saturday night knowing the job has been done and done well. That is all that matters to me." **John Lyall**

Bell's Whsky Second Division Manager of the Month award, January 1980.

John with Mayor of Newham, Marjorie Edith Helps

East End heroes

John in full flow before extra-time against Everton, FA Cup semi-final replay 1980

West Ham United won the FA Cup for the third time in their history. Many maintain that the 1-0 victory over Terry Neil's Arsenal was John Lyall's finest moment during his 15-years in the hot seat.

Stuart Pearson was signed for £220,000 from Manchester United. Pearson's former teammate and England International defender, Brian Greenhoff, was also a target of John Lyall. However, an offer of £350,000 was declined and he signed for Leeds United, instead.

Jimmy Neighbour joined from Norwich City for £140,000. Dutch International Kees Kist was another target. West Ham offered AZ Alkmaar £600,000 for his services. He eventually went to Paris St Germain and remains fourth on the all-time scoring list in the Eredivisie.

West Ham paid £400,000 for Dundee United right-back, Ray Stewart. The final piece of the successful FA Cup winning team has arrived.

Programme masters, Helliar and Sons, became the first company to sponsor a West Ham United match – a League Cup encounter against Barnsley at Upton Park, which the Hammers won 3-1.

In the FA Cup 3rd round against West Bromwich Albion, Phil Parkes played his finest game for the Hammers: "Phil's performance was a world class show, as good as I have seen from anybody," asserted John Lyall during his post-match comments.

West Ham went on to beat Arsenal in the final but their promotion chances were surrendered as a consequence. A third season in Division Two awaited.

John Lyall introduced six new players to his first team – Stuart Pearson, Dale Banton, Ray Stewart, Jimmy Neighbour, Paul Allen and Mark Smith.

Here is their story...

36 – STUART PEARSON

"Many thought that John Lyall had wasted his money on me because of my age and injuries. But I won three medals in as many years at West Ham, so I couldn't have been too bad. I wish I'd played for John at my best."

Born: Cottingham, East Riding of Yorkshire, June 21, 1949 • **Position:** Striker • **Games played for West Ham United:** 50 (1979-1982) • **Goals:** 10 • **Honours:** 1980 FA Cup winner, 1981 Second division champion, 1981 League Cup runner-up

Debut: Wrexham (a) L 0-1 () Att: 13,036

Wrexham: Niedzwiecki, J Jones, Dwyer, Davis, J Roberts,* Giles, Sutton, Vinter, McNeil, Whittle, Cartwright. Sub: Fox*

West Ham United: Parkes, Lampard, Brush, Pike, Martin, Bonds, Holland, Devonshire, Cross, Brooking, **Pearson**.

Stuart James Pearson joined West Ham United with a winner's mentality, 15 England caps and a couple of dodgy knees. Remarkably, his medal haul at Manchester United was equalled during his three year stay at Upton Park. He won an FA Cup winners' medal with both clubs, a promotion medal with both clubs and a runners-up medal in two other major finals, too. (The 1976 FA Cup with Manchester United and the 1981 League Cup for the Hammers).

Pearson was known by his Old Trafford teammates as 'Pancho,' a curious nickname for a Yorkshireman: *"Tommy Docherty called me Pancho at Manchester United. There were two other Pearson's at the club before me and they had that nickname, so Tommy decided to call me Pancho, too."*

A firm fan's favourite, Pearson etched his name in Hammers' history when scoring against Everton in the 1980 FA Cup semi-final at Villa Park. He was the perfect foil for strike partner David Cross and a key link in the approach play of Alan Devonshire and Trevor Brooking.

Having lived in Spain for eight years, Pancho returned to these shores in 2011. Now 68, he continues to put in a round of golf and maintains strong links with both Manchester United and West Ham: *"I still work in the lounges at Old Trafford along with Jimmy Greenhoff, Sammy McIlroy, Lou Macari, Arthur Albiston and Frank Stapleton. I also meet up with my old West Ham pals at various reunions. It was a*

special time in my life and I love to stay in touch with them."

Pancho had the following memories of John Lyall:

I had a great time with John Lyall and enjoyed a brilliant relationship with him. It couldn't have been any better. He was the instigator of everything that was good about West Ham United. He was the one who got the team together, the one who got the tactics right. Just an all-round good guy and one of the nicest men I've met in football.

John came up to see me when I was at Manchester United. He was with his trusted lieutenant, Eddie Baily. Dave Sexton, the United manager, had only offered me a one year deal which also meant I couldn't get a club car, which disappointed me. John was very articulate in what he said to me and I knew West Ham had some very good players. He offered me a two-year contract and nearly doubled my wages so it was a no-brainer for me in the end.

I'd played against West Ham for Hull City in the FA Cup and also remember scoring for Manchester United against them. It was the week before we played Liverpool in the 1977 FA Cup final. We lost 2-4 in a game West Ham needed to win to stay up.

If I had my time at West Ham again I would only change one thing. I wish I'd ask John to miss training on Friday's because it was just too much for my knees. We'd play five-a-side on the astroturf, which I absolutely loved, but it took

Loving life at West Ham United

its toll on my knees. Most Saturday's I'd wake up hobbling around. I should have spoken to him about it because he would have been absolutely fine, but I think I loved those Friday sessions a bit too much!

John's door was always open and I could have spoken to him about anything. I was an experienced pro, married with two kids and enjoying my football, so I didn't really have any major issues to discuss with him. He extended my contract by an extra year, so he did so much for me and I've got nothing but the highest respect and praise for the man.

John did love his training sessions. When I first went to Chadwell Heath, we did a couple of hours in the morning and then went back out again in the afternoon. I was totally exhausted!

John's team which won the FA Cup in 1980 were a great bunch of lads. They could really play. We had such a strong defensive spine with Alvin Martin and Billy Bonds. The midfield was fantastic with Trevor Brooking and Alan Devonshire. In my opinion, he was the best winger in the country at the time. Dev and I had a great understanding. I knew when he'd be jinking left or right past the defender and pinging it into to me. I'd either lay it back to him or have a go

myself. It was just lovely. To top it all, David Cross was the ideal strike partner for me. We were a very good team.

In the final, Crossy did so much running and I got in all the holes he created. It was great to see Brian Talbot not knowing what to do - the big-nosed Gooner!

I played under Tommy Docherty at Manchester United and he was quite different to John. Tommy didn't get involved in the coaching side of things and put together a team of players who knew how to play. He'd usually set up a 4-4-2 formation with two wingers – Gordon Hill and Steve Coppell – bombing on and putting in loads of crosses. The midfield would be supporting those attacks. It was total football and we all loved playing for Tommy. John was a little bit more structured and had his own vision of how his team should play. Dave Sexton was a little bit different, too. He was one of the nicest men I've ever met but I didn't always enjoy his coaching sessions.

When I came down from United I had undergone three operations on my knee. I'd missed the 1979 FA Cup final which we'd lost 2-3 to Arsenal. When I joined West Ham I honestly believed my knee would hold up and be ok. I remember Frank Lampard wasn't at all convinced about my

On familiar territory, Pancho walking out at Wembley once again, May 1980

fitness. I can still hear him saying: "John's done his money on you!" but I won three medals in as many years, so I couldn't have been too bad. I'm very fond of the goal I scored against Everton in the FA Cup semi-final, too.

In the end, my knees gave up completely. I had to have two more operations but I knew I couldn't perform as I wanted to. John was really good about it and said he wanted to keep me around the club. He had quite a few young players coming through and he wanted me to pass on my experience, which I tried to do. It's not right to take good money and not play so I retired in 1982.

John was a true gentleman of football. One of the nicest guys you could meet. Good coach. Good manager. Good man.

Stuart Pearson

There was no shortage of comments about Pancho:
Stuart scored in the big games. His goal in the FA Cup semi-final against Everton was vital and in the final I think he was our best player. It was certainly his best game for West Ham.
David Cross

He was great for me because he was all one-touch. I knew that when I played it into him I'd get it back straight away. A pleasure to play with.
Alan Devonshire

What a legend! An absolute legend! His attitude was fantastic. In training and in matches he was so full on. Hard-working, aggressive, strong and full of northern grit. I don't think many centre-backs liked playing against him. I'm not surprised he won medals at both Manchester United and West Ham.
Ray Houghton

He had so many injuries he was like a broken man. But

Flying high with the Hammers, FA Cup semi final v Everton, 1980

what a good player and a great professional. He gave me a lot of help with a couple of football things and a couple of personal things for which I am very grateful. An all-round good fella. When his leg was in plaster, he went and bought an automatic car so he could still drive!
Phil Brignull

He turned up at training once wearing a mauve fur jacket. He looked like a chick with the wrong coloured feathers!
Everald La Ronde

In the early 1970s, Pancho played in the Hull City team which beat West Ham in the FA Cup. When we signed him he called everyone: "Love." I always thought that was a bit strange. Billy Bonds certainly didn't like it!
Rob Jenkins

For someone who had won medals with Manchester United, he was very down to earth and unpretentious. He was very precise in the way he spoke and the way he prepared for a game. A great link-up player. He really took to West Ham and it's great to see him at various reunions.
Paul Brush

Stuart was one of the best one-touch players I saw at West Ham. He was just fantastic to watch.
Warren Donald

He took me under his wing a little bit and we used to train together. Quite injury prone, but a great striker. He gave me quite a few tips on how to train and keep fit.
Dale Banton

Stuart was one of my heroes. He was such a clever, tidy player. I love that 1977 Manchester United team he played in, with Coppell, Hill, Greenhoff, McIlroy and Buchan. I actually roomed with Pancho at West Ham which was an absolute pleasure.
Bobby Barnes

Pancho had real quality but picked up several niggling injuries. In training his technical ability was fantastic.
Alvin Martin

I played against Pancho when he was coming through the ranks at Hull City and I was coming through the ranks at Sunderland. He was a good player in his prime, but he's legs had gone by the time he came to West Ham. Nevertheless, he was a key player in the FA Cup final. Arsenal are still trying to work out what to do with him even now!
Mick McGiven

Just the two FA Cup winners medals, 1977 and 1980

With Paul Allen and Geoff Pike at the London Bridge Hilton Hotel for a reunion of the 1980 FA Cup winning team, 2016

37 – DALE BANTON

"John was always very constructive in his assessment of a situation even when he was clearly disappointed by a performance. There is no doubt that he was ahead of his time."

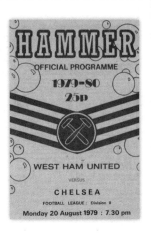

Born: Kensington, London, May 15 1961 • **Position:** Striker • **Games played for West Ham United:** 6 (1979-81)

Debut: August 20, 1979 v Chelsea (h) L 0-1 (Johnson)

West Ham United: Parkes, Lampard, Brush, Bonds, Martin, Holland, Pike, Pearson,* Cross, Brooking, Devonshire. Sub: **Banton.***

Chelsea: Borota, Locke, Stride, Nutton, Droy, Harris, Britton, Bannon, Langley, Johnson, Fillery.

Dale Conrad Banton was another product of West Ham United's Youth Academy. Born to parents Donald and Darley Banton, he grew up in Wembley, attended Alperton High School and played for the Middlesex county side. *"My dad was an engineer and my mum worked for the computer firm IBM."*

Despite playing only a handful of games for the Hammers, Dale went on to become a prolific scorer at both Aldershot Town and York City.

"When I left football I entered the world of sales and for the past ten years I have been the national sales manager for a company called Resin Surfaces which specialises in industrial flooring. Our clients include Mars, Nestle and United Biscuits as well as the big pharma companies such as GSK and Pfizer."

Nowadays, Dale lives and works in York, but he made the trip down for the last ever match at Upton Park in 2015-16. Like so many other youth team products from the John Lyall era, the memories have lasted a lifetime:

My first thought of John Lyall comes from when I first signed as a 15-year-old-schoolboy. It took place on a coach at Chadwell Heath. There had been a friendly match at the training ground and both my mum and dad came along to watch. There was an aura around John and after the match he took me and my parents onto one of those Laceys' coaches with the tables on them. He sat us down and said that West Ham wanted to sign me as an apprentice. I remember my

mum saying that although she didn't have a problem with that, she wanted me to stay at school. So I was given an arrangement where I had a two-day release during that time in order to go to college. John was very understanding which is why we all warmed to him.

In a nutshell John was one of the best coaches I ever played for and I was a bit of a journeyman throughout my career so experienced plenty of different styles. He loved to play one and two-touch football and really looked after the young kids coming through at the club.

I had quite a bit of pace, could use both feet and wasn't arrogant or anything like that and liked to listen and learn so there was a bit for John to work with. I could play anywhere across the midfield as well as up front so I suppose he also liked my versatility.

At the end of the 1981-82 season, John put a sheet up on the board giving details of the date and time when all the young lads were invited in to talk with him and discover if they were going to be kept on by the club. When the day came, I was due to go in after Ray Houghton, who was a very good player, but was released. When I went in John said that he felt that there wasn't a lot more he could do for me. He thought that I needed regular first-team appearances and couldn't guarantee that. He said that he could take the soft option with me but thought it would be better if I left the club and made my mark elsewhere. It was disappointing, of course, but that is how it happened.

Paul Brush gave me a bit of advice just before I left West

Back row, second from right. 1978-79 South East Counties League Cup winners

Ham. He said that I should think about the position I wanted to play and believed that playing up front would have been best for me. In midfield there was Trevor Brooking, Alan Devonshire and Geoff Pike with Paul Allen breaking though. Patsy Holland was still playing on the right so there was tough, tough, competition. Brushy was right and when I left West Ham I only ever played up front. That was my position at both Aldershot Town and York City and I scored a combined total of over 100 goals.

Ronnie Boyce looked after the young kids at that time. What a player he was! Bill Lansdowne Snr was also coaching and I was so pleased to see him at the last ever match at Upton Park against Manchester United. I also caught up with Everald LaRonde, young Billy Lansdowne, Paul Goddard, and quite a few others. It was a terrific night.

My debut came in 1979, against Chelsea, in the old second division. I had been o substitute in the previous match at Wrexham but didn't get on. Then, John put me on the bench again for the visit of Chelsea. There were over 30,000 fans packed in that night under the floodlights and I came on for Stuart Pearson. I thought I played well. There was a moment in that game when I played a one-two with Alan Devonshire on the edge of the penalty area and David Cross had peeled off into some space, but instead of laying off a simple pass,

I went for glory and missed. It didn't help that we lost the match 0-1. Afterwards, John told me not to worry and that my chance would come again. Sadly, even though I played a few more games I never scored a goal for West Ham. I started a few games, came on as sub in a few but was also left on the bench for more than I would have liked, which is always disappointing.

The atmosphere at the club in the run-up to the 1980 FA Cup final was electric. I actually started in the match before the final itself. We beat Charlton 4-1 and John had decided to rest a few so I got my chance.

I lived in Wembley at the time so arranged with John to make my own way to the stadium for the final and I watched the match from the stand. After the game I made my way home which was only a mile down the road.

It is no surprise that West Ham United was renowned for its one and two-touch football because that was such a big part of the training. We would also play keep-ball and John would always pair me off with Billy Bonds who could run for England!

We would always do a lot of running and John could see that some of the younger lads didn't really like it so it was important to him that they understood why it was crucial. He told them that putting those miles into your legs was the same concept as a bank account. He explained we would

Putting in a cross against Preston North End, September 1979

need to draw on those miles during a match in order to be the best we could be. If you don't have any money in the bank you had nothing to draw on. It made perfect sense of course and the running didn't feel so bad after that!
Dale Banton

Following are some player and coach recollections of Dale's time at West Ham:

I was so pleased to see him at the final match at Upton Park. He was a quick winger but didn't have any tricks. He might have been better off being an energetic midfield player but he wanted to play as a winger. Unfortunately, West Ham had some exceptional wingers at the time who were very, very quick, with great individual ability and first-class crossing skills.
Mick McGiven

He was a very quick player. A good lad. I loved his fuzzy mop.
Alan Devonshire

Dale was a very good table-tennis player.
Greg Campbell

I played against Dale quite a bit in the lower leagues, when he was at Aldershot Town and York City, two clubs where he is highly regarded as a prolific striker.
Phil Brignull

He had a bouncy stride and it all seemed to be going well

for him at the beginning but when he stepped up from the reserves it just didn't seem to click.
Paul Brush

Everything Dale had was bright and sparkly. I remember he had a metallic lime green Ford Capri Ghia. You can't get any louder than that!
Everald La Ronde

Dale the salesman

38 – RAY STEWART

*"A total gentleman and a legend.
I miss him dearly. "*

Born: Stanley, Perthshire, September 7, 1959 • **Position:** Right-back • **Games played for West Ham United:** 432 (1979-1991 - 15th on the all-time list) • **Goals:** 84 (14th on the all-time list) • **Honours:** 1980 FA Cup winner, 1980 Charity Shield runner-up, 1980-81 Division 2 Champion, 1981 League Cup runner-up, 1985-86 – Member of highest finishing league team (third), 1981-87 10 Scotland caps • **Testimonial:** May 6, 1992 versus Ipswich Town

Debut: September 4, 1979 v Barnsley (a) W 2-0 (Cross 2) League Cup 2nd Round 2nd leg. Att: 15,898

Barnsley: Pierce, Flavell, Collins, Glavin, Dugdale, McCarthy, Little, Riley, Pugh, Banks, Bell. Sub: Millar

West Ham United: Parkes, Lampard, Brush, Bonds, **Stewart**, Holland, Pike, Banton, Cross, Brooking, Morgan.

Raymond Struan McDonald Stewart is the most successful Scottish player ever to pull on the claret and blue shirt. No Hammer from north of the border has played more, won more or been capped more, than Ray. Fellow Scot, John Dick, certainly scored more goals but Ray's penalty taking prowess will live long in the memory. A whole generation of West Ham fans were catapulted into the realms of ecstasy after his spot kicks against Aston Villa in the quarter-final of the FA Cup, Liverpool in the final of the League Cup and at home to Ipswich Town during the famed 1985-86 season. John Lyall's £430,000 investment was money well spent.

During his 12 years at West Ham 'Tonka' converted 76 spot kicks which will safely sit in the record books for some considerable time to come.

The highlight of his time at West Ham came at the end of his first season with the club – victory over Arsenal in the 1980 FA Cup final. "My medal is my pride and joy and something I'll never part with."

Ray had the opportunity to apply some of John Lyall's coaching methods after he entered management and took charge of Livingstone, Stirling and Forfar Athletic.

Following open heart surgery in 2015, Ray has returned to full fitness and is pivotal to the network of Hammers from the John Lyall era. "West Ham will always be special to me."

Following are Ray's recollections of John:

I'd never met John Lyall in my life until both he and Eddie Baily came to up to Scotland to chat with me. It took place at a service station on the Dundee to Perth road. West Ham had been watching me for quite a while but it was only when I met John that I realised they were the club for me. I liked it that he'd look me straight in the eye when outlining the vision he had for me as a West Ham player. He talked a lot of sense, listened to what I had to say and told me directly what he was thinking. To me that is the behaviour of a totally honest man.

The following day we all flew down to London. I sat in between John and Eddie and felt thoroughly exhausted from all their talk about football. They discussed and analysed everything.

I was just a young boy leaving home so it was important that I could trust somebody and I felt I could trust John. Nothing happened during my ten years playing for him to change that view. John was clever in that he invited my parents down to watch me play and I think that's why I never felt homesick.

How to take a penalty

I stayed at John's house on my first night in England. His wife, Yvonne, told me to hang up my clothes in their wardrobe but I couldn't fit anything in it because of John's shirts and suits. They really looked after me and became my family in England.

The following day we drove to Chadwell Heath and when

Wembley elation. Ray equalises against Liverpool in the last minute to force a League Cup final replay, March 1981

we got to the junction at the Moby Dick on the A12 I couldn't get my head around just how many lanes there were. I was used to just two lanes with a few cars but this was bigger than any other road I'd ever been on.

John stuck me into the action straight away, playing me at centre-half up at Barnsley in the League Cup. There was nothing on the game really, because West Ham had won the home leg 3-1. We ended up winning 2-0 and I thought I did alright.

My first home game was against Sunderland and I think the fans took to me. We won 2-0 and from that point on I had a fantastic relationship with the fans.

My penalty taking responsibility came about when Geoff Pike was out injured. He took the penalties at the time but John asked if anyone else fancied the job, so I stuck my hand up. It was the making of me really because I took some vital ones and made a name for myself. It was lucky that John believed in me. I had taken a few for Dundee United so I knew what needed to be done. I was only a young lad taking them up there but I wanted to give it a go because everyone was missing them. They even gave Hamish McAlpine, the Dundee United goalkeeper, a go - that's how bad it had got.

The first really important penalty I scored was against Aston Villa in the FA Cup sixth round – that stands as my best penalty. It was a special day on a very muddy pitch. The atmosphere was so much better back then and the fans were allowed to express themselves. Someone was holding up a banner during that game which read: 'Jesus Saves – But

Cross gets the rebound!' I miss all that in the modern game.

John Lyall and Jim McLean were the two best coaches I ever had. They were both brilliant. Jim was a very good coach at Dundee United and I had another fantastic coach in John. Everything he did was top quality. I learned something every day and I think he liked my determination, endeavour and versatility. He played me at right-back, centre-half and even left-midfield so he liked the fact I gave him an option as a utility player. I was prepared to play in any position for him and gave everything I had in each and every game. He liked the Scottish character and signed a few Scots at West Ham. He had Scottish heritage himself and knew how to make the most of our steel and ruthlessness on the pitch.

John had a good rapport with most of his players and was a master at building confidence. He made quite a few of us believe we were better than we actually were and that's no bad thing. He was very thorough and had a good group of players to work with. He'd never let anyone get too big headed and knew how to keep a strong ego in place. When Tony Cottee started scoring quite a few goals as a youngster, he started to get a bit mouthy in the dressing room. John knew how to keep him in check and would say something like: "You're still in nappies, son," or "You've still got a long way to go." It was a good thing because it kept your feet on the ground. Tony has still got too much to say!

He understood that players liked to have a drink but told them to call him up rather than drink and drive. He was prepared to get up at any hour to look after his players. That is why he was so disappointed when Steve Whitton crashed his car.

John spent hours and hours with me out on the training pitch and improved my game no end. He set up situations in which I'd have to beat a player and put in cross after cross after cross. I was doing that hundreds of times every week. Frank Lampard also helped me tremendously because he'd put in endless days of hard work himself. Frank was amazing and testament to what you can do with the right work ethic. He earned two England caps for his effort.

John was always very passionate about his players performing for their country. He took great pride in that and travelled up to see me play for Scotland. Jock Stein was the manager of the national side. He was a big character and got on very well with John. People used to say that when Jock walked into the forest, all the foxes ran out! I'd have a joke with John and asked him not to use the 'Old Pals' Act' to get me a cap for my country. He'd shoot me down straight away: "I'm not kissing anyone's a*** to get you a cap, son – you'll do it on your own merit."

John loved talking about football and I have to repeat just how thorough he was. It wasn't enough to say how good a player was at getting to the touch-line and putting in a cross. He had to comment on the technique, how the player

Tonka - West Ham United's greatest ever penalty taker

received the ball, his pace, awareness, posture, touch…the list was endless, but John was assessing that in a matter of seconds. He had a brilliant mind.

John commanded respect wherever he went. He was also respectful of others. Whenever we stayed at a hotel, wither at home or abroad, he would never walk in expecting to be treated differently. He was big time but he didn't give it big time, if you know what I mean. Similarly, if anyone came to see him at the training ground or Upton Park he would make them feel welcome. He was a total leader and like all good leaders he knew everyone. He was on first name terms with the police, the media, just about everyone.

Winning the FA Cup in 1980 was the greatest moment I had in my career. I know Trevor's goal made the difference but John Lyall's brain won it really. He'd changed his tactics ten minutes before kick-off. He left David Cross up front on his own and put Stuart Pearson in a five man midfield. Arsenal didn't know how to play against us. It was a stroke of genius. Sadly, no one rates the FA Cup these days and yet we had a finest hour winning that competition.

I treasure the goal I scored at Wembley against Liverpool in the 1981 League Cup final. Every kid dreams about scoring a winning goal in a cup final and that was the closest I got. John said he felt cheated by the decision to allow Liverpool's goal,

On Father Christmas duty.

He asked me to join him at Ipswich Town but my knee wasn't right and I didn't want to mislead him. I should have asked him to help develop me as a coach because he was one of the great coaches and I would have learned a great deal from the best. I was disappointed it didn't happen but there comes a time in life when you have to learn to stand on your own two feet.

I always stayed in touch with John right up until the very end and I send Yvonne a card every year. I'm still in touch with his brother, Jim. He lives in Norwich but has a property near me in Stanley up in Scotland. In fact, it was Jim who called me to tell me that John had died. When I heard his voice, I thought this is a bit strange. "John passed away in the night," he said. I broke down crying. It crushed me. I didn't really know what to do. My mind was all over the place. I decided there was only one thing to do. I called Billy Bonds. I called my captain.

All those boys from the John Lyall era still keep in touch and we are very close. We meet up from time to time and are always there for each other. Long may it continue!

Ray Stewart

Possibly the best right-back West Ham has ever had. Mr Dependable in the Billy Bonds mould. Strong in the tackle with a great right foot. He could chip balls into space, place them over the top or pass into feet. His crossing was first class and his penalty taking was the next level up from first class. There was no one better.

Mick McGiven

even though Sammy Lee was in an offside position. John never called Clive Thomas a cheat, he just said he felt cheated.

John developed a team mentality in everyone. He made every player a team player and worked tirelessly to promote a team ethic. He could be very firm in his manner and on one occasion I had to challenge his authority. Not many people stood up to John and it was noticeable that he wasn't used to people questioning what he wanted to do.

It all came about when I bought a new car and was looking at houses to buy in the area. John said he'd come along with me and we took my car. On the way, he lit up a cigarette and I asked him not to smoke in my car. He simply replied that I didn't tell him what to do but I explained that it was my new car, I'd paid for it, and I'd gladly stop for him to have a smoke but I didn't want him, or anybody else for that matter, smoking in my car. He backed down in the end and I think he admired my strength and determination in standing up to him. We did make a lot of stops, that's for sure. It probably doubled the length of the journey! I can't remember the cigarettes he smoked. Yvonne would know – she was probably rolling them for him every day!

I was in a hospital near Woodford with a damaged knee when someone said there was a phone call for me. It was John. He told me he'd just lost his job and that he was going to pop in and see me. I cried, because I couldn't understand how something like that could happen to such a man as John Lyall. It was typical of John to still be thinking of others at one of the worst times in his life. He promised my parents that he'd look after me and he was still doing that even though he'd been sacked.

Frank Lampard, Stuart Pearson and the whole of Upton Park celebrates with Super Jock

One of the best penalty takers I have ever seen. He was so confident and just smashed them in. Strong, competitive and a good passer of the ball.
Ray Houghton

People say that West Ham's defence of Phil Parkes, Ray Stewart, Frank Lampard, Billy Bonds and myself enjoyed the success we did because of our communication across the back line. Well, Phil, Frank, Bill and me could communicate! Anytime we conceded, it was Tonka's fault!
Alvin Martin

When I first saw Ray and watched the way he played he reminded of everything I'd heard about John Lyall as a player. It seemed to me that John had bought himself. A tough tackling, hard-working type of player, lacking finesse.
John McDowell

He was one year older than me but played like he was ten years older. He was so powerful and talented.
Phil Brignull

He never stopped moaning at me!
Paul Hilton

I honestly don't know how he scored all those penalties, especially the high pressure ones against Aston Villa and Liverpool. Phenomenal!
Alan Dickens

I love Ray, there are no airs or graces with him and we always pick up from where we left off. I scored four goals in the reserves once and he asked me about them. I started to give him a bit of detail about each goal and at the end of it Ray absolutely slaughtered me: "Hark at him going on about his goals. What a big headed twat! He's got a head as big as Beachy Point!" He still calls me Beachy today.
Greg Campbell

Top, top man and the best right-back I've seen. I had a very good relationship with Tonka.
Alan Devonshire

I'm very close to Ray and count him amongst my best mates.
Steve Bacon.

He loves West Ham, the fans and the area. He is always enjoyable to be around and made a lot of friends down here. Nice as pie off the pitch and hard as nails on it.
Paul Brush

The final encounter. L-R David Cross, Ray, Alan Devonshire and John, Britannia International Hotel, 2005

With captain Bill during the last ever season at Upton Park

39 – JIMMY NEIGHBOUR

"The goal against Coventry was probably the highlight of my West Ham career and the biggest memory that most fans have of me."

Born: Chingford, London, November 15, 1950 • **Died:** Woodford Green, April 11, 2009 • **Position:** Winger

Games played for West Ham United: 96 (1979-1982) • **Goals for West Ham United:** 6 • **Honours under John Lyall:** 1981 League Cup runner-up, 1981 Second Division Championship • **Debut:** September 15, 1979 v Sunderland (h) W 2-0 (Cross, Pearson) Att: 24,021

West Ham United: Parkes, Lampard, Brush, Bonds, Martin, Stewart, **Neighbour,** Pearson, Cross, Brooking, Devonshire.

Sunderland: Siddall, Whitworth, Bolton, Clarke, Elliott*, Buckley, Ashurst, Rostron, Brown, Robson, Arnott. Sub: Chishom.*

James Edward Neighbour was signed from Norwich City by John Lyall for £150,000 in September 1979. In 2005 EX Hammers magazine interviewed Jimmy and gained the following insight into the move: *"I was quite settled at Norwich City at the time but after spending half-an-hour in the company of John Lyall, I knew that it was the right move for me."*

Jimmy had started his career at Tottenham Hotspur in the early 1970s and won a League Cup winner's medal after beating Aston Villa, 2-0, at Wembley. Indeed, Jimmy knew West Ham's chief scout Eddie Baily, who he'd worked with at Spurs. "Eddie was another reason I joined West Ham. He was helping John to rebuild a team following relegation in 1978. They had already signed the likes of Phil Parkes, Stuart Pearson and Ray Stewart, so there was clear ambition at the club."

Jimmy had a clear recollection of John Lyall following his debut for the Hammers – a 2-0 victory over Sunderland at Upton Park. "After the game, John said to me: You were great, because you gave us the shape I've been looking for." Remarkably, of the 96 appearances Jimmy made for West Ham United, 43 of them were played at Upton Park, and the Hammers remained unbeaten in 38 of them.

The stand out result, of course, was the 2-0 victory over Coventry City in the second leg of the League Cup semi-final in 1981. "The goal against Coventry was probably the

Being greeted by John at Chadwell Heath, September 1979

highlight of my West Ham career and the biggest memory that most fans have of me. I can remember the goal quite well. Frank Lampard played it in for the left and it was flicked on by David Cross into the box. Before I knew it I'd made the run in behind Crossy and the ball just dropped for me about 10 yards out. I just managed to prod it past their keeper, Les Sealey. It was a great moment because I knew and the crowd knew that it was the goal that would take us to Wembley."

Interestingly, no Hammer has scored a winning goal in a League Cup semi-final since Jimmy's effort, and, it is only Marlon Harewood who has scored a winning goal for the Hammers in any semi-final – in the 2006 FA Cup, against Middlesbrough, at Villa Park.

Jimmy Neighbour suddenly died from a heart attack on April 11, 2009. He was recuperating from a hip operation. Martin Peters read the eulogy at his funeral.

Since 2010, a Charity Golf Day has been held in Jimmy's honour. Details can be found by emailing Barry Neville – info@jimmyneighbourgolfday.co.uk

Out on the wing

Following are some player comments about Jimmy, along with a photographic collage of his time at West Ham United:

Jimmy got on well with John Lyall. He had a good relationship with all the boys at West Ham. We used to say that John was too nice to be a manager. I have quite a few photos of my brother, including the one of him scoring the winning goal against Coventry City in the League Cup semi-final. That was one of the magic moments. He was never really a goalscorer and was expected to go jinking down the wing and putting over a good cross. He did this for Martin Chivers and Alan Gilzean at Tottenham Hotspur and David Cross at West Ham United.

He got on very well with Billy Bonds. We were at an event once and it was during a time when Jimmy was thinking of leaving football altogether. Billy Bonds came over to me and said: "Oi, Ron, have a word with your brother, he's thinking of jacking it all in." It was a shame what happened really, because Jimmy had always been a very popular winger. But, towards the end of his time at West Ham, he received a lot of aggravation from the fans. The Chicken Run turned on him completely and he wasn't used to being an unpopular player. That was one of the main reasons why he decided to leave West Ham.

It was tragic to lose Jimmy so young. He was only 58. He'd had a hip operation and seemed to have made a good recovery. He was in the hospital, getting ready to leave, when he came over faint and passed out. They said he'd developed blood clots which brought on a heart attack.

Ron Neighbour

His finest moment in a West Ham shirt - scoring the winner against Coventry City to take the Hammers to Wembley, February 1981

I got on well with Jimbo. He played in the reserves with me a few times and always helped me out and gave me good advice. I had the impressions that he never really believed in himself as a player. When we went to Dinamo Tbilisi to play in the European Cup Winners Cup we had to stop in Moscow on the way and the authorities were adamant that Jimmy wasn't the chap in his passport because he had a moustache!
Ray Houghton

I got to know Jimmy really well when he joined West Ham. He couldn't remember that I marked him on my West Ham debut against Norwich City. He was a friendly, easy going, fun loving bloke. We roomed together a few times and he just loved being a footballer. Later on in his career he coached with Pat Holland at Spurs.
Paul Brush

He was very quiet and unassuming, a really nice guy.
Everald La Ronde

Jimmy was a very nice man – a smashing bloke. I brought him in to look after the youth at West Ham when I was manager and he did a great job for us.
Billy Bonds

They brought in Jimmy to replace me but it didn't affect our relationship at all. He was a terrific person.
Pat Holland

I liked Jimmy. We played golf together along with Graham Gooch and Stuart Pearson.
Billy Lansdowne

He was an old fashioned winger. Loved the ball at his feet and would look to beat defenders on the outside. Didn't like being man-marked and was at his best when he had a bit of space. He wasn't blessed with electric pace but could whip in really good crosses, none better than the cross for Goddard's goal in the League Cup final replay in 1981. So sad that he has gone.
Mick McGiven

We're on our way to Wembley - celebrating with Ray Stewart and fellow scorer, Paul Goddard, February 1981

Showing Everton a clean set of heels, January, 1982

Jimmy with mum Joyce, sister Sally and brother Ron

40 – PAUL ALLEN

"John's funeral was a very poignant occasion and I reflected on my time with him at West Ham United and the fact that he put his faith and belief in me, as a 17-year-old, to play in the FA Cup final. That must have been a very big decision for John."

Born: Aveley, Essex, August 28, 1962 • **Position:** Midfielder • **Games played for West Ham United:** 197 (1979-85)

Goals for West Ham United: 11 • **Honours under John Lyall:** 1980 FA Cup winner, 1981 FA Youth Cup winner, 1980-81 Division Two Champion, 1984-85 Hammer of the Year • **Debut:** Football League Cup. September 25, 1979 v Southend United (h) D 1-1 (Cross – Pountney) Att: 19,658

West Ham United: Parkes, Stewart, Brush, Bonds, Martin, Holland, **Allen**, Lansdowne, Cross, Brooking, Devonshire.

Southend United: Cawston, Dudley, Moody, Cusack, Yeats, Stead, Otulakowski, Pountney, Morris, Tuohy, Gray.

Paul Kevin Allen remains the youngest ever player to collect an FA Cup winner's medal, aged just 17 years and 256 days. Emphasis needs to be place on the word winner here as he is no longer the youngest player simply to appear in an FA Cup final. Allen was born in the family home at 28 Alfred Road, Aveley to parents Ron and Irene or 'Reney' as everyone calls her. *"My dad played football, too, and was a very good athlete. Unfortunately, he damaged his knee whilst on national service in Germany. That put paid to his playing aspirations but both my mum and dad were so very supportive throughout my football career. I was one of three sons, the others being David and Peter, and a sister, Irene."*

Paul spent almost 10 years at West Ham and left for Tottenham Hotspur just before the record-breaking 1985-86 league season. There cannot be many players to win the FA Cup at two different clubs and be voted Player of the Year at each one, too. A mark of quality if ever there was.

Paul Allen is also a member of another very exclusive club. Both he, and the great John Sissons, are the only two Hammers to win both the FA Cup and the FA Youth Cup. Remarkably, Sissons remains the youngest player ever to score for a winning FA Cup side at Wembley after contributing to the 3-2 victory over Preston North End in the 1964 final.

Nowadays, Paul continues his fine work at the Professional Footballers Association and made himself available to discuss John Lyall:

My earliest memory of John Lyall came after I was taken to the club as a 13-year-old by a scout named Len Hurford. At the time, West Ham's Youth academy needed to be bolstered so they brought in a lot of school kids and set up a Possibles versus Probables match. There was Ron Greenwood and Eddie Baily watching on, with their clip boards, and John Lyall, too. I was invited back and that was the start of it all for me.

I began taking the bus to the ground and John's car was always in the car park when I arrived. He would always say: "Hello," and called me by my first name. As a young kid that made me feel very special, very important and valued. I remember thinking: "Blimey, he knows my name!" It had a huge, positive impact on me.

Even at primary school, all I wanted to do was play football. I'd be in the playground either kicking a ball or swapping football stickers. I watched my uncle Les – Clive and Bradley's dad - play for Queens Park Rangers, and was at the game when he played against West Ham in the late 1960s. It was televised and Bobby Moore scored a goal after a long run and shot. In fact, the player who gave the ball to Bobby for that goal was Trevor Hartley who was a coach at Spurs under

February 1980 - Closing down cousin Clive - The Allen family are one of the most successful in the history of football

David Pleat when I was there. He mentioned it a few times!

During my first week as an apprentice, John's son Murray was at Chadwell Heath training ground driving a tractor. I was really impressed by that because it sent out the message that we all muck in together and that there was no gravy train. I went home and told my family and they were also really impressed. He liked to keep his players level-headed and well grounded. After we won the FA Cup, he told me that it didn't mean I could turn up at pre-season training in a Jaguar. He asked me if I had opened up a savings account and if I was going to buy a flat or a house. He was very good at giving practical advice and had general concerns about his players above and beyond football.

Every Saturday morning when we played youth team football at Chadwell Heath, John was always there and it was just so impressive to have the first team manager watching. I was only 15-years-old and my friends at Aveley Comprehensive didn't believe it when I told them because they knew he'd be with the first team in the afternoon. John

knew every player at every level at West Ham and how they were progressing. When I got into the England Youth team I remember leaving Lilleshall to watch the England Under-21s. Back then, players like Glen Hoddle, Ray Wilkins, and Kenny Sansom were playing at that level and we took the bus to Coventry to watch the game and I remember looking up and seeing John in the stand. He was always at a game, always assessing players, always looking at the opposition.

When I was 16 - a first year apprentice - Ronnie Boyce brought in his 1964 FA Cup winners' medal, which was an amazing moment. Little did I know that I would have my own one in little over a year's time? Unbelievable when I think about it. In fact it was Ronnie who said to me that I'd done it the wrong way round because I won the FA Cup in 1980 first followed by the FA Youth Cup the following year. Ronnie was a big influence on me. He had played in midfield with Bobby Moore and was a big inspirational figure to me then and still to this day.

My nickname, 'Ollie,' came about when I was a first-year apprentice. Back then the apprentices had a lot of chores to do around the club so after training we would take a shower, have a bite to eat and then tidy the changing rooms, clean the boots or whatever else was needed on that particular day. On one occasion I came out of the dressing room after my shower and the apprentice goalkeeper at the time, Graham Moseley, noticed that my hair was sticking up. He started calling me 'Ollie' from Laurel and Hardy, but someone corrected him and said don't you mean Stanley? It was Stan Laurel who used to tease his hair up on his head. But his mistake with Ollie was the name that stuck and I've been called that ever since.

Everyone I dealt with during my formative years at West Ham were very hands-on, very attentive and took the time to explain why things were done the way they were. Ron Greenwood, Eddie Baily and Len Hurford were all like that and John was just the same.

I think John liked my enthusiasm, my energy and my determination. I would like to think that my desire to do well was something that registered high on his list of important attributes to possess. My earliest memory is one of wanting to be a footballer. I was always looking to learn and develop myself as a player. I felt I was a team player rather than an

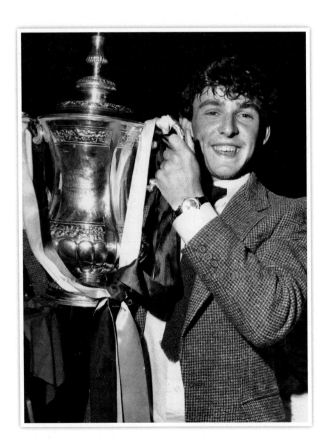

Still the youngest player to win the FA Cup

individual, which is why I probably didn't score as many goals as I should have done.

I always loved to watch Rodney Marsh, Gerry Francis and Stanley Bowles because I was a bit of a closet QPR fan on account of my uncle, Les Allen, playing for them. He also managed them, too. However, when I started to watch West Ham, it was always Trevor Brooking and Billy Bonds who were the two I admired the most.

I think people often under-estimate just how hard John Lyall's training sessions were. People confuse the West Ham way as being all tippy-tappy but it was far more sophisticated than that. I was learning about the weight of pass and receiving the ball sideways on. Physically, it was really tough with plenty of running, five-a-side matches and one and two-touch football in the grids. So it was very, very, hard and very, very, thorough. John was extremely good at slowly integrating the youngsters with the senior pros. For example, John would call me over to put in some crosses for part of the session, which was great for getting valuable experience. He always made it entertaining and expected a high tempo.

John instilled good habits into the apprentices at the club. Things like cleaning up after yourself and others, dressing correctly for the right occasion and showing respect to others. These are the good habits that I took through life.

Regarding my debut, John told me I was in the squad for a League Cup match against Southend United at home. He said I wouldn't be playing but I might be on the bench. I was delighted with that and went home and told my parents. Before the match, I was feeling very self-conscious just being in the first team dressing room and I sat in a corner all by myself. When the team sheet was handed round I noticed I was starting! John came over and talked to me and told me to get the ball to Trevor Brooking or Alan Devonshire and to ease myself into the game that way. Basically, he wanted me to keep it simple.

John would always be in the dressing room the whole time. Some management styles are not like that but John liked to have a one-on-one with his players. He was always very thorough and would tell you a bit about certain opposition players and how they were likely to play. At half time, he would let you know if you weren't playing well individually or as a team. He would tell you what you had to do to change and improve things. He always did this in a calm and assured way.

I was very fortunate in that I played under Peter Shreeve, David Pleat, Terry Venables and John Lyall. They all had their different styles but were all very good in their own way.

Even though I played in every game of the 1980 FA Cup run, John did drop me to the bench for the game against Swansea City in the fifth round. Jimmy Neighbour came in for me and although John just said he felt I needed a rest, I still felt very

Leading the way against Politechnica Timisoara of Romania, November 1980

disappointed. Thankfully, I got on and scored, when following up a David Cross shot which the 'keeper could only parry. It was with my left foot which was something of a collector's item.

Turning to the FA Cup final itself, John had been talking to the press at Chadwell Heath the Wednesday before and he asked me if I knew I might be the youngest player ever to play in an FA Cup final? I think Howard Kendall was the youngest at the time and had played for Preston North End against West Ham in 1964. The following day, my brother Peter asked if John had actually confirmed that I was in the team but he hadn't. I'd also been dropped for the league match against Charlton Athletic on the previous Monday so my emotions were up and down throughout that week. We did think for a moment that he was using the story as a smokescreen to take the pressure off the team and complicate Arsenal's preparations. It wasn't until Friday that John put up the team sheet for the final. It was funny because I worked my way down from Phil Parkes at Number one, and when I got to Number 7 and saw my name I didn't bother looking any further. My family asked me who was playing up front but I could only name the first seven!

From the final, people always remember the Willie Young moment, when he brought me down as I was through on goal. My thoughts on that have always been the same. It had no impact on the game or the result, whatsoever, so I am just proud to be part of that winning team. I've never seen Willie Young since that day.

The spine of that FA Cup team with Phil Parkes, Alvin Martin, Trevor Brooking, Bill Bonds and Alan Devonshire, David Cross and Stuart Pearson was such very high quality and could beat any team on its day. No second tier club has won the FA Cup since, so John had a lot to be proud of. I was very lucky to be surrounded by those players who protected me and passed on their experience. To this day, I am grateful to them for that.

The following season we played in Europe. I played in Romania against Politechnica Timisoara and at home to Dinamo Tbilisi, who were the best side I ever saw at Upton Park. They had two players in particular – Chivadze, who kept playing the ball out of defence, and Kipiani, who ran us ragged all night long. To be fair to John, it was during an era when it was hard to get any knowledge of clubs behind the Iron Curtain in Russia and Eastern Europe. To his credit, once he assessed how they played in the first leg he put out a team that beat them in Georgia, in the return.

I left the club during the 1984-85 season. I was only 22-years-old but had been at West Ham since I was 13. I felt that it was maybe time, rightly or wrongly, to test myself elsewhere. My contract talks didn't start until quite late in March and there had been a bit of press coverage that both Liverpool and Spurs were interested in signing me. I didn't get the impression that the club was doing everything in their power to keep me and I made the decision to leave. It was difficult for my family, particularly my dad, because they lived in a predominantly West Ham area.

When I played for Tottenham against West Ham I always made sure I had a chat with John and Boycey because I'll never forget what they did for me. I've always admired both those men and the club and don't feel that we left on bad terms. I actually phoned John after he lost his job at West Ham. I just wanted to tell him how sorry I was to hear the news and wished him well for the future.

One of the last times I saw John was when he came to Spurs in a coaching capacity. Terry Venables had appointed him so it was great to catch up. John was involved in both the youth development side and on the scouting side. He stayed for about six months before getting the job at Ipswich Town.

I also remember going to see Ipswich Town play at Portman Road. I've always loved watching football and was living in Brentwood at the time and they were doing really well under John. I was impressed by Chris Kiwomya, Simon Milton and Jason Dozzell. John had put together a really useful side and was surprised to see me there but we just picked up from where we left off. It was always comfortable talking with John.

The very last occasion I saw John was at a reunion of the 1975 and 1980 FA Cup winning teams at the Britannia Hotel on the Isle of Dogs. That was an amazing evening and everyone made the effort to be there. The fact that John passed away the following year makes it all the more poignant.

I went to John's funeral at Ipswich Cathedral and there was a superb turnout which was the very least he deserved. People travelled from all over to pay their respects. Paul Ince and his wife were there and Sir Alex Ferguson delivered the eulogy.
Paul Allen

Ollie was such a down to earth lad. Even after he won the FA Cup as the youngest-ever player he never gave it the big 'I am'. He still played in the youth team and wanted to do all the things a young lad does. He didn't want to grow up too quickly and I admired him for that.
Ray Houghton

I've known Paul for a very long time and we've worked closely together at the PFA for almost 20 years. He still hasn't forgiven me for ruining his sheepskin coat at West Ham. I used to spray oil in my hair and fell asleep on his coat on our way back from a game!
Bobby Barnes

I thought Paul was an outstanding player. He could play attacking midfield, defensive midfield, he could score goals, he could beat people and he had terrific passing range. He wasn't the tallest but what a competitor. I was disappointed when he went to Tottenham.
Mick McGiven

Mr Happy I call him because he's always smiling.
Everald La Ronde

We're all still waiting for his voice to break!
Alan Devonshire

We roomed together a few times. He was a really nice, polite, young lad and very determined.
Paul Hilton

He had a great attitude to the game and always trained long and hard. I've got nothing but respect for Paul Allen.
Dale Banton

He was a wide-eyed kid who played on the big stage as if he was playing in the park. He played bigger and stronger than he looked. I also know the family quite well – Bradley, Martin and Clive in particular. Paul is a very thoughtful type of guy and we like to have a chat about Bruce Springsteen, who he has seen a couple of times and is my musical hero, too. Paul epitomised the idea of taking your chance when it comes.
Paul Brush

I've never told Ollie this but he is a few years older than me and when he got into West Ham United's first team I used to pretend to be Paul Allen in the park!
Alan Dickens

Ollie

41 – MARK SMITH

"He was one of the loveliest men I have met in my life. Encouraging, supportive and a steadying influence. It felt like playing football for your dad. I could sit and praise him all day long."

Born: Plaistow, London, October 10, 1961 • **Position:** Left-back • **Games played for West Ham United:** 2 (1979)
Debut: October 8, 1979 v Southend United (h) W 5-1 (Lansdowne 3, Holland, Stewart – Gray)
West Ham United: Parkes, Stewart, **Smith,** Bonds, Martin, Holland, Allen, Lansdowne, Cross, Brooking, Pike.
Southend United: Cawston, Dudley, Moody, Cusack, Walker, Stead, Otulakowski*, Morris, Pountney, Hadley, Gray. Sub: Hull.*

Mark Smith's West Ham United story is the most poignant I have heard from the Greenwood and Lyall era. Having interviewed every surviving Hammer from the 1960s, 70s and 80s, it is Mark's experience which has had the greatest emotional impact. His upbeat resilience and first class company is a joy to behold and the quicker I am back round his living room in Plaistow reminiscing in Claret and Blue bliss, the better.

Born in Plaistow to parents Roy and Beryl, Mark grew up at 45 Malmesbury Road in Canning Town with his sister, Jill and brother, Keith: "I was blessed to have such fantastic parents, both of whom left this world far too soon. My dad was a lagger and boiler fitter which is how he picked up asbestosis. He died from the illness at just 51-years-of-age. My mum passed away at 47 from breast cancer. She was a very special person in my life. We were all West Ham mad."

Mark played for Star Lane School, Eastlee Secondary School, Newham District, Essex County and a Sunday team called Poplar: "All through my school experience I played centre-half, except for the district side, where I took a central-midfield role."

Mark's dream of playing in the Claret and Blue became a reality in 1979, but a closely-guarded secret overshadowed his progression and ultimately decimated his football aspirations.

Today, Mark still resides in Plaistow with his lovely wife Laraine. The walls are adorned with photos of the other great passions in his life – The Beatles, Gilbert O'Sullivan and West Ham United.

Following are the recollections preserved from A Day in the Life of Mark Smith:

My first memory of John came when I played for Newham District at Terence McMillan Stadium. After the match, I was told there were representatives from West Ham United wanting to have a chat with me. I went outside and Ron Greenwood, John Lyall and Eddie Baily were all waiting to see me. At that time, Ron Greenwood was like a god to me. It was 1974 so I didn't really know John or Eddie that well. My dad was at the game, because he came with me absolutely everywhere and watched all my matches. It was funny because Eddie Baily had brought along a catalogue with all the latest styles of football boots. He said to me: "Pick out any pair of boots you like and West Ham will buy them for you." No sooner had Eddie finished saying it than my dad chimed in and said: "I'm his dad. I buy his boots!" That was that! Later in life, I discussed that moment with my dad and he said it felt like a bribe so his instinct was to push back immediately.

I first went to see West Ham when I was a very young kid, maybe three or four-years-old. My dad was a big fan and went to every home game and many away matches, too. I've still got memories of Bobby Moore and Geoff Hurst playing.

Winning the ADO Youth Tournament in Holland, 1979 (Back Row - Far Left)

We were living in Malmesbury Road, Canning Town and I used to go along to the ground with my mum and queue up outside the South Bank so that we could stand behind the goal. The gates would open at about half-past one but we would get there about four or five hours earlier. That thrill of going up the steps and seeing the pitch and taking our place on the wall will stay with me forever. Just that simple walk through the turnstile to our spot was super exciting, it really was. Bobby Ferguson, the goalkeeper at that time, always came over to us and said a few words or gave a high five. He was a cracking bloke, Bobby, and I liked him a lot.

I signed schoolboy forms for West Ham in 1974, when I was 13-years-old, but Eddie Baily came round to our house and said they couldn't process it because I had to be 14 to sign. It was West Ham's mistake and the FA had obviously rejected the forms.

I'd started training at West Ham when I was 12. I absolutely loved football and loved West Ham even more. The feeling I got going to the ground with all those great players, was absolutely unbelievable. It was beyond exciting.

One of the early conversations I had with John was over at Chadwell Heath. He'd heard good things about me and told me he was going to keep an eye on my progress. He said I should keep practising and working hard, and that he was expecting to see a lot more of me in the future. It was just a beautiful thing for me to hear.

It was only when I joined West Ham that I started playing at left-back. I was predominantly left-footed but, to be honest, I didn't really feel comfortable playing in the Number 3 role. It doesn't matter now, of course, but if things had been less complicated, I might have developed into a different position.

Bill Lansdowne was our reserve team manager. What a beautiful bloke he was! The thing I loved about him was that he was mild mannered and never shouted at the players. He was so patient and usually gave sound advice rather than criticise. It made me really want to play well for him because he was such a diamond.

In 1978, I signed apprentice forms, which meant I did a lot more training at Chadwell Heath. That was an amazing place and sometimes ex-players like Bobby Moore, Geoff Hurst and Martin Peters dropped in. We'd all be standing there, in awe of our heroes. Bobby took time to talk to us, which really impressed me because he didn't have to hang around with a bunch of kids but he did. He was always encouraging and Geoff and Martin were the same, which is why they are West Ham gods to every proper West Ham fan.

I took over from Phil Brignull as head apprentice at that time and one of the first things the players asked me to organise was more Luncheon Vouchers. We were given 40p each to spend in Cassettari's Café, but that barely paid for a cup of tea and a slice of toast, let alone a proper meal. I

Training at Chadwell Heath with David Cross, Bobby Ferguson and Bill Lansdowne looking on

went and saw Albert Walker to ask for more: "How many do you need?" he said. "Two pounds should do it, Albert" I replied. I might as well have asked for the Crown Jewels. "Two pounds!" he said, raising his voice. "I'll have to talk to Ronnie Boyce." The next day I was called in to see Ron: "I hear you've been causing a bit of a stir at the club?" he said. "It's only Luncheon Vouchers Ron," I pleaded. "We need a good meal before we clean the changing rooms, the boots and stands and everything," I continued. He looked at me and said: "Look Smudger, I scored the winning goal in the 1964 Cup final and I didn't get as much as that. It's been 40p for some time and there has never been any fuss. I'll have to take this right to the top." That was classic Boycey, god love him. He took any opportunity to mention his winning goal in the FA Cup final! He told everyone he had it set up on a Super 8 film projector at home and watched it every night before he went to bed! In training he'd ask someone, anyone, to put in a cross and he'd head it home and say: "That's what I did at Wembley in 1964!" The truth be told, I loved to hear it because those FA Cup and European Cup Winners Cup winners were my heroes. Anyway, we didn't hear anything about the Luncheon Vouchers for a few days and then Albert Walker came in with more than he could carry and from then on we got two pounds every day. What a different world! It is so comical now but was so serious to us at the time.

My first team debut came against Southend United in a League Cup second replay. John told me to be at the ground no later than 6pm because he was putting me in the squad. I walked to the ground because I was living in Plaistow and can remember turning the corner and seeing an Evening Standard billboard with the headline: 'Young local lad Mark Smith to make debut for Hammers.' When I got there, John called me to one side and asked me if I was feeling like a game of football because I was in the starting line-up. I said

I was ready and that I'd just seen the news on an Evening Standard poster. He told me I should have grabbed the poster as a keepsake because it would be something to look back on later in life. How right he was because I'd love to have that framed on my wall.

During the match, I got cramp in both legs so Rob Jenkins, the physio, told me to go down so that he could treat me. I did exactly that, right near the dug out, so Rob only had to walk about six feet to tend to me. He started massaging my legs and said: "You tart, you're like an old woman going down like this. You've been playing crap anyway and I'd have taken you off ages ago. The whole crowd is saying how crap you are! My nan could play better than you." He was hilarious! Then he turned to John and shouted: "He's fine to carry on!"

I always had belief in my ability and never once thought I wasn't good enough. I looked around at the other players and felt confident that I had a part to play. As a Canning Town boy, I just wanted to play for West Ham United all my life.

One of the memories which chokes me up a bit, came after my league debut against Swansea City in November 1979. The following day I was carrying an injury so went and saw Rob in his clinic at the ground. When I arrived, Trevor Brooking, Billy Bonds and Alvin Martin were all there and quite a few others, including John himself. My dad had come along with me, too. Rob liked him and always said: "Bring your dad down and we'll have a cup of tea." My dad was in the dressing room while I was having some treatment when all of a sudden John said: "I'm nicking your dad for a little while, Mark." So off they went together and a short while after, Rob took me out through the tunnel, towards the pitch. I couldn't believe my eyes! My dad was having a kick about with Trevor Brooking, Billy Bonds and Alvin Martin. I get quite emotional when I think of what John did there because my dad is no longer with us. That sight is one of the most beautiful and greatest things in my life. My dad, who was a West Ham fanatic, playing football with his heroes on the same pitch where he'd watched Moore, Hurst, Peters and all the greats in the club's history. When they came back to the clinic John said to me: "Smudger, I've just offered your dad a five-year contract because he's better than you, son!" When I think of my league debut, which we won 2-0, I cannot separate it from the memory of my dad playing on the same pitch with the same players that following day.

There were so many great characters at West Ham. There was the cook at Chadwell Heath and her husband. They were known as 'Bubbles' and 'Bert.' Bert cleaned the dressing room and was a general handy man. They were a lovely couple and, for whatever reason, Bubbles took a liking to me. We teased each other and got on so well together. One day, she pulled me to one side and said: "What are your favourites, Mark?" I told her I liked apple pie and jam roly-poly. The next day Bubbles called me over and said she'd prepared some jam roly-poly for me. John caught sight of us and in a loud voice said: "What's all this going on here, Smudger? Why is it one rule for you and another rule for the rest of us? Why can't I have some jam roly poly?" Bubbles replied: "My Mark doesn't like custard and rice so I've made him some jam roly-poly?" John teased the hell out of the situation. "Your Mark! Your Mark! We can't have favourites at this place! What about me? You've never asked me if I like jam roly-poly? I've never said I liked custard and rice..." He went on and on trying to get others involved in the humour and asking their opinion: "Ernie, do you know anything about this jam-roly poly racket Smudger and Bubbles have got going on?" It was just so funny.

My memories of West Ham centre on two extremes really. On the one hand I'm incredibly proud and honoured to have risen up through the ranks to play for the first team yet, on the other hand, I think about how I nearly lost my life and the serious health issues I've endured ever since.

I noticed that I had something wrong with me when I was a little boy. My bladder and bowel started hanging outside of me and I had to tuck them back in. I played all my schoolboy football like that and had to find ways of keeping my bowel and bladder from falling out of my rectum. On the night of my debut I wore four women's sanitary towels and three pairs of pants to stop, what I would describe as a football bladder pouring of blood, from falling out. At half-time, Trevor Brooking said to me: "Smudger, you've got blood dripping down your legs." I had to go somewhere and change all the bandaging and replace it with new sanitary towels and pants. I know now that it was a life or death situation because if the bladder had burst during the game I would have probably died.

That was the same ritual I had been going through for years but it was getting harder and harder to stop the bleeding and it was affecting my health. One day, Boycey called me in and told me I was looking grey, lacked energy and wasn't as sharp as I used to be. He said: "I've known you since you were a young boy and you're not leaving this room until you tell me what is going on." Eventually, I told him about my condition but he didn't really understand it and wanted to see what I was talking about. When I showed him he simply couldn't believe it: "How long have you had this?" he said. "Since I was six-years-old." I replied. In the end he called Dr Roper, who worked for the club. He couldn't believe what he was seeing either and quickly sent me to see a specialist in Harley Street.

West Ham then put me up in Fielding House which was the private section of London Hospital. I'll never forget the words of the specialist, because for the first time I felt my world of problems was about to be lifted from my shoulders. He said: "We'll bring you in on Thursday, you'll have an operation on Friday and you'll be back training on Monday." These words were sent from heaven, as you can imagine, because I'd been trying to keep my condition a secret for 12 years.

I had the operation, but on the Monday I was still bleeding, so the specialist told me to rest for another week. That Thursday I woke up in the middle of the night and I called out to my mum and said: "Mum, I'm so sorry but I think I've got diarrhoea and I can't stop it. When she turned on the light she screamed because there was blood everywhere. I was haemorrhaging. The ambulance came and the next day I was in intensive care. They said that another half-an-hour and I would have been dead. They actually told my mum and dad to get any family members to the hospital because they didn't think I would survive the night.

Over the next few months, I had a dozen operations because they just couldn't stop the bleeding. It is such a rare condition. I spoke to a leading surgeon from the United States, once, and he said he had operated four times on people with my condition and three of them hadn't survived.

Remarkably, I did make a comeback in the reserves and things appeared to be going ok. Trevor Brooking played in one game because he was returning from injury. He came up to me afterwards and told me how great I looked and how well I had played. He told John that I'd be ready for the first team in about a month, once I got back to full fitness. John was delighted at this and said to me: "Smudger, I've heard good things from Trevor and it sounds as though you're back on track, son?" Devastatingly, during the next training session, I went in to a tackle and felt everything inside give way and that was that. All the surgery and stitching was undone and I was back to square one. I knew then, my career was over.

I went to see Doc Brill and both Rob Jenkins and John Lyall were there, too. I could tell by the look on their faces that they knew what I already knew. John explained that he had spoken with the specialist at London Hospital and they felt they had tried everything and that there was nothing more to be done. John got really choked up and said that in all his years as a manager he hadn't felt this upset about a player. He said there was no doubt that with a clean bill of health I would have been West Ham's left-back for a long, long time. I left that meeting knowing that I would never play professional football again and, to this day, after more operations than I care to remember, and with all the latest technology, they have never been able to put it right. Even now, I only sleep for a couple of hours every night, because I still bleed and have to change the bandaging. My circulation is all wrong and I have shaking fits but they won't operate on me anymore. Most specialists are amazed that I played any type of football at all. They are convinced that I could have dropped down dead on my debut, or for that matter, any game that I played in. When I hear what they have to say I feel lucky to be around to tell the story.

A big memory I have of John comes from that time when I was critically ill in London Hospital. I had tubes hanging out of me and was seriously ill. He came to visit me and the excitement which spread through the hospital, just from his presence, was electrifying. The Sister, Elizabeth, came dashing in, all flustered saying: "Guess who's coming in to see you? It's John Lyall and he is on his way up!" Now, I wasn't as excited as everyone else in that hospital because I saw John every day, but it was amazing to see the effect John had on the staff and the patients. I was having blood transfusion after blood transfusion so it was a welcome distraction and when John came walking into the room it was full. He looked at me and I'll never forget what he said: "The things this boy will do to get out of training!" Well, there was an uproar of laughter and he we had a lovely bit of banter going on:

"Smudger," he smiled. "All you had to do was ask me for a bit of time off."

"Would I have got it, John?" I asked.

"No!" he quickly replied.

It went on like that and he was signing autographs for everyone and posing for pictures. John was just amazing. All the top doctors came in because of who he was and the fact that West Ham had won the FA Cup six months earlier. John was a hero to everyone and he visited me three times in hospital and I'm forever grateful to him for that.

In the face of all the terrible things I've been through, I still look back and tell anyone who will listen that I've had an amazing life and fulfilled all my dreams. I married an amazing woman in Laraine and we have two beautiful kids, Clair and Mark. I always wanted to meet the Beatles and I've met both Paul McCartney and Ringo Starr. I've also met Gilbert O'Sullivan a few times who is another hero of mine. Last but not least, I played for West Ham United, the team I love. What more could I ask for?

Mark Smith

Following are some player recollections of Mark:

Smudger was a great left-back with a very educated left foot. There weren't too many naturally left-footed players around so they always stood out. He was a good lad with a dry wit and absolutely bonkers about the Beatles.

Ray Houghton

I got on really well with Mark. I identified him as one of the better players, who would be challenging me for the left-back position. He played well in the couple of games I missed because of injury.

Paul Brush

Smudger came to my wedding. He was a very good player

and who knows just how far he could have gone? But for an unfortunate condition with his health, he would have been one to remember at West Ham.

Phil Brignull

Everyone used to say what a talented footballer he was.

Alan Dickens

If he'd stayed fit and healthy, Smudger would have been West Ham's left-back for ten years. He had such a cultured left foot. He could put the ball anywhere with it. The fans were denied seeing a player who could have been the best ever in that left-back position. A total Beatles nut as well.

Everald La Ronde

He was one of the best players of my generation at West Ham. I played in his debut against Southend United and he did really well. But for his health problems he could have gone all the way.

Paul Allen

Now there's a boy who should have had a long and successful career.

Bobby Barnes

Mark was not only one of the best left-backs at West Ham United, he was amongst the top three or four in the country.

Mick McGiven.

Smudger at home in Plaistow

Back row: Martin, Banton, Parkes Ferguson, Morgan, Lansdowne.

Middle row: Brush, Smith, Stewart, Bonds, Brooking, Cross, Cowie.

Front row: Neighbour, Allen, Pearson, Pike, Lampard, Devonshire, Holland.

They Played For John Lyall – The West Ham Years

CHAPTER SEVEN
1980-81

"I didn't go near Mr Thomas. He walked at least 20 yards to approach me. I wasn't the aggressor but I felt I was entitled to my opinion. I told him: "Don't say anything to me, we feel we were cheated." **John Lyall**

Liverpool manager, Bob Paisley keeping John away from Clive Thomas, League Cup final, 1981

Enjoying the FA Youth Cup and Second Division Championship trophy, May 1981. L-R Yvonne and John Lyall with Ron and Dawn Boyce

Division Two Manager of the season, May 1981

John Lyall signed a new five-year contract. West Ham played in competitive European competition for the first time since 1976. Lamentably, crowd trouble against Real Castilla overshadowed the club's first every match in the Bernabeu Stadium.

UEFA decided that West Ham must play their second leg tie against Castilla behind closed doors. Only 70 people from each club were allowed to attend the match - including players, journalists and other official observers. 252 was the official attendance. It was the first game to be played behind closed doors in the UK since 1921, when Stockport County met Leicester City at Old Trafford.

West Ham arrived at Wembley, for the Charity Shield against Liverpool, in a shiny new Lacey's coach, bought from the proceeds of last season's victorious FA Cup campaign. The state of the art coach had a service area at the rear, an on board toilet and a treatment bench.

Paul Goddardd joined from QPR for £800,000. He had an inauspicious start to his Hammers' career when he limped off in the opening day defeat at home to Luton Town. Lyall's initial impression of 'Sarge' was a good one: "He could have scored three goals. It's early days, but I think he will be a very useful asset."

Albert Walker retired from the club he described as: "The best in the land." Having played as a full-back for the Hammers between 1932 and 1938, he returned in a coaching capacity in 1952. Billy Bonds made a presentation to him at Chadwell Heath.

West Ham won the Division Two championship at a canter. Furthermore, the youth team won both the FA Youth Cup, beating Tottenham 2-1 on aggregate, and the South East Counties Division One Cup. Unfortunately, the club was denied another when losing to Liverpool in the League Cup final. John Lyall was incensed when referee Clive Thomas allowed a goal, even though Sammy Lee was in an offside position.

A record breaking season which saw just two new debutants in Paul Goddard and Bobby Barnes.

Here is their story...

42 – PAUL GODDARD

"John didn't mince his words. When he signed me he said: "We're spending all our FA Cup money on you, so you'd better be good!"

Born: Harlington, Middlesex, October 12, 1959 • **Position:** Striker • **Games played for West Ham United:** 213 (1980-1986)

Goals: 71 (15th on the all-time list • **Honours:** 1981 League Cup runner-up, 1985-86 Member of highest ever league finish (third)

Debut: August 16, 1980 v Luton Town (h) L 1-2 (Stewart pen – Moss 2 pens) Att: 28,033

West Ham United: Parkes, Stewart, Brush, Bonds, Martin, Devonshire, Holland, **Goddard,*** Cross, Brooking, Pike. Sub: Lampard*

Luton Town: Findlay, Stephens, Donaghy, Grealish, Saxby, Price, Hill, Stein, White,* Antic. Sub:

Paul Goddard was signed by West Ham United in August 1980, for a record transfer fee of £800,000. His 71 goals from 213 appearances ensured a good return on that investment. His flying header against Liverpool at Villa Park in the 1981 League Cup final replay was a big highlight of his time with the Hammers.

Nicknamed 'Sarge', on account of his time spent in the Boy's Brigade, Goddard was a firm favourite at Upton Park.

Since 2006 Paul has worked as a football intermediary with Stellar Group, a sports consultancy. The football journey continues…

Today, Goddard lives just around the corner from John Lyall's wife, Yvonne: "She is a lovely, pleasant lady, who has got so much love for John. She can't speak three sentence without mentioning John and that is a tribute to John and the love they shared."

Following are Paul's memories from his time at West Ham:

John is not only one of the best coaches I've ever worked with but he is one the best coaches I've ever seen. He was one of the best men in football and a first class person. A proper man.

All I'd ever wanted to do was play football. As a young kid, living at number 18 Bedwell Gardens in Hayes, I'd kick a

John spends West Ham United's 1980 FA Cup winnings!

Goddard's flying header against Liverpool in the League Cup final replay at Villa Park, April 1981

tennis ball, every evening, against a huge Library wall along from my house.

My first memory of John is from when I was 20-years-old and I'd just got married. He and Eddie Baily came to my house in Beech Avenue, Lane End, High Wycombe. I was a QPR player at the time but West Ham had made a record bid of £800,000, which had been accepted. We'd received a phone call to say that John Lyall was on his way. My wife completely panicked because we had a house full of borrowed furniture and she was frantically trying to make everything presentable. John and Eddie sat on an old leather couch which we'd borrowed from my auntie.

It was a great time to be joining West Ham. The atmosphere around the club was electric following the FA Cup success over Arsenal. There was a great team spirit and some tremendous players. Match of the Day wouldn't have enough time to analyse some of Brooking's passes or Dev's mazy runs, taking on three or four players. It was a place of enjoyment and the emphasis was on entertainment and not just winning, like in today's game. There were many times that we won games and John was disappointed because we hadn't stuck to the style of play we worked so hard at in training. Similarly, we might lose a match but he'd find so many positives in how we had played in line with the principles he had laid down. Personally, that approach gave me a lot of confidence. I felt part of something special, which had a clear vision. We were all in it together as a club and that just doesn't exist today.

My first training session was a real eye opener. We went for a run and there was this great big thundering bloke at the front powering away into the distance – Billy Bonds. He did everything ten times quicker and ten times stronger than any other player. I realised I'd have to up my own effort even further.

At QPR I'd had some very good coaches. Frank Sibley, Theo Foley and Brian Eastick were all excellent. They were good football men but John Lyall was the first coach to make my brain work in a different way. He would ask me my thoughts on a specific move or approach. We would discuss the options, create certain scenarios and always analyse cause and effect. He was forever saying "What if?" and "Why don't we try this?" That is why I improved so much as a player during my time at West Ham. He gave me a clear understanding of what I was good at and what I wasn't good at. He made me aware of my role in the team and why my skill set was important. Nobody was better than Trevor Brooking at passing the ball so it made sense to ensure he did most of the passing. Nobody was better running with the ball than Alan Devonshire so it was important to ensure we enabled him to do that. I had a very good first-touch and was a great back-to-goal player, so John made sure these skills were utilised during a game. If you listened to John it was impossible not to improve your game. When the team linked all these assets together and played one-touch football with plenty of movement, we were unstoppable.

I had a very strong relationship with John. I spent seven years with him at West Ham and another four years at Ipswich Town. Even in the final few weeks of our time together at Portman Road he was still putting on training sessions that I'd never seen before. How is that even possible? The man was a real visionary who had an insatiable appetite to improve, explore and create. I was 35-years-old at Ipswich and he was still inspiring me with new ideas and highlighting my strengths. He was extraordinary. I briefly worked with Dave Sexton and Terry Venables as part of the England set up and they were definitely from the same mould as John.

I can remember quite a few of my goals. The ones that stand out are the 25-yarder against Coventry City in the League Cup semi-final, which got us back into the game, and the flying header against Liverpool in the League Cup final replay at Villa Park. I'm not a statistician but I'm pleased with my goals to games ratio. I think it is better than a goal in every three matches.

I got on really well with Phil Parkes, Alan Devonshire and Kevin Keen because we all travelled in together each day. Some of those car journeys were hilarious. Dev would be talking about his greyhounds and we'd stop off for some breakfast in our favourite café. They'd have all our food ready for us. Dev would polish off a big old gut buster and then, half an hour later, he'd be gliding past half a dozen players at Chadwell Heath. We had great comradeship.

I played with some terrific strikers – Clive Allen, David Cross, Tony Cottee, Frank McAvennie, Peter Beardsley, Dean Saunders, Teddy Sheringham and Chris Kiwomya. It is impossible to pick a favourite from that lot and I like to think that it highlights just how adaptable I was as a player.

When the news of John's sacking filtered through the football world, it was massive news. Today, someone seems to get sacked every week and life goes on. That wasn't the case with John's dismissal. Time seemed to stop for a while.

It is quite remarkable, the impact John had on Ipswich Town. I still keep in touch with Bryan Klug who is the current Academy Manager at Portman Road. He was a coach under John and when we chat he still says: "I wonder what John would have made of that?" It is quite remarkable really, given that 25 years have passed since John was at the club. Charlie Woods is another great personality at Ipswich Town and was a top class coach under Bobby Robson at Portman Road, and later with England. Whenever we chat it will not be longer than 15 minutes before he makes a reference to John. Quite incredible.

Paul Goddard

I still stay in touch with 'Sarge' and we exchange Christmas cards. He scored goals wherever he went.

Eddie Gillam

He had exceptional ability but often did something that used to really annoy me. When he fell over, or went down under a tackle, it would take him an age to get back up. It used to drive me nuts! He would be sitting there in the mud, gesticulating about how he should have got a free kick or whatever.

Ray Houghton

I played with some very good strikers during my career. Laurie Cunningham and Cyril Regis at West Bromwich Albion and Colin Stein at Coventry City. Colin is a legend at Glasgow Rangers and was still a very good player at Coventry. I had

Completing his hat-trick against QPR, April 1981. The first of three hat-tricks for the Hammers

They Played For John Lyall – The West Ham Years

Collecting an Evening Standard Player of the Month award from John Lyall, September 1981

a good understanding with Stuart Pearson and the most technically gifted player was certainly Pop Robson, but my most productive partnership was with Paul Goddard. During the 1980-81 season we scored 58 goals between us.
David Cross

Sarge was a very good one-touch two-touch player. I was disappointed when he went to Newcastle because he definitely made us a stronger team.
Alan Devonshire

We used to say that wherever he went there was always a cloud over him!
Paul Hilton

Paul was a proper striker and just what West Ham needed at that time. They broke the bank to get him. He was young, enthusiastic and could score goals on a regular basis. A great signing and a good character.
Mick McGiven

Sarge and Psycho at a John Lyall tribute evening in 2016.

43 – BOBBY BARNES

"John was always dispensing good advice. The two nuggets of wisdom he shared with me were: "Train harder!" and "Get your hair cut!"

Born: Kingston-upon-Thames, December 17, 1962 • **Position:** Winger/Striker • Games played for West Ham United: 54 (1980-85)

Goals: 6 • **Honours under John Lyall:** 1981 FA Youth Cup winner, 1980-81 Second Division championship, 1985-85 Squad member of West Ham United's highest ever league finish • **Debut:** September 17, 1980 v Real Castilla (a) L 1-3 (Cross - Paco, Balin, Cidon) Att: 40,000

Real Castilla: Miguel, Juanito*, Casimiro, Salguero, Espinosa, Sanch' Lorenzo, Balin, Alvarez, Paco, Bernal, Cidon.* Subs: Chendo*/Blanco*

West Ham United: Parkes, Stewart, Lampard, Bonds, Martin, Devonshire*, Morgan*, Goddard, Cross, Brooking, Pike. Subs: Brush*/**Barnes***

David Oswald "Bobby" Barnes grew up in Leytonstone and took the 58 bus to West Ham United's ground. *"It dropped me off at the Boleyn pub. Eddie Baily often gave me a lift, too. He was a real mentor to me."*

Born to Thomas and Dorothy, Bobby was one of seven kids growing up in the East End: *"My dad worked for Scholl, the famous footwear company, for almost 40 years. My mum was originally a school teacher but then worked for NatWest Bank."*

Nicknamed 'Digger' after a character in the 1980s US hit drama, Dallas, Bobby was just 17-years-old when scoring on his home debut against Watford on September 20, 1980.

Bobby played for no fewer than 13 different football clubs, enjoying his best spell whilst at Northampton Town, where he played over 100 games and scored over 40 goals.

His parents' insistence that he continued with his schooling paid dividends after Bobby hung up his football boots in the mid-1990s: *"Since 1999 I've been working at the Professional Footballers' Association. I'm now deputy to Gordon Taylor at the PFA in England and President of the European equivalent. We have offices in Geneva, Zurich and Lausanne so I split my time between London and Switzerland."*

In 2015 Bobby followed in the footsteps of Sir Geoff Hurst when receiving an honorary science doctorate from the University of East London.

The interview took place at the PFA headquarters in London and 'Digger Barnes' was on top form:

In recent times it has only been Alex Ferguson who, like John Lyall before him, has run a football club from top to bottom. It takes a lot of confidence to actually believe you are going to be at the club long enough to have that impact.

I started at West Ham United as a young teenager and the thing that first struck me about John was how he would be watching the youth team games in the morning before going on to watch the first-team in the afternoon. He even knew which district and county teams I'd played for before joining West Ham. So, by the time I made my debut, I'd known John for over five years. That is one of the reasons nobody called him 'Gaffer' or 'Boss.' He was always 'John' to everyone at the club. Premier League clubs don't have the luxury of knowing a player for that length of time because it is a results driven business. It is quite sad to note that the average age of a debutant these days is 22, which is ridiculous really. In my day, if you were any good at 15 or 16, you might have got a game in the reserves. I actually made my first-team debut at 17-years-of-age. It is so hard for young kids to play at the very top these days. Look at Manchester City who have just spent £200 million on three defenders. Those positions are now closed to any young lads trying to make their mark.

There was a strong familiarity at the club. When I returned

Jumping for joy after scoring on his home debut versus Watford, September 1980

for pre-season training, it was more or less the same playing personnel at the club. There wasn't the high churn of players you see at West Ham United these days, or the Premier League clubs at large, for that matter. Mark Noble will probably be the last ever West Ham United player to have a Testimonial and yet there must have been at least a dozen from the Lyall era. The notion of a local boy playing for his local club has all but disappeared from the game. The concept of schoolboy football, district and county football – which was second nature to us – doesn't really function as it should today. Nowadays, players are scouted at eight or nine years old and aren't allowed to play for their school teams or anything like that. They are swept into the academy system at a very early age. Understandably, the drop off rates are very high indeed because it is hard to sustain interest in football for such a lengthy period of time.

John had a quiet authority but he certainly let you know about it if you upset him. However, very few people did

Hitting the headlines

upset him because he was held in such high regard. His son, Murray, played cricket for Abridge, the village where John lived. Sometimes, during the summer, Murray would be a few short so John would call me up to ask what I was doing. Before I knew it, there were two or three of us playing cricket in Abridge! I'd been a left-handed batsman for Essex schoolboys so I actually enjoyed it as well as wanting to help out John. It was like your dad asking you to do something, you didn't want to let him down. Tony Cottee and George Parris were decent cricketers so we'd all go along and support Murray.

I was discovered by Eddie Baily. I had been keenly pursued by both Crystal Palace and Millwall but John and Eddie came to my house and impressed my family. I was quite academic and my parents were keen for me to continue with my schooling and Eddie gave them peace of mind on that point.

At the time I was quite a quick and direct player who liked to take responsibility on the pitch. John must have seen an opportunity to mould me into his team ethic. What he didn't realise, was that I had poor eyesight and didn't wear contact lenses so I couldn't actually see anyone on the pitch! It was John and Eddie who arranged for me to wear contact lenses.

I think it's safe to say that I am the only Hammer in West Ham United's history to have made his debut in the Bernabeu Stadium. It was always going to be downhill from there really! That was a horrible experience actually. There were so many ugly scenes with fans fighting and urinating from the top of the stand. It was the only time the fans turned on Billy Bonds. He was quoted in the papers, calling West Ham fans 'Scum' for travelling over there and behaving like that. At the next home game the fans were chanting: "Bonzo, Bonzo, wer're not scum."

There was a hierarchy at West Ham and I was the new young kid. It's funny because even now when we meet up for a reunion or whatever, I am still treated like the youngster in the dressing room and I'm 55!

John somehow managed to pay a world record transfer fee for a goalkeeper whilst in the old second division. It will never happen again.

Part of me will always be at Upton Park. I helped to paint those stands, ran up and down those terraces, cleaned the toilets and worked in the club shop selling memorabilia. I worked with Bradley Walsh's mum in the old portakabin near the main gates. When we got to the FA Cup final in 1980, the club simply couldn't cope with the huge wave of interest in the club so all the apprentices at the time were asked to help out. I even helped Pauline Moss run the payroll in the club office.

John's training sessions were very structured. The early part of the week was devoted to physical stuff such as running and weights. Then, Thursday and Friday would be all about passing drills, team shape, one and two-touch football, third man runs and a five-a-side game to finish off the week. John's training sessions were never behind closed doors. The gates at Chadwell Heath were always open and anyone who came in to watch, was always made welcome.

On Friday afternoon, John would take all the coaching staff

into his office at Chadwell Heath and, for all the youngsters, that is when the nerves would start – waiting for the team-sheets to be pinned up. Ernie Gregory used to crack a few funnies when those sheets went up. One of his phrases was: "If you're in the reserves, you're not earning your keep!"

I called John up once I'd heard the news about his sacking. I was playing for Swindon Town and I just couldn't believe it because that sort of thing never happened at West Ham United.

When he took the job at Ipswich Town, I trained with him and Mick McGiven on Monday and Tuesday. I was playing for Partick Thistle and would fly up to Scotland on Wednesday until after matchday. It was great at Ipswich, there was a mini West Ham enclave there with Phil Parkes, Stuart Slater and Paul Goddard.

After John died a whole generation of Hammers were paraded on the pitch at Upton Park as a show of respect. I thought that was a very touching tribute to the great man.

After I retired from playing I started watching quite a bit of football and I could always tell if a player had been through the West Ham Academy just by how he behaved with a ball on the pitch. There were certain mantras that had been passed down from Ron, to John – Sideways on, one-touch football and know what you are going to do with the ball before receiving it. We had all grown up in that culture and it served so many West Ham United players really well wherever they ended up playing. Any kid who went to West Ham United during the John Lyall era was schooled properly. They learned the basics and they learned them well.

John Lyall was the last of the dynastic managers at West Ham, just like Alex Ferguson was the last at Manchester United. Once Arsene Wenger's time at Arsenal comes to an end, I think the notion of managerial dynasties will be over.

Bobby Barnes

Following are players' comments about Bobby:

I think he spent more money on hair products than he was actually earning! His hair would be smelling of strawberries one day and apples the next. He was a great laugh and is doing very well nowadays in a senior role at the PFA.

Ray Houghton

He was a quick winger but a real enigma. One week he was nine out of ten and could do nothing wrong and then the following week he'd be six out of ten and contribute very little. He had a good left foot and could beat people. He had a swagger about him and knew where the goal was but the consistency just wasn't there.

Mick McGiven

We played together at Northampton Town. He was very

Enjoying promotion with (L-R) Paul Brush, Ray Stewart, Geoff Pike and Trevor Brooking, May 1981

quick. He used to wear so much oil on his hair that when he scored I didn't really want to cuddle him!
Warren Donald

Michael Jackson lookalike! On one occasion, after a youth team match, someone set light to his hair!
Alan Dickens

Digger permed his hair and applied so much oil and spray that it used to drip everywhere. He'd come to training with a towel around his neck to stop it dripping on his neck! We called him Soul Glow after the spray he used.
Everald La Ronde

He had a dodgy taste in music. He liked The Smiths if I remember rightly. We played a tournament in Japan and by the end of it we were all sick of The Smiths. Give me soul music anytime.
George Parris.

We played up at Newcastle United and Digger was getting so much racial abuse you could see it was starting to get to him. In the dressing room at half-time, the lads rallied around and made him captain for the second half. He was visibly lifted by the gesture. When we went back out, the lads deliberately held back and let him run out by himself to a torrent of abuse!

We were all pissing ourselves in the tunnel! Another time, we played together and it started raining. It turned the Soul Glow in his hair white. He looked like something out of the Wizard of Oz!
Greg Campbell

Digger Barnes

Back row: Morgan, Brush, McAlister, Martin, Parkes, Brooking, Bonds.

Middle row: Lampard, Cowie, Goddard, Devonshire, Stewart, Cross.

Front row: Pearson, Holland, Alen, Barnes, Pike, Neighbour.

CHAPTER EIGHT
1981-82

" I always talk more about what we can do to the opposition rather than what they can do to us." **John Lyall**

Belgian superstar Francois Van der Elst signed for the Hammers

Neil Orr joined from Morton

West Ham United returned to the top flight after a three year absence. They enjoyed a flying start and topped the table early on after a 4-0 thumping of Tottenham Hotspur at White Hart Lane. The players stretched their unbeaten run to 27 games, until tasting defeat at Aston Villa in the middle of October.

John Lyall signed 27-year-old Francois Van der Elst from New York Cosmos for £400,000 and 22-year-old utility player, Neil Orr, from Morton for £375,000. West Ham were also linked with Dundee's Paul Sturrock (£500,000), Ayr United's Steve Nicol (£250,000), and Derby County's Steve Buckley (£300,000). Early in the season the club pulled out of a race to sign Manchester United's Steve Coppell who was rated at £1m. Crystal Palace defender Jim Cannon was another to be considered but nothing materialised.

Six new apprentices joined the club – Tony Cottee, George Parris, Greg Campbell, Gerhardt Ampofo, Alan Dickens and Warren Donald. All played first team football for West Ham with the exception of Ampofo, whose career was cut short through injury.

For the first time since 1966, West Ham had four players selected for the England squad – Trevor Brooking, Alvin Martin, Paul Goddard and Alan Devonshire were all called up by Ron Greenwood. They emulated the history made by Geoff Hurst, Martin Peters, Bobby Moore and Johnny Byrne. High times for West Ham.

FA Cup winner and slayer of Spurs, David Cross decided to leave the club. John Lyall cannot hide his dismay: "I'm very disappointed David is going. He may not be the greatest player, but he scores goals."

The following Hammers made their debuts for the club: Tom McAlister, Francois Van der Elst, Neil Orr, George Cowie, Everald La Ronde and Ray Houghton

Here is their story...

44 – TOM McALISTER

"McAlister's late saves were spectacular. He's done exceptionally well for us and made key stops in many games. He certainly deserves a pat on the back."
John Lyall

Born: Clydebank, December 10, 1952 • **Position:** Goalkeeper • **Games played for West Ham United:** 100 (1981-88)

Debut: October 3, 1981 v Birmingham City (a) D 2-2 (Cross 2 – Langan, Dillon) Att: 22,290

Birmingham City: Wealands, Langan, Dennis, Dillon, Broadhurst, Todd, Brocken, Whatmore, Worthington, Gemmill, Van Mierlo*. Sub: Handyside*

West Ham United: McAlister, Stewart, Lampard, Bonds, Martin, Devonshire, Neighbour, Goddard, Cross, Brooking, Pike.

Thomas Gerald McAlister made exactly 100 appearances for West Ham United. The quiet Scot spent eight years at Upton Park, having had spells with Sheffield United, Rotherham United, Blackpool, Swindon Town and Bristol Rovers. He could so easily have been one of the famed 'Boys of 86,' during West Ham's greatest ever league campaign, but first team 'keeper, Phil Parkes, remained ever-present during that historic season.

To me, Tom McAlister will always be 'The one that got away.' Having searched high and low for him during the two years it has taken to research this book, he remains the 'lost man.' His former teammates are unaware of his whereabouts, his former clubs could offer no leads and I even employed the services of a genealogist, but without any success

Over the past five years I have tracked down and interviewed every first team Hammer between 1958 and 1989 – the Golden Age. That involved everyone who played with Bobby Moore and all who played for John Lyall. Those interviews, including the families of those Hammers who are sadly no longer with us, now reside in two books – my life's work. Tom McAlister thwarted my efforts to preserve his memories. He is my Scarlet Pimpernel, my Irene Adler, my Tom McAlister!

Following are photos from his time at West Ham along with recollections from his teammates:

If you wanted a dependable keeper who could play in the top division, then Tom McAlister would fit the bill. It was just bad luck that he happened to be at West Ham during the prime of Phil Parkes, the club's greatest ever goalkeeper. When Phil was injured and Tom deputised, he was outstanding and didn't let anyone down.
Mick McGiven

The last time I saw Tom was when I played with him in Graham Gooch's testimonial. Bobby Moore also played.
Paul Brush

I played a lot of games with Tom in the reserves. He was a good pro, with a good attitude, but just not in the same bracket as Phil Parkes.
Ray Houghton

We shared digs together and he was really great fun. He loved a good night out.
Greg Campbell

Tom was a lovely guy. We stayed in digs run by Mrs Cross in Barking Road. We had a good laugh together. I'd love to see him again.
Stuart Pearson

Tom signs for West Ham United, 1981

I played against Tom when I was at QPR and he was at Sheffield United. He was being touted as the next best thing and Scotland's next goalkeeper for many years to come. Sadly, a couple of bad injuries put paid to all that. John liked him and brought him in as my understudy when Bobby Ferguson was coming to the end of his time at the club.
Phil Parkes

The Christmas Party L-R Parkes, Bonds, Neighbour, McAlister and Pike. Notice young Frank Lampard at the front with a toy gun

Under the watchful gaze of Billy Bonds

45 – FRANCOIS VAN DER ELST

"You just knew something special had turned up when he arrived."
Greg Campbell

Born: December 1, 1954, Opwijk, Belgium • **Died:** January 11, 2017, Aalst, Belgium • **Position:** Right-wing • **Goals:** 17

Games played for West Ham United: 70 (1982-83) • **Debut:** January 16, 1982 v Brighton & Hove Albion (a) L 0-1 (Ritchie) Att: 22,591

Brighton & Hove Albion: Moseley, Shanks, Nelson, Grealish, Foster, Gatting, Ryan, Ritchie, Smith, McNab, Thomas.

West Ham United: Parkes, Stewart, Lampard, Bonds, Martin, Devonshire,* Neighbour, Goddard, Cross, Brooking, Pike. Sub: **Van der Elst***

Francois 'Swat' Van der Elst tragically passed away on January 11, 2017. He was 62. He had suffered a heart attack on New Year's Eve but lost his battle for life 12 days later. Over 1000 people attended his funeral, including a West Ham United contingent. He was described as 'Mister Europe.'

Van der Elst was signed from New York Cosmos in January, 1982 for £400,000. He spent 16 months at West Ham United and his affection for the club lasted a lifetime. He returned to Upton Park on many occasions and he occasionally brought along his beloved grandson, Yarne.

Swat was well known to West Ham United supporters prior to him joining the club. Many had seen him, and his Anderlecht teammate, Rob Rensenbrink, dismantle their team in the second half of the 1976 European Cup Winners' Cup final.

Sadly, that scintillating form was not reproduced by Swat in the West Ham United shirt. However, he did plenty to endear himself to the fans – scoring at both White Hart Lane and Highbury, claiming a hat-trick at Notts County and finding the net on four consecutive winning occasions, which took the Hammers up to second place in the league, in October 1982.

He remains the only Hammer to have gained a cap for Belgium. Of his 44 International caps for his country, eight of them were gained whilst at Upton Park.

Following are photos and memories of Swat from those who remember one of Belgium's finest ever players:

Swat was a very simple man who didn't want to be in the spotlight. He loved to talk about his memories with his friends while he smoked a cigarette and drunk a Carlsberg. I knew Swat from Anderlecht and regularly visited his snooker club. His son was one of my good friends before he died and I went to kindergarten with his daughter. Swat was an honorary member of our supporters club.
Kevin Jacobs (President of The Purple Stars, Opwijk)

Francois looked after all the lads when we played pre-season in Belgium. He was treated like a king wherever he went. He laid on a barbeque at his house. He loved a cigarette and a Gin & Tonic.
Bobby Barnes

Later in life, Frank travelled over from Belgium to watch West Ham. He was giving an interview outside the ground for Belgian TV when he spotted me, stopped the interview, and gave me a big hug.
Eddie Gillam

I got on well with him. I called him 'Swat' because everyone else knew him by that name.
Rob Jenkins

Celebrating his first goals for the Hammers, against Stoke City, February 1982

Scoring against Arsenal, May 1983

Scoring at Spurs, November 1982

Franky had been a superstar at Anderlecht and played with Beckenbauer and other greats at New York Cosmos. Like most truly great players, he was a really lovely guy and very modest. I was often in Francois' company out in Brentwood and we'd enjoy a drink together. He liked a Gin and Tonic and a cigarette. I was so shocked and upset to hear that he'd passed away.
George Cowie

It is fair to say that his prime was behind him by the time he joined West Ham. He never really fitted in. He had been a fantastic, attacking goalscorer, with great skill, but it didn't work for him at West Ham. He would make one or two runs but if he didn't receive the ball that was him finished! His pace was gone and he lacked stamina. I remember we went up to Liverpool, which was always difficult, and we really needed him to be on the boil but he just didn't perform.
Mick McGiven

I'll never forget that he was in the line-up for my debut. I have a photo at home of the goal I scored on my debut and Franky is in the background.
Alan Dickens

You just knew something special had turned up when he arrived.
Greg Campbell

46 – NEIL ORR

"I enjoyed a good rapport with John and we discussed our respective Scottish heritages. John felt that a good football team needed two or three Scotsmen in the side. I called him Mr Lyall first of all, to which he replied: "My name's John. Call me John."

MANCHESTER UNITED v WEST HAM UNITED
WEDNESDAY 27th JANUARY 1982
Kick-off 7.30 p.m.

TICKET & MATCH INFORMATION

Born: Greenock, Scotland, May 13, 1959 • **Position:** Defender/Midfield • **Games played for West Ham United:** 175 (1982-1987)

Goals scored for West Ham United: 5 • **Honours under John Lyall:** 1985-86 Member of West Ham United's highest finishing league team (third) • **Debut:** January 27, 1982 v Manchester United (a) L 0-1 (Macari) Att: 41,291

Manchester United: Bailey, Duxbury, Albiston, Wilkins, Moran, McQueen, Robson, Birtles, Stapleton, Macari, Coppell.

West Ham United: Parkes, Brush, Lampard*, Bonds, Martin, **Orr,** Van Der Elst, Stewart, Cross, Brooking, Pike. Sub: Goddard.

Neil Ian Orr was the son of Tommy Orr, the Morton legend and Scottish International. Sadly, Neil's father passed away when he was just 13-years-old and he was raised by his mother, Ishbel, in the family home at Craigmuschat Road in Gourock, Inverclyde.

In 1975, Neil signed schoolboy forms for Morton, where he spent seven years, making 196 appearances

John Lyall paid Morton a fee of £400,000 to bring Orr to West Ham United. Neil reflects amusingly on the impetus behind the transfer: *"John always told me that he signed me to replace Billy Bonds who was 35-years-old when I joined. The irony of course was that Billy was still playing after I left the club in 1987!"*

Neil's time at Upton Park was his only experience of football south of the Scottish border and he returned to his homeland in 1987, where he played out his career at Hibernian, St Mirren and Queen of the South.

Today, Neil works in Australia as a technical director for Valentine FC, a National Premier League club. *"I also work for ex-Hammer, George Cowie, out here. George is the Oceana Director for West Ham United, while I run a football clinic twice-a-week in New South Wales. I pass on my recommendations to George. I must say that I still apply several of John Lyall's training techniques so, even today, there is a little bit of the Lyall influence having a positive role to play in Australian football. One example is that I try and*

In the snow with fellow Scot, Ray Stewart

Celebrating with John

encourage the kids to see things quickly and play the ball early."

In May 2016, Neil returned to the East End to attend the last ever match at Upton Park where he caught up with fellow Scot, Sandy Clark. "Beating Manchester United in an entertaining match was the best sign-off anyone could have wished for."

Despite living 9,000 miles away, Neil was very generous with his time and recollections of John:

I first met John when I was on Scotland Under-21s duty. I was playing for Morton at the time. Both John and Eddie Baily had travelled up to watch Ray Stewart - I used to play with Ray in the Under-21s and against him when he was at Dundee United. From that moment John kept an eye on me.

The transfer to West Ham United came completely out of the blue. It had been a particularly bad winter in Scotland which blighted the fixture list. We eventually played a game against Kilmarnock one Friday night. The following morning, my manager at Morton, Benny Rooney, called me up and said that a potential move was on the cards. I knew it was important because Benny called me at home, which was very unusual. When I got to the ground I was told that John Lyall and Eddie Baily were coming up to talk with me. As it turned out, they got delayed in London because of the weather and I ended up going to the Excelsior hotel at Glasgow airport to meet them. There were no agents in those days but the proposition was straight forward - deciding between playing full-time at West Ham United or part-time at Morton. It was very clear cut and the decision was an easy one for me to make. John told me the terms and what they were going to offer me and I signed there and then. The following day I was in London and starting my time as a West Ham United player so it really was a whirlwind transfer.

On the flight down, I was reading the newspaper and there was speculation that Southampton, Aston Villa and Nottingham Forest were also interested in me. John and Eddie were reading the same article knowing that the deal had already been done! John didn't like to get into bidding wars with other clubs and preferred the personal approach. Back then, the club was the dominant influence in any transfer, whereas now it is the player. Just like Phil Parkes and Paul Goddard before me, John made the offer and the player had a decision to make.

The culture at West Ham was a world apart from Morton where, as a part-timer, I only trained two-nights-a-week.

In London, the weather was too bad to train outside and there is a photo of me and Ray Stewart in a sleigh at Chadwell Heath. So, in the early weeks we did all our training indoors.

My first involvement with the first team, came in a match at Brighton & Hove Albion in January 1982. John sometimes watched the match from the stands, so he put me on the bench even though I wasn't playing, just to get a feel for the experience. Frank Lampard snr got sent off early in the game and the next minute John appeared and asked me to sit in his seat in the main stand. He wanted to direct things from the bench with Mick McGiven and Ronnie Boyce. So I went upstairs and sat next to Ron Greenwood, who was England manager at the time. He was oblivious to my presence at first and was talking to me as if I was still John! When he saw me he said: "You're the new boy Orr, aren't you?" I thought that was really impressive.

I made my debut up at Old Trafford, which was a bit of a baptism of fire. John was very calm and encouraged me to go out and play my game. It was a great experience for me even though fellow Scot, Lou Macari, scored United's winning goal late on. Their strike force that day was Gary Birtles and Frank Stapleton, who were both big signings at the time. I felt I did okay and remember Phil Parkes having an exceptional game.

I'm no different to most other West Ham players in thinking that Bonzo, Dev and Trev were the three best footballers at the club. But please don't ask me to pick an order!

I picked up a niggling hamstring injury which meant I missed pre-season training and ended up playing only nine league games the following year. Most of those were from the sub's bench and it affected my psychology. I began picking up little injuries and started trying to avoid situations where that might happen. Instead of trusting my pace, I guess I started cutting corners and keeping away from having to sprint, in fear of damaging my hamstring. Consequently, I wasn't as influential in matches as I should have been.

I started off in central-defence but there was fierce competition with Billy Bonds, Alvin Martin, Gary Strodder and Joe Gallagher so John moved me into midfield. He wanted me to get more involved in the game. I'd seen how Billy liked to charge forward and I think John wanted me to do the same

The joy of scoring for West Ham United

so it was a bit of an experiment. I was familiar with the position because I'd played there for a couple of seasons at Morton.

I enjoyed a good rapport with John and we discussed our respective Scottish heritages. John felt that a good football team needed two or three Scotsmen in the side. At the time Liverpool had Graeme Souness, Alan Hansen and Kenny Dalglish. Nottingham Forest had John McGovern and John Robertson, while Manchester United had Joe Jordan, Gordon McQueen and Lou Macari. John admired Scottish players and had signed quite a few in Ray Stewart, George Cowie, Sandy Clark, Tommy McQueen and, of course, Frank McAvennie.

West Ham had a bit of a reputation for being 'Southern softies' and John was keen to address that. I must say that while I was at the club I didn't feel we were out-muscled or a soft-touch in any game, especially during that 1985-86 season. We were turning up for games feeling confident and believing we could win every match. People often say that the home defeat against Chelsea that season ultimately cost us the title. I made a big mistake which allowed Nigel Spackman to score. To lose that game 1-2 having been ahead 1-0 was a big blow and some of the fans got on my back after that, but, at the end of the day, we lost the league by four points and not the three we should have taken from that game.

After that, I started to pick up injury after injury and John then brought in Stewart Robson and Liam Brady. The club did offer me another one-year contract but I felt my opportunities were becoming limited and that it was probably time for a move. Hibernian came in for me so I ended going back to Scotland. I left on good terms with John and actually trained with the boys a few times when I came back down to sell my house.

I was really surprised when the club sacked John but I was even more shocked when they brought in Lou Macari - somebody from outside of the club. I don't know if West Ham saw it as a bold move or wanted to send out a message that West Ham were moving in a different direction. It clearly didn't work and they quickly got back on track by appointing Billy Bonds.

John was a lovely football man who created a proper family feeling at West Ham United. Everyone felt part of it and contributed to it. He was approachable, knowledgeable and concerned about each and every one of his players and staff.
Neil Orr

Honest, hard-working and versatile. Neil gave you everything he had. I preferred him as a defender but he did play midfield for us, too.
Mick McGiven

I liked Neil and got on well with him. He spent a lot of time in the treatment room with Rob Jenkins.
Alan Dickens

Neil loved tackling players. We used to say he liked to give the ball away so he could tackle someone else! He was so fit that he was one of the first to think he could take on Billy Bonds at running. I think he stayed close for the first 20 minutes and then Bill just cruised away from him. He is another one who got into coaching because of John's influence.
Paul Brush

How's your hamstring Neil?
Greg Campbell

Prior to the last ever match at the Boleyn Ground, May 2016

47 – GEORGE COWIE

"John had a lot of charisma and set the standard for decency, respect, trust and honesty. I coach a lot in Australia these days and when I am talking in the dressing room at half-time, I can still hear the words of John Lyall from when I was a young lad."

Born: Buckie, Scotland, May 9, 1961 • **Position:** Midfield • **Games played for West Ham United:** 9 (1982-83)

Debut: April 13, 1982 v Ipswich Town (a) L 2-3 (Cross 2 – Brazil, Wark (pen), Osman)

Ipswich Town: Cooper, Burley, McCall, Mills, Osman, Butcher, Wark, Muhren, Mariner, Brazil, Gates.

West Ham United: Parkes, Stewart, Allen, Orr, Martin, Devonshire, Van der Elst, Goddard, Cross, Brooking, Neighbour.* Sub: **Cowie**

Alexander George Cowie was born to parents James and Nancy and grew up in Buckie on Scotland's Moray Firth coast. Despite playing only a handful of first team matches for West Ham United, the experience has served him well in a long coaching career which continues to this day: *"I've spent 20 years in Australia and have been a full-time coach for much of that time. I actually managed the Solomon Islands for over three years and became the technical director of Queensland for another three years. I also had a spell at Papua New Guinea."*

His six years at Upton Park have left a long standing affection for the club and former teammates: *"I arrange football tours to the UK and I've seen quite a bit of Patsy Holland and Trevor Brooking. Trevor played in my testimonial match between Hearts and Dunfermline many moons ago. I try and catch up with Sandy Clark and Ray Stewart when I'm back in Scotland. Neil Orr works on the West Ham programme out here and, for the past five years, I've been running football camps for West Ham United in both Australia and New Zealand."*

George visited these shores in October 2017 and watched his first match at the London Stadium – a 1-0 victory over Swansea City. He is always keen to meet up with any Hammers from that era.

I was just a young kid when I first met John Lyall. I had a trial

George in his Scotland youth shirt, 1978

George in the youth team - Back row, second left

when I was 15 and signed apprentice forms when I was 16. I had five years training with the first team before making my debut in 1982.

I have a couple of stand-out memories with John, which probably differ a bit from the experiences of the more senior players at that time. The first occurred just two weeks after I joined the club. My mum and dad came down to see me, to check that I was okay. Ron Greenwood and John Lyall took them out to lunch in a restaurant in Barking. It was a Friday afternoon and, with a match the following day, Ron and John would have had plenty to do but they spent over two hours with my parents. My dad was a fisherman in the north of Scotland and John's father was from the Outer Hebrides. They spoke more about the fishing industry in Scotland than they did about football. They were so impressed and knew I was being looked after by very good people. They went back to Scotland with total peace of mind.

The other memory also came very early on during my time at West Ham. I was feeling quite homesick and knew I'd have to ask John for his permission to go back home to Scotland. We were playing Brighton in an FA Youth Cup match which we ended up losing. John came into the dressing room afterwards and gave us all a rollicking. I couldn't sleep at all that night. After

training at Chadwell Heath, I took the bus to Upton Park to see John. I was really nervous and was seriously thinking of pacing it all in and going back home to Scotland for good. I knocked on his door and he invited me in. He got me some tea and biscuits and I started to tell him how I was feeling. He spent two hours with me and removed all my worries. In many respects that conversation changed my life. Without it, I might not have played for West Ham, Hearts or pursued a career in coaching.

The players were so good to me. I felt I was in a dream. Pop Robson and Trevor Brooking invited me to play golf with them at Chigwell which was a fantastic experience for a 16-year-old. When I got my first car – a second-hand white Ford Cortina Mark III – I'd pick up Phil Parkes, Alan Devonshire and Paul Goddard at Barking station. I was a young pro at the club but did that for two years. It was brilliant to start my day with those guys.

I only played nine games for West Ham but I was lucky because my dad came down to see me play against Spurs and Manchester United over a three day period. We drew both games so he went home very happy. I also played in a League Cup quarter-final against Liverpool up at Anfield which I'll never forget, even though we lost 1-2. I liked playing in midfield and felt I could pass well and was good in the tackle. Mick McGiven played me as a sweeper in the reserves and John put me in at right-back for a few games.

I have adopted a lot of John Lyall's training techniques which I use at the West Ham football camps in Australia. John kept things very straight forward. Everything was uncomplicated and simple to follow. The basics were so very important to John – first touch, passing, shooting, scoring and so forth. It was absolutely paramount that these were mastered.

I was a bit disappointed not to be in the full squad for the FA Cup final. Nicky Morgan, Dale Banton and myself had been in the 18-man squad for most games that season. For some reason this was reduced to a 15-man squad for the final. Of course, we were not in the reckoning to play, but it would have been great to have been in the full squad for the experience. I've never known why it was reduced to 15 because most FA Cup final teams took 18-man squads to Wembley. Curiously, a couple of months later, John took an 18-man squad to Wembley for the FA Charity Shield. Nicky Morgan was actually named amongst the substitutes and played but I sat on the bench as a squad member.

I ended up leaving West Ham in 1983 when I was only 22-years-old. John had offered me another year but I was impatient to play regular first team football and Rangers wanted to take a look at me. It wasn't about money or the terms of the contract. I simply wanted to play. I ended up signing for Hearts but I've often wondered what might have happened if I'd stayed at West Ham because, shortly after I left, Patsy Holland, Frank Lampard and Trevor Brooking all retired.

I wish I'd played more games under John, but I'm so thankful to have spent six years at the club.

George Cowie

George was a very good runner. There were four of us who would generally finish ahead of everyone else in the cross country runs. Billy Bonds was streets ahead of us all but George Cowie, Tony Cottee and I would have some good battles to finish second.

Ray Houghton

He was the noisy Jock in the corner!
Greg Campbell

George and Paul Allen were the England Under-18 captains, which was an achievement the club was very proud of. George was a high energy, high octane player but, sadly, another midfielder at West Ham so was up against it given the rich seam of talent at that time.

Mick McGiven

George is a well-respected coach in Australia and it's great to work for him given our roots in West Ham United's history.
Neil Orr

Chairman Reg Pratt enjoying an historic moment at West Ham United. Paul Allen and George Cowie are youth captains of England and Scotland

George Cowie at The London Stadium, September 2017

48 – EVERALD LA RONDE

"John lived for football and there wasn't anything he didn't know about the game. A well-loved football great."

Born: January 24 1963, Plaistow, London • **Position:** Left-back • **Games played for West Ham United:** 7 (1982)

Honours: 1981 FA Youth Cup winner (Captain) • **Debut:** April 17, 1982 v Coventry City (a) L 0-1 (Hateley) Att: 13,466

Coventry City: Sealey, Thomas, Roberts, Butterworth, Dyson, Gillespie, Whitton*, Jacobs, Hateley, Thompson, Hunt. Sub: Homantschk.*

West Ham United: Parkes, Stewart, Cowie, Orr, Martin*, Devonshire, Van Der Elst, Goddard, Cross, Brooking, Allen. Sub: La Ronde.*

Everald La Ronde was one of five sons born to Peter and Daphne. His father was of Dominican Republic descent and worked at Fords of Dagenham, while his mother was a matron.

Born in Plaistow in 1963, a year before West Ham United won their first ever FA Cup, La Ronde lived at 36 Chesterton Road before moving to 36 Chester Road in East Ham.

Having shown great promise, when captaining West Ham United to only their second ever FA Youth Cup final victory - over Tottenham Hotspur in 1981, La Ronde left the club barely one year later. Sadly, his football career was cruelly cut short by injury and, after brief spells at both A.F.C. Bournemouth and Peterborough United, he retired from playing in 1985.

Subsequently, Everald worked as a Security co-ordinator at Canary Wharf for 21-years but was made redundant in 2010: *"I now work as a supervisor at Forest Environmental, which specialises in asbestos removal. I'm married to Michelle and have two children, Theo Everald La Ronde and Mia Nicole La Ronde. I'm a big fan of tennis and golf but rarely get time to play."*

Like all good captains, Everald keeps in touch with his former teammates and organises the occasional reunion. The Gaucho restaurant in Canary Wharf is usually the venue of choice.

Everald attended the last ever match at The Boleyn Ground and is always generous with his time to discuss West Ham matters:

A scout by the name of Dave Wally spotted me playing district football. Playing at that level placed you in the upper echelons of schoolboy football. I played for Newham and we won the Schools Trophy in 1978 which hadn't been done for ages. Kevin Hitchcock played in that side and so did Jermain Defoe's father, Jimmy. Another team member called Dave Martin also went to West Ham United as a schoolboy but, sadly for him, got involved in some crowd violence at a West Ham match and John saw him get ejected from the ground. He was released soon after that.

I was asked to train at the ground on Tuesday and Thursday evenings. Bill Lansdowne snr and Ronnie Boyce took the sessions. I was first coached by Tony Carr and, in 1981, we lifted the South East Counties Trophy and the FA Youth Cup. The main man that we all talked to was Eddie Baily. He was a funny guy, he'd come and watch us play at Chadwell Heath and when you were about to take a corner he'd urge you to use your other foot. He liked to take a player out of his comfort zone and believed it improved their ability. John Lyall watched a lot of the youth team's matches. He liked to keep in touch with the talent that was coming through.

The club signed my brother, Tony, on pro forms, too. He was a left-midfielder but picked up an injury and had to have an operation on a trapped nerve in his foot. He lost a bit of interest after that. He was a year older than me but we had always played together in the same team as youngsters.

I started training with the first team and can only describe

They Played For John Lyall – The West Ham Years

the experience in a single word: "Frightening!" The senior pros were very good to the youngsters. Trevor Brooking often gave little snippets of advice and Billy Bonds was our great protector on the pitch. John was the father figure behind all this and his office door was always open to discuss any issues. He was always concerned about my wellbeing both on and off the pitch. He was very good with advice, very articulate.

My actual debut came at Coventry City. I thought I might have got my chance a bit earlier up at Molineux because there was an article in the press saying: "Lyall throws kid to the Wolves." Unfortunately, I didn't even travel up for that one. John then put me on the bench for a visit to Ipswich Town but, once again, I didn't play. However, those experiences with the first team helped settle my nerves.

A week later I was on the bench up at Highfield Road. Alvin Martin had injured his collar-bone playing for England a few weeks earlier and aggravated it again so I replaced him at half-time. One of the first things I did was lunge, in vain, to prevent Mark Hateley from scoring the only goal of the game! It actually came off my foot and hit the roof of the net. It wasn't given as an own goal but I certainly touched it before it went in. I was playing centre-half which wasn't my preferred position but I won my first header and our fans got behind me then which eased me into the match.

My home debut, against Leeds United, was a bit special. I walked to the ground from my home in East Ham. I had my boots in my hand and all the fans were completely oblivious as to who I was, and yet I was fully aware that I'd be crossing that white line wearing the claret and blue shirt. The memory still gives me goose bumps now. It was a thrilling game and we beat a very good Leeds United team 4-3.

I would say I was a steady player with a lot of pace, which helped. The best player I marked in my career was Steve Coppell of Manchester United. He made so much space for himself, had a brilliant first touch and was so quick it was very difficult to play against him.

In the early 1980s, John joined the youth team on a pre-season tour to Holland. It is one of my earliest memories of him. We played in the ADO tournament out there and usually won it. On this occasion, John told us to just do the things which come naturally which was quite ironic because on the first night I snuck out the window with a couple of others and had a night out! When we climbed back through that same window in the early hours of the morning John was sitting on a stool in the bar waiting for us! I certainly found out that night how an angry John Lyall behaved! After being severely reprimanded he said that he wanted to see a good performance from us the next day. Thankfully, we went on to win the tournament. John was very fair and honest but very strict and it was best not to get on his wrong side.

John was very much an old school manager, in that he

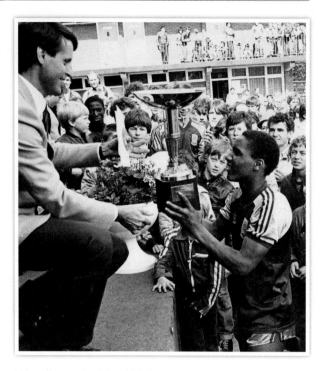

Winning captain of the ADO Tournament Trophy in 1981

stuck by the senior pros. Billy Bonds played into his 40s while Frank Lampard and Trevor Brooking were well into their 30s before hanging up their boots. Today, you don't see that so much in the top flight - 28 is considered old. It was tough for a lot of the youth team and reserve team players to see where an opportunity was going to arise. That's why John released Ray Houghton. 'Scotty,' as we all called him, had the likes of Alan Devonshire, Geoff Pike, Pat Holland, Jimmy Neighbour, Paul Allen and Trevor Brooking, all ahead of him for those midfield shirts. John knew it would be a long time before Ray established himself at West Ham so, instead, advised him to take a different route into football. As we all know, that was the right decision for Ray, who went right to the top.

John didn't over complicate things and used phrases that were easily understood: "It's another winger against another full-back and I'd put my money on you," he'd say. When he talked about team tactics there was a lot more depth and thoroughness. He did his homework and his coaching staff all fed into that. He knew exactly how the opposition was going to play. That approach really worked for me because I felt I was being managed by a man who really knew his stuff, who kept it straightforward and made me feel both confident and capable.

In the dressing room he was very calm most of the time, so long as you were doing what he'd asked you to do. He'd explain things slowly and clearly and go around having one-on-ones with different players. Generally, he delivered what he and his staff had worked hard to put together at the training ground. He expected his players to execute his plan and get something positive from the hard work we had all put in.

I did get fined by John once. He docked me a week's wages after he felt I had let the club down during a trip to Switzerland. We were playing in two tournaments, one in the valley and one in the mountains. The night before driving up the mountain for the second tournament, I was given the responsibility of making sure all the youth players were back at the hotel and ready to leave first thing in the morning. As the senior player, I made sure this happened. However, I didn't bother going back myself! I eventually returned in the morning and, as I turned the corner, all the players were on the hotel balcony applauding my return! I thought it was amusing, but Mick McGiven and Tony Carr took a dim view of it and included it in their report. John fined me a week's wages. I felt hard done by because I had fulfilled my responsibility of getting the younger lads back to the hotel in time.

It usually took an injury or a series of injuries before John selected the youngsters for a first team outing. Paul Allen only got his chance because Pat Holland had broken his leg and Geoff Pike had a long term injury, too. It seemed to improve when Academy boys such as Tony Cottee, Alan Dickens, George Parris and Steve Potts were given a good run in the side at a young age.

John did say something nice about me which I have always remembered. After the seven appearances I played in the first team, I needed an operation on my stomach because I'd torn a muscle. The surgeon told me that I must be a very valuable young man because John had instructed him to ensure I was looked after and returned in perfect shape. That was a nice sentiment.

The culture at West Ham United was terrific. I had such a good group of friends and some of them would crash at my mum and dad's house for the night. Sometimes as many as eight would stay over, especially during the victorious FA Youth Cup run in 1981. After cleaning the boots and washing the van we'd all head back there to play cards and listen to music. There was Johnny Vaughan, Chris Ampofo and his brother Gerhardt, Mark Schiavi, Warren Donald, Keith McPherson, and Adrian Keith. Only the local lads like Robert Wall and Wayne Reader didn't stay over.

There were some real characters at the club. Ernie Gregory was in charge of us for a youth game at Oxford United. His team talk was: "Just make sure you all kick the same way." He was so funny Ernie. He'd take the kid's training session whilst sitting in a deck chair with his shirt off, slapping on the sun cream!

Once, we trained on Christmas Day and it had snowed heavily. John had us practicing diving headers in the snow. It was typical of a Scotsman as well, because he made sure we wore shorts and flimsy shirts, even though the temperature was well below freezing. His sessions had so much variety and some of his ideas around fitness were a bit unorthodox. He introduced silver space suits for us to wear during pre-season training to sweat off the extra pounds. We were fined £1 for every pound overweight. Ernie weighed us every Monday and John handed out the silver foil suit to anyone who was over their target weight. Phil Parkes was never out of that suit! Frank Lampard volunteered to wear one anyway. He liked to maximize the benefit of training.

I'd been to the 1975 FA Cup final as a West Ham fan and it was a very special moment when John included me in the 25 man squad for the 1980 FA Cup final. It meant I sat with a few of the youth team lads and watched us beat Arsenal. I sat next to Dale Banton. It was a very special day.

I never went to John's house or any social events with him, but there was one encounter which was purely coincidental. The summer of 1981, before pre-season training, I went to Marbella for a break. Incredibly, I bumped into John, and his son Murray, on the beach. He thought it was commendable that I'd flown over there by myself. I'd told him I had nothing to do at home and a friend had an apartment so I decided to

In action during the 1981-82 season

book a flight. He invited me to visit their apartment and we all enjoyed a memorable lunch together.

My time at West Ham came to an end quite abruptly. John called me into his office with about five minutes to go on transfer deadline day. Harry Redknapp, who was manager at Bournemouth, had come in for me. Frank Lampard was Harry's brother-in-law and had an interest in seeing me leave West Ham because I had just broken through into Frank's left-back position. John made it clear that he'd prefer me to stay at the club. However, I'd made the decision to leave as I felt it would be in my best interest to get regular football elsewhere, a bit like Ray Houghton. It was very close to deadline so I was under a lot of pressure to make a hasty decision. With hindsight it was one of the worst decisions I've ever made in my life. I should have stayed, because after a couple of months at Bournemouth, I broke my leg.

It was like a time warp at Bournemouth. The equipment was from pre-war days and I had two straightforward injuries handled terribly. My broken leg had to be re set and my hernia was left so long that gangrene set in. It was a forgettable two years because I didn't play for half of it so John's words about keeping me at West Ham still ring in my ears today.

There was no comparison between Harry Redknapp and John Lyall. John was an excellent coach and an excellent manager while Harry was an excellent coach and a terrible manager. He was very raw and his man management skills were awful. Obviously, he has gone on to become a very good manager in the eyes of many.

I didn't find out that John had died for about a year after it happened. I was out of the country and nobody had been in touch. It wasn't until a charity golf day a year later, when I'd bumped into Murray, that the news was shared with me. I was in a state of shock and we stayed up late talking about John and reminisced about the day we had shared in Marbella all those years ago.
Everald La Ronde

Everald's teammates had the following memories:

Both Ev and his brother, Tony, were hilarious. Physically they were very imposing and had these huge legs. They were really nice lads and I got on well with both of them.
Ray Houghton

I thought he was unlucky because he had a great opportunity, having been the winning captain of the successful 1981 youth team. He is a very intelligent guy and technically he was good so I don't really know why it didn't work out for him.
Paul Brush

I saw Ev at the final match at Upton Park. He is a good

organiser and keeps a lot of the players from that era in touch with each other.
Warren Donald

We still keep in touch and it's always great to see him.
George Parris

I remember watching him mark Manchester United's Steve Coppell out of the game.
Bobby Barnes

Ev was my youth team captain so I've always respected him.
Alan Dickens

He was very good to me at West Ham. He lived around the corner and we'd go to his house and listen to vinyl records. Ev liked George Benson and Bobby Womack.
Keith McPherson

When I got my first car - a Regency Green, 2 litre Ford Capri, with a vinyl roof – I'd drive over to Ev's house and we'd have a lot of fun.
Dale Banton

Everald and his brother Tony were probably my best friends at West Ham. Ev and I lived together in Bournemouth when we both played down there. None of my stories about Ev are printable!
Phil Brignull

Ev's final visit to Upton Park, May 2016

49 – RAY HOUGHTON

"I was sitting in John's office, waiting for the moment when I could negotiate a better deal, but I quickly realised that his words didn't quite conform to what I was expecting. I was being released!"

Born: Glasgow, Scotland, January 9, 1962 • **Position:** Midfield • **Games played for West Ham United:** 1 (1981-82)

Debut: May 1, 1982 v Arsenal (a) L 0-2 (Rix, Sunderland) Att: 34,977

Arsenal: Wood, Hollins, Sansom, Talbot, O'Leary, Whyte, Hawley, Sunderland, Davis, Robson, Rix.

West Ham United: Parkes, Stewart, La Ronde, Allen, Orr, Devonshire, Van Der Elst, Cowie*, Cross, Brooking, Pike. **Sub:** Houghton.*

Raymond James Houghton played just fifteen minutes of first team football in the West Ham United shirt and is the great, 'What might have been,' conundrum in the club's history. With the exception of Paul Ince, Houghton is the most decorated player to graduate from the West Ham United Academy during the John Lyall era. Sadly, for the claret and blue faithful, it was Oxford United, Liverpool and Aston Villa who benefitted most from his talents. They have the silverware to prove it.

On the surface, the decision to release Houghton in 1982, at just 20-years-of-age, appears to stand out as John Lyall's most lamentable decision. However, the recollections of both Ray, and his former playing colleagues, help to confirm there was method in the perceived madness.

Nowadays, Ray is a well-respected voice of radio and TV and works for Talk Sport, RTE Sport and SKY Sports. Two of his six goals for the Republic of Ireland have ensured his immortality in the annals of Irish football – the first against England in the 1988 European Championships and the second - against Italy in the 1994 World Cup. On both occasions they were the all-important only goal of the game.

Such a remarkable playing career away from Upton Park has not caused Ray's memory of his time at West Ham United to fade in any degree at all:

I have a very good impression of John Lyall because he gave me my first opportunity to become a professional footballer. I'd played for Islington Boys, and also at Arsenal as a kid, before trialling at Queens Park Rangers, but opportunity just seemed to dry up. I thought my chance had gone. Then, in 1979, when I was just 17-years-old, I got a chance at West Ham United. A scout called Bruce McClelland, who we knew as 'Mac,' asked a good friend of mine, Dennis Phillips, if he knew of any other talented footballers. Dennis mentioned me, so, I too went along to Upton Park to train on Tuesday and Thursday evenings. I did well enough for John Lyall to offer me a one year deal.

My mum, Rita, had passed away just a year before I joined West Ham so my dad, Seamus, took me to West Ham along with all the other families of the young boys who had been offered professional forms. We were all gathered there when, all of a sudden, in walked John Lyall. He came over to me and my dad and said congratulations and well done. That was my first look at John as a manager.

Tony Carr trained the youth team, usually at the ground on the forecourt or in the gym. I was still working as a shipping clerk for Justerini and Brooks, organising the shipping of whisky all over America.

One of the great things about John was just how hands on he was as a coach. You don't see it happening that often in today's game and even the greats like Alex Ferguson weren't as hands on as John. Managers tended to delegate others to

Bottom row, far right - Ray after winning the ADO tournament in Holland, 1981

run their coaching sessions, but John loved the coaching side of it and enjoyed taking those sessions, whether they were for the youth team, reserves or first team. That was one of his great traits as a manager.

Some managers are good coaches, while others are good man managers, but John was both. That is very rare and something I thought was exceptional. He was supported by some highly competent coaches in Tony Carr with the youth team and Ronnie Boyce and Mick McGiven with the reserves and first team. I certainly wasn't expecting to see John at our coaching sessions but he would discuss the strengths and weaknesses of a youth team player with just the same level of professionalism as he would with a first team player. Who wouldn't want to run through walls for a man like that? I thought that was great because, as a player, I wanted to impress the manager. It wasn't something I witnessed anywhere else in my playing career.

I think John liked my hard work and good attitude. I loved training and was hungry to learn. I remember my first training session with the first team. One minute I was on the ball and the next minute I was doing a 360 degree turn in the air after a tackle from Billy Bonds! Every experience, good or bad,

was a great learning curve because, to me, Billy exemplified everything I loved about footballers – He was hard working, no nonsense, and someone who typified everything good about the club.

John's training sessions were without doubt the most challenging I experienced throughout my 20 years as a footballer. He knew football inside out and liked the physical side of the game a lot more than people talk about. If a player pulled out of a tackle he would let them know about it in no uncertain terms. Even now, if I close my eyes, I can see him waving his fist in the air with his face grimacing, telling me to get stuck in and win that ball. It's totally the opposite today, with players preferring to jump out of the way of things.

John had a vision of how the game should be played and he was ruthless in his pursuit of ensuring each player performed in the way he needed them to. Only then could he ensure that his vision became a reality. You only have to look at Trevor Brooking and Alan Devonshire to see how good he was at bringing the best out of a player.

As a youth player I had various duties to perform, like collecting the kit after a match for cleaning. I'd often be outside the changing room, listening to John, and if the first team had

Why Scotty got a "free"

THE success "Scotty" Houghton is currently enjoying with Fulham, whom he joined on a free transfer from Hammers last summer, does not surprise West Ham chief John Lyall.

The young Scot's starring role in the Cottagers' splendid 4-1 win over Newcastle — Kevin Keegan and all — at St. James's Park last Saturday was highlighted in Sunday's Big Match TV screening. Houghton had a part in the first two goals and then fired a spectacular third as Fulham went in three nil up.

Ray has a lot of ability and we youngsters like Alan Dickens and Warren Donald who needed opportunity to progress.

"Even so, we told Ray we would be very happy for him to stay on with us if he could not get another club," reveals Hammers manager.

Leading reserve team goalscorer last season with 13 goals, Ray's sole taste of first-team action came when he went o as sub late in the league gam at Highbury last May.

"At the end of the day you hav to make these kind c decisions . . . Phil Brignul Billy Landsdowne and Da Banton are other players wh have made similar recei moves to get the regular firs team football they deser with other clubs," points o John.

---

lost particularly badly he would hold nothing back in explaining in some detail why it hadn't worked, why it was unacceptable and what was needed to be done to fix it. I soon learned that if you had honesty, effort and a good attitude – the three by-words of most football clubs – then you would be alright.

John always wanted to see determination and desire and more often than not he received that from his players. Every training session was geared towards that and every day you were expected to perform. There was never any cutting of corners or shortcuts. John had established a culture of hard work, with an emphasis on improving his players and ensuring that those improvements benefited the team as a whole. He wasn't stupid either. He knew he wasn't going to get Trevor to work as hard as Billy, because that would have been both ridiculous and impossible. It was another level of John's exceptional management - understanding the players he had to work with and exercising individual management for improved team performance on Saturday – the day when all the hard work and strategizing was put into action.

Everyone at the club believed in that culture wholeheartedly and the senior pros set the right example for the youngsters. The good habits were passed on. Both Billy and Trevor were hugely respected players, real football men with so much experience. They were very different types of player, of course, but in their own unique way they gave everything to the club.

Sadly, all that has largely gone in today's game and yet it was so important to me. There were some outstanding individuals at the club. As a young kid earning buttons I sometimes struggled to find the money to get to West Ham on the train. I'd meet up with Phil Parkes and Alan Devonshire at Mile End station and take the train to Barking. From there, they would pay for a taxi the rest of the way.

Once, I was taken to an away match with the first team, just to gain experience. We got back to Upton Park at 2am and I had nowhere to go and no money to get there. Frank Lampard made sure I was ok and ended up putting me up in his house, cooking me breakfast and taking me to training the next day, even though he had a day off. The people who worked there and the people who played there were all really good people and I believe that comes from the top, from the manager down, and that was all John Lyall. He set the tone.

I loved the football culture at West Ham and the attitude of the players. They weren't in it solely for the money – there wasn't a lot of money around - they just loved to play football and were tough in the tackle. They were like cave men, going out with clubs over their shoulders. It was like war and the players who could play, played, and the rest did all the nitty gritty stuff to keep things going. There were some brutal 50-50 challenges and crunching flying tackles. It was a real man's game whereas today tackling has largely left football and if someone does go over the top it is a major headline on SKY and in the press.

The role of the manager was also different. John was in control of everything at West Ham and nobody dared to question his authority. No matter how big the individual was at West Ham, no matter how inflated an ego a player might have had, John was in charge. The only way to earn decent money back then was to be in the first team and winning games and winning cups, so you had to impress the manager to get picked. It isn't like that at all nowadays and the players have as much power as the manager, if not more. It doesn't matter if they are not being picked because they are earning millions of pounds every year. They don't need a strong relationship with a manager. They will just go elsewhere and get paid the same, usually more. Compare that to Paul Brush in 1980 when John broke the news to him that he wasn't starting in the FA Cup final. He came into the dressing room in tears and was absolutely inconsolable.

John had so much experience and we were lucky that he wanted to pass it on. I'd like to say a bit about Ronnie Boyce as well because he was my type of player. We both played in the middle of the park and he gave me so many little nuggets of advice. He'd been there, done it all and had the medals to show for it. He knew all the situations that I was going to find myself in and coached me in how best to deal with them. He knew so much about every midfielder at every club and gave good advice: "When he turns his back with the ball, and he will, that is the time to tackle him." If you can't learn from someone like Ronnie Boyce you may as well chuck in the towel. Mick McGiven was the same but his focus was more on the defensive side of the game.

The couple of years I spent at West Ham coincided with one of the last great eras at West Ham United. John fashioned a team that won the FA Cup, reached the final of the League Cup, enjoyed a decent European campaign and won promotion to the top flight, at a canter. The atmosphere around the club was electric.

John took me along to Dinamo Tbilisi for a European Cup Winners' Cup match. It was quite an experience because I hadn't been out of the country much at that time, apart from a trip to Den Haag as a youth player for an ADO tournament.

We flew out of Stansted and had to stop in Moscow to refuel. The weather was appalling and the snow drifts were like nothing I'd seen before. They were 40 feet high, even covering trees and we couldn't take off, so we had to find a hotel for a night. When we did eventually get to Tbilisi it was really hot – easily 80 degrees - and we were walking about in heavy coats! It was a harsh place with people queuing for hours to buy bread. It was grey and gloomy everywhere. The Tbilisi fans camped outside our hotel singing songs all night long. Stuart Pearson scored the only goal of the game but we had already lost the tie in the first leg. You have never seen a group of players leave a stadium and city as quickly as West Ham did that night!

John gave me my debut in May 1982, after I'd been playing well in the reserves. I'd scored 19 goals at that level over the course of the season – my last at West Ham as it turned out. In training, a lot of the first team players thought I was ready and deserved a first team opportunity.

John used the dressing room at Chadwell Heath to post all the team sheets on Friday afternoon – first team, reserves and 'A' team. We'd finish our training session and go for something to eat because there was a bit of hanging around, waiting for John and his staff to put the teams up on the board. I'd been hopeful that I would get my chance on a few occasions prior to the Arsenal game but it hadn't happened. Then, just like that, my name was listed in the squad for the trip to Arsenal. I was absolutely delighted.

The game itself was memorable for a couple of reasons - a smoke bomb went off in the North Bank, so we had to come off and, with about 15 minutes left, John brought me on. We were two-nil down at the time and I didn't realise it, but that would be my first and last outing for West Ham. My fifteen minutes of claret and blue fame!

John's decision to let me go was a major shock. All the lads whose contracts were up, had to go and see him in his office. We'd find out if we were going to be signed on again or released, so it was a super-charged moment, waiting outside to hear our fate. I was one of the first to go in and all the lads were telling me not to take all the money and to leave some for them because in their eyes it was a cast iron certainty that I was going to be offered a new contract. I had played with them in the reserves that season so they had seen how good a season I'd had. I can even remember being prepared to ask for a three year contract instead of a two year contract.

So there I am sitting in front of John in his office with both Ronnie Boyce and Mick McGiven close by. I was waiting for the moment when I could negotiate a better deal, but I quickly realised that the words John was saying didn't quite conform to what I was expecting. I was being released! He may have been speaking Chinese from that point because I was totally gutted and lost in a world of disbelief. I've since discovered that John was unsure whether or not to keep me. Mick wanted to let me go and Ronnie wanted to keep me. To be fair to John, he explained that there were several midfielders coming through – in particular Alan Dickens - and along with the current crop of first team midfielders – Brooking and Paul Allen - he couldn't see me breaking through. He suggested I drop down a division and take my chance that way. He also said that if nobody came in for me then West Ham would keep me for another year but I got a chance at Fulham so ended up leaving West Ham for good.

I really was gutted because I desperately wanted to prove myself a success at West Ham. I remember some of the senior pros being shocked by John's decision. David Cross, who was a representative for the Professional Footballers Association, was responsible for handing out pink forms to all those players who were leaving the club. When I asked him for one he told me not to mess about. I kept saying: "I'm serious!" but he wouldn't believe it and explained that the pink forms were only for those players who hadn't received a contract extension and who needed the support of the PFA. "That's me!" I kept saying and he was completely shocked when the news quickly filtered through the club. There was actually a delegation of players who went in to see John to tell him that they thought it was a mistake, but he stood by his decision. Even now, when I meet up with any of those players from that era we always seem to make reference to it. I was playing golf with Trevor Brooking recently and we discussed it once again.

It was hard to leave. I had grown up with that team and had some really good mates like Phil Brignull and Mark Smith. It was funny because I scored a goal for Fulham which was shown quite a bit on TV. It was against Newcastle United and I chipped their keeper from 40-yards. The next time I went back to West Ham, I saw John and he jokingly said that no keeper of his would every let a goal in like that and we shared a laugh.

There were no hard feelings and it was clearly a very difficult decision for John to make. A manager has to make thousands of decisions and he's lucky if only a few backfire on him. A few years later when I was playing for Oxford United, we won the League Cup. I received a lovely letter from John congratulating me and saying how delighted he was that my career was going from strength to strength. Later in life when we bumped into each other at a game, he still called me 'Scotty' and we always maintained the same amount of respect for each other.

John understood what the fans needed and he worked hard to give them something worth remembering. He wanted them to be proud of their team. Similarly, he wanted his players to be proud of the fans. He did so much good at West Ham and had a positive influence on the lives of so many players, staff and fans alike.

John created an environment where the players wanted to train, enjoyed training and were desperate to express themselves in a West Ham United shirt. It is a simple thing, but so difficult to develop nowadays. I am so pleased I had a first team outing during the three seasons I spent at West Ham and that was all thanks to John. Before arriving at the club, I'd been working as a shipping clerk and thought my chance to play had gone, but John gave me that opportunity and without that I wouldn't have achieved the things in football that I did.
Ray Houghton

Player recollections of Ray:

He was one of my close pals and the only one I've really kept in touch with since I moved to Sweden in 1983. We were released from West Ham on the same day. I heard that Billy Bonds went in to see John Lyall when he heard that Ray had not been kept on.
Billy Lansdowne jnr

Scotty was one of my pals at West Ham. Sometimes, I'd pick him up at Kings Cross and drive him to the ground.
Dale Banton

It was a tough decision for John to let him go because Ray was a top player. He scored goals for fun in the reserves. Unfortunately, he had Trevor, Dev, Paul Allen and Geoff Pike in front of him so John let him develop his game elsewhere.
Alan Dickens

I played with Ray in the reserves. You could see he was a talent and could control a game with ease. George Parris
One of the best free transfers in the history of the game. John let him go to further his career. Another great mark of the man.
Greg Campbell

Scotty

In the 'wrong shirt' tackling Alan Dickens at Anfield

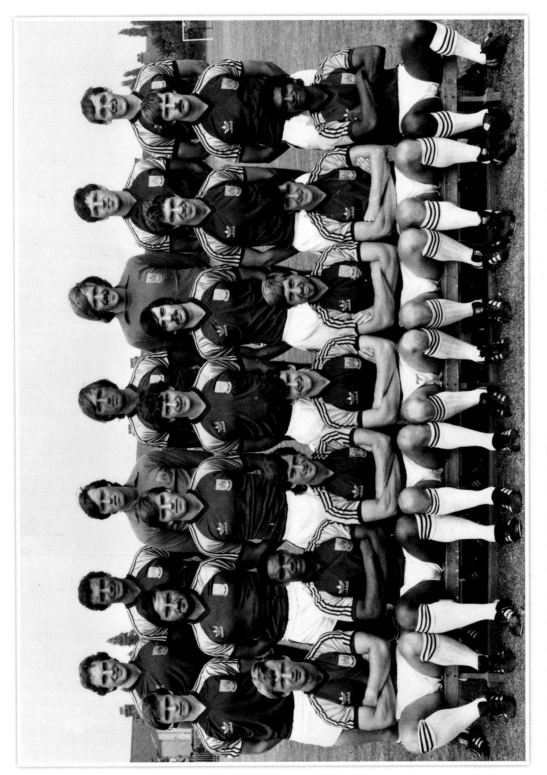

Back row: Brush, Brooking, McAlister, Bonds, Parkes, Martin, Clark.

Middle row: Cowie, Lampard, Morgan, Stewart, Devonshire, Holland, Orr.

Front row: Goddard, La Ronde, Neighbour, Allen, Pike, Van der Elst, Barnes.

CHAPTER NINE
1982-83

"West Ham is a team of young lads, working and fighting for each other, developing together. When boys come to the club, they start learning from the first team players as soon as they arrive." **John Lyall**

John at Chadwell Heath

Billy Bonds overtook Bobby Moore's all-time appearances record of 544 matches, when pulling on the shirt in a 1-1 draw at home to Ipswich Town, in September 1982. He celebrated his 36th Birthday one week later and went on to play until he was 41.

17-year-old Tony Cottee had a sensational debut, scoring against Tottenham Hotspur in a 3-0 home win on New Year's Day, 1983. He was described as the new 'Pop Robson' and went on to score 146 career goals for the Hammers, 42 more than his childhood hero, Pop.

John Lyall bought 25-year-old Scottish talent, Sandy Clark, from Airdrie for £200,000: *"He is a positive player who attacks the ball and is also very quick – not a bad combination in a striker,"* observed John.

John sent shock waves throughout the club when he released Ray Houghton, the leading goalscorer in the reserves. John explained his decision: *"Ray Houghton is now at the point where he needs regular first team football. Continuing to play in our reserve side would not help his progress."*

Dale Banton was another to be released, along with Stuart Pearson, Steve Milton, Adrian Keith, Wayne Reader, Mark Smith and Robert Wall, (the latter two due to injury).

Joe Gallagher was signed on a month's trial to ease the defensive worries, with Billy Bonds, Ray Stewart and Alvin Martin all sidelined. Jimmy Neighbour decided to leave the club.

In March 1983, Dave Swindlehurst signed from Derby County for £160,000 and arrested a worrying slide down the table. The Hammers recovered to finish 8th. However, attendances dropped to below 16,000.

Jack 'the boot' Leslie retired after 15 years looking after the players' boots: John marked the occasion in the press: *"Jack has done a great job for us but, at the age of 80 , he feels it is time to hang up his own boots."* The Hammers beat Manchester United 3-1 in his final game.

John Lyall gave debuts to the following five players – Sandy Clark, Joe Gallagher, Alan Dickens, Tony Cottee and Dave Swindlehurst.

Billy Bonds became West Ham's all-time appearances holder

Here is their story...

50 – SANDY CLARK

"There has been a little bit of John Lyall and Chadwell Heath throughout my coaching career in Scotland. "

Born: Airdrie, North Lanarkshire, October 28, 1956 • **Position:** Striker • **Games played for West Ham United:** 34 (1982-83)

Goals: 10 • **Debut:** August 28, 1982 v Nottingham Forest (h) L 1-2 (Stewart pen – Walsh, Robertson pen) Att: 23,796

West Ham United: Parkes, Stewart, Lampard, Bonds, Martin, Devonshire, Van Der Elst, Goddard, **Clark,** Allen, Pike.

Nottingham Forest: Sutton, Anderson, Bowyer, Proctor,* Young, Todd, Hodge, Wallace, Plummer, Walsh, Robertson. Sub:

Alexander 'Sandy' Clark was bought from Airdrie in August 1982. He stayed at West Ham United until February 1983. Clark had the challenging task of replacing the recently departed FA Cup winner, and fan favourite, David Cross: *"I'd been playing part-time for relegated Scottish Premier League side Airdrie so it was a big step up for me. I wasn't the most talented of players but I was aggressive. I certainly endeared myself to the West Ham fans by scoring nine of my ten goals at Upton Park!"*

It is interesting to note that in 1985-86 when West Ham were within touching distance of their first ever top flight championship, Sandy was playing for Hearts, who missed out on the Scottish title with only seven minutes remaining of the season. A defeat at Dundee on the final day had handed the trophy to Celtic. A famous line from John Cleese was quoted in the press at the time and West Ham fans will nod their head in sympathy: "It's not the despair I mind," said Cleese. "It's the hope I can't stand."

Sandy started the 2017-18 season working as a coach to Allan Johnston at high flying Dunfermline Athletic of the Scottish Championship. His son, Nicky, also plays for the Pars, having had successful spells at both Queen of the South (also under Sandy) and Rangers.

Sandy had the following memories of John Lyall:

John was such an impressive character and I learned so much from him. It was while working under John that I first started to think about a career in coaching. I soon took my coaching badges through the Scottish Football Association.

He liked me to play with freedom. He'd offer some advice on where he thought I should play and the type of runs I should be making, but he let me go out and play my own game. He had a sixth sense when it came to recognising weaknesses in the opposition which is a very handy skill to possess.

Socially, I naturally gravitated towards the Scottish players, Ray Stewart, Neil Orr and my really good friend, George Cowie. We've always stayed in touch and we meet up whenever he comes home from Australia where he is coaching. I also got on very well with Franky Van der Elst and Alvin Martin. I initially stayed in a hotel in Epping but then moved into a house in Shenfield. Van der Elst was my neighbour and liked a drink and a cigarette so we'd often go out for a pint in The Eagle and Child, which was our local. Along with Alan Devonshire, Franky was one the most talented players I ever saw. He was so laid back it was untrue. His response to everything was: "Let's go for a beer." We saw in the New Year together in 1983, the day Tony Cottee scored on his debut in a 3-0 rout over Spurs.

John's Scottish heritage definitely helped cement our relationship. The other Scottish lads at the club - Ray Stewart, Neil Orr, George Cowie and Tom McAlister - also benefited from this. John liked the qualities in Scottish people. A bit later, Tommy McQueen and Frank McAvennie would have enjoyed a similar experience.

John was the type of person who would do anything for his players. Whether it was help searching for a house, or looking for furniture to put in that house, John was always on hand to help and support. He knew that a player's situation off the pitch was pivotal to his performances on it. This is an aspect which I have adopted in my own coaching career. Players are not just robots. They have issues like the rest of us and they need support and advice. John had a keen eye and ear for recognising if a player was not quite right, not quite himself. If there was a problem, he would try to fix it and usually found a solution. He was a strong character and a great leader, so the players knew that confiding in John was trust well invested.

In Scotland I had been playing on really poor quality pitches and training on gravel and just running around a pitch to stay fit, but when I went to Chadwell Heath the facilities there were far superior and they had a great indoor five-a-side area and a weights room. The quality was so much better it really inspired me to try and be the best I could be. There were several pitches and an indoor training area. Everything was geared towards improving the players.

Nowadays West Ham's first team don't train at Chadwell Heath, which I find incredible. When you think of the players that have trained there down the years, what a source of inspiration that should have been for future players joining the club. Just being around John on the training ground and listening to him talk about football gave you a tremendous sense of the grand history of West Ham United. He'd been there since the 1950s and had so many stories about Noel Cantwell, John Bond and Bobby Moore.

There was a very special feeling at West Ham back then. John was vital in maintaining that feeling and it was felt by everyone at the club, including the players, tea ladies, groundsmen, and fans, absolutely everybody. I can't begin to tell you just how special that was.

I had a slow start and it took me five games before I scored, but then I managed to score five in six games which gave me a lot of confidence. I scored against Liverpool and Manchester City which was highly rewarding because it meant I had what it took to score at that level. We were riding high, in second place, around about October 1982. It was a great experience for me.

John was a strong character, a strong leader. He usually knew the team he was going to play by Thursday and would set out the tactics ahead of Saturday's game. This made the team-talk in the dressing room on Saturday much easier because the preparation had been so good. It flowed so well because his communication skills were top class.

After a match, if we had lost – and sadly you can't win

Netting the winner against Norwich City at The Boleyn Ground, November 1982

every game – John wasn't the type to throw cups around and shout at everyone in sight. He was always measured in his analysis and always made a point of sharing his view on where he thought the game had been lost and what needed to be worked on in the next training sessions.

One of my favourite goals for West Ham came at West Brom. It wasn't glamorous or a 25-yard screamer or anything like that, but it summed up the type of player I was. We won 2-1 and I scored the first goal. It was a tenacious effort, riding a few tackles and scrambling for the ball and showing enough determination to make sure the ball ended up in the back of the net. The goal epitomised the type of spirit John had running through the club; hard work, togetherness, inclusion of everybody, working hard for each other, team spirit and putting absolutely everything into the cause, led by John. I'm very proud of that goal.

In May 2016, I returned for the last ever match at Upton Park. I hadn't been there for well over 20 years but I still felt that family atmosphere which I remember from my time at the club. In fact, Mark Noble said a few words that night and he noted that when you play for West Ham United, you are not only joining a football club, but you are becoming part of a family. That really struck a chord with me.

Sandy Clark

The Flying Scotsman, Vicarage Road, December 1982

An intelligent guy who worked his socks off but found the transition from Scottish to English football very hard. In addition, he had to try and take the place of an absolute legend, and fan favourite, in David Cross. Anyone would have been up against it in those circumstances. It was a pity because Sandy had a great career in Scotland and has proven himself to be a very successful coach. John had so much faith in him. He'd take him to one side and say: "Don't listen to the crowd, we both know you can do it." John was hoping that Sandy would break through but sadly it didn't happen for him.
Mick McGiven

When John signed Sandy I went into his office and told him I was a better striker than him! I was only 16. John told me

to get out of his office.
Greg Campbell

I really liked Sandy and I was so pleased to see him before the Manchester United match at Upton Park for the last ever match. We had a good chat at the bar. He's a lovely bloke. He wasn't the best finisher but worked really hard.
Alan Dickens

Wearing the Number 9 shirt at Old Trafford, January 1983

At the Boleyn Ground for the last ever match, May 2016

51 – JOE GALLAGHER

"I had 17 different managers in my football career and there wasn't anybody as good as John Lyall. Jim Smith at Birmingham City was a very good manager and a great motivator but when I think of John Lyall I am left speechless, he was so good."

Born: Liverpool, January 11, 1955 • **Position:** Centre-half • **Games played for West Ham United:** 11 (1982-83)
Debut: December 11, 1982 v Coventry City (h) L 0-3 (Hateley, Roberts, Whitton) Att: 19,321
West Ham United: Parkes, Stewart, Lampard, Orr, **Gallagher**, Devonshire,* Van der Elst, Goddard, Brush, Allen, Pike. Sub: Morgan.*
Coventry City: Sealey, Thomas, Roberts, Butterworth, Dyson, Gillespie, Whitton, Jacobs, Hateley, Melrose, Hunt.

Joseph Anthony Gallagher highlight from his time in the East End was a 3-0 victory over Tottenham Hotspur on New Years' Day, 1983. He narrowly missed out on scoring that day but his header, which came back off the bar, was followed-up by 17-year-old debutant, Tony Cottee.

Gallagher played the bulk of his career with Birmingham City and he enjoy Hall of Fame status at St Andrews. John Lyall signed him as an emergency measure in the midst of a spate of injuries and suspensions.

Today, Joe is kept busy by his three grandchildren – Lydia, Claudia and Noah - and lives in Solihull with Jeanette, his partner for the past 23 years. *"Since 1995 I worked at Jaguar Land Rover as an Ultrasonic Inspector. In layman's terms that means I tested the welding which pinned each car together. I have taken early retirement so that I can spend more time with my loved ones."*

Joe was delighted to share his memories of John Lyall:

My first contact with John came in 1982, under very strange circumstances. I had just been sacked by Wolverhampton Wanderers for not appearing in a team photo. It was a very bizarre situation but I thought the phone would ring and I'd join another club and start playing again. After a few weeks the phone hadn't rung and I was starting to get a little bit anxious. Then, one Sunday evening the phone rang and the man on

In the gym at Chadwell Heath

Joe (left) on his debut against Coventry City, December 1982

the other end of the line was claiming to be John Lyall. He was asking me if I'd be interested in signing for West Ham United. I thought it was a hoax and that one of the lads at Wolves was winding me up! "Come on, who is it really?" I kept saying. He assured me that he was John Lyall and that he wanted to come to Birmingham and talk to me. Within a few hours John and Eddie Baily were in my house talking about a move to Upton Park. He explained to me how they needed cover at the back. Billy Bonds had a broken foot, Alvin Martin was suspended and Ray Stewart had been sent off against Aston Villa in the previous match. Obviously, this was all music to my ears given the situation I was in. Then John told me there was one problem – he needed me to travel to London with them straight away. I didn't see that as a problem and within five minutes I'd thrown some clothes and things in a bag and was sitting in John's car on my way to West Ham. That night I slept in a hotel near Epping Forest feeling really good about life.

I hope John saw in me a good work ethic. I lacked some of the ability that other players had but made up for it with endeavour and fighting spirit.

The training sessions were world class at West Ham. The coaches – Ronnie Boyce, Ernie Gregory and Mick McGiven - were 100% supportive. John Lyall was at the head of all this and was absolutely brilliant. He was a master at getting his point across without pointing criticism at one person. If a player was having an off day, John would highlight the problem while addressing the whole team, not just the player who wasn't performing. John was a great believer in collective responsibility, not individual criticism. If I had to compare him to a manager in the modern game I would have to take the good bits from each of them to get close to John Lyall. He really did have everything.

Initially, I signed on a month-to-month contract because I had been brought in as defensive cover while a few of the first team regulars were not able to play. At the end of season John offered me a one year contract. I was delighted with that because those three West Ham legends – Billy Bonds, Alvin Martin and Ray Stewart – were back in the team and John still wanted me to remain at the club.

I'd like to mention a couple of players who really helped me at West Ham. Ray Stewart was absolutely brilliant to me. He picked me up for training and introduced me to all his friends and associates on the commercial side of West Ham. Alvin Martin was also very supportive and drove me around looking at houses when it looked like I was going to be staying at the club for a while. I am very grateful to both of those great men.

I almost scored a goal for West Ham against Tottenham Hotspur but it came back off the cross bar and Tony Cottee managed to convert the rebound. I was pleased for Tony because we'd room together the night before and it was his debut.

Just before the start of the 1983-84 season, John called me into his office and told me that John Bond at Burnley had come in for me. They were in the third division at the time and I wasn't keen on moving. John was brilliant with me and completely fair. He said he was happy for me to stay but wanted to share the offer with me because it would be a four year contract which would provide me and my family with a lot of security. I agreed to go and talk with John Bond and the offer was one I couldn't refuse. I called up John Lyall from Burnley and explained what had happened and he was perfectly fine for me to go.

My time at West Ham United was very short but I wish it would have been a lot, lot longer because everything about the club was first class. The 11 matches I played in are very special to me.

Joe Gallagher

Joe with his grandchildren, Claudia, Noah and Lydia, November 2017

52 – ALAN DICKENS

"David Beckham once said that even when he played in a Charity match, he tried as hard as he could because he knew Alex Ferguson was watching and he wanted him to think he was a good player. That is exactly the same attitude I had towards John Lyall."

Born: Plaistow, London, September 3, 1964 • **Position:** Midfielder • **Games played for West Ham United:** 234 (1982-89)
Goals: 30 • **Honours under John Lyall:** 1980-81 FA Youth Cup winner, 1985-86 Member of West Ham United's highest ever finishing league team (third) **Debut:** December 18, 1982 v Notts County (a) W 2-1 (Dickens, Hunt og – Worthington) Att: 8,457
Notts County: Avramovic, Benjamin, Worthington, Hunt, Kilcline, Richards, Chiedozie, Fashanu, Christie, Hooks, Mair.* Sub: Clarke.*
West Ham United: Parkes, Lampard, Brush, Orr, Gallagher, **Dickens,** Van der Elst, Goddard, Clark, Allen, Pike.

Alan William Dickens was one of two children born to parents, Alan and Wendy. His father was a lorry driver, while his mother worked as a dentist's assistant and also helped young children in local schools: *"She was always helping someone, my mum."*

Born in Plaistow in West Ham United's FA Cup winning year of 1964, both Alan and his sister, Tracy, were raised in Custom House. 'Dicko' spent the first six years of his life at number 40 Devonshire Road. *"We had an outside toilet and no bathroom. We then went a bit more upmarket and moved to the new builds a few streets away at number 36 Mortlake Road."*

"When I was a little boy, I modelled myself on Johan Cryuff. I pretended I was him in the team photo and brushed my hair forward to look like him. A bit later on, I loved watching Michel Platini, too. They were my two favourite players."

Dicko has his place in West Ham United's history. He is the only Hammer to win the FA Youth cup, score on his debut, and form part of the club's best ever top flight finish - narrowly missing out to Liverpool and Everton in 1985-86.

Today, Alan works as a black taxi driver and lives with his wife Annika s on the Barking Road. *"My first date with Annika was at Alan Devonshire's Testimonial dinner at The Grosvenor House Hotel. She is from Wanstead – her mum just liked the name. We have two sons - our youngest works for the law firm, Macfarlanes, while my eldest wants to become a*

teacher."

Sometimes, West Ham United's history can add an extra layer of pressure to a player – Kevin Lock was cruelly labelled the next Bobby Moore, while both Allen McKnight and David Kelly found it difficult to follow in the footsteps of Phil Parkes and Tony Cottee. Similarly, Alan Dickens was burdened through comparison with Trevor Brooking.

One of many true Hammers from the Lyall era, Dicko took time to share an enjoyable lunch in London to discuss his former manager:

When I first wore Trevor's Number 10 shirt I really enjoyed it. I was scoring goals and everything seemed to be going fine. Then, when I started to think about what it all meant, I didn't cope at all well. I found it difficult. I never spoke to Trevor about it and he never gave me any advice or anything like that. In fact, I don't recall him saying one word to me. I talked to John about things that were on my mind and to be fair to him, he always made me feel better and I usually left his office thinking that my game was ok and that everything was fine. His words made me feel quite good.

John always wanted his players to be smart and well behaved. As a young kid I remember the coaching staff telling us to tuck our shirts in.

I couldn't stop scoring goals in the youth team. I'd get 20-25

Taking on David O'Leary of Arsenal

every season. Even when I got in the first team I remember scoring six in ten games. I liked to play with a bit of freedom.

When I turned 19, I started thinking too much about my game and I think it spoiled my progress a little bit. I worried a great deal and became overawed by the responsibility of playing for West Ham United. Consequently, the goals suddenly dried up and I felt I was expected to add other parts to my game, like defending, just to get into the team.

I was a West Ham fan and had watched the great Eintracht Frankfurt semi final in 1976. I was in the Chicken Run and that is still my favourite game. I went to the FA Cup final in 1980 and was on the roof of the Co-op at East Ham for the open-topped bus homecoming the following day. I went to all the home games and Dinamo Tbilisi was the best side I ever saw play at Upton Park. I spent the whole game just watching them. They were mesmerising. I enjoyed watching Trevor Brooking and Billy Bonds, of course, and have flashes of memory seeing Billy Jennings getting up high and flicking the ball on.

I went to Woodside School and I think a chap called Dave Wooley spotted me playing for Newham at McMillan Stadium. There was a little group of scouts and I think Len Hurford was part of it.

When I was 13-years-old, a fella called Malcolm Fidgeon took me up to Manchester United. He was the same guy who took David Beckham to Old Trafford. Dave Sexton was in charge and I really enjoyed the experience and was all set to sign but ended up deciding to stay closer to home. They offered me a two year apprenticeship and one year pro. I was in digs in Salford with Norman Whiteside. I went to the 1979 FA Cup final when Arsenal beat United 3-2 at Wembley.

I knew I was progressing fast and played in West Ham United's successful FA Youth Cup final in 1981. I was only 16 and most of the lads were 18. I went back to school the next day!

I made my debut at Notts County in December 1982. John told me on the Friday before the match. The day of the game, I arrived at Upton Park at 9am and was asked if I needed any tickets. I asked for ten, because I had quite a few family and friends coming up to see me play.

I had a dream debut and scored a goal in the first half. Sadly, all my friends and family were caught in traffic so didn't get to the ground until half-time. It was only a tap in from six yards so they didn't miss much! People often recall the goal I scored against Ipswich at the end of the 1985-86 season, but I always remember my first goal with greater affection.

I didn't really think about my situation at West Ham. If I had thought about it, how Trevor Brooking was about to retire and how I started really well and seemed good enough to be in the

Scoring a belter at Norwich City, March 1983

team, then maybe I would have managed my situation a bit better. I didn't even think about the money I was earning. Only now do I realise that I earned nothing at West Ham – I was on about £110 on my debut and eventually got up to £400 or £500-per-week. I basically agreed to whatever John put in front of me. If West Ham could pay you the bare minimum, then they would. Looking back, the young lads who worked hard to get into the first team had a raw deal, financially.

I should have been a bit more like Tony Cottee. He was knocking on John's door all the time asking for a better deal. His father, Clive, understood how the finances worked and made sure Tony was earning his true value. I just trusted John to give me more money if he thought I deserved it, so I didn't earn any decent money at West Ham. That wasn't my priority anyway. My priority was to play football.

John's training sessions were simple but always varied and entertaining. I did a lot of training with Ronnie Boyce. I wanted to try my best for both of them. Boycey would tell you straight. If he felt you were playing rubbish he'd tell you. Mick McGiven did a lot with the defenders and Tony Carr looked after the kids. Ernie Gregory would look after the 'keepers.

When I left West Ham for Chelsea in 1989 I thought the training was awful. I had three years at Stamford Bridge and

Dickens of a day!

A headline writer's dream

it just wasn't good. It was far too intense and not nearly as enjoyable. We played against each other rather than together. There was far too much competition and not enough camaraderie. They taught you to be selfish rather than a team player. Ironically, it only improved when I dropped down into the reserves and was coached by Frank Sibley who was a good coach. Then Don Howe came in for one pre-season and it was like being back at West Ham. Don was a very good coach.

At West Ham, John looked after everyone – the quiet ones and the noisy ones, whereas at Chelsea, if you didn't quite fit in with what they wanted, you got lost and I felt lost most of the time. I suppose I'm talking about man management and John was excellent at that. Personally, I needed even more man management than even John could give me. He said things to me which really boosted my frame of mind but I needed so much more. Perhaps he thought I was coping well, but I wasn't and needed that extra support, guidance and self-belief. Maybe the Number 10 shirt was too much for me? Maybe John could have given that to Dev and put me in the Number 6 shirt with Pikey in the Number 7 shirt? I know it sounds odd but psychologically I think that might have made a positive difference to my frame of mind.

Another thing about the training was that if John left the

Stylish

session to his coaches, the players would take it easy and generally fool around. Then, all of a sudden, John would return and the whole atmosphere would change. The tempo would increase, the focus would return and everyone would be giving it their all. It was a bit like naughty kids at school who mess about and then change completely when the headteacher arrives on the scene.

I think John noticed a few flaws in my game. I could be a little bit complicated at times and that is probably the reason why he didn't ask me to join him at Ipswich Town after he left West Ham. I can understand that.

I never went out with John socially and didn't know his family at all. In fact, I only got to know them recently, at a commemorative eventing for John in South Benfleet in 2016. I was really surprised that his wife, Yvonne, knew my name. I sat next to his son Murray and really enjoyed the whole evening. Maybe John and I didn't get to know each other as well as we should have done?

One of the last times I saw John was at Chelsea. He had brought his Ipswich team to Stamford Bridge and was in the manager's room with Bobby Campbell. He saw me and said he thought I was going to score but I didn't.

I'm not surprised that they sacked John. The club had been relegated, the fans weren't happy and the board obviously thought it was time for a change. If I'm honest, I probably didn't give it too much thought at the time. Most players think mainly about themselves and that's what I would have done. If John had remained at West Ham I would have definitely stayed but I'll never know if it was in his plans to talk to me that summer to keep me at the club. Maybe his plan was to move me on?

In 1986-87 John wanted to sign Kerry Dixon. He took me to a hotel to meet Chelsea because I was going to be part of the deal. In the end, Kerry didn't want to leave Stamford Bridge. I think that experience affected the regard in which I hold John. I am always very respectful, but when I see players like Geoff Pike in tears when they talk about him, I don't feel that same level of emotion. I wasn't as close to John as those guys.

I went to John's funeral which was a very sad day. I don't remember too much about it but felt I had to go.

I found John quite inspirational at times. If, during half-time, he said the right things I would really, really, be fired up to go out and do my best. He wasn't the type to throw things around or pin people up against a wall. He would keep you in the dressing room for over an hour after a game if he wasn't happy. No one would every answer him back.

I really admire John. To sit in front of 30,000 fans and make decisions takes a lot of bravery and responsibility. Every game he was trying to pick a team to entertain and create the things worth remembering. He knew the tea lady through to the Chairman and that is the best way to run a club.

When I heard that only 77 played in his first team over 15 years, I felt quite privileged.
Alan Dickens

Dicko is remembered with fondness by his former colleagues:

He's still got those golden feet. We play for Dev's charity from time to time and Dicko can still pick a pass and has those lovely touches. He was very much in the Trevor Brooking mould, with two great feet and first class vision. He was very shy and perhaps a lack of confidence affected him.
Everald La Ronde

A class player. Dicko should have played for England without a doubt. I liked playing with Dicko because he always wanted the ball and rarely wasted it.
Tony Gale

What a good player he was! What a very good talent! To this day I still don't know what happened to him. One minute he was riding high with the Hammers and the next he was playing for Chesham. The move to Chelsea was a mistake. That was not the right club for Dicko. He needed a West Ham type family club with a manager who would put his arm around him or kick him up the backside when he needed it. A manager who would be honest with him. The West End socialites were no good for him. He was the best one-touch player I'd seen in a long time. Great vision and I'm just disappointed that his career didn't progress to the very top because that is where he should have gone.
Mick McGiven

He should have been a top West Ham legend. What a player! Why on earth he went to Chelsea I do not know.
Paul Hilton

We played against each other at Redbridge and Newham. I've known him since the age of 11 and we still keep in touch. A quality player.
George Parris

He was quite simply the best schoolboy footballer I have ever seen. Havering played Newham and there was this young kid gliding around the pitch in absolute control of the ball and the pace of the game. Graceful and magical. We lost 1-4 and I scored our goal. Dicko scored all four for them. Sadly, even though he had the skill and technique of ten players, he lacked self-belief.
Tony Cottee

Dicko in his taxi cab

53 – TONY COTTEE

"Everything I've achieved in my career goes back to half past one on New Years' Day, 1983, when John Lyall called me into his little office and told me I was playing against Tottenham Hotspur. He asked me if I was up for it and I looked at him and said: "Of course I am. I'd love to play for West Ham."

Born: July 11, 1965 Forest Gate, London • **Position:** Striker • **Games played for John Lyall:** 256 (1982-88)

Games played for West Ham United: 336 (1982-88 and 1994-97) • **Goals:** 146 (5th on the all-time list behind Victor Watson (326), Geoff Hurst (249), John Dick (177) and Jimmy Ruffell (166))

Honours under John Lyall: 1983-84, 1984-85, 1986-87, 1987-88: Club's leading goalscorer; 1985-86: member of West Ham United's highest finishing league team (Third), 1985-86; Hammer of the Year, 1986; PFA Young Player of the Year, 1986-89 Seven England caps

Debut: January 1st, 1983 v Tottenham Hotspur (h) W 3-0 (Cottee, Stewart, Pike) Att: 33,383

West Ham United: Parkes, Stewart, Gallagher, Dickens, Martin, Devonshire, Van der Elst, **Cottee**, Clark, Allen, Pike.

Tottenham Hotspur: Clemence, Hughton, Mazzon, Price, Villa, Perryman, O'Reilly, Archibald, Brooke, Hoddle, Crooks.

Anthony Richard Cottee was a statisticians dream. He is the last West Ham United striker to register goals in such numbers to challenge the great goal getters in the club's history. But for a six year sojourn at Everton between 1988 and 1994 the sharp, instinctive striker, may well have challenged both Geoff Hurst and Victor Watson for greater prominence in the club's list of most prolific strikers. Instead, the cheque book dashed the hopes of the claret and blue dreamers, anoraks and historians, and no other striker has troubled the history books since. Even Paolo Di Canio's relatively modest 50 goals in the top flight, between 1999-2003, have not been challenged by any subsequent striker in the claret and blue.

Cottee's strike partnership with Frank McAvennie in 1985-86 yielded a combined haul of 54 goals, and you would have to go back to the 55 scored by Geoff Hurst and Martin Peters during 1968-69 to find a better single-season return. The 63 scored by Victor Watson (50) and Jimmy Ruffell (13) in 1929-30 remains the highest ever achieved. Suffice it to say, we now live in an age where good strikers remain for only one or two seasons so such lofty records will remain in short supply. Football is all the poorer for it.

Today, 'TC' is a respected pundit for SKY sports and regularly hosts various West Ham reunions with his good friend, Tony Gale.

Everything I have done in my playing career and as a pundit for Sky Sports is off the back of John Lyall believing in, and giving a chance to, a young 17-year-old.

I started training with the first team at West Ham when I was 15-years-old. Prior to that, I had been tasked with doing plenty of chores. I had to cut the grass, creosote the fences and clean the toilets - all those things that players don't do today. It gave me a good grounding, but the most amazing thing of all was that John was doing many of those same jobs with me. He was there overseeing things and helping out with the painting and things like that.

John knew that I was a goalscorer and that I had talent. He also knew that he'd need to harness that talent and bring me on in the right way. Tony Carr looked after me at youth level but John oversaw everything at the club. He was the big power.

All managers need a goalscorer in their team and John was

no different. He liked my pace and movement and I like to think that I had a good football brain. The challenge for John was to make me a better all-round player because I was only interested in scoring goals. I was like that in the youth team, the reserves and the first team and I suspect all my playing colleagues will say the same thing about me – goals first and everything else a distant second.

I wasn't interested so much in putting in the hard graft for the team, unlike Frank McAvennie, who was a real team player. It came naturally to him and he put in a lot of hard work. I can still hear John's words: "When we haven't got the ball we've got to challenge their defenders so that we are defending from the front." During the famous 1985-86 season, John knew he had two good goalscorers on his hand. The ethos in training was to get the ball to us in dangerous areas because he knew we would score and wanted to keep us sharp.

As a left-sided striker, I was very lucky in that I had Georgie Parris and Steve Walford vying for the left-back position. Galey was at left centre-back and Dev was in left midfield, so the supply to me was tremendous and I thrived on that. Similarly, McAvennie had Alvin Martin, Ray Stewart and Mark Ward working the same magic down the right-hand side. It was a very exciting time because everything just clicked and it was John who put all that together.

People go on about Barcelona all the time and, as great as they are, and they are fantastic, they are basically playing pass and move and one-touch football. They have great players who can create and score goals. John Lyall was doing that over 30-40 years ago as was Ron Greenwood before him. Perhaps not always with the right players but they were way, way ahead of their time.

John was a fantastic man to work for. He was an incredible coach, a very good manager who could spot things if they were going wrong. He invariably made the right team selection and substitutions. He also had a hard side to his character. If he needed to put his foot down he would and he was notoriously difficult to deal with when negotiating contracts. I felt frustrated with that because I was progressing at a rate of knots. By the time I had signed one contract I felt that I had out grown it after a couple of months and wanted something better, something more in line with the improvement I was showing.

From John's perspective he had West Ham's best interests at heart and had to find the right balance between the board and the player. He would come back to me and say that he'd managed to get the board to agree a really good three year package on good money but then I'd be banging on his door asking for a four year deal on more money, and then a five year deal and it went on like that so we were locked in contract talks a lot of the time!

John could be very strong in those discussions and my dad, Clive, always helped me. He worked in insurance and knew

Potty about Cottee

1982-83 Youth Team - Cottee is bottom row, second from the left

the art of negotiation. He also enjoyed a good relationship with John, Eddie Baily, Ronnie Boyce, Mick McGiven and Tony Carr.

John loved to pit players against each other and he knew I was 800m Essex champion at aged 15. I think my best time was two minutes and three seconds. One pre-season John measured out an athletics track at Chadwell Heath and decided to set up an 800m race. Now Billy Bonds was the king of running and had been pretty much undefeated over any distance for many years. John was chuckling inside because he knew he had an 800m champion in the field this time and after I'd won he went over to Bill and explained. They shared a good laugh together.

When John signed Frank McAvennie in 1985 I wasn't exactly sure which position he was going to play. In the press, they were promoting him as a striker. The season before I had played up front with Paul Goddard so all of a sudden it seemed as though John had brought a third striker to the club. Even though I had been top scorer for the past two seasons I was still worried about where I stood. I was only 21 so needed a bit of certainty about my position at the club. I spoke to John and he could sense that I was worried so he invited me over to his house: "Come over and have a cup of tea and we'll talk about

it," he said. John was always so approachable and wanted his players to talk to him. His door was always open. When I visited his house, he was up a ladder doing some DIY as he often did during the summer. Yvonne and Murray were there and, true to his word, we had a cup of tea and a chat. He told me that he hadn't brought Frank in to replace me. He initially saw Frank's role as that of an attacking midfielder, offering support to both Paul Goddard and me.

John was always trying to think outside the box and some of his training sessions were a little bit unpredictable as a consequence. I'd reflect on some of them and think what was he trying to achieve there? One example came when it was snowy and the pitches were hard. John decided to play a game with a rugby ball. It was impossible to control and, although John was trying to prepare us for the ball bouncing unpredictably, he could have done that with a normal football. Anyway, Wardy picked up the ball and drop-kicked it so hard we lost it! So that was that.

John was very good at keeping the training sessions fresh and interesting. This was before the days of team breaks to Dubai or long rest periods due to International breaks. All credit to John for being inventive and creative on the training ground because ten

Debut goal versus Tottenham Hotspur, January 1st 1983

months is a long time to keep a team focussed and committed.

Although it is very difficult to draw comparisons with modern day managers I would put John in the same category as Mourinho, Guardiola and Wenger. He was a football purist and understood the importance of winning games. The modern day coaching sessions with quick, accurate and effective passing is a variation on what we were doing in the 1980s. Don't forget, nowadays the top coaches are looking after players who in most cases are already the finished article. They also have the financial resources to buy top class talent whereas John employed his knowledge of the game to improve the vast majority of those 77 Hammers you are going to interview for the book. The club gave him the time to put his theories into practice. That is time which is not given in the modern game. The cheque book is used instead.

John was given free rein to put the infrastructure into place to support his vision for West Ham. You only have to talk to the academy boys such as Alan Dickens, Paul Ince and myself ,for that matter, and we will all agree that John improved us as players. Similarly, those players John signed, such as David Cross, Ray Stewart, Tony Gale and Frank McAvennie, will all say the same. People wanted to play for him and it is no coincidence that there were so many testimonials during John's time at the club.

John had great presence. When he walked into the dressing room there was an aura of authority. You knew your manager was there. He was very tactically aware so you always felt that you were part of a well thought through game plan. If things went terribly wrong on the pitch he would think nothing of keeping us all behind for over an hour to explain what went wrong, why it went wrong and what we all needed to do to ensure it didn't happen again. He would also praise a player if he'd had a particularly good game and said things like: "Well done, son." Or he'd point out a particular move which gave him satisfaction. Whether you are 17 or 32 you still need that pat on the back sometimes and John was good at that.

John did try to keep me at West Ham. The great Alan Devonshire always maintains that I should have stayed longer at the club. I just thought it was in everybody's interests that I moved on. I had become very frustrated after the 1985-86 season and disappointed that we hadn't strengthened the team. I'd also been selected for England and was talking to players who had won things or were challenging for trophies and were on better money than me. I wasn't convinced that my future remained at Upton Park.

It was a very tough decision to leave a club that I'd loved and supported since a boy. But while my personal head was telling me to stay, my professional head was urging me to leave. When I did move on I received a lovely personal letter from John. In it he thanked me for all that I had done for West Ham and he wish me all the best going forward. It was a hand written letter signed by John and a very special item which I've still got today amongst all my memorabilia. It is a reminder of how great a man he was. Another cherished part of my

Kid Cottee is a winner as Lyall smiles

Ipswich 0   West Ham 3   By ALAN LYONS

VETERAN Trevor Brooking and youngster Tony Cottee brought the smiles back to West Ham in an uncompromising victory at Ipswich.

They were the only two to show traditional Hammer qualities as the side played on Ipswich's lack of confidence by keeping a tight hold on midfield and defence.

It was the speed and tenacity of 18-year-old Cottee aligned to the brain of Brooking which simplified the task of ending a three-match losing run.

After only four minutes, Cottee forced Russell Osman into a mis-header and was then held back by Terry Butcher as he controlled the loose ball.

Brooking, back after missing six weeks with a hamstring injury, curled his cross to evade Paul Cooper in the Ipswich goal and Paul Hilton's header brought his first goal for the club.

From then on West Ham were happy to let Ipswich come at them without disturbing Phil Parkes in goal.

Manager John Lyall admitted: 'We got men behind the ball knowing they lack confidence and tried to catch them on the break. We set out to play a short passing game and we were tight and solid.'

Both sides have their injury problems, but Lyall has been able to call on the likes of

Cottee, who is adding a sense of all round awareness to his known scoring skills.

He had a hand in the second goal which again came from a Brooking cross. Cottee got a foot to the ball before it bounced into the net off the unhappy Butcher after 48 minutes.

Then Cottee's burst of speed earned him a dramatic if bizarre goal after 57 minutes.

He was the first to judge the strength of a Parkes' clearance and controlled the ball on the first bounce before scoring in the top corner.

Lyall added: 'After three defeats people were beginning to write us off. It was nice to bounce back.'

Ipswich manager Bobby Ferguson said he was hoping to discuss terms with Arsenal for on-loan striker Alan Sunderland.

Press plaudits

Champs slip...and ace Cottee closes the gap

HAMMERS KEEP TITLE DREAM ALIVE

WEST HAM are still clinging to the vision of the First Division

The last serious brush with immortality

collection is a photo of me John and Eddie Baily on the day I signed as a 14-year-old.

I couldn't believe it when John was sacked. I think it was the worst decision in the club's history. They missed a big opportunity to continue the tried and tested and successful approach of both Ron Greenwood and John Lyall. They had a ready-made successor in Billy Bonds, who was already at the club. John could have been a guiding hand as Director of Football. I must say that when I did return, some six years later, the club was pretty much the same as when I had left it. Harry Redknapp was in charge and he was a Greenwood boy and familiar with the West Ham traditions. A lot of the personnel were still at the club. Alvin Martin and Steve Potts were still there along with Tony Carr, Stevie Bacon, Eddie Gillam and even Shirley, who was still serving the dinners! The training ground was much the same and it felt like going back into a John Lyall time zone but, obviously, without John being there.

I always stayed in touch with John and when I became manager of Barnet, in 2000, he was one of the people I called for advice. He'd retired from football and I don't think he was overly fussed about what was happening in the game. He wished me luck and advised me to do things my way and to be myself. He rightly believed that it is better to succeed or fail doing things your own way. I really appreciated the fact that he took my call because after he finished at Ipswich Town he became quite reclusive. It was a crying shame that John was largely overlooked at that time and, just like Bobby Moore, all that experience and first class football knowledge was not put to good use. John had a unique bank of knowledge that shouldn't have been ignored.

I don't think John had a sense of the high esteem in which he was held by the players and the fans. He only ever talked in terms of the club doing this or the players doing that. He would never talk about himself and I never heard him say: "I did this" or "I did that."

In 2005, Galey and I hosted a reunion of the 1975 and 1980 FA Cup winning teams at the Britannia Hotel in London's Docklands. We weren't sure if John would come along because he had been out of the game for ten years. He seemed to find it hard to believe just how adored he was by so many West Ham people. There were over 500 people there that night and the standing ovation John got will live long in the memory.

I was in Florida when I heard the news that John had died. I receive a text saying: "Sorry to hear about John." I had to stop and think what it was about. Then a few more texts filtered through and the worst imaginable thing was starting to dawn on me. I called Galey and he confirmed the terrible news.

The funeral was something I couldn't miss under any circumstances and judging by the number of people in Ipswich that day, a lot of people felt the same. It was incredibly moving and great to see Alex Ferguson and so many people from

West Ham, Ipswich and the football world at large. He clearly had a positive effect on many, many people. It was just an unbelievable turnout.

I'm often asked, at various functions and reunions, about my favourite manager. Now, I played under some really good ones in Howard Kendall at Everton, Bobby Robson at England and Martin O'Neill at Leicester City, but I always come back to John Lyall as being the best. Basically, he was the man who gave me everything. Without him there may not have been anything else.
Tony Cottee

Player's comments;

He was a better player than people gave him credit for. Sure, he'd get you a goal but he had a broader skill set than that. Marin O'Neill and I had him at Leicester City later on in his career and he was great for us.
Steve Walford

'Poacher' we called him and it was obvious he was going to score goals at all levels. Strong, fit and fast, and a clinical finisher.
Ray Houghton

Tony was one of my first room-mates on away trips and he looked after me. I thought we had a good connection on the pitch but didn't play enough games together because, obviously, he moved to Everton.
Kevin Keen

He was always doing extra training, always out there with a bag of balls, knocking them in with his left foot and right foot. He was very dedicated from a very early age.
Dale Banton

I taught him everything he knew about scoring goals! It doesn't get any better than scoring against Tottenham on your debut.
Greg Campbell

A top goalscorer who loved scoring goals. I was very disappointed when he went to Everton. I don't think he handled it well but there you go. I should add that John was the reason we got what we did for him. The board wanted to accept a lot less but John convinced them to wait a bit longer for a better offer which they did and the club ended up getting a lot more. Whenever we played Coventry City he scored. I think I took charge of West Ham against Coventry on one occasion when John was ill and they had Dave Sexton in charge. We beat them that day and TC scored.
Mick McGiven

He was a damn fine striker.
Derek Hales

We've known each other since we were kids. Always handy to have a striker who only needs one touch.
George Parris

Even from a very young age, TC was the most single-minded of strikers. In his autobiography he criticises me for not passing to him in a reserve team match! If we won 3-0 but Tony didn't score, he'd be sulking for a week.
Bobby Barnes

I've known Tony since we played Under-11s football together at Chadwell Heath. I also played with Kerry Dixon at Chelsea and always felt they had the same striker's mentality.
Alan Dickens

I used to kick him and McAvennie in training and they got the hump about it. John told me to get after them to keep them on their toes.
Paul Hilton

If every player was like Tony Cottee there wouldn't be any need for physios. I don't think I saw him once in my surgery. When he scored a hat-trick on his debut for Everton, West Ham had just lost 0-4 to Southampton at the Dell. When I heard the news my instinct was to shout: "Yes!" because Cottee was a friend of mine. John Lyall was very bemused and turned round to me and said: "You alright, Rob?"
Rob Jenkins

With Frank McAvennie - the last great West Ham United strike partnership, Hornchurch, 2017

54 – DAVE SWINDLEHURST

"A great man, sorely missed."

Born: Edgware, Middlesex, January 6, 1956 • Position: Striker • Games played for West Ham United: 71 (1983-85)

Goals: 18 • Debut: March 26, 1983 v Norwich City (a) D 1-1 Att: 17, 639

Norwich City: Woods, Haylock, Downs, Mendham, Walford, Watson, Barham, O'Neill, Deehan, Bertschin,* Channon. Sub: Jack

West Ham United: Parkes, Stewart, Lampard, Bonds, Martin, Devonshire, Orr, Goddard, **Swindlehurst**, Dickens, Pike.

David Swindlehurst was bought from Derby County for £160,000 in March 1983. He joined West Ham United with a burgeoning reputation, having been a prolific goalscorer at both Crystal Palace and Derby County.

During his time at Upton Park, West Ham enjoyed top spot in the league for two months and spent over half of the 1983-84 season inside the top three. A spate of injuries to several key players eventually burst the bubble.

David suffered from his own series of injuries and was transferred to Sunderland in 1985.

For the past 20 years David has been working at Harrodian School in Barnes. *"I primarily head up the football there and also help with rugby and cricket."*

David lives in Surrey and had the following memories of John Lyall:

John was a very nice man. His man-management skills were fantastic. He had a calm authority about him so it was easy for the players to talk to him. He was very professional in everything he did.

Eddie Baily had been up to watch me at Derby County a few times, but I was in talks with Aston Villa and it looked for a time that I would sign for them. John came up and talked to me and the thought of returning to London and being with my family had a strong appeal. It was an easy decision in the end and I

Celebrating with Tony Cottee after scoring against Coventry City, September 1983

moved into the Bromley area. Billy Bonds lived in Chislehurst, so we'd travel in to Chadwell Heath together. The Blackwall Tunnel made sure we weren't always on time!

Training was enjoyable with plenty of shooting practice, keep-ball sessions and set piece plays. John planned everything very thoroughly and kept us fit and sharp ahead of matchday. It makes me laugh nowadays, because the Premier League commentators give the impression that football is being played properly for the very first time. What were we playing then? They have completely forgotten everything that occurred prior to the Premier League and bundle us into categories such as 'Hoofers' and 'Chasers.'

That is a gross injustice because we played some very good football at West Ham. Parkesy played it out to Frank Lampard, who'd run with it before playing it to Alan Devonshire. Dev used his pace to take on a man before putting me in on goal. We enjoyed some great link-up play between us and I certainly had plenty of chances.

My debut at Norwich City was a tight game and there weren't too many chances flying around. I have fonder memories of my home debut against Watford because I scored the winner. Franky Van Der Elst scored a good goal that day, too.

During my first full season at Upton Park – 1983-84 – we got off to a really good start. I scored six goals in five matches and we were top of the league throughout September. I always say that you are only as good as the people around you and, unfortunately, Dev picked up a bad injury and both Billy Bonds and Trevor Brooking were out for long periods. To cap it all, Steve Whitton and Alvin Martin were injured in a car accident so the results started to fall away. We finished ninth but, at full strength, would have been a lot higher.

I managed to score 18 goals for West Ham so there are some good memories to reflect on. I scored against Spurs at White Hart Lane and at home to Manchester United. The hat-trick I got against Coventry City gave me a lot of satisfaction. All strikers welcome those. It was a shame that I picked up a couple of injuries which kept me out for a while, otherwise my record would have been better.

I think John liked me because I was hungry to play and was scoring goals with my head and either foot. I'd also played in midfield for Crystal Palace and Derby County so that would have given him another option, too. I was easy to get on with and slotted in well with the team. I was lucky in that West Ham had a very high calibre of player at that time. Billy Bonds, Alan Devonshire, Trevor Brooking and Frank Lampard were all top pros. It was a terrific time.

I loved the dressing room atmosphere before kick-off. John was very calm because he knew that all the hard work and preparation had been done at Chadwell Heath during the week. Ronnie Boyce and Mick McGiven were there making sure everyone knew their job and what was expected of them.

We just had to go out there and produce on the day.

I got on well with all the lads but spent quite a bit of time with Alvin Martin and Steve Whitton. Phil Parkes was another top man and I went on one of his end of season trips to Guernsey. Parkesy loves that part of the world and we played against a local team which was great fun.

At the beginning of the 1984-85 season I had a problem with my cruciate knee ligament, which kept me out for three months. I came back and played a few games but then fractured my ankle at Tottenham Hotspur on Boxing Day.

I would place John Lyall alongside Terry Venables as the best managers I played under. Venables coached me at Crystal Palace and, like John, was very innovative in his approach.
Dave Swindlehurst

Dave was a good target man and very similar in style to John Radford. Very strong, with excellent aerial ability. I thought he was a good player and did very well for West Ham. His link-up play was excellent. He was a man's man.
Mick McGiven

Dave had the biggest shoulders I've ever seen!
Paul Hilton

I played up front with Swindles. He was underrated and a real powerhouse. We had a good team during that 1983-84 season and were flying high for a while. Unfortunately, Dev sustained a bad injury and both Alvin Martin and Stevie Whitton were ruled out after a car accident.
Tony Cottee

Dave at home in Surrey, November 2017

Back row: Dickens, Brooking, Parkes, Bonds, McAlister, Swindlehurst, Martin.

Middle row: Whitton, Brush, Donald, Devonshire, Stewart, Orr, Walford.

Front row: Lampard, Goddard, Pike, Allen, Barnes, Cottee.

CHAPTER TEN
1983-84

"We have certainly reached the end of what I would call a memorable era. With Trevor now gone, and Frank and Billy no longer first team regulars, we have a lot of experience to replace." **John Lyall**

Trevor Brooking brings the curtain down on 19 years as a player. Seen here with Barry Simmons at the start of his journey

Trevor Brooking retired at the end of the season. His 102 goals from 642 appearances from midfield are numbers which are unlikely to be posted for some considerable time to come. He was voted Hammer of the Year for a record fifth time.

West Ham topped the league for much of the early part of the season but eventually fell away and finished 7th. A combination of injuries and a car crash, which involved Alvin Martin and Steve Whitton, accounted for the dramatic loss of form.

Alan Devonshire suffered an atrocious injury during an FA Cup match against Wigan Athletic. Three ligaments were snapped in his right knee.

In the League Cup, the club registered its highest ever victory, beating Bury 10-0 at home and 12-1 on aggregate. In a strange twist of fate, John Lyall signed their centre-half, Paul Hilton, four months later.

A new, larger, style programme was launched. It marked the end of a 60-year association with local printers Helliar and Sons.

Steve Walford joined from Norwich City for £160,000 and local boy, Steve Whitton, signed from Coventry City for £200,000. Francois Van der Elst returned to Belgium.

West Ham signed a £150,000 shirt deal with Adidas. Avco Trust become the first ever shirt sponsors.

There were four new debutants during the season: Steve Walford, Steve Whitton, Warren Donald and Paul Hilton.

Here is their story...

John with representatives of Avco Trust, West Ham United's first ever shirt sponsor

55 – STEVE WALFORD

" The atmosphere at West Ham United was tremendous. It was very friendly and easily one of my most enjoyable times at a football club. John looked after the players and their families. When my wife was poorly and had to go into hospital, there was always a bouquet of flowers from the club by her bedside."

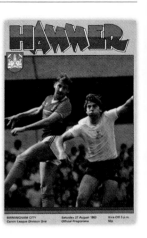

Born: Highgate, London, January 5, 1958 • **Position:** Defender • **Games played for West Ham United:** 147 (1983-87)

Goals: 4 • **Honours under John Lyall:** 1985-86: Member of West Ham United's highest ever league finish (third)

Debut: August 27, 1983 v Birmingham City (h) W 4-0 (Cottee 2, Martin, Swindlehurst). Att: 19,729

West Ham United: Parkes, Stewart, **Walford**, Bonds, Martin, Devonshire, Whitton, Cottee, Swindlehurst, Brooking*, Pike. Sub: Orr.*

Birmingham City: Coton, Hagan, Stevenson, Blake, Wright, Broadhurst, Handysides*, Phillips, Harford, Van der Hauwe, Hopkins Sub: Rees.*

Steven Joseph Walford grew up in Tollington Park, North London. *"My parents split up when I was 11. My dad had been a milk man and my mum had done various jobs to support us."*

"Wally," as he is affectionately known by his teammates at West Ham United, had a good football pedigree by the time John Lyall paid Norwich City £160,000 for his services in 1983. He had played for Arsenal in their FA Cup final victory over Manchester United in 1979 and won promotion with the Canaries in 1982.

The six years he spent at Upton Park are defined by the 'almost men' of the 1985-86 season. Steve made 33 appearances in defence during that historic season. Sadly, recurring problems with his knee, combined with a loss of form, saw him leave the club in 1989.

Steve is married to Theresa and they have two girls, Katy and Emma, and a boy, Joseph. He stays in touch with many of his West Ham teammates and attends various reunions.

"Nowadays, I am a semi-retired old codger with a metal knee and a metal hip! Since 1994 I've always been part of Martin O'Neil's coaching team and we have enjoyed a fair amount of success at Wycombe Wanderers, Leicester City and Celtic. We continue in that role with the Republic of Ireland and the big aim is to qualify for the 2018 World Cup finals."

Despite his busy schedule with the Republic of Ireland's

World Cup qualifying campaign, Steve took the time to discuss John Lyall:

I went to school in North London and, as an 11-year-old, I was invited to watch a match at West Ham United. It was against Sunderland in 1969, the season after Geoff Hurst had scored six against them in an 8-0 rout. It was a terrific day and afterwards I met Ron Greenwood and all the players. It was quite an experience for a young lad. I then started training at Chadwell Heath and Upton Park. John was coaching the evening sessions at the ground and was a really nice man and a very good coach. It was ironic really because Frank Lampard snr was helping John on those evenings and little did I know that John would choose me to be Frank's successor at left back some 14 years later!

It was through that experience that I developed a soft spot for West Ham. They gave the young lads a free pass to watch the first team and we'd stand in the players' pen near the tunnel. I only trained with West Ham for about a year because I found the travelling horrendous. I had to get to Mile End and take the green line to Chadwell Heath, which was miles for me as a young kid. Tottenham asked me to train with them. It was only a 20 minute bus ride to White Hart Lane, so it was a lot easier for me, even though I preferred West Ham.

John signed me as a left-back from Norwich City but I much preferred playing centre-half. I always felt a bit isolated at left-back but I wanted to return to West Ham so I agreed to play left-back.

John's training sessions were very tough – it was the hardest I've ever trained at any club. It was enjoyable but very physical and the only time it petered off a little bit was on Friday when John would set up a five-a-side kick about. John was very hands on and usually attended every session. On Thursday he'd ask Mick McGiven to coach the defenders while John and Ron Boyce took the attackers for some shooting practice.

John was very good at assessing your strengths and weaknesses and passed on very sound advice. He said something to me which I still share with young players today and have always passed on to others throughout my coaching career. Because I was playing left-back I was expected to put in more crosses which wasn't a particular strength of mine. It was another reason why I preferred to play centre-back. In training, most of my crosses were going behind the goal so John took me to one side and advised me to bend my run. It was such a simple piece of advice but made so much sense. I'd been running up to the ball and hitting it far too straight. Some players, like Trevor Brooking and Alan Devonshire, could cross a ball running straight on, but mere mortals like me couldn't wrap their foot and body around the ball to get the bend. So I started to arc my run before crossing and I had a lot more success after that.

Once, when we were practicing volleying the ball, John shouted: "Shoulder!" At first I didn't have a clue what he meant, but then he explained that when volleying a ball it helps to drop your shoulder because your leg will naturally come up over the ball, making it a lot easier to control and get the right direction

I had a flying start at West Ham. We won the first five games I played in and I managed to score a couple as well – the first one was a fluke up at Everton. I went to cross it with my right foot and it just looped over the keeper's head. I think Jim Arnold was in goal and he never played again. Neville Southall replaced him.

It was funny because after our fifth straight win I remember being in the bath after the game and Steve Whitton, who had a very good sense of humour, asked if we were safe yet! He had spent quite a bit of time at Coventry City so avoiding relegation was the only thing on his mind!

I played in the 10-0 victory over Bury in the League Cup, which was a strange night. We had beaten them 2-1 at their place in a tightly fought match, but they just lost all heart in the second leg. West Ham had been scouting Bury's centre-half, Paul Hilton, prior to those games, but a lot of eyebrows were raised when John signed him. Thankfully, Hilts did all right for us, so it was a good decision to sign him.

One of the big coaching decisions John made while I was there came during the famed 1985-86 season. In the very first game of the season, he played Frank McAvennie in a midfield role behind Paul Goddard and Tony Cottee. Unfortunately, Goddard picked up an injury so John brought on Alan Dickens in midfield and moved McAvennie up alongside Cottee. Just

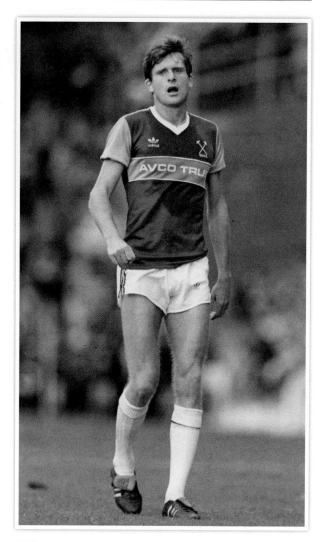

Wally

'WHY WE WANTED WALFORD' — LYALL

WEST Ham manager John Lyall revealed this week why he signed defender Steve Walford from Norwich.

"I wanted to strengthen our squad—you can never have a big enough squad. We also have to cater for the future, too. We were looking at a number of defenders and Steve was one of the quality we wanted and at the price we could afford." he declared.

But he denied that the latest signing means an early departure from Upton Park of either the veteran Frank Lampard or Paul Brush. "Steve's arrival merely helps to increase the competition for first-team places, which is always a healthy thing." said John.

Battling with Manchester United's Arthur Graham at Old Trafford, April 1984

like that, one of the greatest strike partnerships in the club's history was formed.

If we lost badly, John kept us in the dressing room for a long time after the final whistle. Once, we lost up at Leicester City, so he kept us in the dressing room for a big inquest after the game. I piped up and made a couple of points which John addressed and explained his own position. When we did eventually take our showers, Frank Lampard came over to me and told me not to ask any more questions because they only kept us there much longer. I kept quiet after that!

Prior to the 1985-86 season, John changed things around during the pre-season. He took a different approach to running and we did fewer long distance runs around Hainault Forest and a lot more sprints over 100 metres, 200 metres etc. He brought in a fitness coach to facilitate this and I think it helped to keep us fresher and sharpened our instincts. We didn't seem to burn out as quickly, and, if anything, got a lot stronger as the season progressed. I think our unbeaten run of 20 odd games remains a record in the top flight for West Ham. It still very disappointing when Tottenham Hotspur ended the run on

Boxing Day. I'd always liked to beat them and it always felt that little bit worse when they beat us.

John always treated me very fairly and I was very surprised when the club sacked him. Nobody saw that coming, least of all John. I had already left the club. John had told me that they were not going to renew my contract and I understood all the reasons why and left on very amicable terms with John.

I was very fortunate in my career in that I was coached by some top people and John is right up there with the best of them. Don Howe was a terrific coach at Arsenal and I also liked Mel Machin at Norwich City. If John did have a downfall as a coach it would be the fact that he didn't praise players very much. I don't recall him ever coming into the dressing and saying well done you and what you did was great. I found that sort of thing gave me a lift. Mel Machin was quite good at that.

In 2006, I had just landed in Singapore on holiday when a friend called me up to say that John had died. I just couldn't believe it. Thankfully, I was home in time to attend the funeral in Ipswich. I remember chatting with Bonzo and Pop Robson on that day.

It was a shame John died so young, and that he left the

Repelling the advances of Manchester City's Gordon Smith, November 1984

game so early, because he had so much experience to pass on to the next generation. I'm starting to feel a bit like that as I approach 60. I think the FA or the football clubs themselves should make sure that experienced coaches like John Lyall, like Don Howe and like so many others, are given a role in preparing the next generation to play the game in the right way and with the right code of conduct.

Too many top class football brains are allowed to leave the game and John was certainly one of those. It is ridiculous to treat such people as if they are old dinosaurs because the English game needs as much help as it can get, especially the national team. To ignore great minds with 50 years of first class experience is simply wrong.

Steve Walford

I loved playing with Wally because he was such a great organiser and was always talking during a game. I'm not surprised he has had such a successful career in coaching. Long may it continue!

Tony Gale

I've seen Wally quite a lot during our respective coaching careers and he has a very astute footballing brain. The image I have of him as a player, shows him sitting in the changing room after a game, legs crossed and saying to no one in particular: "We could have done this, we could have done that. This could have been better, if only we'd done this."

Kevin Keen

He loved a cigar did Wally.

Warren Donald

We both wanted to wear the Number 3 shirt. Wally was a dedicated pro who gave me some good advice.

George Parris

Wally is the most laid back fella you're ever going to meet in your life. Loved a 'La Di Da' before and after a match!

Greg Campbell

We were flying home from a pre-season tour and Wally was trying to throw himself out of the plane! They had to restrain him because he was having a panic attack.

Alan Dickens

He had an excellent left foot and a good understanding of the game. I remember we went to Everton where we hadn't won in donkey's years and Wally scored with his right foot to win the match. It just couldn't happen but it did! He'd switch off sometimes and if he made a mistake he would be very hard on himself. It was like the world was crashing in on him but that was because he loved the game so much. A really good guy.

Mick McGiven

Wally was the reason West Ham players' first started to change their shirt at half-time. Before he arrived, nobody had ever asked for a clean shirt, but Wally kept going on and on about how Arsenal did it. In the end the club started buying more shirts.

Eddie Gillam

At a West Ham reunion, September 2017

56 – STEVE WHITTON

"I remember waking up in Newham Hospital at about six o'clock in the morning and John was standing there. He'd heard about the car crash and had driven to check on me and Alvin, immediately. Once he knew it wasn't life threatening, he gave us both a few harsh words, that's for sure!"

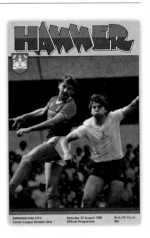

Born: East Ham, London, December 4, 1960 • **Position:** Striker • Games played for West Ham United: 46 (1983-85)

Goals: 8 • Debut: August 27, 1983 v Birmingham City (h) W 4-0 (Cottee 2, Martin, Swindlehurst) Att: 19,279

West Ham United: Parkes, Stewart, Walford, Bonds, Martin, Devonshire, **Whitton**, Cottee, Swindlehurst, Brooking Pike. Sub: Orr.

Birmingham City: Coton, Hagan, Stevenson, Blake, Wright, Broadhurst, Handysides, Phillips, Harford, Van Den Hauwe, Hopkins. Sub: Rees.

Stephen Paul Whitton was one of four sons born to parents, Les and Maureen. *"Both my mum and dad worked for the Thames Water Authority. I was born in Mountfield Road, East Ham and grew up in Darwell Close, just off the Flanders Playing Fields, where I played football as a kid."*

Whitton was a Newham Schools product who always wanted to play for West Ham United. Ironically, in 1978, he was lured away by the scouting system and youth team set up at Coventry City. It would be five years before 'Whit' would return to the East End and finally pull on the claret and blue shirt. Sadly, Steve was involved in a car crash with Alvin Martin, which limited his first team opportunities. After just two seasons he moved on to Birmingham City.

"For the past 15 years I've been living and working in Marbella, where I run a car hire company. There are a few ex pros who live close by. John Gidman, who played for Villa, Everton and Man United and Larry Lloyd of Liverpool and Nottingham Forest. I first came out here 35 years ago so I always knew where I wanted to be. I haven't seen any of the lads from my West Ham days for quite some time. Be sure to remember me to all of them. There's a beach out here anytime they need one!"

Following are Steve's recollections from his time at West Ham:

The first thing John talked to me about was family. He was happy that I was married and I felt I could talk to him about anything.

I first met John when I was playing for Coventry City. Bobby Gould had just been appointed manager and my contract was up. Gouldy asked me to talk to him before making any decisions about my future. John Lyall called me up and I said: "Yes" straight away! I really couldn't turn down John's offer and the thought of playing for my home town club excited me. Gouldy had been at West Ham himself so understood why I wanted to go there.

I actually joined West Ham as a schoolboy. There were six of us playing for Rippleway Newham, but bizarrely, we all signed for Coventry City because they looked after us really well. They had a very good youth system. Gordon Milne was the manager when I joined but it was his successor, Dave Sexton who gave me my chance. He put me in the first team straight away.

I don't think I fulfilled my potential at West Ham. I could cross the ball well and was a good passer but I couldn't run so John certainly didn't sign me for my pace! My favourite position was right-side midfield.

I had a great first year, but was then involved in a car crash with Alvin Martin which put me out of action for six months. By the time I got back to full fitness John had bought Frank McAvennie and Mark Ward. It was always going to be difficult for me after that. John did tell me he wanted me to say, but I wanted to play first team football so ended up signing for Birmingham City where I had a really good three years. From there, I signed for Ron Atkinson at Sheffield Wednesday before being reunited with John at Ipswich Town.

I don't remember much about the car accident. I was out with Alvin late one night and he was driving. He drove a sponsored Toyota Super at the time which was built for speed. I remember going around a long, left-handed, bend in Bow. It was pouring with rain and then everything went black. We hit a lamp post and a tree. I broke my shoulder and Alvin smashed six ribs. It was the beginning of the end because I struggled to get back in the side.

John knew how to relate to his players throughout the different stages of their career. He was attentive, supportive and full of advice for the young kids and more relaxed and less hands-on with the experienced pros. At all levels he was the perfect man-manager. Even when a player was injured he'd always make a point of asking how they were. Some managers don't have so much time for injured players but John was never like that. When I was playing in the reserves he was always interested in how I was getting on. I never felt left out or marginalised. He knew when to coach you and when to leave you to your own devices. I adopted a lot of John's coaching style when I managed Colchester United.

I scored eight times for West Ham and one that springs to mind came against Coventry City. I cut in from the right and hit a screamer into the top corner with my left foot. It was against all my former teammates so it felt great.

I embraced the social side of football a bit too much while I was at West Ham. I was a local boy and everyone wanted to buy me a pint. I was a young kid so I didn't see the point of saying, "No."

I got on well with Frank Lampard and spent quite a bit of time in his pub, The Britannia. I had three elder brothers so it was hard for me to say no to a drink, which probably wasn't the best thing for my career at West Ham. Frank had a nightclub called Reflections and we went in there quite a bit, too. I got done for drink driving so wasn't exactly the model footballer, but John was there to help me through those times. Anything I needed, he was there. Unfortunately, he was also there with things I didn't need – like several fines for being overweight! I didn't' mind, because I was having a great time. West Ham was my club and I wouldn't change my time there for the world. It's just a shame that I played all my best football after I left West Ham. The fans gave me quite a lot of stick and rightly so! After a good start the goals had dried up. I'd have behaved just like them in their shoes. I was probably a bit too laid back at West Ham.

There was a big difference between the John Lyall at West Ham and the John Lyall at Ipswich. He was so much more relaxed at Ipswich.

When I remember John, I think: "He signed me twice." It gave me so much confidence because he must have really

Outjumping Chris Hughton at White Hart Lane, a game in which Steve scored his first goal for West Ham, September 1983

believed in me.
Steve Whitton

Whit left his mark on his colleagues:

A local West Ham boy who had skill in abundance. The only problem was that he was asthmatic and he found it difficult to get up a full head of steam. He had great ability on the ball but there was fierce competition at West Ham at that time. If you look at his record after he left West Ham, he scored his fair share of goals for every team he played for.
Mick McGiven

He was the best five-a-side player I ever saw. On Friday mornings when John set up a five-a-side match, Whitton was just brilliant. He held the ball, scored loads of goals and did lots of little tricks. I think he struggled with his fitness a bit because he didn't have the same control on a full size pitch.
Tony Cottee

Whit was playing for Coventry City before we bought him. He had a good game against West Ham once, but it felt as if he took on a couple of our players so we signed him! Eddie Gillam
I liked Whit. He liked the other side of football and enjoyed a drink. He had a great sense of humour.
Steve Walford

He was hilarious, but wasn't the most politically correct of characters. We played out in Japan in the Kirin Cup and Whit kept saying: "What you chink you're doing? What you China do?" Every time he signed his autograph he'd say: "Remember Bobby Moore." At half-time, in one of the games out there, he did a session of keepie-uppie and had 20,000 fans applauding him. He had a lot of skill.
Greg Campbell

He had masses of talent.
George Parris

The crowd called him 'Nelly the Elephant' so we did, too. He had a lot of natural talent and should have done a lot better than he did. Off the field he was a bit of a loose cannon, otherwise he could have been a top quality player.
Tony Gale

Whit was a clever player, but the fans got on his back and they never saw the best of him. He should have been a top player.
Alan Dickens

Steve enjoyed a lager. John would often have him in his office reprimanding him about one thing or another. It was usually

drink related. Whit had a great time at the club he loved.
Everald La Ronde

He made me laugh. Every pre-season he would sit in the changing room and say: "Let the runners run and the players play." Whit could not run! He had a good football brain, a shot almost as powerful as Julian Dicks but, athletically it was a bit of a struggle for him at times.
Kevin Keen

I had to share a room with Whitto and Dave Swindlehurst in Guernsey for four days. What an absolute pair of first class jokers! They were so funny. Whit had one of the hardest shots I've ever seen.
Paul Hilton

If Whit had got himself a lot fitter I think he could have been a world beater. He had all the attributes. He was a local boy who wanted to play for West Ham so could have left a big legacy.
Bobby Barnes

'Whit' with son, Stanley in Marbella

John at work

57 – WARREN DONALD

"I can still see John getting out of his jag, wearing his suit. I was really impressed by him and his coaching staff."

Born: Hillingdon, London, October 7, 1964 • **Position:** Midfield • **Games played for West Ham United:** 2 (1983-84)

Debut: December 26, 1983 v Southampton (h) L 0-1 (Wallace) Att: 22,221

West Ham United: Parkes, Stewart, Lampard,* Walford, Martin, Devonshire, Whitton, Orr, Cottee, Brooking, Dickens. Sub: **Donald.***

Southampton: Shilton, Mills, Dennis, Armstrong K, Agboola, Williams, Holmes, Curtis*, Worthington, Armstrong D, Wallace. Sub: Puckett.*

Warren Ramsey Donald enjoyed a long career in football, playing in over 350 matches spanning 15 years. The journey started at West Ham United and although his first team appearances were limited, the experience has left him a lifelong Hammers fan. *"I went back to Upton Park for the final match. I've never known an atmosphere like it."*

His father, Clive, was a brick layer while his mother, Frances, worked for Honeywell Computers. In fact, it was his mother who gave him his nickname, 'Wozzer,' when growing up in the family home in Morello Avenue, Hillingdon. *"Everyone at West Ham called me by that nickname, even John."*

Today, Warren lives with his wife, Vanessa, and their son Alex in York: *"I do a lot of scouting with Graham Carr who managed me at Northampton Town. He has been very good to me and takes me all over the country and overseas to watch players for Newcastle United. We've developed a really good friendship. He has been in the game for so long and knows so many players and scouts so it really is a fantastic education."*

Wozza had the following recollections of John Lyall:

I was spotted by Eddie Baily playing local football in Hillingdon. He invited me along for a trial at West Ham United and they offered me an apprenticeship. I'd been to Chelsea, Watford and Leyton Orient, too, but it was West Ham that really took a keen interest. As a boy I took the 207 bus to watch QPR play,

Wozza

Scoring against Hamish McAlpine of Dundee United in a friendly at Upton Park, February 1983

but my experience at West Ham has left both me and my son, Alex, supporting the Hammers.

When I first met John he was a very professional man, very smart and softly spoken. I can still see him getting out of his jag wearing his suit. I was really impressed by him and his coaching team. Initially, I was coached by Tony Carr, who was excellent at bringing through the young lads into the first team.

I lived in digs in Barkingside with Mrs Cross which was great but I felt a bit lonely. After training I would go back to my digs and didn't really know what to do. I watched a bit of telly but very little else. It was all part of learning to become a professional footballer. I had to sacrifice a few things in order to get on. I later shared a place in Whipps Cross with a lad called Robert Wall. Then, from 1981 until 1985, I lived in Collier Row with Tony Cottee and his mum and dad. I got on well with Tony.

A few of the senior pros really looked after me. Phil Parkes, Paul Goddard and Alan Devonshire let me share their taxi from Barking to Chadwell Heath. Alan Dickens and George Parris were two other good guys I really liked.

On the training ground John liked to make sure we understood what we were doing and why we were doing it. If he wasn't happy with something he'd stop and take it back until we did it properly. Sometimes, he'd split the group up into defenders, midfielders and attackers so that the training had a greater focus on those positions. I was only a young boy and wanted to learn quickly and it all seemed very exciting. I was learning the West Ham way which was passing and moving and playing entertaining football. John really brought me on and I developed into a decent footballer. There was a great camaraderie amongst the youngsters and the senior pros. The

club had a policy whereby everyone ate together so we were all bonding and getting on.

I preferred playing in central midfield because I got more involved but West Ham had some very good midfielders at the time with Trevor Brooking, Paul Allen, Geoff Pike and Alan Devonshire, so it was always going to be difficult to make my mark. I thought I was a very good tackler and liked to go in hard without worrying about getting hurt. My passing was very good and although I wasn't super quick I had a good level of fitness and could get through 90 minutes without any problem.

John and his coaching staff certainly moved my career forward and helped to keep a lot of the young lads level-headed at an important time in their careers.

I found him to be a very calm character. In the dressing room he spoke calmly and got his point across clearly, even if things weren't going our way. He wasn't one for putting players down. Instead, he was all about encouraging players. Ronnie Boyce and Mick McGiven could be quite the opposite and would blow their top if they thought we were letting ourselves down.

John liked me to pass the ball quickly and then make an angle to receive the ball. He didn't want me to hold on to the ball too long. Just little bits of advice like that helped me to play confidently and with a clear vision.

I played against Dundee United in a pre-season friendly and I managed to score which was a great moment for me in front of the fans at Upton Park. Then, on December 26 1983, I was listed in the 16-man squad to play Southampton at home. I was really excited, but thought I would only be there to look after the kit and watch the game. However, when I got to the ground, John told me I was one of the substitutes which was a real bonus. Fate seemed to take over because Frank Lampard picked up a nasty cut on his head and had to come off, so, just like that, I was running out for my first team debut. I just couldn't believe it and even though we lost 0-1, it was an unforgettable experience. John told me to enjoy myself and to pass the ball like I had been doing on the training ground. I feel like I did that and hopefully didn't disappoint the 22,000 fans.

After that first taste of top flight football, I went back in the reserves for a few months before playing my second - and final - match for West Ham. It was against Everton at the end of the 1983-84 season. This time I started the match but once again we lost 0-1. Everton were a strong team so it was another really tough experience for me.

John did offer me a new two-year contract but I decided to leave. The money wasn't going to increase unless I got in the first team so I thought it would be better to move on. I went out on loan to Northampton Town and Graham Carr, the manager, came and watched me a few times before making a bid of £12,000. John called me into his office and asked if I wanted to go? That's how it came about and that was the last time I saw John.

A short while later, another lad from West Ham also signed for Northampton. His name was Keith McPherson and we struck up a good friendship and shared digs together. I missed the East End, and the football at Northampton was very different. At that level a more direct approached was required and we won promotion playing that way.

I wish I had stayed at West Ham because players like George Parris and Steve Potts eventually got their chance and became regulars in the first team. However, I don't regret leaving because I went on to have five good years with The Cobblers.

I had great times at West Ham and have only good memories of John. He instilled me with the right discipline, taught me the skills I needed to become a professional footballer and led by example when it came to the right way to treat people properly.

I wasn't around John as much as the established players but I could see he was a decent and fair minded man. I hope he is having a good life up there. Rest in peace.

Warren Donald

Energetic, honest and hard working right-sided midfield player. He could make a goal and score a goal. I bumped into Wozza at the final match at Upton Park and was pleased to hear he is doing a bit of scouting with Graham Carr who he played for at Northampton.

Mick McGiven

We played in midfield together and he was tenacious and passed the ball well, but he wasn't quite ready to hold down a first team place at West Ham.

Alan Dickens

Wozza was my boot boy at West Ham. I bumped into him not so long ago and was pleased to hear he is doing some scouting.

Tony Gale

We played for the England Schoolboys together. He was a tough tackler and hard worker.

George Parris

Warren used to live at my house when he was a first year apprentice. We travelled into work together. He was a dependable midfield player but sadly his career didn't take off at West Ham. I haven't seen him for years but as youngsters we were good friends.

Tony Cottee

It was great to catch up with Wozza at the final match at the old place.

Greg Campbell

He was only small but he wasn't scared of anyone and would always get his foot in and make his presence felt in midfield.

Everald La Ronde

Warren in March 2017

58 – PAUL HILTON

" It was lucky West Ham didn't beat Bury 11-0 because John might not have signed me! "

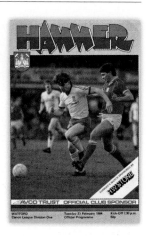

Born: Born: Oldham, Greater Manchester, October 8, 1959 • **Position:** Central-defence/midfield

Games played for West Ham United: 79 (1984-89) • **Goals:** 8 • **Honours under John Lyall:** 1985-86: Member of West Ham United's highest finishing league team • **Debut:** February 21, 1984 v Watford (h) L 2-4 (Swindlehurst, B Barnes – Johnston, J Barnes 2, Callaghan) Att: 19,241

West Ham United: Parkes, Stewart, Lampard, Bonds, Walford, **Hilton,** Barnes, Cottee, Swindlehurst, Allen, Dickens.

Watford: Sherwood, Bardsley, Rostron, Sims, Franklin, Taylor, Jackett, Callaghan, Johnston, Barnes, Atkinson.

West Ham's new signing, Paul Hilton last night. Picture : ROB TAGGART

Lyall snaps up bargain boy Hilton

BY HARRY HARRIS

Paul Hilton was playing for Bury and living with his parents in Oldham's Union Street West, when, in February 1984, John Lyall made the call to sign him for £100,000. *"My parents, Tommy and Doris, were greengrocers and my dad was also a Jazz trumpet player. His band actually played at the Manchester United Christmas ball once!"*

Nicknamed, 'Spider', Hilton's opportunities in the claret and blue were restricted to 79 matches over six years. This was largely due to the strong central defensive pairing of Alvin Martin and Tony Gale.

Like several players from the John Lyall era, Hilton entered the world of coaching after injury forced him to retire from playing. He worked for West Ham United during Billy Bonds' time as manager in the early 1990s.

"Today, I live in Great Dunmow and deliver cars for BMW. I had a knee replacement in 2015 so am now back to full fitness but I haven't been involved in coaching for a few years. I'd like to get back into the game but it is very difficult at my tender age of 58. Sadly, that is the same story for so many experienced coaches. It doesn't help that quite a few work for nothing."

Paul's affection for John Lyall hasn't waned over time and his recollections of West Ham United clearly represent a

Hilts

special time in his life:

John was a great man and a great manager. Even on the phone when I first spoke to him he was just so down to earth. He was trying to sign me and came across as very impressive indeed. I was playing for Bury and the manager, Jim Iley, informed me that both Portsmouth and West Ham United had come in for me. He advised me to sign for West Ham because of their impressive reputation. He told me that John Lyall was going to call me at four o'clock and he rang dead on time. We had a chat and I agreed to join. John arranged my train ticket from Manchester and both he and Eddie Baily picked me up at Euston station. I sat in John's Jag and he was asking me about all the players I'd played against and I found his knowledge of players, and the game in general, a few steps up from what I'd been used to. I was 24-years-old at the time and he said that he'd been watching me for about 18 months. The scouting reports had described me as a hard working type who could play in several positions and John obviously liked that about me. At Bury I'd played up front and in midfield, as well as at centre-half. I'd also scored a few goals in the lower leagues so had a few strings to my bow.

From the moment I signed, John was always asking about me and my family and how I was settling in. I felt so wanted that when a couple of other club's came in for me I didn't consider them at all because I wanted to play for John.

When I broke my nose in a reserve match, John actually drove to my house in Ilford and took me to the hospital near Epping so that my wife didn't have to drive in the evening. Judy was pregnant at the time so John was a terrific help. That was over 30-years ago but you just don't forget gestures like that.

I didn't know I was making my West Ham debut until I got to the ground, which was probably a ploy of John's in order to keep me calm. We were playing Watford and he called me into his office and told me he'd decided to play me: "I'm going to stick you in the middle of the park tonight with Alan Dickens," he said. I didn't have time to get nervous to be fair. I'd played against Watford in a lower division so I knew they took a very direct approach. John Barnes got a couple that night and although I had a hand in one of our goals we lost 2-4.

John's approach to training and coaching was a real eye opener. I'd played schoolboy football and had been a pro since the age of 17 but it wasn't until I was coached by John Lyall that I realised just how much I didn't know about the game. He was so inventive, uncomplicated and full of belief in everyone at the club. I really enjoyed all the technical training we did and was so enthusiastic about what I was being asked to do, that I'd go home and write it all down.

John even put a lot of thought into the warm-up and training was so interesting every day that I couldn't wait to discover

The thrill of scoring against Tottenham Hotspur at White Hart Lane

Liverpool. I always joke with my friends that I marked Ian Rush up at Anfield and that he never scored against me. I forget to tell them that Steve McMahon scored the only goal with a 20-yard strike!

John was always trying to instil good habits and offered sound advice to the young kids coming through. The emphasis was always on hard work and just how much practice and dedication it was going to take for them to earn their chance. He cared so much about everyone progressing in one way or another.

There was such a family feeling around the place. The physio, Rob Jenkins, always called me 'Spider' which is a name I was given up north. I saw him at Dave Gladstone's funeral and he still calls me it now. Rob was one of many great characters at the club.

John actually played the role of an agent for me once. A team came in for me and he said that he'd try and broker a deal on my behalf. He was so genuine and gave me peace of mind by saying that if he couldn't get some decent money for me, then I'd be able to stay at West Ham.

I did actually submit a transfer request once but after chatting for about 45 minutes I tore it up! He understood my frustrations about not playing all the time and he knew how to resolve the situation.

I've done quite a bit of coaching since I hung up my boots in 1989 and still use some of John's ideas and technical drills. John shaped a lot of my life because I still live in the south with my wife and we've got two kids and a grandson now. I got into coaching in the early 1990s so he had a tremendous impact on my professional life as well. A lot of players from John's era pursued a similar course to me. It would be interesting to see just how many from those 77 Hammers you mentioned, who played under John, went on to perform some level of coaching.

I was in digs with Kevin Keen at West Ham and we lived with Mrs Cross in Barking. Kevin has gone on to become a very well respected coach himself. He was a 16-year-old apprentice at the time so was brought up in that excellent environment which John had cultivated.

I coached at Ipswich Town's Academy for six years, so I know the high regard in which John was held by the staff and players there. He laid a foundation for their youth academy which still exists today. He had a positive influence on everything he did.

When I heard that John was sacked I called him up straight away. It was typical of John in that he was more concerned about thanking me for all my efforts. He was just such a selfless man. Sacking John was something that you thought would never happen. How could it even cross someone's mind? That is not the way to treat someone who gave as much to a club as John Lyall had invested in West Ham.

the next thing he was going to introduce. On top of that I was playing with a group of players who were so talented, with great knowledge and experience, that it really was the best thing that could have happened to me.

Even though I wasn't playing week in week out, I knew that John had belief in me and my game. I was learning so much I didn't want to be anywhere else. I managed to get a good run in the side after Alvin had damaged his shoulder in a car crash with Steve Whitton. I knew I wasn't going to be a regular which is why the two games I played during the famous 1985-86 season really stand out above all the others.

Beating Chelsea 4-0 at Stamford Bridge and then Spurs 2-1 at home, are two very special memories which I'll keep forever. Another sweet memory is going back up north and beating Manchester United 3-2 at Old Trafford. The lads scored some great goals that day. I should also mention my first goal at Ipswich Town - a header from a cross by the great Trevor Brooking. We ended up winning 3-0. That was a very special moment for me as was scoring at Arsenal in a 3-3 draw.

I played against some top quality strikers. Mark Hughes at Man United, Cyril Regis at Coventry and Ian Rush at

He was taken away from West Ham too soon and he was taken away from life too soon. There were so many great people at this funeral and quite rightly so.

I've still got folders full of John's training schedules. Even in the modern game they could teach young players a hell of a lot. Basically, those folders represent the coaching methods of one of West Ham United's most successful managers.
Paul Hilton

He was honest, hardworking and totally committed to the team. He could play centre-back or centre-midfield. He was very dangerous in the air and gave West Ham everything he had.
Mick McGiven

He had a good sense of humour but couldn't run. He had bad knees.
Steve Walford

Spider covered for Alvin on a couple of occasions during that 1985-86 season. We beat Chelsea away 4-0 and Spurs at home 2-1 so he didn't let us down.
Tony Gale

Hilts was a scream. He was a great teammate. A very funny guy.
Greg Campbell

We roomed together and lived nearby. Hilts and his wife, Judy, were always very good to me.
George Parris

He was a good laugh. I'm not sure which one of us has lost our barnet the quickest!
Alan Dickens

Hilts

JOHN
LYALL
WEST HAM UNITED Manager

WEST HAM UNITED
JOHN
LYALL
MANAGER

WEST HAM UNITED

JL
W.H.U.F.C.

JOHN
LYALL
MANAGER

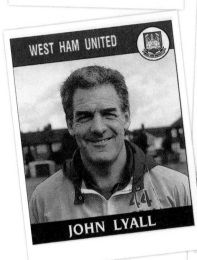

WEST HAM UNITED

JOHN LYALL

WEST HAM UNITED
JOHN
LYALL

WEST HAM UNITED

MANAGER
JOHN
LYALL

Football
League

First
Division

JOHN
LYALL
WEST HAM UTD. Manager

JOHN
LYALL
WEST HAM UNITED

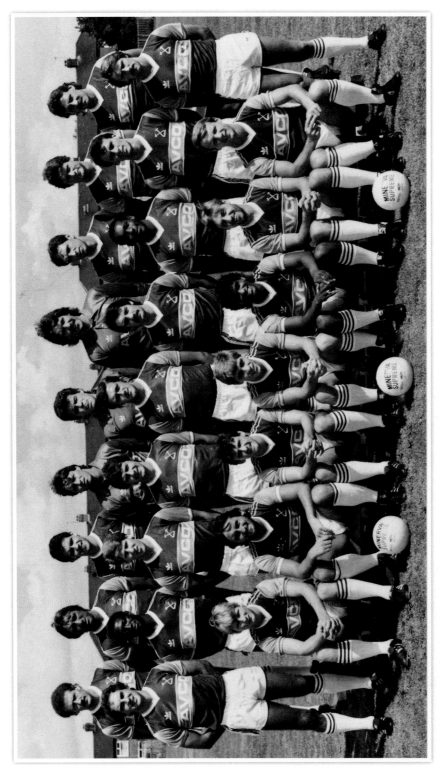

Back row: Hilton, Bonds, Gale, McAlister, Vaughan, Parkes, Martin, Walford, Swindlehurst.

Middle row: Brush, McPherson Campbell, Stewart, Whitton, Devonshire, Parris, Dickens, Orr.

Front row: Donald, Lampard, Allen, Cottee, Barnes, Pike, Goddard.

CHAPTER ELEVEN
1984-85

"The game of football is all about tomorrows and not yesterdays." **John Lyall**

Captain of West Ham United

Dev returned to action

Alvin Martin was appointed club captain. He followed the legendary line of Bobby Moore and Billy Bonds.

It was the first time since 1966 that West Ham started a season without any one of Frank Lampard, Billy Bonds or Trevor Brooking in the line-up. The season was a rollercoaster, with a top five placing early on, quickly replaced by a relegation battle that went down to the penultimate game, when Tony Cottee scored the only goal against Ipswich Town at Portman Road.

Tony Gale joined from Fulham for £200,000. He is the only signing made by John Lyall who missed out on winger Peter Barnes of Leeds United. He trained with the club for one week but the deal fell through. Former Holland World Cup final star Johann Neeskens was also linked with a move to West ham. Once again the club missed out. John turned towards his academy, giving debuts to four young professionals. Alan Devonshire made his return to first team football.

John Lyall was linked with a move to QPR. He had been offered a £70,000-a-year salary to replace Barcelona-bound, Terry Venables. John decided to stay but many felt he was never quite the same manager and his relationship with the Board was weakened.

Tony Gale, Greg Campbell, Steve Potts, Keith McPherson and George Parris all made their West Ham debuts.

Here is their story...

59 – TONY GALE

"Gone but never forgotten."

Born: Westminster, London, November 19, 1959 • **Position:** Defender • **Games played for John Lyall:** 197 (1984-89)

Games played for West Ham United: 368 (1984-1994) • **Goals:** 7 • **Honours:** 1985-86 – Ever present member of highest finishing league side (third), 1990-91 Promotion to top flight, 1992-93 Promotion to top flight • **Testimonial:** May 8, 1994 v Republic of Ireland

Debut: August 25, 1984 v Ipswich Town (h) D 0-0 Att: 19,032

West Ham United: McAlister, Stewart, Walford, Allen, Martin, **Gale**, Whitton*, Cottee, Goddard, Dickens, Pike. Sub: Hilton.

Ipswich Town: Cooper, Burley, McCall, Zondervan, Osman, Butcher, Putney, Brennan, D'Avray, Sunderland*, Gates. Sub: O'Callaghan.

Anthony Peter Gale was born in Westminster. *"My mum, Val, was a civil servant and my dad, Peter, was a taxi driver. We were living in Page Street at the time but soon moved to Lupus Street in Pimlico just around the corner."*

Gale began his football journey with Fulham in 1977 and was an unused substitute in one of the 150 matches Bobby Moore played for the Cottagers. It was during this time that Gale first encountered John Lyall: *"While I was playing for Fulham under Bobby Campbell we faced West Ham on several occasions. What struck me about John was that he was always the same towards Bobby regardless of winning or losing. If West Ham lost he wasn't full of animosity and if they one he didn't rub it in."*

Gale joined West Ham United in 1984 and played 10 years in the claret & blue which culminated in a testimonial. Nicknamed 'Reggie' by his teammates due to his wicked, 'Reggie Kray' sense of humour, Gale eventually moved on to Blackburn Rovers. The 15 appearances he made earned him a Premier League winner's medal during the club's successful campaign in 1994-95. He mentions it from time to time…

Nowadays, Gale continues his work in the media and is a well-respected match analyst. He is regularly engaged to host various West Ham reunions and his rapier wit and

humorous observations elevate every occasion.

The approach from John came right out of the blue. I was out of contract at Fulham and he came round my house in East Molesey, Hampton Court and knocked on the door. Fulham had offered me several new contracts but I was advised to let my contract run out which meant I could chat with other clubs. On the same day I had a visit from both Chelsea and West Ham; Ian McNeill and John Neal from Chelsea and John Lyall and Eddie Baily from West Ham.

On paper, and given my background, I should have signed for Chelsea. My dad had been a season ticket holder at Stamford Bridge and I had supported them as a kid although that had been diluted somewhat once I'd signed for Fulham and the rivalry which comes with that. Furthermore, the traveling from East Molesey to Chelsea was nothing compared to daily slog of getting to Chadwell Heath and Upton Park.

So it is a testament to John that having met him I was in no doubt that West Ham was the best option for me. He said he had been watching me for quite some time, had good knowledge on my career to that point and I think he liked me because I was a footballing central-defender. They had seen me play for Fulham against Spurs in the FA Cup the previous season and Eddie Baily was impressed by the way in which I had dealt with Garth Crooks and Steve Archibald. They said I was the same on the ball in the big, high pressure games as I was in the less important games. John knew the travelling would be a bit of an issue and it was funny because he did offer for the club to pay my removal fees to make the traveling that bit easier. I took him up on those removal fees but moved a few miles in the opposite direction to Weybridge!

Thankfully, I quickly struck up a friendship with Phil Parkes and Alan Devonshire so travelled in with them. I would drive from East Moseley to Pimlico and have a cup of tea with my mum. That would also help to stagger the journey before picking up Phil at Waterloo Station – I can still see him running out of the old sandwich shop with a bacon roll on the go. Then we would travel down to Barking station where we would pick up Dev. I can still see him now wiping the fry up away from his moustache!

John's training sessions were always innovative and interesting and nearly always with a ball. He would focus more on midfield and attack rather than defence. The defenders would spend time with Mick McGiven doing heading practice and defending sessions. If I had any criticism at all I would say that we could have been a bit more defensively minded but having said that, between Alvin Martin, Ray Stewart and myself we had a lot of experience and more often than not organised the defence amongst ourselves.

The 85-86 season was incredible and as good as it was and as cohesive and well organised and skilful a team as we had, people still say that if Julian Dicks had been left back with Paul Ince in midfield as well as a full fit Billy Bonds we would have won it all. Personally, I think that we didn't have any weak spots in that 85-86 team and everyone played their part.

John had all those little personal touches which elevate a person from the run of the mill to the category of 'special'. He knew the names of every players' parents, what they did for a living, the name of our wives and children. He always arranged a Christmas party for the kids each year and even dressed up as Father Christmas some years and handed out all the presents. John had a strong, loving family of his own so he knew how important it was and he invested a lot of time into that side of a player's life.

I remember I got concussed in a game once and was taken to London Hospital. My dad came with me and never forgot the moment when John turned up at the hospital after the game. My dad was so impressed by that because he knew John would have been super busy after the game and could have left it to a club doctor to check up on me but no, John came to the hospital himself and made sure I was alright and that my dad was ok to get me home.

When I discussed my contract with John I didn't have an agent or anything like that so you tended to trust that what was being offered was the best deal available. Now, John talked me through the contract and said that if I started well

Playing it out from the back

and had a good couple of months then the club would consider a pay increase. Anyway, that season – 84-85 – we had a good start and I was playing well. We were fifth in the league and about to go to Old Trafford so on the Friday before the game I went to see John and reminded him of the offer of a pay increase. "Tone", he said. "It's a wrong move to come in asking for an increase before we've played Manchester United. Come and see me on Monday." So we went up to Old Trafford and I played a stinker. We get beaten 1-5 and I'm to blame for at least a couple of them. Gordon Strachan and Mark Hughes tore us to pieces. However, on Monday I pluck up the courage to go and see John and as I walk in he greets me and

Scoring his first goal for the Hammers, against Coventry City, August 1986

said; '10/10 for bravery Tone. Now, I expect you've come in to discuss a wage reduction!"

John was a good talker. He was never a shouter or a bawler and always talked good common sense. Some of his talks after a defeat were legendary. He would address us all and say things like; "I wouldn't wanted to be jumping over the trenches with you. You'd be hiding at the back not facing up to your responsibilities, not doing what was expected of you, what you've been trained to do…" He would go on and on like that. "I wouldn't want to be beside you in a war. You'd be the last to fix your bayonet and we'd all be in danger", "If a car full of kids was heading over a cliff you'd bottle it and be the first one out…" There were so many similes like this and we used to have a little chuckle about most of them.

John treated his players like men and he expected them to behave like men. If you let him down he wouldn't be slow in letting you know about it in very strong terms.

I remember once when we were in a bit of a bad patch and John came into the dressing room before a game and said 'I've had enough, you're not listening to me. You need to hear a different voice. Galey, Alvin, you can give the team

talk today…" and with that he walked out. So Alvin and I had to give the team talk. We just repeated everything John used to say!

John was such a huge influence on the club. There will never be another one like him. He spent over 30 years at West Ham and had done absolutely everything. He had played for the club, worked in the ticket office, ran the youth team and the reserves, was assistant to Ron Greenwood and then became the manager. He had done the wages bill, set up the whole structure, the budget for the club, man managed the players, coached the players and when he wasn't able to be at Chadwell Heath, he would tell the coaches how to run the sessions. Everything was either done by John or had to be run by John. He would even ask Shirley, who worked in the canteen, to tell him what we had all been eating throughout the week!

I don't think he would have liked the media spotlight we have on the game today. Making all those radio, TV and press interviews as well as the club website and twitter and all that. I don't think he would have enjoyed it or even seen the point of much of it. He had his friends in the media and he trusted them and journalists such as Michael Hart, Ken Dyer and Trevor Smith would be on the coach with the team for away games. They'd all be playing Trivial Pursuits together! Club photographer Stevie Bacon was another one whom John trusted implicitly. He treated the press boys really well and would invite them into his office after a game to discuss the game and any issues. A lot of journalists from that era will either be West Ham supporters or have a big soft spot for the club.

Obviously, I played under Kenny Dalglish when Blackburn Rovers won the Premier League and he was quite different to John. Kenny had been a world class player which commands a lot of respect but he was also a good man manager. However, he left all the coaching to his right hand man, Ray Harford whereas John was a good man manager and an even better coach.

I was never fined by John and was never sent off during his time at the club. Bill was in charge when I got sent off by Keith Hackett in the FA Cup semi-final against Nottingham Forest in 1991. On the contrary John felt comfortable giving me the captain's arm band on those occasions when Alvin and Ray were injured.

I was playing golf at Silvermere in Surrey when I heard the news of John's sacking. There were no mobile phones back then but my wife had got a message to the course and someone came running out to tell me. I stopped what I was doing immediately and made my way home. It felt like someone had died. I rung him up immediately to find out what had happened and to thank him for all that he had done for me. He just told me to get on with my football and that I was playing for a great football club and that he'd always be on the end of the phone if I needed him. He also wrote a nice letter to me and I think he did the same for all the players.

Such was John's dedication and work ethic, he had already arranged all the pre-season games which Lou Macari obviously had to honour. John and Lou were like chalk and cheese and Macari must be the worst appointment in the club's history. It felt like being part of a rudderless ship. The first bit of advice Lou gave me was to practice heading for distance, so it went downhill immediately. I don't think the club has ever felt the same since John left. The logical thing to have done was for John to bring through Billy Bonds and maybe Alan Devonshire onto the coaching team and prepare them to be the next faces of management at the club. Alvin could have graduated to the role at a later stage but that would have been the West Ham way. Thankfully, Billy was eventually given the job but we have now lost all that experience and club culture which Ron and John had both developed.

I had helped to arrange the evening for John's final appearance in a West Ham environment. All the boys turned up in the Docklands and we were absolutely delighted to have persuaded John to come along. Both Parkesy and I went to his house to ask him to come. He smiled and said that if all the boys were going to be there, he would be delighted to come. That night was magical. The reception John got from the fans will stay with me forever. He was so chuffed and the whole evening was full of fantastic memories. He thanked us for inviting him and said that he wouldn't have missed it for the world. There was one other occasion when I saw him when Tony, Phil and I went down and spent the day with him at Wallers Farm. He signed some Boys of 86 memorabilia that we had and he showed us all his own bits and pieces. He had all the programmes beautifully bound from his time at the club, I seem to remember. That day has grown in importance given that John passed away soon after. I remember him saying that we had to keep going with all the West Ham reunions. He felt it was important to keep the history of the club alive.

Tony Gale

He was the best man at my wedding in 2016 and we have become very close friends over the years. I love his sense of humour and he has a special talent of saying what everyone is thinking and saying it in a humorous way. He is a scream a minute and we've had some fantastic times together. Let's not forget either that he was a very good player. Another one who was unlucky not to win an England cap.

Tony Cottee

Galey was never an athlete but he was a wonderful player who taught me a lot. Because he lacked pace he read the well better. He could put the ball on my chest or is some space for me to run onto. He has a rapier wit but he is fair with it and is a great entertainer. It was because of people like Galey that you looked forward to training and being in the dressing room. There was a lot of fun and a lot of laughter. John was good at bringing in decent people with the right attitude and Galey was certainly one of those.

Leroy Rosenior

He always had a story to tell and was usually taking the mickey out of someone. He was a wide boy and is still like that on the telly today.

Steve Walford

Galey was the perfect John Lyall player. Good attitude, good player who put his foot in and liked to bring it down and play it on the floor.

Ray Houghton

Galey is fantastic. He can say things to raise your spirits but you try and avoid eye contact just in case you are next! A great

comedian. Dev is usually on the butt of his jokes. It makes me laugh when he says; "We've got Alan Devonshire's dad here tonight" when introducing Dev to an audience. I love Galey. He was a great passer and a very good footballer. If I had to be ultra-critical, he just lacked a little bit of pace.
Alan Dickens

A great player who should have won an England cap. He had a cutting wit in the changing room which, as a young player coming through, introduced me to dressing room banter in a very harsh manner. A great fella with a fantastic football brain. I think he is great and how he didn't play for England is beyond me.
Kevin Keen

He always goes on about winning the Premier League with Blackburn Rovers but says I won the Mickey Mouse league with Celtic. Well, at least I played my games. He sat most of that season on the bench!
Frank McAvennie

Galey and I go back a long, long way. My dad gave him his debut for Fulham and sold him to West Ham. During his managerial career my dad looked after Liam Brady, Tony Gale and George Best. Galey and I differ as to who was the best out of those three!
Greg Campbell

Reggie was easily the biggest mickey taker ever to enter a West Ham dressing room!
Paul Hilton

Galey was a very good player. His reading of the game, his distribution and positioning were all excellent. At set plays he was always a threat in the air. Great at flick-ons. I remember when he was a young kid playing for Bobby Campbell's Fulham and they beat us 2-3 at Upton Park. Two of their goals were identical. Corner, flick-on by Galey and goal.
Mick McGiven

A great player who has found his forte in the world of media. He's brilliant at it.
Ray Stewart

Galey the host (far right) with great friends Phil Parkes, Frank McAvennie and Tony Cottee

60 – GREG CAMPBELL

"John had loads of theoretical stories which he would roll out to make you think about the type of person you were."

Born: Portsmouth, Hampshire, July 13, 1965 • **Position:** Striker • **Games played for West Ham United:** 5 (1984-85)

Honours under John Lyall: 1985-86: Member of West Ham United's highest ever league finish (third)

Debut: September 4, 1984 v Coventry City (h) W 3-1 (Stewart 2 (1 pen) Cottee – Pearce) Att: 14,949

West Ham United: McAlister, Stewart, Walford, Allen, Martin, Gale, Barnes, **Campbell***, Cottee, Dickens, Pike. Sub: Bonds.*

Coventry City: Ogrizovic, Stephens, Pearce, Jol, Kilcline, Peake, Bennett, Gynn, Latchford, Gibson, Platnauer.

Gregory Campbell was born in Portsmouth to parents Bobby and Sue: *"My dad was one of 12 kids and played inside-right for Liverpool and scored a couple of goals. He played with Tommy Lawrence and Billy Liddell and had a long career in management. He managed Portsmouth, Fulham, Chelsea and a couple of clubs in the Middle East. My mum took me to watch all his matches and was a big influence on my own career."*

Following trials with both Liverpool and Manchester United, Campbell signed apprentice forms with West Ham United. He was quickly earmarked as another leading light in the club's Academy. Unfortunately, two freak accidents were to blight his fortunes and his appearances were restricted to just five matches. Furthermore, Greg was distracted by the social side of a footballer's existence which had a detrimental effect on both his professional and private life: *"I'd go to Stringfellows with Frank McAvennie, Mo Johnstone and Charlie Nicholas. You can imagine what they were getting up to. I embraced that side of the game a bit too much and, later in life, I ended up in Tony Adams' clinic for drink and drug abuse. I lost a hell of a lot from that experience."*

Today, Greg works as a chauffeur and is putting off a hip operation a bit longer than he'd like to. The interview took place at Chelsea's Stamford Bridge ground and Greg's time at West Ham with John Lyall walks tall in his life's experiences:

"West Ham are my team. My dad wanted me to support Liverpool and I usually followed whatever team he was playing for or managing. But when I went to West Ham it was my decision and it felt like my club. The fans were fantastic and nothing comes close to that atmosphere at Upton Park. Running out on that pitch, well, it was just magnificent."

Following, are Greg's memories of John Lyall:

One big story about John relates to the Tate & Lyle factory in Silvertown. He took every player at West Ham to that factory and I mean Trevor Brooking, Billy Bonds, and Frank Lampard, as well as first year apprentices. We were taken on a tour and all given a tin of syrup and a bag of sugar. On the coach back John made us aware of just how hard they were working in that factory and how we should make the most of the opportunity we had. He wasn't demeaning or detrimental in any way, but he felt we were privileged to be footballers and that we shouldn't waste our talent. He urged us to strive to be the best we could be. Can you imagine Slaven Bilic doing the same with the likes of Lanzini and Payet? You could've left Za Za there!

I loved football and trained everywhere as a school kid – Fulham, Millwall, Chelsea and QPR. I spent a half-term at Liverpool and a half-term at Manchester United. I signed school boy forms with United - that is a special club. I took the

In the gym with Chris Ampofo. Ray Houghton and Warren Donald are to the rear

Regarding my debut, John called me into his office about an hour and half before kick-off and told me I was starting. We were playing Coventry City and I was going to be marked by Brian Kilcline. 'Killer' they called him. We won 3-1 and I did everything but score. Early in the game, I did Killer for pace and put in a cross for Cottee who hit the post. Killer came over to me and said that he'd break my leg if I did that again. I just ignored it but Cottee shouted back at him: "You'll have to catch him first you old c***!" I thought cheers TC and sure enough Killer caught me with a few naughty challenges, poleaxing me on one occasion about waste high.

I had a set-back in my second match, against Watford at home. Tom McAlister kicked the ball out and it ended up in their penalty area so I went up to head it. I only bothered going for it because I'd heard their keeper, Steve Sherwood, couldn't catch a cold. He ended up punching me in the face and breaking my jaw in three places and fracturing my nose. He must have been blind as well as clumsy!

I was in a lot of pain and I remember Bonzo, who was on the bench, coming on for me. We passed each other as I came off and he looked at me and slapped me around the face and said: "You'll be alright, son." I was taken to Mile End hospital where they made a tannoy announcement asking for my mum and dad. My mum thought I was dead!

After the match, I had four visitors at the hospital. Cottee, Wozzer, Dicko and George – my good pals. They had brought

me a copy of Penthouse and some toffees!

train up to Old Trafford from Euston and I'd be training with the likes of Butch Wilkins, Gordon McQueen, Gary Bailey, Steve Coppell and Joe Jordan. Dave Sexton was in charge and he was very much like John Lyall. He trained the kids as well as the senior pros. Sadly, it didn't work out for me there because Dave Sexton got the sack and Ron Atkinson came in so I ended up training with West Ham and lodging at Mrs Cross' digs near the Fly House on the Barking Road. Stuart Pearson and Tom McAllister stayed with her and they loved to party. They could put McAvennie to shame sometimes. One afternoon, John came round and had a chat with me and I signed for West Ham. I was so impressed by him.

I worked hard to be a good player but feel I was unlucky. I think John liked the progress I was making in the youth team when I was 15. Tony Cottee, me, and a lad called Alfie Wright scored over 100 goals between us. TC got the bulk of them, of course, but we were all filling our boots.

When I played my first game for the reserves I thought I'd been dropped from the youth team because I didn't recognise anyone! Anyway, old Frank Lampard was playing and so was Mark Dennis for Birmingham. We hadn't even kicked off and Frank flew for Dennis. They hated each other.

In action against Watford

My jaw was in a bad way and it affected my confidence for a while. John knew how to help me psychologically. When I returned to training, he got Frank Lampard to throw the ball in my face. "Nothing to fear now son," John said. "Welcome back."

The following season was the famous 1985-86 campaign. I had a few outings early on, including a substitute appearance up at Manchester United. Coming on at Old Trafford was an experience to die for. John actually gave me a ticking off on the following Monday because I had spent most of the game warming up in front of him, I was that desperate to come on. I wanted to play against Bryan Robson, who was captain of both United and England at the time. 'Captain Marvel' they called him. John relented and brought me on late in the second half. We lost 0-2 and I hardly got a kick but it's still one of my treasured memories. Over 50,000 fans were there. It was Boy's Own stuff.

The next injury I suffered was far worse. I had played in a 1-1 draw at Southampton and was starting to feel confident about my chances of playing regularly. Little did I know, but that outing at The Dell would be my last for the club.

We were training at Chadwell Heath on an area of land we seldom used. We called it Wembley because we never played on it! I went into a sliding tackle on Everald La Ronde and felt my knee jar. The next thing I remember was looking down at my ripped track suit bottoms and staring right at the patella in my knee. I was in a state of shock, looking at this deep, open wound with blood oozing from it thinking how did that happen? An angle iron from some old tennis nets had been left in the soil, but had re surfaced over time and I'd ripped my knee across it. Rob Jenkins, the physio, patched it up the best he could with some towels but I needed to get to hospital. John said he'd take me in his jaguar which he had only taken delivery of that week! It was a beautiful burgundy jag with cream leather seats and now my blood was all over the back seat.

I spent a night in hospital and John came to see me and asked if I wanted to sue the club: "Sue West Ham United?" I replied, "You've got to be joking. I only want to play football." John looked at me and said: "Correct answer, you're on first team wages for the rest of the season."

I was never the same player after that and John did me a favour by nudging me towards playing on the continent. He offered me a free transfer. There was so much talent at West Ham it was always going to be difficult for me to get back into the first team. Goddard, Cottee, McAvennie, Stuart Slater and a lad called Paul McMenemy (nephew of Lawrie McMenemy) were all very good players so it was going to be tough. John was very honest with me and explained that Slater would play first. He never misled me and was always straight down the middle. That is when I signed for Sparta Rotterdam and my time at West Ham was over.

I had already spent one pre-season on trial at Real Zaragoza

Rob Jenkins tends to Greg's broken jaw with his magic sponge

GREG: 'TRUE GRIT'

MANAGER John Lyall paid glowing tribute this week to the courage young striker Greg Campbell showed after fracturing his jaw in three places during Saturday's home win over Watford.

for six weeks which was just amazing. It was the most unbelievable football I'd ever been involved in. They had the captain of Spain called Luis Costa playing for them, Pepe Diaz and Ruben Sosa, who ended up playing with Gazza at Lazio. He was some player. I played in a couple of pre-season friendlies against Valencia and Seville. I was still a West Ham player and went back after the six weeks were up.

John was a feared, well respected, father figure and feared in the right way. You always wanted to do well for him. If you got a "well done!" off John Lyall you went home happy. He didn't have to say much but you knew to take it on board. It might be; "Oi, raise your game, son", or "Buck your ideas up" or, in my case: "Don't go out with McAvennie anymore!"

I felt the wrath of John's anger when I was 19. I'd just got a new car and McAvennie asked me to take him to

Stringfellows. I didn't have a drink and didn't misbehave and was just looking at all the beautiful birds. On the way home I got stopped by the police. McAvennie was pissed and thankfully I was sober but John found out about it. He called me into his office, slapped me around the face and ordered me not to go out with McAvennie anymore.

John reminded me a lot of my dad in that he was honest, hard and straight talking. They were both good coaches and improved the players they looked after. I haven't seen Mourinho improve too many players because they are already the finished article by the time he signs them. It is a lot like that at West Ham nowadays. Cheque book football.

John was a great man and a great man manager. He'd tell you in no uncertain terms if your first or second-touch wasn't good enough. If you weren't the type to respond to criticism he'd put his arm around you and ask you why you felt it didn't go to plan.

The only other manager I can compare John to was Alex Ferguson. They were miles better than anyone else. Mourinho couldn't lace John's boots. Mourinho has never made a player and never improved a player.

It was a joke when they sacked John. He should still be there now. He'd only be in his 70s.

I was very sad when John died. The feelings were very similar to those I felt when my own father died. I loved them both to bits.

One other thing about John is that he had to juggle the club's finances which was a skill in itself. It wasn't like today where a club is given £100m just because it exists. John had to worry about the pennies as well as the pounds. There was a photo in the newspaper recently showing the entire workforce at West Ham out on the pitch at the old Boleyn Ground. There must have been over 300 people in that photo. It just underlines the magnificent job John and his staff did running West Ham United.

My last words on John would be that a lot of what he said to me as a kid has stayed with me throughout my life. John was everything to his players: their mum, their dad, their agent, everything. He was a big man, a hard man, an honest man, a great coach, a good friend and a trophy winning manager.

Greg Campbell

He was a very confident kid and had all the clothes and a fast car even before he started playing in the first team.

Steve Walford

Greg only played a couple of first team games for West Ham but was part of the most successful league side in the club's history. He attended a lot of the Boys of 86 evenings we organised over the years. He can always say he played centre forward for West Ham.

Tony Gale

Greg was a very confident young player. His dad, Bobby, was a top manager and knew all the stars like Jimmy Tarbuck, so Greg grew up around all that. He joined as an apprentice in the same year as me and everyone had high hopes that he was going to make a big name for himself. He broke his jaw against Watford and pick up a terrible injury at the training ground and was never quite the same. A real shame.

Tony Cottee

We called him 'Son of Bobby.' He came through the system and worked very, very hard. He had a lot of injuries but could take them on the chin. It was big enough!

Paul Hilton

Greg was very unfortunate. He was honest, hard-working, long-legged, quick and really enthusiastic. He had a really good debut and seemed set to be a prominent West Ham striker for some time. But a terrible training ground accident ruined his leg and he was never the same player.

Mick McGiven

We still keep in touch. We played in the youth team together and Greg was highly regarded. He's had his ups and downs but stays on top of everything.

George Parris

Greg with his debut programme

61 – STEVE POTTS

"John ticked all the boxes. I was at the club for 17 years and John was the best manager I had during that time. He ran the club from top to bottom, knew everyone, all the players, their kids and all the staff. He was a totally decent man. "

Born: Hartford, Connecticut, United States of America, May 7, 1967 • **Position:** right-back/centre-half

Games played for John Lyall: 65 (1985-89) • **Games played for West Ham United:** 506 (1984-2001) • **Goals scored for West Ham:** 1

Honours: Hammer of the Year: 1993 and 1995. Promotion 1991 and 1993 • **Debut:** January 1, 1985 v Queens Park Rangers (h) L 1-3 Att: 20,857

West Ham United: McAlister, **Potts,** Brush, Dickens, Martin, Gale*, Allen, Hilton, Goddard, Cottee, Orr. Sub: Whitton.*

Queens Park Rangers: Hucker, James*, Dawes, Waddock, Chivers, Fenwick, McDonald, Fillery, Bannister, Byrne, Gregory. Sub: Robinson.*

Steven John Potts was born in Hartford, Connecticut in the United States of America. In the early 1960s, his parents, John and Jean, had emigrated to the States where they lived for six years. *"I was just a babe in arms when the family returned to England. We lived for a brief spell in Romford."*

The Potts family then moved to Porters Avenue in Dagenham where Steve lived until his early twenties. Steve's father worked at Fords while his mother ran a florists. The whole Potts family are good West Ham supporting stock.

"Pottsy" was spotted by West Ham's club scout Ronnie Gale and his signature was secured for the Hammers ahead of Arsenal. *"I grew up playing with Tony Adams and he played in the same position as me but opted for Arsenal over West Ham. He found himself more comfortable at Highbury and I felt more at home at Upton Park."*

Steve usually roomed with either Kevin Keen or Paul Ince and was very much a part of the next generation of quality footballers produced by John Lyall's Academy. He went on to play 506 games for West Ham United over a 17 year period. He served under four manager and Steve maintains that John Lyall was the cream of the crop. *"John gave us all a master class in coaching. There were no grey areas. He knew what he wanted from his players and he helped as much as he could without compromising your natural ability to go out*

there and play your own game. He had it all really."

Today, Steve remains one of the few links to the John Lyall era. He looks after the Under-18s at West Ham and trains the new generation of budding professionals at Chadwell Heath. He has also passed the knowledge and is one of two Hammers from that era to earn a living as a black taxi driver - the other being Alan Dickens.

Initial contact with Steve was made at the funeral of the late, great, Peter Brabrook and subsequently Steve took the time to share his memories of John Lyall:

The club was set up very differently back then. Nowadays, West Ham take on kids as young as six and seven, whereas I joined the club as a 15-year-old apprentice. It was immediately obvious that John had a great knowledge of the game and talked endlessly about football.

He was a man who I wanted to play well for. If I had a bad game I felt that I had let him down. He had that type of connection with all his players. He was a manager, yes, but he also had a very personal side to him and was definitely seen as something of a father figure for quite a few of the players. He went to great lengths to get to know you and your family.

I made my debut in 1985 and it still feels like it was only yesterday. John called me in to his office and asked if I was ready to play. I simply answered: "Yes." He responded by saying:

Youth Internationals produced by West Ham United. Back row - Ince, Dolan, Martin, Dickens and Parris. Front row - Cottee, Keen, Slater and Potts

"Ok, you're playing." I left his office and celebrated the New Year by playing in the first team against Queens Park Rangers.

John constantly changed his training regime. No two sessions were the same and the variety definitely help to maintain high levels of enthusiasm. Each day, I drove home thinking about the session and the new things he was introducing. I've always liked to think about the game and I think John liked that about me.

He was always trying to push the barriers by trying something new, something different. He understood the physical and mental side of the game. If we'd put in a bad performance on the Saturday, he'd have us all in early on Monday. He created one-on-one situations in the gym and it was clear that he was making it awkward for some of the players who may not have been on top of their game. The unspoken message was that bad performances had consequences. Those were the type of mind games he played.

In football there are a lot of kids with bags of ability, but very few with the mental strength to go with it. That was the bit John worked on tirelessly. He wanted his players to think about what they were doing, why they were doing it and how

it benefitted the team. When he walked out on the training pitch the atmosphere and tempo would change. He had a tremendous presence about him. He was great at solving problems, working through situations and making sure that everyone was learning the right lessons along the way.

On pre-season tours, some of the players flouted the curfew so John would stay up for as long as it took until he felt everything had been resolved to his satisfaction. He set good boundaries for his players and although a handful would be quite comfortable crossing those boundaries, the vast majority worked hard to earn his respect. He was so good to me that I felt I owed him something all the time and I think that was the same for most of the players.

John went out of his way to support his players and be part of their football journey. He had a hard side to him but mainly he was all about being supportive and understanding. I remember playing for the England Youth team and he came and watched me in a match at Craven Cottage. It was funny because he called me into his office the next day to have a word with me about the game. At the time the England Youth team were playing a very direct style of football in the long ball style of Charles Hughes: "Don't bring any of that back to West Ham," laughed John. He had received a very good football upbringing under Ron Greenwood and wanted to continue to develop that. He certainly resisted anything that would dilute it. It was a philosophy which he so firmly believed in and it made it an exciting time for everyone. You felt part of something important, something that had been successful and needed to be preserved.

As a youth player I had played at centre-half quite a bit and John was aware of that. However, of the 60 odd matches I played under him, all of them were in that full-back role. I didn't play too many games because Ray Stewart was the established right-back. It wasn't until Ray left the club and Billy Bonds took over that I started to play centre-half. I always thought my main strength was reading the game and dealing with the situations which arose from that.

John's team talks were very good. Once, he took me along as part of the squad to play Manchester United. It was the FA Cup match when Geoff Pike scored a brilliant header from the edge of the penalty area. I was just a young kid sitting in the dressing room up at Old Trafford and I heard John addressing the team and I thought: "Wow, this is a whole

Pottsy on his debut against QPR, January 1985

different level, now." It was so impressive. He knew he had a team to beat United that day and he tapped into the minds of each player and sharpened their focus. He knew exactly what he wanted from them, both individually, and as a group. I'd never heard anything like it and it has always been something I've remembered. The players left that dressing room absolutely spot on both mentally and physically. It was so impressive to witness and not surprising at all that we beat Manchester United 2-0 that day.

It was a very upsetting time when John left the club. There was a very strange atmosphere, that's for sure. Ok, the team had been relegated, but only a few years earlier we had finished in the top three so it underlined just how quickly things can unravel. They change even quicker in the modern game as we saw with Claudio Ranieri at Leicester City.

There were some very good players at the club and I looked up to Billy Bonds, Alvin Martin and Tony Gale. If I had to pick one player who stood out above all others, it would be Alan Devonshire. He was magnificent to watch. In training, he'd just keep the ball under total control wherever he went. Most of the time I was thinking: "What a player, what a player!"

John commanded a loyalty in his players which doesn't exist today. The number of testimonials which many of his players earned is testament to that. It felt like there was one every year. The players loved being at West Ham and being part of what John had created. He improved their skill set and a virtuous cycle had evolved. Young kids learned from the senior pros before graduating to the first team. They, in turn, would then pass on their experience and knowledge to the next generation of young kids. It was a strong family unit and John was the paternal figure in the centre of it all.

I don't think John was too keen on agents which were starting to proliferate the game at that time. He handled them well and was very strong in his dealings with them. What I think he might have found more difficult is the amount of money in the game today. It has lost touch with reality and challenges a player's loyalty which John would have found frustrating.

The only coach I could compare to John would be Alex Ferguson, because he is another manager who ran his club from top to bottom. Nowadays, managers are not around long enough to really spread their influence and personality throughout the club, the players, the families, the staff and the fans. John did that every day for 15 years.

One of my standout memories of John came when he called me into his office to discuss my contract. I was 17-years-old and didn't have an agent to help broker a deal for me. He called me in, told me that he was delighted to offer me a three year contract paying £150 per week in the first year, £175 in the second year and £200 for the final year. He told me that I should be walking out of his office six feet tall

and that I should sign the forms before the club reconsidered. He had such a way about him that I felt I was getting the very best deal available, where in fact I was getting a really bad deal! I look back and think that he had me over a barrel there but at the time I didn't want to say anything that might offend him. I respected him too much. My mates were earning more than me as electricians and plumbers!
Steve Potts

Steve was a very quiet lad but a good lad. I'm pleased he is back at West Ham coaching.
Steve Walford

We are the same age and grew up together. He is one of the nicest people you will ever meet. Totally underrated as a player by the wider footballing public but not by the West Ham fans. A top, top bloke and a proper legend in my book.
Kevin Keen

A proper West Ham man. He came up through the ranks and must be in the all-time top ten for appearances at West Ham. His son Danny also played in the first team.
Tony Gale

I love Pottsy. He's such a decent bloke. West Ham through and through.
Alan Dickens

Steve played in the Under-13s and Under-14s for Barking. Tony Adams was also in that team and we had Tony at West Ham for a while but for some reason he went to Arsenal. I loved Steve and thought he had everything. He played centre-back for his school team and centre-back for his district team. He could play either centre-back or right-back at West Ham and was quick in the tackle and even quicker to recover. He was good in the air without being outstanding and always wanted to be a winner. I'm not surprised at all that he played 500 games for the club. One thing that does surprise me is that his son, Danny, is all left foot. I don't know where that came from!
Mick McGiven

A very quiet lad but quick, dependable and read the game well. Another one who is progressing well as a coach. 500 games, one goal!
Tony Cottee

Shortest centre-half there has ever been! Very quiet but very good.
Paul Hilton

A very, very, good cab driver!
Greg Campbell

Mr Reliable. He was a class player. You only really knew just how good he was when he missed a game. Thankfully, he didn't miss too many.
George Parris

At the funeral of West Ham legend, Peter Brabrook L-R Anton Ferdinand, Joe Cole, Ken Dyer and Pottsy

62 – KEITH McPHERSON

"My opinion of John is one of a fair, honest and very loyal man. As a young pro I didn't have much contact with him and it was a big thing if he talked to me."

Born: Greenwich, London, September 11, 1963 • **Position:** Centre-half • **Games played for West Ham United:** 1 (1984-85)
Honours under John Lyall: 1981 FA Youth Cup winner • Debut: May 20, 1985 v Liverpool (h) L 0-3 (Walsh 2, Beglin) Att: 22,369
West Ham United: Parkes, Stewart, Brush, **McPherson**, Martin, Lampard*, Barnes, Parris, Goddard, Walford, Pike. Sub: Gale.*
Liverpool: Grobbelaar, Neal, Beglin, Molby*, Nicol, Hansen, Dalglish, Whelan, Rush, Walsh, Wark Sub: Lee*.

Keith Anthony McPherson was born in Greenwich and grew up in Brockley where he attended Samuel Pepys School: *"My mum was a nurse in Lewisham and my dad worked for Greenwich council. I played Sunday football for the Orpington Eagles."*

In 1981, McPherson was a member of West Ham United's successful FA Youth Cup team, which overcame Tottenham Hotspur 2-1 in the two-legged final. Despite a bright looking future with the Hammers, the central defensive positions were the mainstay of Alvin Martin, Billy Bonds and, later, Tony Gale. However, Keith did get that all important first team appearance in the claret and blue – the dream of millions. It came against Liverpool at Upton Park in May, 1985. Subsequently, he continued his playing career at Cambridge United, Northampton Town, Reading and Brighton & Hove Albion.

Today, Keith lives near Purley in Surrey and works in IT at Reigate Grammar school. He occasionally meets up with his youth team mates and, in 2016, returned to Upton Park for the final ever match played there.

Following are Keith's recollections of John Lyall:

To be honest I find it quite amusing, but really nice, that I am remembered at all by West Ham fans. I only played the one game even though I was at the club for six years, having joined as an apprentice in 1980. A few years ago Tony Cottee and Tony Gale invited me along to an FA Cup reunion at the London Bridge Hilton Hotel and I was amazed that people were asking me for my autograph and had photos and books about my time at West Ham. It is all very flattering.

I was 16 when Eddie Baily asked me to trial at West Ham. I was a bit cheeky and turned him down at first because I lived in Brockley, South East London, and didn't know how to get there! In the end, I took the bus to New Cross and a train to Upton Park, via Whitechapel, on the District Line. Training took place every Tuesday and Thursday evenings. My parents were quite worried because I had to get the bus home from New Cross and usually returned after 11pm. My mum would always be checking out of the window to make sure I got home safely.

Once I started my apprenticeship I trained at Chadwell Heath in the morning and then took the bus to the ground to clean the boots and kit in the afternoon.

My opinion of John is one of a fair, honest and very loyal man. As a young pro I didn't have much contact with him and it was a big thing if he talked to me. John had a very good coaching team. Tony Carr, Mick McGiven and Ron Boyce all had a big influence on my development as a footballer.

West Ham was very good to the youth players. I went on day release to study professions such as surveying and accountancy. Obviously, there were no guarantees in football and the club gave us a taste of alternative careers that we could fall back on. I eventually got into IT after I left Reading.

Macca at Chadwell Heath

team and I'm proud of that achievement because West Ham has only won it three times in its history. My mum has still got my medal. I also won division titles at both Northampton Town and Reading. My parents had a trophy cabinet in their living room displaying everything. My mum also kept a scrap book.

I made my debut in the very last match of the 1984-85 season, at home to Liverpool. It was played on Monday evening and George Parris also made his debut in that match. There were quite a few injuries and Neil Orr didn't play and Tony Gale was on the bench so John started with me. There wasn't a lot on the game so John obviously decided to blood a couple of youngsters. We lost 0-3 and that ended up being my one and only first team appearance for West Ham. It was a great experience to play against Kenny Dalglish and Ian Rush.

I had a terrific time at West Ham United and was surrounded by some very good players in Everald La Ronde, Paul Allen, Bobby Barnes, Alan Dickens, Tony Cottee, Steve Potts, Kevin Keen and Paul Ince.

There were a lot of players ahead of me for those centre-half positions. Alvin, Galey, Bonzo, Hilts and Orr meant that it was always going to be hard for me and I ended up going out on loan to Cambridge United before a permanent move to Northampton Town in 1986. In 1990 I was ready to step up a level and went on to Reading where I played around 300 games. I spent almost ten years there.

I went back to Upton Park a couple of times during the last ever season there and I was introduced to the crowd on the pitch at half-time and it gave me a buzz. I felt really good being out there again. I hadn't been back for 30-years so it

I preferred playing centre-half even though I was only 5 feet 10 inches. I had some decent spring and played quite a lot in the reserves. As a player, I think my strengths were my pace and agility. I was good in the air but my distribution could have been better. I felt that I read the game well.

I mainly played for the reserve team in the Football Combination league which was great because there were quite a few pros appearing in those matches, either coming back from injury, or having lost a bit of form. It was a great way to pick up some valuable experience against seasoned professionals.

Very early on in my time at West Ham I was part of the youth side which won the FA Youth Cup in 1981. We had a very strong

Keith originally turned down Eddie Baily - John Lyall's chief scout

was a very special occasion and something I'll never forget. These things become more important the older I become.

John worked hard and deservedly holds his place in West Ham United's history.
Keith McPherson

Macca was a good, solid, player. He was very comfortable on the ball and had a lot of pace for a centre-half. He was the type of player who needed confidence instilled in him. Almost 40 years on and, physically, he hasn't changed one little bit. He's like the Peter Pan of the our 1981 youth team!
Everald La Ronde

We played a lot of reserve games together and I enjoyed playing with him. He was a wholehearted, dominating, centre-back who went on to have a very good career at Reading. A really great bloke.
Kevin Keen

I think I only played once with Keith but what a nice fella he is. We invited him along to an evening at the London Bridge Hilton Hotel in 2015. He looks exactly the same as when he played.
Tony Gale

I played with Keith in the 1981 Youth Cup final. He was so good in the air, but didn't quite develop that extra bit of quality in time to play regularly for West Ham.
Alan Dickens

A good young pro. I was sorry to see him leave because he was a lovely lad. I saw him at the final game at Upton Park and couldn't believe how fit and young he still looked.
Paul Hilton

We only played one first team game together and that was when we made our debuts against Liverpool.
George Parris

Keith was very quiet but totally committed.
Bobby Barnes

He had fantastic heading ability and tremendous spring. He was unlucky to have been at West Ham at the same time as Alvin Martin but he went on to have a fine career at Reading where he is very highly regarded. If you were playing against Keith McPherson you knew you were going to be in for a very hard game.
Mick McGiven

KEITH SIGNS FULL PRO

Keith McPherson, Hammers promising young youth team centre-back, signed full pro this week. He joined West Ham as an apprentice last summer and was in the team which won the FA Youth Cup last

Signing full pro

Back at the Boleyn in 2016 - (L-R) Everald La Ronde, Paul Allen, Bobby Barnes and Keith

63 – GEORGE PARRIS

"It was always going to be a tough gig for anyone to replace John. Some would argue he has never been replaced."

Born: Ilford, Essex, September 11, 1964 • **Position:** Defender/Midfielder • **Games played for John Lyall:** 149 (1984-89)
Games played for West Ham United: 298 (1984-93) • **Goals for West Ham United:** 18 • **Honours under John Lyall:**
1985-86: Member of highest finishing league team (third) • **Testimonial:** April 22, 1995 v Ipswich Town (h) L 2-3 (McAvennie,
Parris – Tanner, Mathe, Marshall) Att: 1,379 • **Debut:** May 20, 1985 v Liverpool (h) L 0-3 (Walsh 2, Beglin) Att: 22,369
West Ham United: Parkes, Stewart, Brush, McPherson, Martin, Lampard,* Barnes, **Parris,** Goddard, Walford, Pike. Sub: Gale.*
Liverpool: Grobbelaar, Neal, Beglin, Molby, Nicol, Hansen, Dalglish, Whelan, Rush, Walsh, Wark. Sub: Lee.

George Michael R. Parris took the Redbridge, Essex, London and England Under 15s route to West Ham United. He played both cricket and football for Redbridge: *"I was more into cricket as a kid to be honest. I thought I was a better cricketer than I was a footballer. I started out as a bowler but then I saw the light and switched to batting! I didn't get into the Essex side for cricket but I did for football so that sort of swayed me more towards football."*

Signing apprentice forms for West Ham United in July 1981, 'Smokey' spent 12 years at the club before seeing out the remainder of his career, mainly at Birmingham City and Brighton & Hove Albion.

He played 35 games during West Ham's celebrated 1985-86 season and enjoyed further success after the John Lyall era, when helping the club to promotion in 1990-91. He scored eight goals that season and only missed out to Ludek Miklosko for the Hammer of the Year title.

Today, George works as a football director for the women's regional talent at Brighton & Hove Albion. *"In West Ham parlance we'd call it a Women's Academy. In my role as a coach I try to pass on a bit of John's advice. He always told me to play with a smile on my face and people generally perform better at something if they are enjoying it."*

George frequently attends various reunions and remains a firm fan's favourite. Following are his recollections of John Lyall:

The first experience I had of John occurred when he watched me train soon after I had joined the club. I wasn't blessed with a great left foot but John spent a lot of time with me in the gym. He'd hang these numbers from the goal and get me to hit them with my left foot. He'd feed the ball into me and call a number and I'd try to hit that number with my weaker foot.

Regarding my debut, John didn't tell me I was playing until about an hour before kick-off. I'd been in and around the squad for the previous few games but hadn't got on, so it was a big moment for me. I played well, even though we were beaten convincingly by a very good Liverpool side. We lost 0-3 but it could have been a lot worse. I was just pleased to be out on the pitch with so many great players like Kenny Dalglish and Ian Rush.

John was always very straight with his players. We knew if he was upset about something. During the 1985-86 season, we beat Newcastle United 8-1. We were all laughing and joking in the dressing room but John came in and let us know that he wasn't happy with the decision to let Alvin Martin take the penalty for his hat trick. Ray Stewart was the club's penalty taker and John thought goal difference could come into play at the end of the season. He felt it showed a lack of professionalism to pursue one person's glory at the possible expense of the club's success.

The 1985-86 season was easily the highlight of my time at the club. We were unplayable at times and the momentum was irrepressible. Because of the bad weather, the games were coming thick and fast towards the end of the season. It was just a whirlwind really but we kept our focus. Ultimately, we had two very good teams in front of us - Liverpool won the double that year and Everton went on to win the league the following season.

I was in the dressing room up at West Bromwich Albion in 1986 when we heard our fate. Kenny Dalglish had ended all our dreams by scoring the only goal to win the title against Chelsea at Stamford Bridge. I was also in the dressing room up at Anfleld in 1989 when we were relegated after losing 1-5. On both occasions, John was philosophical and talked to us as a group. He was very positive and reassuring. We stayed up in Liverpool that night and John had a drink with us in the bar and was analysing the game and contemplating the next season. He was already preparing for the new challenge ahead. John was at his happiest when talking about the game. Nobody had the slightest notion that he'd managed West Ham for last ever time. It just wasn't a consideration. .

Like everyone else I was really shocked when the club sacked John. It was totally unexpected and I remember he wrote a letter to me thanking me for my time and effort. It was very strange around the club afterwards, which was to be expected given John's colossal involvement. The first training session without him felt flat to say the least.

I think Phil Parkes gave me the nickname 'Smokey.' We're not sure if it was after Smokey Robinson the singer or Smoking Joe Frazier the boxer. I'd like to think it was after the singer.

I scored a few goals for West Ham, which I look back on with fondness. I got one at home to Millwall which is always a good one to get. People often remind me of the last minute winner at Watford as well. Dev, Bonds and TC were the three best I played with at West Ham.

John fined me a couple of times but only for small indiscretions, like turning up late for training or keeping the coach waiting for an away game. Those occasions pale into insignificance when I consider the advice he gave me both in terms of football and my personal life.

After I left West Ham I developed a serious gambling habit. Even though I was gambling at West Ham, it wasn't as big a problem as it became later on. John didn't really have to talk to me about it because it wasn't the life changing issue it developed into.

John was the type of manager who looked after his players

Smokey

both on and off the field. Paul Ince is a good example of that. John kept him on the straight and narrow because it was all too easy for Incey to go off the rails.

As a player, I'd like to think that John liked my energy and enthusiasm. I was a good tackler and did the simple things well. He coached me to use my left foot as well as my right and, it is testament to John's skill as a coach, that I played all those games at left-back. Most people couldn't tell the difference between my left and my right.

John was a great manager and a great man. I can't thank him enough for all that he did for me. He gave me my career.
George Parris

Smokey received the following comments from his former teammates:

I think they called him 'Smokey' after Smoking Joe Fraser, but he used to work so hard in training that smoke would literally be coming out of his head during the winter months.
Steve Walford

In FA Cup action against Sheffield Wednesday, February 1987

One of West Ham's proper one hundred percenters. The Chicken Run loved him. He'd slide in on opponents from ten yards away. Just as Dev could get the crowd going with a touch of brilliance, George could do the same with a tackle.
Tony Gale

I played against George when he was ten years old. At the time I was only about three feet two inches! He was like a giant in defence, very athletic and very difficult to play against. When we played together at West Ham I had caught up with him a bit and there wasn't too much height difference between us.
Tony Cottee

George was a big barrel chested player and people thought he was unfit but he could run. He had a great attitude and absolutely loved West Ham. We soon realised the gaping chasm between John Lyall and Lou Macari when West Ham were playing Torquay away in the FA Cup. Both George and I were carrying injuries and Macari told us to go and stand in the sea late at night. It was absolutely freezing. Picture the scene of two black boys in Torquay, standing with the sea above our knees, at 10 o'clock at night for what seemed like an eternity! We both woke up the next day with stinking colds and ended up losing the match 0-1.
Leroy Rosenior

Smokey gives everything his all. He has had to contend with quite a few challenges and overcame a gambling addiction which says a lot about his will and determination. He's a great

character and good fun to be around.
Everald La Ronde

George looked after me West Ham. He has a massive heart, is West Ham through and through and one of John's boys that came through the ranks. We still stay in touch.
Kevin Keen

My mate George! I got on so well with him. He was a top player but slightly overweight!
Paul Hilton

Mr Dependable and Mr Versatile. He could play left or right and gave you everything he had. He'd make mistakes but correct them. Fantastic guy and honest as the day is long.
Mick McGiven

George was my best mate at West Ham. We went to the betting shop all the time and I was the one who had the problem because I loved the horse racing. I was absolutely stunned when I heard he had developed a gambling problem. Thankfully, he has put all that behind him. He drove a white Morris Marina and he'd sit so low in the seat you could barely see his head above the dash board! I still call him up. He's a really good friend.
Alan Dickens

A good pal of mine. A very good pal.
Greg Campbell

With Everald La Ronde (left) at Ernie Gregory's funeral reception, Boleyn Ground, 2012

Smokey, Dicko and Pottsy at a John Lyall tribute evening, South Benfleet, 2016

Back row: Swindlehurst, Martin, Bonds, Gale, Walford, Parkes, Vaughan, McAlister, Campbell, Devonshire, Hilton, Dickens, Whitton, Goddard.

Front row: Orr, Stewart, McPherson, Pike, Barnes, McAvennie, Cottee, Donald, Potts, Keen, Parris, Brush.

CHAPTER TWELVE
1985-86

"I have no problem stopping a training session as many times as it takes to get something right. It might be a basic technical skill but it has to be done right.." John Lyall

West Ham achieved their highest ever league placing in the club's history, when they finished 3rd, to Champions Liverpool and runners-up, Everton. Press headlines such as: 'Vintage bubbly,' and 'Best Ham' returned to journalistic parlance. 'West Ham crush Chelsea' was a new gem to add to the scrapbook. The Hammers kept their title hopes alive until the final weekend of the season.

New signings, Frank McAvennie from St Mirren and Mark Ward from Oldham Athletic, proved to be the catalysts behind a sublime season. Ward was described as the next Alan Ball. West Ham were also linked with Tosh McKinley of Dundee but no deal was reached.

The glorious season was awash with records: 17 home wins and 25 overall victories broke the previous single season records from 1958-59. Nine consecutive wins was

a new record as was five consecutive away wins. 24 goals conceded on opposition grounds was the lowest mark since 1923-24. 40 goals conceded overall also bettered that season. Tony Cottee and Frank McAvennie combined to score 54 goals. No other West Ham strike partnership since has been anywhere close.

English clubs were banned from competing in Europe, following disgraceful scenes between Liverpool and Juventus fans in the previous year's European Cup final. Consequently, West Ham missed out on a continental tour.

Chief Executive, Eddie Chapman, retired after 49-years' service as player and club secretary.

Frank McAvennie and Mark Ward were the only two debutants that season.

Here is their story...

McAvennie joined the greats. (60 goals from 190 matches) alongside Vic Keeble (51 goals from 84 matches)

Eddie Chapman retired after 49 years service. Seen here with one of West Ham United's proud achievements - the 1940 War Cup

64 – MARK WARD

"He was always in control, always thinking about football and always impressive. I went out and played not just for myself and the club, but for John Lyall."

Born: Huyton, Liverpool, October 10, 1962 • **Position:** Right-wing • **Games played for John Lyall:** 184 (1985-89)
Games played for West Ham United: 209 (1985-1989) • **Goals:** 14 • **Honours under John Lyall:** 1985-86: Member of West Ham United's highest ever league finish (third) • **Debut:** August 17, 1985 v Birmingham City (a) L 0-1 Att: 11,164
Birmingham City: Seaman, Ranson, Roberts, Wright, Armstrong*, Daly, Bremner, Clarke, Jones, Geddis, Hopkins. Sub: Kuhl.
West Ham United: Parkes, Stewart, Walford, Gale, Martin, Devonshire, **Ward**, McAvennie, Goddard*, Cottee, Orr. Sub: Dickens.*

Mark William Ward was one of seven children born to parents Billy and Irene: *"My Dad worked as a labourer on various building sites and my mum was a housewife."*

John Lyall signed "Wardy" for £250,000 from Oldham Athletic in the summer of 1985, having earlier received £400,000 from Tottenham Hotspur for the services of Paul Allen. It was a fine investment as Ward went on to play in every game of West Ham United's finest ever league season in 1985-86: *"I could have continued playing that season. I loved every minute of it and didn't want it to end. It was the only team I have ever played in where I wasn't thinking if we were going to win, but by how many."*

Ward left West Ham in 1989, following the appointment of Lou Macari as manager. He played out the rest of his career at Manchester City, Everton and Birmingham City.

In 2005, Ward fell from grace, when he was jailed for his involvement in the supply of cocaine. He served four years of an eight year sentence. The story of his playing and post playing experiences were chronicled in his autobiography: 'From Right-Wing to B-Wing.' In it, Ward explains the scenario which sealed his fate: *"I knew that although the drugs and paraphernalia were not mine, and nor were they put there by me, I'd be held responsible because the property they had been discovered in was rented in my name. What a dickhead I'd been!"*

During the final few years at The Boleyn Ground, Ward was

a regular in the annual Charity match between ex Hammers and The Great Ormond Street Hospital. Since the move to The London Stadium, he has hosted pre-match entertainment at the East Ham Working Man's club and occasionally attends reunions of the famed, Boys of '86.

Wardy, readily gave his memories of John Lyall:

My transfer to West Ham United was quite rushed because it was just a few days before the start of the season. Both John Lyall and Eddie Baily had showed an interest in me. I was at Oldham Athletic at the time and their manager, Joe Royle, called me up to say that West Ham had paid £250,000 for me. Joe said that John Lyall would be at my house within the hour! How many managers would pick up their new signing like that? He'd driven all the way from Essex to my house in Liverpool.

Joe trusted John and I was given a very good first impression. He was a real gentleman and had great presence. I found him so impressive and knew I wanted to play for him. He drove me down to London in his jaguar. John and Eddie had so many great stories about the club and the characters who worked and played there. They told me they wanted to sign me when I was at Northwich Victoria but the West Ham board weren't comfortable paying the asking price of £9,500 for a non-league player!

The transfer to West Ham meant a big change in my

circumstances. I think John liked me because I stayed wide and created opportunities. It was a gamble for John because I was taking a big step up and hadn't proven myself in the top flight. I was 22-years-old and £250,000 was a lot money. Along with the £340,000 signing of Frank McAvennie from St Mirren, John really was putting his reputation on the line. Thankfully, we didn't let him down.

Both Frank and I were quick and aggressive players and John was hoping we would ignite the good players around us. Frank was from Glasgow and I was from Liverpool and we were hungry to be the best we could be. We were a little known Jock and a little known Scouser, but we became good mates on and off the pitch. The training facilities at Chadwell Heath were so much better than I'd been used to at Oldham.

The coaching team at West Ham were excellent. They created situations for me whereby I could take on a full-back and put in a cross. Ronnie Boyce played the ball in to me and I'd have a one-on-one and get to the line before getting in my cross. We didn't have big, imposing strikers at West Ham so I would try and put my crosses in hard and low for Cottee and Frank to feed off.

Everyone at West Ham could play. Even the centre-halves, Alvin Martin and Tony Gale, brought the ball down and played it out of defence. Dev was just brilliant to watch and being around those players certainly made me a better player. John was very astute as well in that he asked Alvin to look after me. We were both from Liverpool and became firm friends. Both Alvin and his wife, Maggie, really helped to settle me and my wife, Jane, into the area. Alvin was club captain and gave me a very sound piece of advice: "Just give 100% and the fans will love you."

I didn't have a very good debut up at Birmingham City, but John stuck by me and I set up a goal for Alan Dickens in the first home game of the season, against Queens Park Rangers. I didn't look back from there and John picked me for every game. I think Parkesy, Galey and me were the three ever present players in 1985-86.

That record breaking season was all down to John. He knew that he had the nucleus of some very good players at the club and didn't want to bring in any superstars to spoil the mix. He found the right blend to fit his plan and it was almost perfect. Almost. We just ran out of games. There was a great Karma at the club during that final run in. We could have beaten anybody.

John liked a settled side and there were strong relationships all over the pitch. Obviously we had Cottee and McAvennie up front but Galey and Alvin worked so well together in defence. Me and Ray Stewart also had a great partnership down the right side. Everyone seemed to click.

I was surprised John smoked so much because he never seemed nervous to me. In fact, he was quite the opposite.

Doing battle with Mitchell Thomas of Tottenham Hotspur

He was always in control of any situation. The dressing room was usually filled with smoke because Boycey liked a cigarette as well. Those two could have smoked for England and Scotland!

John was very direct with any criticism he had for the team. He said things like: "You know that's a disgrace out there and you've got to go out and put it right." He didn't care how well you had been playing in other games, or even if you were one of the younger lads, he would let you know if you weren't performing. On one occasion, Tony Cottee, was singled out for criticism. TC was a fantastic striker, but didn't like tracking back and defending from the front. McAvennie did it really well but John had noticed that TC wasn't defending the opposition's right-back or centre-half when they were bringing out the ball. John flagged this as the reason we were being so overrun and let Tony know about it.

I was managed by some top managers in my career. Joe Royle at Oldham Athletic and Howard Kendall at Everton were brilliant. I had a great relationship with Howard who was a very special person. John was the one who was like a father figure to me. They were all proper football men with many fine qualities. John spent time with me, took an interest in my life and was always asking after my family. My happiness genuinely meant a lot to him. Through this, I really got to know the man. I went to his house and met Yvonne and Murray, so I felt part of something special. That was a big thing for me because I went out and played not just for myself and the club but for John Lyall.

I could be quite an aggressive character both on and off the pitch. John said to me once: "What does your wife feed you on, raw meat?"

I do remember a time when John lost his temper. A journalist from the Sun named Steven Howard had asked John if he could interview me and he'd given his consent. I think Steven was new at the Sun and John liked to foster lasting relationships with the press. I'd been playing well and we both thought it was going to be a piece about my England chances.

John told me to be careful because he knew any journalist from the Sun might have an ulterior motive. Anyway, the interview went well and was mainly about football and how I was playing. He did ask me if I thought I should be in the England squad and I said I was happy with my form but that was something for manager Bobby Robson to decide. We ended the interview and had a general chat about London and Liverpool and the things I missed, that sort of thing. On Saturday, I realised I'd been duped because the big headline in the Sun read: 'Homesick Hammer.'

John went absolutely mad. He knew that I was going to be on the radar of all those clubs in the north and he was in a total rage about it: "That so and so at The Sun will never be allowed inside West Ham again!" he fumed. He was

shouting and swearing and kept calling The Sun to talk to the culprit but they wouldn't take his call. They had written a pack of lies and John felt betrayed. He had opened up the club and given access to one of his players and now he felt they had gone behind his back. He didn't blame me for anything and I felt as though I hadn't done anything wrong. "I'll get him," he kept saying. I don't know if he ever meted out any kind of revenge but he was really annoyed about the whole episode.

John was very clear in his approach to football. The defenders would supply the ball to me and, in turn, I'd keep the strikers supplied and amongst the goals. I never played in a better team than that 1985-86 side. We just gelled so well together. Dev was the best player I ever played with. You just don't see players like him anymore. It takes my breath away just thinking about what he could do with a ball. We were particularly good away from home. How many games did we win 1-0? We defended high up on the pitch and were super quick on the break. Dev was quick, I was quick, and so were Cottee and McAvennie. We could destroy defences in a matter of seconds. The 4-0 thumping of Chelsea at Stamford Bridge was a good example of that.

I think I got very close to an England cap. I had a really good game against Nottingham Forest and people were saying that I'd destroyed the country's best left-back in Stuart Pearce. I felt I was definitely in the reckoning at that time but the call never came. It's a shame that Ron Greenwood didn't keep the England job for another ten years!

John spent a lot of time with me after training and often dropped by to my hotel to make sure everything was fine. He was so good at all those little touches and they made you feel comfortable and needed. He was so much more than a manager, I would have run through a brick wall for him. He invested so much trust and time and energy into making me feel part of West Ham. If any family matters arose, John would be there for me. I just didn't want to let him down. I was lucky in that Howard Kendall was a lot like that as well.

I didn't score many goals at West Ham, I think I got 14 and the pick of them would have to be my first goal for the club. It came at Oxford United from a 35-yard free kick. I'd also set up Cottee with a 10 yard pass in that game and we came from behind to win 2-1. That was my best goal for West Ham. John signed me as a good source of supply for the strikers and I certainly set up a good share of the goals, too.

I was absolutely devastated when I heard they'd sacked John. I just couldn't believe how they had treated him. I never felt the same about the club after that to be honest. When they decided to appoint Lou Macari, I just thought: "Why?"

I bumped into Macari in Loughton just before he got the job at West Ham. I was going into a bookmakers to back my mate Mickey Quinn's horse. It was called 'Town Patrol' and I'd already lost a few quid on it, but Quinny assured me it had

Playing in a Great Ormond Street Hospital Charity match at Upton Park - L-R Stuart Slater, Keith Rowland, Kevin Keen and Wardy

a very good chance. Macari had seen me enter the Bookies and came over for a chat. Before he left, he said to me: "I'll see you sooner than you think." He'd obviously already been given the nod by the club. By the time I got to the counter I was too late because the race was off and Quinny's horse won! That was a bad omen right there.

I didn't click with Macari at all. I never liked the way he spoke to people. If you were looking for a personality that was the precise opposite to John Lyall, then look no further than Lou Macari. He was unethical, hopeless at man-management and spread unhappiness like confetti. He gave me £400 once to put on a horse in the local bookies 20 minutes before kick-off. How can a West Ham United manager be thinking of such things at 2.30 on Saturday afternoon? If Bonzo had taken over from John I probably would have stayed at the club.

I was in prison when I heard the news that John had died from a heart attack. I was absolutely gutted and made a request to the prison governor to attend the funeral but it was declined.

He wasn't just a great manager he was a great friend.
Mark Ward

Wardy was a good player, a good lad and a typical Scouser. West Ham missed him when he was sold. I sometimes wonder if John would have played Wardy or Paul Allen on the right in his best 11 from that era.
Steve Walford

A really good friend of mine and I won't have a bad word said about him.
Tony Gale

When I was trying to break into the team I was trying to dislodge Wardy on the right and Dev on the left so I was really up against it. A great crosser of the ball, a great striker of the ball and a real team player. He had that little bit of nastiness in his play which the Chicken Run loved.
Kevin Keen

I played with Wardy at both West Ham and Everton and he always wanted to take on the world. We still keep in touch and it is always good to see him. One defender I didn't like playing against was Stuart Pearce at Nottingham Forest. When things started to get nasty I'd shout: "Wardy!" and leave him to have some titanic battles.
Tony Cottee

We all knew he was a bit of a scallywag but he always put a smile on your face.
Leroy Rosenior

I love Wardy. He's got a winner's mentality. He was one of the main reasons we did so well in 1985-86. He worked hard, loved to tackle and was a quality player.
Alan Dickens

A funny, Scouse nutter!
Paul Hilton

Started off brilliantly for West Ham but after a season just seemed to disappear. The work rate, accuracy and flamboyance all vanished and I don't know why. Perhaps his desire had gone but we had a terrific season out of him. He had quick feet and his crossing ability was first class and he could score goals, too.
Mick McGiven

Wardy is one you would want in the trenches with you.
George Parris

Back at Upton Park with Billy Bonds, 2016.

65 – FRANK McAVENNIE

"Sometimes I would wake up on Monday morning and look at the stunner lying next to me and think: "Sorry, John - I'll take the fine!"

Born: Glasgow, November 22, 1959 • **Position:** Striker • **Games played for John Lyall:** 116 (1985-89)

Games played for West Ham United: 190 (1985-1987, 1989-92) • **Goals:** 60 (23rd on the all-time list)

Honours: 1985-86: Member of West Ham United's highest ever league finish (third), 1985-88; 5 Scotland caps (1 goal)

Debut: August 18, 1985 v Birmingham City (a) L 0-1 Att: 11,164

Birmingham City: Seaman, Ranson, Roberts, Wright, Armstrong,* Daly, Bremner, Clarke, Jones, Geddis, Hopkins. Sub: Kuhl.*

West Ham United: Parkes, Stewart, Walford, Gale, Martin, Devonshire, Ward, **McAvennie**, Goddard*, Cottee, Orr. Sub: Dickens.*

Francis 'Frank' McAvennie grew up in Ensay Street, Glasgow, and attended St Augustine's Secondary School in Milton. His father, Benny, was in the Navy before becoming an upholsterer. His mother, Jean, was a machinist. In 1981-82, while playing for St Mirren, Frank was voted Scotland's Young Player of the Year.

In the summer of 1985 West Ham United paid £340,000 to St Mirren for his services, initially as a midfielder, but most memorably as a striker. His partnership with Tony Cottee during 1985-86 yielded 54 goals and no West Ham strike force has come anywhere remotely close since.

In 1987, West Ham more than doubled their investment when McAvennie was transferred to Celtic for £750,000. He returned to the club in 1989, just a few months before the club sacked John Lyall: "One of the worst memories I have from my time in football was the sacking of John Lyall. I think a lot of people felt betrayed by the club over the way he was treated."

McAvennie gained all five of his Scotland caps while at West Ham and is one of only three Scottish Hammers to have scored for his country whilst playing for the Hammers - Ray Stewart and Christian Dailly being the other two.

Nowadays, McAvennie is a popular name on the after dinner circuit and holds shares in several companies: *"I'm keeping nice and busy which is good for me. I manage to put*

in a round of golf each week so my handicap is coming down. My goal is to get down to single figures."

Frank had nothing but praise for his former manager:

The first contact I had with John Lyall was at Toddington services on the M1. I was actually in talks with David Pleat at Luton Town and was going to sign for them. My agent called me and said that West Ham's manager John Lyall also wanted to talk to me. It was awkward because Luton had paid for my flight from Scotland and the directors at St Mirren, too. Obviously, we couldn't tell Luton what we were up to so I ended up meeting John and Eddie Baily at 2am in Toddington services.

Immediately, I could see that John was a total football man. He talked a lot of sense and was so easy to listen to. I have to laugh now because I was so tired that I was arguing with him over a couple of pounds! I knew there and then that I was going to sign for him. I asked John if he'd been watching me at St Mirren and apparently Alex Ferguson had recommended me to him.

John liked Scottish players because they showed a lot of aggression and loved to win. I absolutely hated losing. Even now when I play in a Charity match, I simply have to be on the winning side. Both Neil Orr and Ray Stewart were the

Scoring against Oxford United, April 1986

same. They had a strong will to win.

After signing for John, I went down to West Ham and had my first pre-season training session. I was absolutely gobsmacked because they got the ball out straight away. In Scotland, I didn't see a ball for three weeks. John laughed when I told him: "This is the tool of your trade," he said. "You'll do plenty of running this afternoon!" he joked.

It was just magnificent to get the feel of the ball again because I'd just had five weeks off. I soon found out that if I did put on a bit of weight, John would make sure I wore a bin bag to get up a good sweat. He was a real hands on manager. He liked the physical side of the game but his favourite was the one and two-touch sessions in the small grids at Chadwell Heath. That experience gave me so much confidence when playing on a full-sized pitch. It made everything that bit easier. I thought the West Ham players were first class at one and two-touch but when I watch Barcelona with Messi, it is as if they are playing half-touch, they are so good!

John had bought me to play in the Number 10 role, behind the two strikers – Paul Goddard and Tony Cottee. However, when Goddard got injured, during my debut at Birmingham City, I was pushed up front and Tony and I just clicked immediately. John couldn't change it from there. Who knows how it would have played out had 'Sarge' not got injured? He was one hell of a player.

John said to me that after I'd scored two goals against QPR

during my home debut, he knew that he wasn't going to change the partnership. It's ridiculous nowadays when you hear the media going on and on about how players have to adjust to their new surroundings and need time to forge a partnership with the players around them. What a load of nonsense that is! You can either play football or you can't play football.

When I came down to West Ham no one could understand a single word I was saying because I had a really strong Glaswegian accent. TC certainly couldn't understand me. He thought I was picking a fight with him every time I spoke! But we could play together and we knew each other's strengths and made sure we got the best out of each other.

Tony and I had such a good understanding that we believed we were going to score in every game. We were so confident that we once struck a bet for £500 to see who could score the best goal. We were playing against Aston Villa at home and I thought I had a chance because, as you know, Tony rarely scored from outside the box. However, on this day, it was just my luck that he smacked one in from 25-yards. I thought I'd lost the bet. But then I got an opportunity. Wardy put me through and I was in on goal with only their keeper, Nigel Spink, to beat. Instead of sliding it by him I tried to chip him and the ball didn't look like it was going to make it. If it went in I was convinced I'd done enough to win the £500. It was one of the most beautiful sights when it crossed the line

During the famous 4-0 victory over Chelsea at Stamford Bridge, March 1986

for a goal. Unfortunately, John found out about the bet and fined us a grand each!

I shared the same agent as George Best, so when I came down to play for West Ham United Georgie looked after me. He ran a club called Blondes and it was full of the most beautiful women you have ever seen. I used to pop in a few times a week just to make sure George was ok! I actually got engaged twice in that place. What a night that was!

John was so far ahead of his time. The positional play they rave about these days in the Premier League was something John had us doing in the 1980s. I think that managers nowadays owe a big thank you to John Lyall. There isn't anyone to compare John to in the modern game because he was a one off. He ran the whole show at West Ham. He was such a lovely guy and a great advert for how a club should be managed. That is why it was such a massive shock when they sacked him. I couldn't believe it and the club was never the same. His replacement, Lou Macari, was so far off the mark for West Ham it wasn't even funny. They were trying to

do things in a different way and basically f***** up the club.

John was great to me. He gave me the freedom to go out and play my game, to express myself. No other manager had ever been like that to me. He believed in me so much that I always felt good about my game. He loved it that I didn't give a monkeys about the defenders I was coming up against. He liked it that I had a little bit of arrogance about me, too. I always felt I was a team player first before an individual player which was another feature that John admired. If I had a one-on-one and TC was in the clear I would pass it to him to guarantee the goal. My philosophy was team first - win the game and showboat afterwards.

John believed in all his players which cultivated a brilliant team spirit. We were all good friends and knew each other's game inside out. Tony was the out and out striker and to this day we are still very close pals. You really can't buy that with any amount of money. When you get a group of players as close as that 1985-86 team, then something good will come from it. We should have won the title. It was only the weather that beat us because we were the best team in the league at that time. It was very disappointing because I would have loved to have given the title to John.

I should have won the Golden Boot easily that season but missed out to Everton's Gary Lineker. He was a good player and had the advantage of taking the penalties. If I'd done the same at West Ham I would have won that boot easily. We had Ray Stewart and he never missed penalties so that was another aspect of the team John wasn't going to change. I scored 26 league goals and I was one or two behind Lineker, but he scored over 10 penalties that season. Anyway, it's not a problem. I might have got a crisp advert named after me, that's all!

The pick of all my goals for West Ham would have to be the one at Chelsea when we battered them 4-0. I also remember lobbing Peter Schmeichel from a free kick up at Old Trafford. Sadly, we lost that one so it doesn't count!

One thing I'm very proud of is taking the time and effort to see John at a reunion in London's Docklands. It was at the Britannia hotel and he died the following year. I wanted to have a chat with John because I'd been in a bit of trouble after my playing days and needed him to know that it wasn't as bad as it seemed. He told me that there was nothing to explain. He was such a gentleman. He said: "I'm just proud of you and that's all we need to know." He died shortly after that so I was so happy and grateful that I saw him that evening.

There are only two managers from my playing career that I would still call 'Gaffer.' One is Billy McNeil of Celtic and the other is John Lyall. Funnily enough, John wouldn't let me call him Gaffer. He always preferred to be called John. I told him he could call me Frank but my behaviour meant he called me quite a lot things! I certainly can't share those for a good family read such as your book! Generally, he called me Frank or Frankie. He knew I didn't do half of what was written about me and that is good enough for me.

John was good at letting you know if things weren't as he expected them to be. He certainly wasn't as soft as some might think and had a hard edge to him. A lot of the players described John as a father figure and that is absolutely correct but he was also like my wife because he was always right! We discussed it once and I've never forgotten his words: "Frank," he said. "Women are always right. Even when they are wrong!" It is just so true. John expected you to respect others.

There was a big mirror on the dressing room door before you walked down the tunnel and out onto the pitch. John would look at me and say: "Frank, take a good look at yourself on the way out and then again after the 90 minutes are up. If you can justify the amount of effort you have put in during that period then that is fine by me." He also said that not every player can play well in every game, but that it was important to remember that every player can still do important things for the team.

Two-goal Frank is a winner for Lyall

West Ham ....3 QPR 1

By COLIN GIBSON

TWO-GOAL Frank McAvennie last night repaid some of the £340,000 gambled by John Lyall when the West Ham manager plucked him from obscurity of Scottish football this summer.

When the opportunity arose for me to join Celtic, John didn't really try to make me stay. He knew that Celtic were my club and that if I was going to leave West Ham, it would only be for Celtic. Furthermore, things had started to change at the club. I couldn't really play with Stewart Robson in midfield because his skill set didn't work for me. I knew I had to go and when Celtic came in for me my mind was made up.

John did so many great things for me and there are so many good memories I can draw to mind quite easily. When I won my first cap for Scotland against Australia, John drove all the way up to Hampden Park to see me play and wished me luck. I get emotional when I think about that.

I was in Glasgow when I heard that he'd died. I still miss him now. He is one of the nicest guys I've ever met in my life. To this day I still miss John. He is a man I would have always kept in touch with. I'd love to have a wee chat with him every week. He was such a lovely guy and a great advert for how a club should be managed. A total gentleman.

Frank McAvennie

There was no shortage of comments about Frank:

There is a football show in Glasgow which they produce every year called 'Only an Excuse'. They take Frank off to a tee and it is full of innuendo about Frank and his womanising ways. Luckily for Frank he could perform on the pitch as well and was a very good striker.
Steve Walford

Frank is the same age as me. We were born within four days of each other. He is one of life's real characters. In 2015, we flew out to Dubai together for Tony Cottee's wedding. We flipped a coin to see who was going to be best man. I lost so had to do it and Frank just went on the piss for a week!
Tony Gale

I played with some great strikers - Peter Beardsley, Graham Sharp and Marco Boogers, obviously! But Frank was my best strike partner and our 54 goals during 1985-86 is something we're both very proud of. I love Frank. He was and still is one of my best friends.
Tony Cottee

Full of fun. Full of joy and always smiling. When he stepped out on a football pitch, the serious work began. What a work rate he had as well. I've got a lot of respect for Frank.
Leroy Rosenior

I roomed with him once. Never again! You just never know what he is going to do next. He always lights up a room when he walks in.
Paul Hilton

Everyone loved Frank. He was a great player and worked his socks off for the team. He got away with whatever he wanted because he was so well liked and did the business on the pitch.
Alan Dickens

The wilder things were, the better he played! George Parris
Quite a remarkable transformation because Frank was just about getting into the team during the pre-season as a right winger.
Paul Brush

I actually think he had a bit of Denis Law about him. Just a little bit, but it was definitely there. Great touch, great finisher and hard as nails.
Greg Campbell

Frank was our equivalent of George Best. He did it on the field and he did it off the field!
Eddie Gillam

One of the leading lights at West Ham. He was a fantastic player and could score goals with his left, his right or with his head. He saw things others couldn't and made terrific runs. He was quick and fearless and was everything we needed at West Ham. The fans will always love someone who can score goals and Frank certainly knew how to do that.
Mick McGiven

He changed the culture at West Ham. I remember Charlie Nicholas and Mo Johnstone coming into the players' lounge after a match to see Frank who was with The Sun's Page Three girl, Jenny Blyth.
Neil Orr

I roomed with Frank at West Ham and it was a miracle that I got any sleep. We'd be having dinner in a hotel the night before a game and I'd wake up in the middle of the night to see the woman who had served our food in Frank's bed!
Mark Ward

With Ronnie Boyce before last ever Saturday match at Upton Park - Swansea City, April 2016

Ernie Gregory - One of the great West Ham characters.

Back row: Walford, Hilton, McAlister, Vaughan, Parkes, Martin, Gale.

Middle row: Dickens, Orr, Campbell, Bonds, Parris, Stewart, Whitton, Devonshire, McMenemy.

Front row: Ward, Pike, Goddard, McAvennie, Cottee, Keen, Potts.

CHAPTER THIRTEEN
1986-87

"We have a reputation for good, attacking football, but getting things right in defence is also important." **John Lyall**

West Ham returned to their unpredictable form, riding high in the early months of the season before plummeting to the lower reaches of the league after Christmas.

Billy Bonds celebrated his 40th birthday. The previous Saturday, he had turned out for the reserves against Oxford United, at a rain-drenched Upton Park: *"I am enjoying every minute of playing my football with the youngsters,"* declared the club legend: *"They are full of enthusiasm."* Billy was in his 19th season as a Hammer.

Phil Parkes was no longer the most expensive goalkeeper, after Graeme Souness, manager of Rangers, paid Norwich City £600,000 for Chris Woods.

Phil's mentor, Ernie Gregory, ended his 51-year association with the club, following a tearful farewell at Chadwell Heath.

The first ever 'Who's Who of West Ham' was published by Jack Helliar and Tony Hogg.

'West Ham United – The Making of a Football Club' by Charles Korr, was also published. It was the first-ever detailed inside history of a football club and remains one of the best books ever written about West Ham.

Following an alarming post-Christmas slide down the league table, West Ham bought Stewart Robson from Arsenal, Liam Brady from Ascoli, Gary Strodder from Lincoln City and Tommy McQueen from Aberdeen. John Lyall also gave debuts to home-grown talent: Kevin Keen, Paul Ince and Eamonn Dolan.

Here is their story...

John addressing the next generation of Hammers

Paul Ince signed for West Ham instead of Fulham because of the indoor training facilities

66 – KEVIN KEEN

" I was coached by Tony Carr at youth level and then developed further under Ron Boyce, Mick McGiven and John Lyall. It is impossible to measure the positive impact those four great minds had on West Ham United. "

Born: Amersham, Buckinghamshire, February 25, 1967 • **Position:** Midfield • **Games played for John Lyall:** 75 (1986-89).

Games played for West Ham United: 278 (1986-93) • **Goals:** 30

Debut: September 6, 1986 v Liverpool (h) L 2-5 (Stewart pen, Cottee – Whelan, Johnston, Dalglish 2, Rush) Att: 29,807

West Ham United: Parkes, Stewart, Parris, Gale, Martin, Pike*, Ward, McAvennie, Dickens, Cottee, Orr. Sub: **Keen.***

Liverpool: Hooper, Venison, Beglin, Gillespie, Whelan, Hansen*, McDonald, Johnston, Rush, Lawrenson, McMahon. Sub: Dalglish.

Kevin Ian Keen grew up in a family football culture. His father, Mike, enjoyed a 25 year association with the game, both as a player and manager. "After my dad retired from the game, he ran a sports shop in Wycombe. It was called 'Mike Keen Sports' and was sold to Mike Ashleigh in 1994. It is now part of the Sports Direct chain of stores and, remarkably, my mum still works there!"

Keen grew up in High Wycombe and was soon placed on the radar of several scouts: *"I was first discovered by Mike Dove at just 12-years-old. I'd been playing for High Wycombe district Under-12s in a tournament on the Isle of Wight. Soon after, Charlie Faulkner, the West Ham scout who had discovered Alan Devonshire, started to keep an eye on me."*

Keen would eventually sign apprentice forms and lodged with Rose Cross in Barking, mother of ex Hammers striker, Roger Cross: *"It was a fantastic time for me. My dad had been a professional footballer and had shown me how to play the game properly. I enjoyed nine happy years at West Ham."*

Today, Kevin is a well-respected coach and has had spells at West Ham United, Liverpool, West Bromwich Albion, Reading and Crystal Palace, as well as a management role at Colchester United.

Following are Kevin's memories of John Lyall:

The reason I chose West Ham United was because the club's

philosophy was very close to what my dad had believed in. My father, Mike, had played over 600 matches in the lower divisions with QPR, Luton Town and Watford. He knew John Lyall and they shared almost identical beliefs in the way the game should be played.

I had five or six offers from other clubs, some a lot nearer to my home, but I chose a club which I believed played the game the right way. John Lyall and Eddie Baily visited my house in Wycombe and talked with my parents about how I would be looked after. Arsenal, QPR, Birmingham and, Manchester United were all possible destinations for me, but John's visit and talk with my parents gave West Ham the advantage and I signed for them.

John was a top manager, a fantastic coach and a father figure to so many young lads at West Ham United. There was a generation of excellent youth players coming through – Alan Dickens, George Parris, Tony Cottee, Steve Potts, Paul Ince and so many others. The club had great senior pros, too. Players who I could really look up to like Billy Bonds and Alan Devonshire. Paul Goddard was particularly helpful to me.

John upheld a certain style of football. He was an advocate of the passing game and the expression of individual quality within a team framework. The one-touch play that was drilled into us day after day has largely disappeared from the way West Ham play football these days. As the club goes through evolution after evolution, the great standard bearers of the West Ham way – Ron Greenwood

Kevin's first league goal, versus Southampton, December 1987

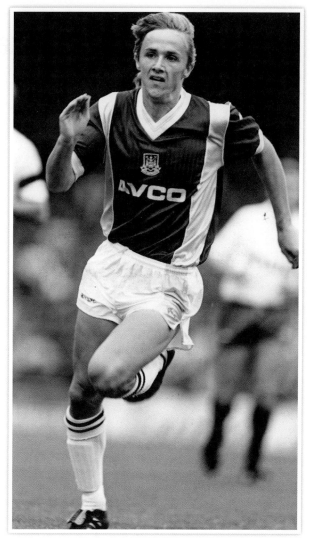

Keeno in action

and John Lyall – become more and more diluted.

I made my debut against Liverpool in September 1986. I came on as a substitute for Geoff Pike and we lost 2-5. Kenny Dalglish got a couple. I have fonder memories of my second match, at QPR, because my dad had played over 400 times for them. It was on a plastic pitch but we ran out 3-2 winners.

John really cared about his players. Once, I asked him why he kept digging me out. He replied: "If I didn't care, I wouldn't be digging you out. The time to get worried is when I stop digging you out because that's when I've given up on you!" He was always giving me little snippets of advice – "You should have stayed wide when that happened" or "An extra touch might have helped there."

One of the strong images I have of John is from the training ground. Every morning he'd be sitting with Ronnie Boyce and Mick McGiven greeting all the players as they arrived. There'd be a thick cloud of smoke because John and Boycey were chain smokers. They always smoked in the dugout during a match. It really was a different era.

I don't have a very good memory of John's final match in charge of West Ham United. It was up at Anfield at the end of the 1988-89 season. I had started in the previous six matches and we'd won five of them. We now had a slim chance of survival. We needed to win at Anfield where we hadn't won for over 25 years. Surprisingly, John dropped me for that game and, instead, opted for Liam Brady. To say I was upset would be an understatement. We lost 1-5 and were relegated. Even though I don't think we would have won that game, because Liverpool were going for the title, I just wish it wasn't my final memory of John as West Ham's manager.

In the summer of 1989, I was 22-years-of-age and had been called up for jury duty in Ayelsbury. The court had been showing evidence all morning, so, when we had a break I went out to my car to clear my head. I switched on the radio and was thinking about the court case when, in the background, I heard John's name on the radio. I turned it up

and was totally shocked when they announced that he'd been sacked. I just couldn't believe it and when they appointed Lou Macari as his replacement, I couldn't believe that either.

It is one of my biggest regrets that I didn't ring John at the time. We weren't living in the mobile phone age back then so it was a bit more difficult. I was only young, but really wished I'd called him to thank him for everything. I put it down to immaturity but I do regret not taking the time to talk to him.

The next time I saw John he was in charge of Ipswich Town and I was playing for Wolves. It was a big cup game and I must say that it was my best game for Wolves by an absolute distance. I wanted to show John that one of his boys had become a good player. We won 2-1 at Portman Road and they were in the top flight whereas we were in the league below. It was weird talking to both John and Mick McGiven after the game. Out of all the coaches, it was Mick who had the most respect for me as a player. That respect was reciprocated and it just felt strange talking to them outside of a West Ham environment. That conversation should have taken place at Upton Park.

When I think of all the players John coached while I was at the club, the two stand-out talents were Billy Bonds and Alan Devonshire. I had a great football education as a young kid because I drove in every day with Alan Devonshire and Paul Goddard. We were the three west London boys who drove in together. Phil Parkes also travelled in with us sometimes. I sat in that car listening to them discussing football so it was a fantastic learning experience for me.

Bonzo was a phenomenon, an absolute one off. I've spoken to Stuart Slater and Steve Potts about this. Because we were at the club for the last four or five years of his playing career and then played for him when he became manager, we were brim full of respect for him. We had seen him train, and had benefitted from the terrific attitude he had for the game generally, and West Ham in particular. When he became manager we would have done absolutely anything for him. Any young kid who had been on a training pitch with Billy Bonds or played with him in the first team would have ran through brick walls for him. I was so lucky to bump into him at one of the last matches at Upton Park and it was just fantastic to shake his hand and say hello. He said he was following my career in coaching and wished me all the best. What a player! What a man! If you had him on your team in training, you won. That is a cast iron fact.

I left West Ham for Wolverhampton Wanderers when I was 27. Graham Turner was the manager and at my first training session he announced to the players that they were going to play three-touch football in the first session. I had to ask what that was because I simply had no idea!

When I think of John, I keep coming back to the notion of him as a father figure to all those youth team players that were coming through. He cajoled them, encouraged them, praised them and dug them out when he needed to. That's my biggest memory of John Lyall and what he contributed to West Ham.

Kevin Keen

Keeny was an underrated player and one of football's nice guys. Always wanted the ball and knew what to do with it once he got it.

Tony Gale

A very good player. Bags of energy and very creative.
Mick McGiven

I liked Keeny, he was a fantastic footballer but a very quiet lad. It is often the quiet ones who go on and pursue a career in coaching and that has been the case with Kevin. Good luck to him.

Tony Cottee

He was a quality player. When he first came over to train with the senior pros you could tell after a couple of minutes that he was going to make it to the first team. A typical West Ham player - great touch, saw things early, always thinking about position and good pace.

Alan Dickens

Kevin is an honest, hard-working, lovely family man.

Paul Hilton

He walked a bit like John Wayne! Didn't get the recognition he deserved.

George Parris

A proper West Ham player.

Mark Ward

I think Kevin is one of the nicest guys that I have ever met in football. His dad, Mike, played for QPR and my dad, Bill, used to treat him when he picked up any injuries.

Rob Jenkins

Kevin played in a really old pair of boots which were falling apart. He'd never want to play in anything else. I'd tape them up and paint them black! He loved those boots.

Eddie Gillam

Back at the Boleyn Ground, 2016

67 – PAUL INCE

"John was a great influence on my life. When I look back on my career, he is the man who started it all for me. If it wasn't for John, I would never have made it and would probably have spent time in prison. "

Born: Ilford, Essex • **Position:** Midfield • **Games played for John Lyall:** 96 (1986-1989)

Games played for West Ham United: 95 (1986-1989) • **Goals:** 12 • **Honours:** 1989 Hammer of the Year

Debut: November 25, 1986 Full Members Cup v Chelsea (h) L 1-2 (Cottee – Dixon, Spackman (pen) Att: 12,140

West Ham United: Parkes, Walford,* Parris, Gale, Hilton, **Ince,** Ward, McAvennie, Dickens, Cottee, Keen. Sub: Potts*

Chelsea: Niedzwiecki, Rougvie, Dublin, Isaac, McLaughlin, Pates, Nevin, Spackman,* Dixon, Speedie, Bumpstead. Sub: Wood.

Paul Emerson Carlyle Ince should have left behind one of the great midfield legacies at West Ham United. Instead, his time at Upton Park was cut painfully short following the sacking of John Lyall, the very man to whom Ince looked up to. The departure of Ince to Manchester United, in 1990, could have been viewed as an unwanted by-product of Lyall's sacking. However, his decision to wear a Manchester United shirt whilst still a West Ham United player, meant he left the club, in the eyes of many, as a pariah.

Ince went on to enjoy a glittering career and played for some of the best clubs in the world – Manchester United, Inter Milan and Liverpool. He also gained 53 England caps, seven as captain.

On reflection, Paul Ince was the first Hammer to win an embarrassment of riches at other clubs – His football CV sings of Premier League titles, FA Cups, European trophies and League Cup success. It is a crying shame that other starlets from West Ham United's Academy have trodden a similar route – most notably, Rio Ferdinand, Michael Carrick, Joe Cole and Frank Lampard jnr. Undoubtedly, West Ham United have been denied another era to compete with Moore, Hurst, Peters and Brooking Bonds and Devonshire.

After hanging up his boots in 2006, Ince entered the world

of management and had spells with Macclesfield Town, MK Dons, Blackburn Rovers, Notts County and Blackpool. He is also a highly respected media pundit:

"I work for BT Sport on Saturday's and a bit for ITV, too. I keep myself busy and like to watch my son, Thomas, play, which is always nice. I turned 50 in October, 2017 and all is going well."

I joined West Ham United mainly because of their indoor astroturf! I was 14 years-old and training at both Fulham and West Ham. At Fulham, they trained outside on coarse gravel, and I didn't fancy that at all. It was cold and I was grazing my legs every time I made a tackle. At West Ham, they had a modern indoor facility, so it was warm, spacious and well-lit. I much preferred that so decided to join West Ham.

I had a tough upbringing and lived in a rough area where trouble seemed to find me quite easily. There were several occasions when John Lyall could have lost faith in me. On one occasion, I got into trouble for fighting and the police turned up at the training ground. Some kid had reported me because I had broken his ribs and ear drum. Mick McGiven pulled me out of training and told me that John wanted to see me. There were two policemen sitting in John's office and they wanted to take me to the police station. John spent a good hour convincing them why that was a bad idea. He explained how he would take full responsibility for me. They ended up

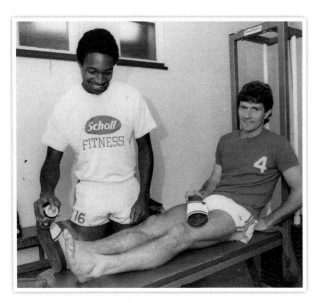

Sharing a joke with Ray Stewart

leaving without me which was a huge relief. John spent just as long talking to me about the situation. He told me how he believed in me and that I had a great chance of being a very good footballer. I'll never forget that conversation because he called me a "Pipsqueak!" He said it would be the last time he would defend me and gave me one final chance. That was the first time I had seen him really angry and it gave me a big wake-up call. He told me I had to get to the training ground early over the next two weeks and paint the gates. At 7am I'd be there, paint brush in hand, watching all the apprentices and senior pros arriving for training. That was the time when I started to think seriously about what I was doing and how I was going to turn my career around. John was a fair man but he was a hard man. I certainly didn't want to mess about with him or get on the wrong side of him anymore. There were certainly people at West Ham who were telling John that I was more trouble than I was worth. But John believed in me and stuck by me. He got me through my early years in football.

I think John liked me because I was a bit of a challenge. I was a cocky upstart and very outspoken. I sometimes said the wrong things and got into trouble, but behind it all, I could play. It was interesting because John actually changed the way I played. Before I joined West Ham, I was playing Saturday and Sunday morning football for Elmshaw Colts and Ford Rovers. I was scoring 30-40 goals every season from midfield. When I got into West Ham's first team I was bombing forward, taking shots and being really aggressive. John called me in and told me to just sit in the middle of the park. It was like someone throwing me a strait jacket. "Just

sit in the middle?" I said in disbelief: "I've been scoring for fun at every level I've played and not once has anyone asked me to do that." But he was adamant. "For now, I want you to win the ball and give it to Alan Devonshire or Alan Dickens." It completely changed my role as a player, because I'd never been a holding midfielder and now he wanted me to break up the play and set up attacks. It was a mark of his experience and knowledge that he saw something in me that not even I had seen. I spent the rest of my career doing exactly what John had described to me in his office at Chadwell Heath. Sometimes it was frustrating, but I carved out a good life from John's advice and have a lot to thank him for.

He had so much respect for his players and they idolised him. He was Mr West Ham to everyone. When I was 16, I went in to see him, expecting to sign a two-year professional contract like most of the other apprentices, but John said he was only going to offer me a one year Youth Training Scheme arrangement. I thought: "Only one effing year? I'm the best player here!" It was 1985 and I'd just captained the youth team to winning the South East Counties league. I was gobsmacked to say the least. He said he wanted me to knuckle down and show him how much I wanted to be a professional footballer. He wanted me to prove that I could

Dictating the play

keep out of trouble and not run with the pack which I'd been doing all my life with the kids I'd grown up with.

A lot of people remember my two goals against Liverpool in the 4th round of the League Cup in 1989, but my best memory is my home league debut. We beat Southampton 3-1 and I scored one and set up one. John told me on the previous Wednesday that I would be playing. He wanted me to prepare myself and not to tell anybody. I was so excited that I went and told Steve Potts straight away. Steve was my best mate, and best man at my wedding. I was buzzing and had to share the news. I was very nervous, like any young kid would be, but once I'd scored, well, it was the best feeling in the world. I felt like the next stage of my career was underway. The two goals against Liverpool were all a part of that.

I'd actually made my first team debut against Chelsea in The Full Members Cup a week earlier. John had also given me a run out up at Newcastle United. I came on in the last ten minutes when we were already 0-4 down. I thought: "Thanks John – that's not quite the memory I wanted to look back on!" After the match, John was lambasting all the players and he said that I'd done more in 10 minutes than the rest of them had done throughout the entire game. There was always method in everything he did and bringing me on as a substitute that day clearly had an ulterior motive.

Pottsy and I were a deadly duo. We were always cracking jokes, taking the Mickey, and having a laugh whenever we could. Kevin Keen was a top lad, Georgie Parris was a good friend of mine, as was Gary Strodder. As I grew into the first team, Alan Dickens became a very good friend, as did Paul Hilton. Alan Devonshire took me under his wing and was always looking after me and trying to keep me on the straight and narrow. He took time out for me and guided me through my first couple of years at West Ham. Not all the senior players took to me. I was too strong minded and outspoken for some of them.

I had a punch up with Alvin Martin when we played at Luton Town and a few 'handbags at six paces' with a couple of other West Ham players. That was the type of player I was. If I felt something was right I'd stand up for that as loud and physical as I needed to. It was all character building. My upbringing made me a stronger person. I had an inner belief that I was going to be a professional footballer and wasn't going to listen to anyone who would interfere with that. I was ultra-determined and was lucky to have John Lyall and Alan Devonshire at West Ham, and Alex Ferguson and Bryan Robson at Manchester United. They gave me all the advice I needed to make it to the top.

I'd like to talk a little bit about the infamous episode with the Manchester United shirt. That never would have happened if John hadn't been given the sack. It was a disgrace to sack

Beating Derby County's Geraint Williams, November 1987

John. I never wanted to leave West Ham. I'd agreed a four year contract with John Lyall just before the end of the 1988-89 season. I was living in a rough area in Dagenham. My car was being scratched, my tyres punctured and I was a target for all sorts of aggravation. John was as keen as I was to get me out of that situation and that meant more money. I was engaged to be married and was ready for a fresh start living somewhere else. He must have put his reputation on the line with the board because he managed to get a deal worth £1,000 per-week. He said I was doing really well and the fans had voted for me as their Player of the Year, so we agreed terms.

A couple of months later John was sacked. When I went back for pre-season training, I met Lou Macari to sign the contract. That's when he said it was too much money for someone my age. Everything changed for me after that meeting because I felt as though the club had reneged on the agreement I had with John. If John had stayed, I'd have stayed. Who knows what we might have gone on to achieve?

When I saw what they did to John Lyall it made me think they could do that to anybody. I was so angry with how John was treated. It was very much a feeling of someone mistreating my dad. I certainly didn't want to play for Lou Macari and didn't see why I should show loyalty to the club

In action against Nottingham Forest

their presence. You only have that air of authority if you are a truly great manager, which they both were. Players give their all for great managers.

Throughout my own experience as a coach, I've used their advice, along with bits and pieces from other people that have influenced my career. My own style of management places great emphasis on being fair. That definitely comes from John. He was hard, but he was fair. Another trait of John's was to have a good relationship with all his players, not just six or seven of them. Furthermore, I'd always try and analyse a situation before putting across my point of view. John was very good at that. It was extremely rare for John to shout at his players. When he did, his players knew he really wasn't happy. That is very important when trying to get your point across. John treated his players like men, not like little boys. He'd never try to belittle anyone. When I sat in his office it was a man-to-man situation. That is how I have always been during my managerial career. He allowed me to put my point across and then he'd put his point across. The conclusion was normally weighted in John's favour but I felt like I had been heard and my points taken on board. Players respect that approach. They may not always like the outcome, but they respect it.

I always stayed in contact with John after our time at West Ham. He came to my wedding which was an unbelievable day. I can't believe it's almost 30 years ago. He was a special guest as he had been so pivotal in my career. I felt I could phone John anytime and it was always great to see him, his wife Yvonne and son, Murray. He created a family environment at West Ham which you simply don't see at football clubs these days.

Every time I think back to when they sacked him, it still disgusts me. Football was his life and they knew that. It is easy to tell what a great manager John was because everyone at the club was devastated. Absolutely everyone. Usually, when a manager loses his job, there's always a group of players happy with the decision and pleased to see him go. The opposite was the case with John. The whole club was frozen in disbelief.

Paul Ince

when they hadn't shown any loyalty to John or me. That's when the wheels were put in motion for me to leave West Ham. John had definitely spoken to Alex Ferguson about me because when I finally went up to Old Trafford, and became a Manchester United player, Alex called me in for a chat. He told me he'd spoken with John and that he knew all about how he'd looked after me since the age of 12. He'd asked Alex to take over that responsibility and explained that I needed a strong, paternal influence in my life, just like John. Alex ended up doing just that.

John Lyall and Alex Ferguson were very similar. John left the coaching to Ronnie Boyce and Mick McGiven whereas Alex left it to Brian Kidd and Archie Knox. Both John and Alex knew exactly what was going on, of course, and Alex would bang on the window of his office if he thought something wasn't being done right. It was on matchday when they applied their genius. That's when their mastery came to the fore, when they galvanised the players. I've been in changing rooms when the managers have been talking, and the players have been looking at the floor, reading the programme or tying up their boot laces. It was never like that with John and Alex. When they spoke, everyone sat up and listened. They both had a tremendous aura about them. When they walked into any room, not just the dressing room, they filled it with

He's a top man Incey. So what if he wore a Manchester United shirt? So did I! Admittedly, I was only a 15-year-old trialist at the time! Whenever he played for West Ham he bled claret and blue. For me, Incey was the best player at West Ham. To go on and become captain of England was a truly fine achievement. The boy from Ilford did well!

Greg Campbell

I felt a bit sorry for Incey because the club reneged on his contract. Of course he was misguided when wearing that

Manchester United shirt before he left the club, but his loyalty was to John Lyall and the club had just sacked him.
Rob Jenkins

You could tell he was going to be a good player. He was a chirpy little so and so, even when he was young. He always had something to say, but he was always going to be a very good player, without a doubt.
Steve Walford

One of the best young players I have seen come through the system. He had a great England career and we still stay in touch.
Tony Gale

Of all the players John Lyall looked after, Paul Ince is one that stands out. He was a real father figure to him and had a very positive influence on his life and career. Me and my wife got on well with Incey and his wife. We'd go out with them when he was playing for Manchester United and we'd moved back up north.
Gary Strodder

He had the most talent I'd seen in a young player and was the most confident person I'd ever met. He was full of bravado but backed it up with his performances on the pitch. I've seen a lot of players with unbelievable confidence and others who are always bragging about what they are going to do. 99% of them can't pull it off but Paul was definitely in that other 1% that could. That is why he went on to captain Man United, Liverpool and England. There is a lot of pressure being a professional footballer. Some players are very humble, while others are very arrogant. Incey was definitely the latter and got under people's skin. He had a difficult upbringing and John Lyall looked after him.
Leroy Rosenior

It wasn't the greatest way to leave West Ham but he was destined for bigger things.
George Parris

I grew up with Incey. He was a great lad and a couple of years younger than me. I tried to take him under my wing. The best compliment I can give Incey is that if he and Julian Dicks had come through a couple of years earlier, the Boys of 86 would have won at least one league title. I loved playing with Incey. He was a fiery and pumped up kid but a tremendous player.
Tony Cottee

What a scallywag! He was a player with immense ability and football was his life. He was able to beat players, was so creative with the ball and scored some spectacular goals. He loved John and John loved him. He loved coming to the training ground but off the pitch he was a real scallywag and we had our hands full with him. He was very badly advised when leaving West Ham which ruined his relationship with the fans.
Mick McGiven

A top player who overcame a lot to make it to the top and made mistakes along the way. Some say he was arrogant but arrogance can sometimes be a quality which helps you succeed.
Paul Hilton

John looked after Incey who could have lost his way without John's guiding influence. He deserves a lot of credit for that.
Alan Dickens

A lot of great players in football have a 'Me, me, and me' mentality and Incey was one of those.
David Kelly

A class player who had a strength of mind that would take him to the top, an arrogance and a single mindedness that I could have done with to help me fulfil my potential that little bit more. One of the top players at West Ham who lived the career his talent deserved and we got on really well.
Kevin Keen

John at Incey's wedding

68 – STEWART ROBSON

"John was a nice, decent, honest man, which you don't often find in football. West Ham was a very good club because it had decent people running it. Firstly, with Ron Greenwood and then with John Lyall. They made West Ham a club which you had a feeling for."

Born: Billericay, Essex, November 6, 1954 • **Position:** Midfielder • **Games played for John Lyall:** 72 (1986-89)

Games played for West Ham United: 84 (1986-91) • **Goals:** 6 • **Honours:** 1987-88 Hammer of the Year

Debut: January 24 1987 v Coventry City (a) W 3-1 (Cottee hat-trick – Borrows pen) Att: 14,191

Coventry City: Ogrizovic, Borrows, Downs, Emerson, Kilcline*, Peake, McGrath, Houchen, Regis, Gynn, Phillips. Sub: Painter.*

West Ham United: Parkes, Walford, Parris, Hilton, Martin, Devonshire, Ward, McAvennie, Dickens, Cottee, **Robson.**

Stewart Ian Robson joined West Ham United in January 1987 for £700,000. He arrived at the club with a big reputation from his experience at both Arsenal and captaining England Under-21s. "I'd had a couple of casual conversations with John before I signed for him. He wasn't tapping me up or anything like that, but he'd mentioned that he liked the way I played and that he'd like me to play for West Ham."

Despite a promising start, Robson's four years at West Ham were blighted by injury and he was eventually transferred to Coventry City. Remarkably, he was voted Player of the Year at Arsenal (1984), West Ham United (1988) and Coventry City (1992).

A brief spell in coaching has been followed by a career in media where he has commentated for TalkSport, BT Sport and ESPN amongst other media outlets. *"I can easily clock up over 150 commentaries throughout the year."*

Despite having mixed emotions from his time at West Ham, Robson was keen to share his memories of John Lyall:

I have the utmost respect for John Lyall. He was a very honest man. A likeable man, a good coach and someone I was pleased to play for. The move eventually came in January 1987. I was in the England squad at the time but had just fallen out with George Graham who had taken over at Arsenal. He accused me of choosing country over club. This was totally wrong because I had dropped out of four England squads so that I could play for Arsenal. I was carrying a bad injury and ended up in hospital having an operation. When I came home I received a phone call from George Graham saying that John Lyall had put in an offer for me which he found acceptable and that he wanted me to go and speak with him. I went to John Lyall's house and he laid down his vision of me as a West Ham player. I then went back to George Graham and heard his take on things before deciding to sign for John. Even though I had been at Arsenal since the age of 12 I had grown up in the Essex area and always viewed West Ham as a great club in terms of their traditions, great players and fan base. They had just had their best ever league season the previous year. John let me know that he wanted me to be the next stage of the development.

Most managers who have worked with me have mentioned my all round ability. I could do everything on any certain day. If I was asked to be a defensive midfielder I could defend. If I was asked to be a dynamic player running off the front two, I could do that. If it was the right-back position that needed filling, I could fill it. I suspect that John saw this in me as well. Don Howe would certainly say that. I was a good professional who could affect games in a positive way.

He was a completely different coach to Don Howe.

Battling against Sheffield Wednesday, November 1987

John was less demanding and if there was a fault with his management style, maybe he could have been more confrontational with players who weren't giving of their best.

We shared a good rapport during a difficult period in my career. West Ham had dropped from third, before I joined, to the bottom half during my first season. Rather than it being a time of development and improvement it was a time of dramatic change with several key players wanting to leave the club. In my opinion their heads were turned and weren't giving the club 100%. Consequently, the few years or so I spent at West Ham were not that great, especially as I was injured for most of it.

John picked me to play at Coventry City for my debut. They were a decent side but we beat them 3-1. Tony Cottee scored a hat-trick and I remember hitting the post when it was 0-0, so it really was a very good game, especially as I hadn't played for about five months.

John's training sessions were always very technical with a lot of possession football and third man movement. Plenty of passing drills and keep-ball sessions which, when done properly, were very intense sessions as well. When John came out on the training pitch at Chadwell Heath, the work rate improved by 20%. He had an aura about him which prompted players to respond.

John was very thoughtful about the game and would sometimes deliver a long summary of a performance if it hadn't measured up to his expectation. He usually addressed the whole team rather than singling out and having a dig at any one player. This could be very frustrating if you thought you were having a good game because you were bundled in with everyone else. This was very different to other coaches for whom I played. Don Howe for example would think nothing of verbally attacking one player who wasn't performing.

There is a story which illustrates just how committed I was to John Lyall. I broke my nose in a match just a few games before the end of the 1987-88 season. At the time, West Ham were in danger of relegation. Three teams were relegated and the fourth from bottom team went into a play-off with a team from the second tier and West Ham were in the mix. I had the operation on my nose and the hospital told me not to play for a couple of weeks. I had the operation on Monday and was discharged on Thursday. That coming Saturday we had a very important game against Southampton at the Dell. I phoned John up to say not to worry about the risks of me breaking my nose again and that I was ready to play in a face mask if necessary. John had been good so I wanted to help in any way I could. He told me he didn't want to risk me at Southampton because the crunch match was against Chelsea at Upton Park. He picked me for that one and we won 4-1. Chelsea went into the play-off and eventually got relegated so the stakes were extremely high.

John was a very thoughtful coach. He knew what made his players tick and wanted to look after them. He had a tough couple of seasons before the club were eventually relegated in 1989. Performances were poor, all the energy had left the team, there was no confidence, players were hiding and the football was dire. There were two or three players who were desperate not to play. There was one player who told me on a coach coming back from a match against Chelsea that because he'd taken so much stick off the fans, he was going to take a rest for a couple of weeks and not play. He ended up missing a couple of games by feigning injury. So that was the type of thing that was going on. John was right to keep us behind after games but, if he had a fault, I think he should have pointed the finger at those individuals who were clearly having a damaging effect on the team.

Dictating the play at home to Coventry City, April 1988

All the players at West Ham had good qualities. Alvin Martin was an excellent ball playing centre-half, who was as good as anybody in that position. He lacked a bit of pace which may have affected his confidence a little. McAvennie was another very good player when I arrived. He was a workaholic and lightening quick. About a year later, that work ethic dipped a bit and stopped him from being the top class player he could have been. Tony Cottee likewise. Paul Ince was a precocious young talent. I wasn't sure if his attitude and refusal to listen to anyone's point of view would prevent him from making it. During the cross country runs at the start of the season he'd be right at the back. He just wasn't trying. But, pass him the ball and he'd become a totally different character. He ended up being a magnificent athlete and a very good player.

I roomed with Billy Bonds on a couple of occasions and remember a very funny story. We were watching the University Boat Race in our room when Margaret Thatcher's husband, Dennis, came on to be interviewed. He was completely off his trolley which we both found hilarious. He was so drunk it was untrue and he wasn't making any sense at all. We just couldn't stop laughing, it was so funny.

I got on very well with Liam Brady. I saw him play early on in his career at Arsenal and then played with him at West Ham at the end of his career. Admittedly, he was past his best and had suffered a couple of injuries, which meant he had lost that bit of speed off the mark. But when he wanted to, he was still a first class player. He couldn't do it every week because he didn't have the athleticism or fitness anymore, but in terms of his passing, shielding the ball and wriggling away from challenges, he was still top class. It was easy to see why he had been a world class player in his prime.

I think one of the reasons they sacked John was because he had taken his eye off the ball. He'd had that terrific season in 1985-86 but it had all unravelled soon after that and ended up with relegation in 1989. If you look at the history of West Ham, whenever they have a good season they tend to underperform the following year. That is because they think they have made it. The players were performing less well but becoming more dominant in the running of the club. They thought they could run it better than John. The club was getting left behind, a little bit complacent. The scouting system wasn't as good and they weren't picking up those little gems from Scotland that had served them so well with the likes of Ray Stewart and Frank McAvennie. I don't agree that John should have been sacked by any means, but it was becoming a bit easy-osey and the board obviously saw that and decided it was time for him to go. They certainly made the wrong decision in appointing Lou Macari, that's for sure.

John Lyall rates very highly amongst the managers I played for in my career. I had Terry Neil at Arsenal, who did everything for me that he said he would. When I was 15 he told me I'd be in the first team by the time I was 18 and I made my debut – against West Ham – when I was 17. He was magnificent for me, even though a lot of other Arsenal players said that he'd reneged on promises and wasn't to be trusted. My experience was the complete opposite. I also played under Don Howe at both Arsenal and Coventry City and he liked my style of football and attitude. I later played for Terry Butcher, also at Coventry. It was one of his first jobs and he wasn't a very good manager back then, but he looked after me and I ended up being Player of the Year in my first season at Highfield Road.

John is right up there as a manager and he'd be right up there as a coach as well. I learned a lot from him and he was very fair so I hold a lot of admiration for him. He improved me as an all-round player, more on the technical side of the game and not so much on the defensive side.

I scored six goals for West Ham and two of those were against Newcastle United – one at home and one away. The one at St James' Park came in the final game of the season. Before the match, John said to me that he wanted me to man mark one of their players who was being touted as the next best thing. He said that at the time he thought I was a better all-round player than this particular player – Paul Gascoigne. "Go and out-play him," was his advice. After about ten minutes into the game, Gazza brought the ball out of defence and went running up the pitch. I went with him, nicked the ball, turned and scored with a left foot shot.

It is hard to compare John to a modern day coach because John loved football, he loved West Ham and personal satisfaction came first, a long way ahead of personal gain. There are not many managers in the modern game you can say that about.

I was very upset when I heard the news that John had died. I sent a note to his family. I have fond memories of John and you tend to be affected when the good ones pass on.

Despite being at loggerheads with West Ham over my injury and the way it was treated, I still hold fond memories from some of my time there. It was nice of Karren Brady and the West Ham United board to invite me back to Upton Park for the visit of Manchester United in the last ever match. I was honoured to be one of only 38 players to have been voted Hammer of the Year at the old place. The match itself was everything you'd expect from West Ham. A great atmosphere, a high intensity game with the crowd getting right behind their team. That's what Upton Park was all about. I was in one of the taxi's with Tony Cottee and caught up with Paul Allen and Ludek Miklosko, so it was a great night all round.

The best coaches, and the ones you always remember, are the ones who taught you things that stay with you a lifetime. There was a piece of advice John shared which has always

Creating another attack

With his Hammer of the Year trophy alongside Hammers' greats L-R - Frank Lampard, Pat Holland, Geoff Hurst and Billy Bonds, May 1988

I knew Robbo from youth team football and John asked me what I thought of him as a player before West Ham signed him. I told him I thought he was the right player to come to the club but the fact that he was injury-prone was something to think about.
Tony Cottee

Loved himself, played for himself and wasn't really a West Ham player.
Mark Ward

When I think of Robbo I think 'Medical room!' Paul Hilton His West Ham career was full of highs and lows - winning the Hammer of the Year and then having a catalogue of injuries.
George Parris

I got pushed out to play wide when Stewart joined West Ham. He had a good reputation and was one of the best young players in the country at that time. The fans loved him because he was 100% committed, but some of the players felt his ego was too big for West Ham. He often took a few too many touches on the ball as a consequence.
Alan Dickens

At Arsenal he was a high energy midfield player and a leader on the pitch. That is why John bought him but sadly his time at West Ham was dogged by injuries.
Mick McGiven

stayed with me. I often allude to it in my current career as a commentator. We played at Orient in a pre-season match and on four occasions I broke through their defensive line and forced a one-on-one situation with their goalkeeper. Each time he made a save. Afterwards, John pulled me to one side and said: "Good running and great energy but do you know why you didn't beat the goalkeeper?" I put it down to the goalkeeper being on top of his game, but John said it was something more than that: "When you are one-on-one like that, make sure the last touch you have before shooting is to take the ball to one side. That way the goalie has got to adjust which gives you a chance to slot it home." From that day on, whenever I see a one-on-one I have John's advice ringing in my ears.
Stewart Robson

Stewart and I are still very close. He was an incredible athlete, a very good footballer and possessed a really good attitude. He is a straight up guy and is as honest as they come. We spent a lot of time in the gym together at West Ham trying to get back to full fitness following our injuries. He doesn't mince his words. He says it how it is and I respect him for that. We both do a lot of commentary work for the same production company.
Leroy Rosenior

He had a very high opinion of himself as a player. I thought he was alright but I don't think he was as good as he thought. I might be wrong of course.
Steve Walford

He had been a very good player at Arsenal and we thought he could be a top quality holding midfielder but he tried to do everything and it didn't work for the team.
Tony Gale

1988 Hammer of the Year

69 – LIAM BRADY

"John was a thoroughly decent person in a world that can often make you cynical about people in football. "

Born: Dublin, February 13, 1956 • **Position:** Midfield • **Games played for John Lyall:** 75 (1987-1989)

Games played for West Ham United: 119 (1987-1990) • **Goals for West Ham United:** 10

First game under John Lyall: March 14, 1987 v Norwich City (h) L 0-2 (Bruce, Drinkell) Att: 21,531

West Ham United: Parkes, Stewart, Parris, Gale, Bonds, Dickens, **Brady,** Ince, Pike*, Cottee, Robson. Sub: Keen.*

Norwich City: Gunn, Brown, Spearing, Bruce, Phelan, Butterworth, Crook, Drinkell, Rosario, Putney, Gordon.

Liam Brady was 31-years-of-age when John Lyall brought him to West Ham United. His left foot, which had matured at both Arsenal and at various clubs in Italy, continued to be a valuable asset in the claret and blue. Affectionately known as 'Chippy,' on account of his enjoyment of fish and chips, the midfield maestro spent three years at Upton Park. The experience brought varying degrees of success, with relegation in 1989, along with two League Cup semi-finals in 1989 and 1990.

Away from events on the pitch, the biggest event of Brady's stay at the club occurred at the end of the 1988-89 season, when the board did not renew John Lyall's contract after 34 years of service to West Ham United: *"I was shocked when they sacked John. He had been relegated before and had brought the club back up. I spoke to him and told him how sorry I was. I think John was very, very disappointed how it finished up at West Ham."*

Unsurprisingly, a player of Liam Brady's stature and pedigree, has been in demand as both a manager and coach – initially with Celtic and Brighton and Hove Albion, and later, as Head of Youth Development at Arsenal and assistant to Giovanni Trapattoni at Republic of Ireland.

Liam has a long pedigree of providing insightful football comment and analysis or RTE Sports and is regularly invited to attend various football events. It was during one such

event – a West Ham United reunion at The London Bridge Hilton Hotel in December 2016 - when Liam agreed to share his memories of John Lyall.

He continues in his role as Ambassador of The Arsenal Foundation and was very supportive and generous with his time to help preserve player memories of John Lyall.

John was one of the best coaches that I worked with in my career. The fact that he didn't tell you one thing and mean something else sets him apart from a great many other managers. He told you how he felt and was honest with it. You can build a relationship with a man like that. In terms of honesty and integrity he was right up there with Giovanni Trapattoni, who managed me at Juventus. There were also similarities between the two men in terms of getting on with players and creating a group of people who wanted to play with each other. Trapattoni was the more cautious of the two coaches and was luckier with the players he had at his disposal. John would have enjoyed working with the likes of Marco Tardelli, Michel Platini, Paulo Rossi and Zibi Boniek. I played with six players at Juventus who went on to with the World Cup in 1982, so Trapattoni had a very rich pool of talent to call upon.

My move to West Ham United came about because I was becoming disillusioned at Ascoli, which was the last

Lyall gets his man

club I played for in Italy. I was having some problems with the President of the club over finance and things which were promised to me that never materialized. I realised half way through the season that he was going to renege on my contract. This was a surprise and a shock to me because every other club I had played for in Italy – Juventus, Sampdoria and Inter Milan – had always delivered on their commitments. Unfortunately, the guy I was dealing with at Ascoli was a bit of a loose cannon and I wasn't enjoying being there so I was looking to get back to England as quickly as I could. It was 1988 and Ireland were trying to qualify for the European Championships, which ultimately, they did.

I met with John, in London, on a couple of occasions, on my way from Italy to Dublin. It was quite common for a manager to get in touch with certain players through a journalist and that is how John tracked me down. In my case, it was Reg Drury at the News of the World, a man I trusted implicitly. I could have also gone to Celtic, where I eventually ended up as manager. The manager, David Hay, was very keen to sign me but, after I'd met John and spoke with him, I had pretty much made up my mind that I wanted to play for West Ham. The club had almost won the league in 1985-86

Arsenal, Juventus, Sampdoria, Inter Milan, Ascoli, Republic of Ireland and West Ham United

The caption within the newspaper clipping reads:

A CLEARLY delighted West Ham chief John Lyall with Liam Brady before the newcomer's first training session at Chadwell Heath last Thursday. Picture by Steve

but were struggling with injuries the following season. There were still a lot of quality players at the club so I saw it as a great opportunity.

John's style of football was always creative, always trying to score goals. In a phrase, it was possession with a purpose. His teams always passed the ball from the back, with plenty of one-twos and third man running situations. There were plenty of near and far post crosses, a lot of reliance on movement and passing to score goals.

Players such as Alan Devonshire and myself didn't need a lot of coaching. We were experienced players and knew how to play. Whether we were playing in the middle or outside, we knew our duties and performed them as best we could. John used to say: "Just go out there and express yourself."

I think John had a problem at West Ham when I was there because quite a few of the players wanted to leave and were being tapped-up by other clubs who were prepared to pay a lot more money. Agents were proliferating the game and that was a real problem for John. Frank McAvennie, Tony Cottee and Mark Ward were all being offered something or other to turn their heads away from West Ham United. Similarly, it happened with Paul Ince a couple of years later. This just wasn't John's kind of world.

I'd like to think that John wanted me to play for West Ham because he knew I could create things, make goals and sometimes score goals. John knew that the result came first but he wanted his teams to play entertaining football and I think he thought that I fitted in with that.

John's conversations were always about football. He knew I had built up a lot of experience in Italy so he was always asking me things about the football culture over there. He was the type of guy who always wanted to learn new things, to add more to his bank of knowledge and to introduce different skills and techniques to his players, which would help to enhance and improve, create and entertain.

We often had a bit of banter about the 1980 FA Cup final. I said to John that Arsenal obviously wanted to win it, but once the dust had settled, I felt that a good group of lads won it on the day. Trevor Brooking, Billy Bonds and Frank Lampard were stalwarts of the game and I'd grown up playing against those guys. Good pros, great players and worthy winners. Arsenal had won it the year before but we were hugely disappointed to lose against West Ham because we were heavy favourites to win. West Ham were popular winners because they have always tried to play good football.

John was pretty black and white in the dressing room. He said what he felt. He would let you know if the performance wasn't good enough. He wasn't frightened to stand up to people. He didn't have any favourites and I think that is what made him thoroughly popular with the players. I was happy to stay at the club even though we'd been relegated. I'd

Recieving a Player of the Match award from Dennis Hughes, Managing Director of AVCO Trust, the club sponsor

picked up a bad injury at Derby County in November 1988 which kept me sidelined for six months so I felt as though I hadn't contributed as much as I could have done. I felt I owed John something.

Some people say that John maybe brought me in to see out my playing career and then perhaps prepare me for management. Perhaps, in a role with Billy Bonds but it was never in my head at the time to enter the world of management. It was only when I retired from the game that I missed it so much that I wanted to get back into it. That was when I thought about management and certainly not during my time with John.

When I did eventually become a manager I wanted to coach in much the same style as Johh Lyall, Johnny Giles, and Giovanni Trapattoni, overseeing attractive, attacking football. Sadly, it didn't work out for me up at Celtic where I was outgunned by a stronger Rangers situation. Similarly, at Brighton, I did what I could under extremely difficult circumstances. I always tried to play entertaining, creative football, to win matches. Sadly, the game was moving towards the long ball approach in the late 1980s onwards. The game became very physical and lacked creativity. It was all about brawn rather than brain.

John really looked after me. He personally showed me around the area where I was going to live and I had a couple of dinner evenings at his house with his family. I went to his funeral. I wouldn't have missed that for the world.
Liam Brady

Class player and person. We still keep in regular touch.
Tony Gale

Scoring from the spot against Manchester United

Most Hammers' fans will remember his final kick in football – a 20-yard screamer against Wolves at Upton Park. What they might not remember quite as clearly is that Liam came on for me as substitute in that game. After the game in the dressing room he was so happy, he came over and said: "Thanks Kevin" and gave me a big kiss. Another little known fact is that I scored the first goal in that 2-0 win – a diving header!
Kevin Keen

His left foot was still world class at West Ham. I was impressed by how he knew exactly what he wanted from the game. He'd been in Italy for many years and just seemed so in control of his career.
Alan Dickens

He was obviously at the end of his career at West Ham but he still did things in training which left you thinking: "Wow!"
George Parris

What a great experience it was to watch him train and play and to see how he conducted himself.
Paul Hilton

My dad was a coach to Bertie Mee at Arsenal so looked after Chippy Brady when he was just starting out in the game. Liam's left foot was still a wand when he joined West Ham.
Greg Campbell

I put Liam in the top four players I ever played with or against along with Paul Gascoigne. Glen Hoddle and Andy Cole, with whom I played with at Bristol City before he went to Newcastle. No disrespect to Ireland, but If Liam had been English he would have been king of the country. He was an incredible talent, easily one of the best.
Leroy Rosenior

At London Bridge Hilton for a West Ham United reunion, December 2016

Liam Brady was the man! You couldn't go anywhere with West Ham without him being mobbed. The fans adored him.
Eddie Gillam

70 – GARY STRODDER

"I was disappointed when they sacked John. He was the manager who had signed me and I trusted him. I enjoyed his style of management, bought in whole-heartedly to his footballing beliefs, and really enjoyed being part of all that coming together on the training pitch."

Born: Cleakheaton, West Yorkshire, April 1, 1965 • **Position:** Centre-half • **Games played under John Lyall:** 58 (1987-89)
Games played for West Ham United: 81 (1987-1990) • **Goals:** 2 • **Debut:** March 21, 1987 v Chelsea (a) L 0-1 (Nevin) Att: 25,386
Chelsea: Godden, Clarke, Dublin, Wicks, McLaughlin, Wood, Nevin, Hazard, Durie, West, Jones.* Sub: Dixon.*
West Ham United: Parkes, Stewart, Parris, Gale, **Strodder,** Brady, Ward, McAvennie, Pike, Cottee, S Robson.

Gary Strodder was born to parents, Colin and Janet. *"My dad, Colin, was a professional footballer. He played for Halifax Town and Huddersfield Town. Sadly, he broke his leg quite early on in his career which forced him out of the game. My mum brought up me and my sister but also took a few part time jobs as a secretary and shop assistant. When I was two, we moved to Moortown in Leeds and I grew up there."*

Strodder began his playing career with Lincoln City and was inside Valley Parade on May 11, 1985 – the day of the tragic Bradford City fire. *"I'd broken my ribs playing for Lincoln City in the previous game, so I was sitting with my dad in the actual stand where the fire took hold. The stadium was packed because Bradford had won promotion as Champions. When the fire started it just seemed to be small and nothing to be alarmed about. Then, in a matter of seconds, the wind fanned the flames and we were running for our lives. Me and my dad were sitting about seven rows back and there was a scramble to get on the pitch. It was pure luck, based on where you were sitting. Obviously, 56 people lost their lives and many others had terrible injuries. My dad struggled for a while to get over the trauma of the experience."*

After that harrowing experience, Strodder spent two more seasons at Lincoln City before moving to London. After two full seasons with the Hammers he went on to play for West Bromwich Albion, Notts County, Rotherham United

and Hartlepool United. He had a spell coaching at Leeds United's Academy but became disillusioned with the game, feeling that the art of defending has largely disappeared from modern football. *"It's become a bit too much like watching reserve team football or a testimonial game. The prices go up but the entertainment has gone down."*

In 2014, Gary seized an opportunity to pursue a complete life change:

"I moved to Menorca with my family and we run a business called Menorca Car Storage + which does what it says on the tin. We look after cars for residents and Villa owners and manage the process of getting their cars to and from the airport. It keeps us busy and we've got some great clients. We're enjoying life under the Mediterranean sun."

My first encounter with John Lyall happened when he came up to Lincoln City to sign me. West Ham United paid £150,000 for me which was a fair amount of money back then for a player in the fourth tier of English football. John looked like a very smart guy getting out of his car, wearing a Prince of Wales suit. He'd just driven up from London but he looked like a million dollars. He had a strong handshake and a really warm smile. He was someone I respected straight away.

My biggest memory of John comes from that time when I arrived at West Ham. I turned up at Chadwell Heath on a Thursday and John was waiting for me in the car park to welcome me. We trained that day but afterwards I went to

Dispossessing John Barnes of Liverpool, September 1987

his house and met his family. Yvonne made us all some tea and cakes. John lived in a beautiful house in Abridge and I was staying in The Bell hotel in Epping which was just down the road. He went out of his way to settle me in and make me feel comfortable and part of the club from day one. The following day we went out house hunting with Liam Brady and then back to John's house once again. He'd pick me up and take me to the training ground and introduced me to everyone at the club. He was very hands on and was involved in everything at West Ham. By the time I made my debut it felt like I'd been around the club a lot longer than a couple of days and that is all down to John making me feel so welcome.

West Ham were struggling at the time and John was looking for a defender with strength, heart and desire. It was a massive step for me to be playing in the top division but John gave me nothing but confidence and belief that I could make that transition. On Tuesday, I was playing against Torquay United at Sincil Bank, but on Saturday I was lining up with West Ham United against Chelsea at Stamford Bridge. Not many players have taken that journey! I must say, it was a bit nerve-racking in the dressing room before kick-off, looking around at Phil Parkes, Ray Stewart, Tony Gale and

Liam Brady. Those were guys that I'd watched as a kid. The pace was a lot quicker but John put on some very challenging training sessions so I quickly got used to it.

John brought me in to defend. He said to me: "There are plenty of good players around you, so win that ball and get it to the playmakers in midfield." I mainly defended, but I did manage to score a couple of goals for West Ham. I got a header against Portsmouth. The games that stand out for me are those midweek matches, under the lights, at Upton Park. They just seem to generate a very special atmosphere.

I got on well with Julian Dicks, Alan Dickens, Paul Ince, George Parris and Leroy Rosenior. All great lads and we shared some terrific times together. I'd love to catch up with them all some day. I lived in Basildon and Dicksy was living in Billericay so we'd drive in together. He's West Ham through and through and I really hope it works out for him in his coaching role at the club.

During that 1988-89 season – John's last at the club – I struggled with my confidence and picked up a few injuries. I only played about half dozen league matches all season. When Lou Macari came in, he seemed to like me and had another good run in the side.

I played under some very good managers in my career and John would be up there with the best of them. I played for Ossie Ardiles at West Bromwich Albion whose beliefs on football and training methods were very similar to John's. I played under Sam Allardyce at Notts County. He had a different variation on football and how it should be played but I was very successful playing for him. So, I've played on both sides of the fence in terms of football philosophies and enjoyed success from both.

John Lyall is one of the characters I look back on from my career who puts a smile on my face. I have good, warm memories of him.
Gary Strodder

Some memories of Gary from his teammates:

Strods was a good, solid, defender, and a lovely bloke. We had some great nights out together.
Alan Dickens

He was an honest, hard-working, centre-back, who was as brave as a lion. Not the tallest and prone to diving into tackles, but very competitive.
Mick McGiven

A big, uncompromising, centre-back.
Kevin Keen

He was a tough player.
David Kelly

He was a big, strong, boy and football was changing in those days. It was becoming more direct and more physical. John Lyall needed big lads just to head the ball clear. I don't think John liked playing against the long-ball teams of the day, such as Wimbledon, but he would have brought in Gaz to deal with them. John was more of a purist and liked his centre-backs to play the ball out as well as head it. Alvin Martin and Tony Gale were typical John Lyall centre-backs.
Steve Walford

Strods was a bit like myself, a northerner coming south and having to step up a level. He welcomed the opportunity to have a crack at it and gave everything.
Paul Hilton

Wholehearted and someone who always gave 100%.
George Parris

I got on like a house on fire with Strods.
Leroy Rosenior

Up against Cyril Regis of Coventry City, April 1988

Enjoying life in Menorca with wife Alison

71 – TOMMY McQUEEN

" The image I have of John is of him sitting in his office with one leg crossed over the other, his elbow on his knee, smoking a cigarette. I think he'd been smoking since his playing days in the 1950s."

Born: Bellshill, North Lanarkshire, April 1, 1963 • **Position:** Left-back • **Games played for John Lyall:** 26 (1987-89)

Games played for West Ham United: 36 (1987-1990) • **Debut:** March 28, 1987 v Watford (h) W 1-0 (Parris) Att: 17,793

West Ham United: Parkes, Bonds, **McQueen,** Gales, Strodder, Brady, Ward, McAvennie, Parris, Cottee, Robson.* Sub: Dickens*

Watford: Coton, Gibbs, Rostron, Richardson, Sims, McLelland, Bardsley, Blissett, Falco, Jackett, Porter.

Thomas Feeney McQueen was born to parents Bill and Mary and grew up in Bellshill, a suburb of Glasgow: *"My dad was a butcher and my mum was a shop assistant."*

McQueen began his career at Clyde, under Craig Brown, before playing for Alex Ferguson at Aberdeen. It was the close friendship shared by Ferguson and John Lyall which resulted in the Hammers paying £150,000 for the services of the 23-year-old Scot.

His three years at Upton Park coincided with the sacking of John Lyall and the departure of his replacement, Lou Macari. The arrival of Julian Dicks in April 1988 limited McQueen's opportunities and, in 1990, he ended up returning north of the border with Falkirk.

"After football I ran a transport company for about 13 years but we lost a big account when MFI went bust and had to jack it all in. I now help my wife run a cheesecake business. We have three shops and cater for weddings and parties as well as restaurants and ice cream parlours."

Tommy played the majority of his 36 appearances under John Lyall and had the following memories of the man:

John was the quintessential gentleman. A very likeable guy who put you at ease as soon as you met him. He was very level headed. I had played under Alex Ferguson at Aberdeen and, compared to him, John never really lost his temper. Most

players were working class guys, trying to make a living playing football and John knew that and helped in any way he could.

My move to West Ham came as a result of a strange series of events. It was March 1987 and I was sitting at home when the phone rang. It was Ian Porterfield, who had replaced Alex Ferguson at Aberdeen. It was 4pm on Thursday, so very unusual to receive a call from my manager. I thought: "What have I done?" Ian came straight to the point. "Do you fancy a move to West Ham?" I asked him how much time I had to decide and he said half an hour! That evening I was talking to John Lyall and Eddie Baily at Glasgow airport. Eddie was funny because his opening gambit to me was: "Do you, or do you not, want to play for West Ham United?" I replied that I wouldn't be there if I wasn't interested, and he liked that. I think John loved Eddie because he was a real old character. I was very impressed by John and agreed to sign. It was a bolt out of the blue but I later found out that John Lyall and Alex Ferguson had discussed me.

I'd like to think that John saw me as a football playing left-back, someone who tried to get forward when he could. John was very meticulous with everything he did. His training sessions were geared towards whichever team West Ham were playing that weekend.

I remember my debut very well. It was against Watford at Upton Park. My mum and dad drove down from Glasgow to watch me play, but the game was almost called off because of torrential rain. Thankfully, it went ahead, but the pitch was so heavy the game wasn't much of a spectacle. Then, in the last minute, George Parris hit an absolute screamer from 25-yards to win the points. There was relief all round because the team had lost their last six league and cup matches. The atmosphere at Upton Park was absolutely fantastic.

The highlights during my short time at West Ham were victories over Arsenal and Tottenham Hotspur. Arsenal had just beaten Liverpool to win the 1987 League Cup and Tottenham had a team full of internationals. Tony Cottee and Frank McAvennie scored a few between them in those games. They were a fine partnership.

John was a great talker and advised me about things which have stuck with me a lifetime. When I was house hunting he said to me: "It's always better to buy the worst house in the best street rather than the best house in the worst street." He usually made a lot of sense. The house prices were incredibly high at the time and we were discussing mortgages: "If you can't take your wife out for a meal and a bottle of wine at the end of week, you're in too deep with your mortgage," he said.

Some of his half-time talks were memorable. He compared us all to racing drivers once: "If you're driving at 150 miles an hour and don't have any breaks, then you're going to crash." He told us that we were doing exactly the same thing out on the pitch: "It's no good just running about until you crash and burn, because you will always lose. You've got to put your foot on the ball and exercise some composure."

I realised the writing was on the wall for me at West Ham once John had signed Julian Dicks from Birmingham City. Later, Lou Macari made him club captain. However, Lou left the club and Billy Bonds took over. I've got a lot of time for Bill and went and had a chat with him in the manager's office. He was very straight with me and said that he thought Julian was the best left-back in Britain. He recognised that I'd worked hard for the club but told me I'd only play if Julian was injured or suspended. I was only 27, and Julian never seemed to get injured, so I decided to sign for Falkirk and head back to Scotland. There was a cruel irony, because when I made my debut for the Bairns, Julian got injured for West Ham and was out for a very long time.

I didn't always play well but I tried to give 100%. I worked on the theory that every fan in the stands at Upton Park would have given their right arm to play for West Ham. Fans will forgive a lot of sins but one thing they will never forgive is lack of effort. They saw it as an honour to wear the jersey and rightly so. That's why I always tried to give everything I had.

I was very surprised when they asked John to leave the club. He was the first manager West Ham had ever sacked. I am a firm believer that you only sack a manager when you have someone better as a replacement. John's sacking was crude and hadn't been thought through at all. It brought

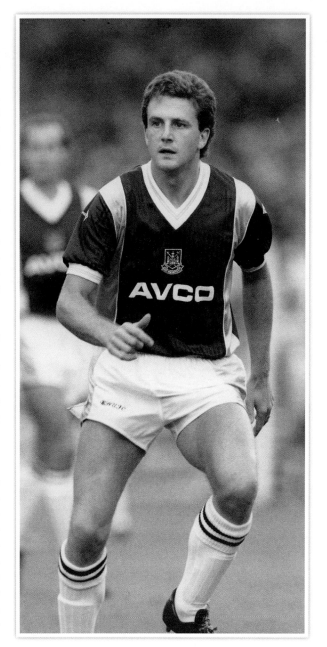

In action

instability to the club which was a shame because there were some good players establishing themselves, like Paul Ince and Julian Dicks. The future under John looked bright, even though the club had been relegated.

Before I went down south I wasn't a West Ham fan, but now I always look for their result first result in England. A lot of that has to do with John. He made me feel part of the club.

Keeping the fans happy

Tommy outside the family run Artisan Cheesecake store in Edinburgh, November 2017

John's door was always open, and whenever you thanked him for anything he'd always reply: "Pleasure."
Tommy McQueen

Left-footed, attacking defender who could cross the ball really well. He struggled with the English game and wasn't the strongest in the tackle.
Mick McGiven

West Ham probably bought Tom a little bit too soon. He wasn't quite ready for the English game.
Alan Dickens

We were playing up at Villa Park and Tommy was slapping on sun cream before the game. I'd never seen anything like that, but coming from Aberdeen I suppose he hadn't seen too much sunshine.
Steve Walford

He played under Alex Ferguson at Aberdeen. I got on well with Tom and liked him a lot.
Paul Hilton

He was another really nice guy at West Ham.
Leroy Rosenior

72 – EAMONN DOLAN

"The image I have of John is of him sitting in his office with one leg crossed over the other, his elbow on his knee, smoking a cigarette. I think he'd been smoking since his playing days in the 1950s."
(Interview with EX Hammers Magazine, December 2004)

Born: Dagenham, Essex, September 20, 1967 • **Position:** Striker • **Games played for John Lyall:** 6 (1987-89)
Games played for West Ham United: 21 (1987-1989) • **Goals:** 4 • **Debut:** May 9, 1987 v Manchester City (h) W 2-0
(Cottee, Brady) Att: 18,413
West Ham United: McAlister, Potts, Orr, Keen, Strodder, Brady, Ward*, McAvennie, Robson, Cottee, Ince. Sub: **Dolan.***
Manchester City: Nixon, Clements, Wilson, Redmond, McCarthy*, Langley, May, McNab, Moulden, Stewart, Simpson. Sub: White.*

Eamonn John Dolan made 21 appearances for West Ham United, six of them under John Lyall – the man who gave him his debut in May 1987, when he came on as a substitute for Mark Ward against Manchester City.

His finest hour in the claret and blue shirt, came, when scoring twice in a 5-0 rout of Sunderland, at Upton Park, in October 1989. John's replacement, Lou Macari, was manager at the time.

It was Eamonn's experience under Lyall which stayed with him throughout his dedicated and successful career as a coach at both Exeter City and Reading.

Having spoken with all of Eamonn's former West Ham teammates, there is a general consensus that if John Lyall had not been sacked, Eamonn would have remained at the club for a lot longer.

Tragically, Eamonn passed away from cancer on June 20, 2016. He was 48. His funeral at Corpus Christi Church in Wokingham had standing room only and was attended by the following Hammers: Kevin Keen, Mick McGiven, Tony Carr, Trevor Lake, Paul Goddard, Geoff Pike, Paul Allen, Bobby Barnes, Martin Allen, Steve Potts, Stuart Slater and Chris Ampofo. There were other notable names from the world of football - Steve Perryman, Shane Long, Martin Keown, Noel Hunt, Alex Pearce, Paul Davis, Nigel Adkins, Dave Beasant, Stephen Reid, Jim Hicks and Michael Gilts, to name but a few.

Following are tributes from his family, friends and former teammates:

Eamonn had passion, drive and determination. He had an ability, not only to achieve the most amazing things, but to believe they were possible in the first place.
Erica Dolan (Eamonn's wife)

Kind, funny, generous and wise do not come close to describing what my dad was like. His approach to life was different to everyone else's. His advice was not always what players wanted to hear but there were many occasions when those same players admitted they should have taken it. He always knew what to do and was a very special man. I am extremely proud to call him my dad. He has gone to a better place but we cannot express the loss we feel.
Grace Dolan (Eamonn's daughter)

Only a few months before he died, Eamonn told me that he wanted to carry on working at Reading for a couple more years. Then, he wanted to become a manager. He readily admitted that he'd probably get the sack quite quickly! So his plan was to become a teacher. Eamonn would have made a great teacher because he always tried to make people feel good. In a world where so many people feel down on themselves, Eamonn would have been a fine antidote. He was always able to spot something in people that could be

Pat Holland with Patrick (centre) and Eamonn Dolan

I am particularly lucky and proud to have been a friend of Eamonn Dolan's. I met him at Exeter City where he was responsible for laying the foundations of the Community scheme and the youth set up, both of which continue to prosper to this day. I know he worked at a few clubs but we consider him one of ours, by the way! He was a total one off. I saw him turn a group of no-hopers, low on confidence, into a very good unit. He did that because of passion, which Eamonn had in abundance.

Steve Perryman

We were first year apprentices at West Ham and were all assigned various jobs to do around the ground. We'd train in the morning, have some lunch, and then complete our jobs in the afternoon. Eamonn's job was to clean the training boots of John Lyall and his coaching staff. That would have

nurtured. Even during his hospital treatment, he reached beyond his own pain to tell others how great they were doing.

Siobhan Wood (Eamonn's sister)

There was a groundsman from the rural part of Longford in Ireland who suggested I use the following motto for a team I was managing. 'Ni neart go cur le cheile' – 'There's no strength without unity.' Eamonn was the embodiment of that phrase. Good players can help but great people get you to where you want to be.

Patrick Dolan (Eamonn's brother)

Celebrating winning the 1984-85 South East Counties League - Eamonn is bottom row, far left, next to Steve Potts and Paul Ince

been Ernie Gregory, Ronnie Boyce, Mick McGiven and Tony Carr. Eamonn was very fastidious in making sure those boots were brilliantly shiny. John commented that they were the best his boots had ever looked. Eamonn was very clever in that he not only got recognition and praise from John and his staff, but he took so long over them, to make them look fantastic, that he didn't have to do any other chores! Eamonn did a great John Lyall impression. I don't think he ever had the temerity to do it in front of John but it really was very good indeed. Even though, at 18, we went our separate ways in life, the bond we had formed at West Ham, meant we remained friends forever.

Trevor Lake

I remember Eamonn when he was about 14 at West Ham. Even though he went on to become Academy Director at Reading football club, he was always a West Ham boy. Everything he did was from his days with John Lyall and he never forgot him.

Pat Holland

During one of the six matches Eamonn played under John Lyall

After the Lyall era - In control against Oxford United with team-mates Steve Potts (left) and Stuart Slater, October 1989

I can't speak highly enough about Eamonn. I spent the last year with him at Reading before he died. I was Assistant Manager and he was the Academy Manager. He was unbelievably encouraging. When I moved on to Colchester United as manager he was really, really ill and yet every week I would get a text from him: "Keep going Kev," he'd write. "You'll turn it around. You're a great coach, just keep going." He really was one of the most amazing men I've ever known.
Kevin Keen

He was the funniest man in football I've ever had the pleasure to know. When I was managing at Torquay he was working at Exeter City so I spent a lot of time with him. He was terrific company. I'm not surprised that he developed so many young careers because he was an excellent coach and had a great presence about him. I paid my respects at a memorial in Exeter they held for him in 2016. He brought 34 players form Reading's youth academy into the first team which is sensational.
Leroy Rosenior

Both Eamonn and his brother Patrick were very bright boys. Very clever lads. It was no surprise when Eamonn became such a great coach at Reading.
Greg Campbell

A very considerate, intelligent guy.
David Kelly

He was a good-hearted, hard-working boy who gave everything he had. He didn't have fantastic ability but he just tried his hardest every time he played.
Steve Walford

He was one of the nicest guys in football and I was so pleased to see him doing such an amazing job at Reading. We always stayed in touch and it is a fitting tribute that Reading Football Club has named a stand after him.
Tony Gale

What a character! He'd drive in on the A12 with Stuart Slater and Tommy McQueen. Always the joker, Eamonn would pull over and pretend the car had broken down!
Paul Hilton

Eamonn and his brother Patrick were 13-years-old when I first met them. After they turned 16, we had to decide who was going to become an apprentice. John, Eddie Baily, Ronnie Boyce, Tony Carr and myself, were all given a vote on who to bring in. We decided to keep Eamonn, but his father, Vince, said that it was both or neither. For a while, they stopped coming to the training ground. John said that he understood Vince's position and that he would behave the same in his shoes. But, on principal, he wasn't going to budge. In the end, Patrick went to Arsenal and Eamonn signed for us. Vince conceded that he didn't want to be the type of father to prevent his sons from progressing. Pat and Eamon were identical twins and sometimes dressed the same. I couldn't tell them apart and they played me up something rotten! As a family they were magnificent. Eamonn loved the game and just wanted to score goals for West Ham and Ireland.
Mick McGiven

A respectful farewell

Back row: Hilton, Strodder, Bonds, Bracey, Parkes, McAlister, Gale, Dolan, Martin.

Middle row: Dickens, Orr, Livett, Parris, Devonshire, Stewart, Robson, Ince, Potts, Walford.

Front row: Keen, McQueen, McAvennie, Brady, Ward, Cottee, Slater, Strain.

CHAPTER FOURTEEN
1987-88

"West Ham is not about John Lyall. It's about a lot of people working together for the club itself, and that's why I've stayed here for so long. Quitting? I don't even think about that sort of thing." John Lyall

"Lyall Out!" was chanted at the Boleyn Ground following a 2-5 home defeat in the Littlewoods Cup against second division Barnsley. Fan favourite, Frank McAvennie, was sold to Celtic which did little to appease John's critics. The West Ham board was described in the press as: 'Quaint and archaic,' for standing by the club's long-serving manager. Terry Venables was mooted in the press as a potential successor.

West Ham were linked with a whole host of strikers: Steve Archibald of Barcelona, Mick Harford of Luton Town, Chelsea's Kerry Dixon, Wimbledon's John Fashanu and Manchester United's Peter Davenport. In the end it was £275,000 Leroy Rosenior who was the unlikely hero. The ex-Fulham front-man scored five goals in nine games which ensured the Hammers' survival. 19-year-old Julian Dicks was also signed from Birmingham City for £300,000.

Speculation in the press suggested that American millionaire, Irving Brown, wanted to buy West Ham. He was quoted as saying: "People want to see winning teams and, with the right cash injection, West Ham can be winners again."

West Ham legend Dickie Walker passed away in Warley Hospital, aged 75. The burly centre-back played over 300 league and cup games for the Hammers, between 1934 and 1953.

Billy Bonds played his 799th and final match for the Hammers, a 1-2 defeat at Southampton.

Stuart Slater, Leroy Rosenior and Julian Dicks all pulled on the first team shirt for the very first time:

Here is their story...

Billy Bonds retired after a 21-year playing career. In 1986-87 he received his 4th Hammer of the Year award, having started only 17 matches

Leroy Rosenior helped the Hammers survive.

73 – STUART SLATER

*"John gave me my career. He had
everything - charisma, respect, discipline.
He could be nice, he could be firm, but he
was always honest. He just had this aura
of excellence about him. It gives me
goose bumps just thinking about
what that man did for me."*

Born: Sudbury, Suffolk, March 27, 1969 • **Position:** Winger • **Games played for John Lyall:** 24 (1987-89)

Games played for West Ham United: 179 (1987-1992) • **Goals:** 18 • **Debut:** October 3, 1987 v Derby County (h) D 1-1 (Brady-Gee) Att: 17,226

West Ham United: McAlister, **Stewart***, McQueen*, Strodder, Martin, Brady, Keen, Parris, Ince, Cottee, Robson. Subs: Hilton*/**Slater***.

Derby County: Shilton, Sage, Forsyth, Williams, Wright, MacLaren, Callaghan, Gee, Davison, Gregory, Cross.

Stuart Ian Slater was born to parents Ian and Margot and grew up in Sudbury: *"Travelling from Suffolk to Upton Park for a trial, as a 13-year-old, was a bit daunting."*

Nicknamed 'Chopper,' by his teammates, Slater gained England Under-21 honours and played twice at England B level, too. However, a full England cap eluded him.

Despite playing in two League Cup semi-finals and helping the Hammers back to top flight football, the highlight of his time at Upton Park occurred when scoring in the 2-1 win over Everton during the 1991 FA Cup quarter-final at Upton Park.

In 1992, Slater joined Liam Brady's Celtic for a fee of £1.5m but, just one year later, he had left Park Head for Portman Road and a reunion with John Lyall, then manager of Ipswich Town.

Slater regularly hosted the corporate lounges at West Ham United's Boleyn Ground and continued with this ambassadorial role at The London Stadium. He also coaches the Under-19s at Chelmsford City.

Stuart has always made himself available to discuss his time at West Ham United and has a special regard for John Lyall:

Because I was a Suffolk lad I had the chance to go to Ipswich Town. They were a massive club at the time under Bobby Robson and had just won the UEFA cup. I was only 13-years-old and hadn't signed schoolboy forms. I was travelling backwards and forwards between West Ham and Ipswich

trying to decide which club to sign for. John went out of his way to ensure that me and my parents were made very welcome at West Ham and that was a big thing to me. He really wanted me more than any other club and he showed it as strongly as he could. He saw the talent in me and used all his charisma and strong intent to convince me that West Ham United was the best option for me. When I signed for West Ham, I had some technical ability but was quite small. However, John looked beyond my size and believed in me. If someone like John Lyall believed in you it gave you half a chance.

Without John, I think I would have been passed over. Plenty of scouts had pigeon holed me as: "Technically gifted but too small and not strong enough." Thankfully, a West Ham scout called Ronnie Gale took an interest in me and John trusted him so I got my chance. The plan was for me to play with Tony Carr's youth team but when I turned up, nobody was there. John noticed what was happening and told me to play with the first team: "I've heard a lot about you and I think you're good enough," he said. That was my first experience of John Lyall. Can you imagine training with Trevor Brooking, Billy Bonds and Alan Devonshire as a kid?

When John heard I was from Suffolk he never stopped going on about how much he loved that part of the world and how he wanted to retire there with a big fishing lake. He told my parents to keep an eye out for a nice property for him in Suffolk. When he saw me in training he'd say "Have you found that place for me yet?" That was one of John's special qualities. He could find something in common with a player to build a bond. John did eventually end up retiring to Suffolk in a big house with a fishing lake, so he's dream came true.

As a second year apprentice at West Ham, long before I made my first team debut, I developed a problem with my knee. I had a small operation and was going to be out for a couple of weeks. They treated me in the Roding hospital. Tony Carr, who looked after the young lads, called the hospital and explained that a car was on its way to take me to my grandparents, which is where I was living at the time. I was sitting there waiting for the car when the door opened and, to my surprise, John Lyall walked in! I hobbled into his big red jag and he drove me all the way to a council estate in Chelmsford. I couldn't believe it but it was just so typical of the man.

John's training sessions were so unique, so varied and so good, you felt like you were learning something different every day. Most of it was with the ball. He set up passing sessions, shooting sessions, keep ball sessions, one-on-ones, two-on-twos, short passing, long passing, the variety was endless. It was quite funny because if John wasn't at a training session

Chopper

a lot of the players wouldn't bother warming up, but as soon as John walked out in his track suit the intensity of the training would go up a few notches! That is not meant as a slight on Ronnie Boyce or Mick McGiven because they were fantastic people - experienced, knowledgeable and with their heart in the club.

John was always looking to improve things. In the late 1980s he brought in a sport scientist called Angela. She applied her knowledge of the body to improve a player's performance. She talked to us about body conditioning, stretching, yoga and diet but a lot of the senior pros didn't really buy into her so it never really took off. They weren't quite ready to surrender their egg, ham and chips for chicken and salad! When you think of sports science nowadays, and the way it has become an integral part of the game, it underlines just how forward thinking John was because it was relatively unknown back then. This was years before Arsene Wenger revolutionised the game with his ideas on training and diet.

I think John liked me because I was a crowd pleaser. I could score goals and create goals and had good technical ability. I would say that to be an attacking player for John Lyall, you had to be a skilful player. He liked all his players to be comfortable on the ball, even the boys at the back, but he expected it from his forward players.

John had a big impression on me during my youth team days because he often came into the dressing room after a game. If someone hadn't played well, he'd let them know. If we had lost, he'd keep us in the dressing room for a long time afterwards. If he singled you out he would make sure you maintained eye contact with him. He'd also ask questions so you had no choice but to concentrate on his words. He was firm but fair and most of the lads were just too scared to take their eyes off him. It was a timely reminder that putting in a good shift, applying everything we had learned in training and winning matches was the reason we were all there.

John was full of great advice. He told me that if I was getting kicked by a defender it meant I wasn't releasing the ball quickly enough. He'd then set up situations in training to help me work on that aspect of my game. If I had to leave the pitch with an injury, he'd say: "What did I tell you? You're not sharp enough".

John was also good at giving a bit of praise. Normally, in the dressing room, he addressed the group as a whole. He'd only dig out individuals if the defeat had been particularly heavy. But, he would usually try and praise those players who'd had a good game. I'd be sitting there and, although he wouldn't single me out by name, he'd say: "Look at this boy, did you see what he did? Only 18 and he's playing like that already. Take a leaf out of his book." I was lucky in that I was a bit of a blue-eyed boy during those five years I had

Scoring at Everton, May 1989

under John. He always treated me fairly and usually with a fair amount of praise. It's funny, because when he signed me at Ipswich Town in 1993, I was one of the senior pros so he was a bit harsher on me!

I made my first full debut against Southampton at the start of the 1988-89 season. I had made a couple of substitute appearances the season before but Southampton was my first start. It was a baptism of fire because Russell Osman smacked me in the ear and I was concussed and bleeding down my face. I had to go off at half time.

Sadly, that 0-4 defeat set the tone for the rest of the season and we ended up getting relegated. Little did we know that the 1-5 defeat up at Liverpool would be John's final game in charge of West Ham United? We travelled up to Anfield the day before but I wasn't feeling at all well. I went to bed shaking and sweating and shivering. Rob Jenkins, the physio, did his best to get me better and John took the decision to

play me. Liverpool took the lead, but, on the half-hour, Leroy Rosenior equalised, which gave us a bit of hope. We then fell behind 1-3 and John took the decision to protect me and put up the board to bring me off. Well, 8000 West Ham fans went mad at the sight of my number being held up and John changed his mind and took off David Kelly instead. It was a massive show of support from the West Ham fans and I've never forgotten it.

When the news filtered through that John had been sacked I was devastated. Why would you sack a man with such tremendous knowledge of the game, of the players and of West Ham? It simply didn't make any sense at all. He was all I had known at West Ham. He had taught me all I knew about football. It was like losing someone in my family. The atmosphere changed overnight and a lot of the boys didn't get on with Lou Macari, although he did like me. The training changed beyond all recognition – lots of running and hardly anything with the ball. It just brought it home how great a manager and coach John had been. That is why the most successful manager of all time – Alex Ferguson – has nothing but praise for John.

John wanted us to play a brand of football which entertained the paying public. He'd always remind us that West Ham supporters were working hard and spending good money to be entertained. He urged us not to send them home disappointed.
Stuart Slater

I gave him the nickname 'Chopper' because he hacked me down a couple of times in the gym! I always remember him doing those 10,000 keepie-uppies in the gym. I'd pop in and out, go and take a shower, eat a bit of lunch and go back in and he'd still be going strong.
Paul Hilton

He was a tough little kid and had loads of ability.
Steve Walford

He should never have left West Ham because he wasn't ready for the goldfish bowl that was Celtic.
Tony Gale

Fans will probably think about him in much the same way as they think about me - he should have done a lot more with

the talent he had. Stuart had great ability as a young player and was a fantastic dribbler. A terrific lad.
Kevin Keen

I went to Buckhurst Hill to see him play for his local team. Ronnie Gale had told me that quite a few teams were interested in him. He was a very good player. He could go left or right and I liked him a lot because he could run with the ball and beat people. He had exceptional ability and he didn't disappoint the West Ham fans.
Mick McGiven

He was as quick with the ball as he was without it. He could run and weave with the ball so quickly and changed direction comfortably, too. That is a difficult skill to perform but it was easy for him.
Leroy Rosenior

A great player. I don't think he knew just how good he was.
Mark Ward

I still see quite a bit of Stuart. He coached the Under-18s at Chelmsford College. Chopper was such a great talent. He had quick feet and a terrific attitude. When I watch Raheem Sterling and Theo Walcott playing today, I just think Stuart was a better player.
Alan Dickens

Back at Upton Park, October 24, 2015. L-R Stuart, Keith Robson, Pat Holland, John Ayris, Trevor Brooking, Harry Obeney and Vic Keeble

74 – LEROY ROSENIOR

"West Ham was a special place because John Lyall was a special man. The two things went hand in hand. If there is a coach in the modern game, who is listened to intently, improves his players immeasurably and commands high levels of commitment and loyalty, then he can be compared to John Lyall."

Born: August 24, 1964, Balham, London • **Position:** Striker • **Games played for John Lyall:** 48 (1988-1989)

Games played for West Ham United: 67 (1988-1991) • **Goals for West Ham United:** 23

First game under John Lyall: March 19, 1988 v Watford (h) W 1-0 (Rosenior) Att: 16,035

West Ham United: McAlister, Stewart, Potts, Bonds, Strodder, Gale, Ward, Keen, **Rosenior**, Cottee, Robson.* Sub: Dickens.*

Watford: Coton, Gibbs, Rostron, Sherwood, Terry, McClelland, Sterling, Allen,* Blissett, Porter, Jackett. Sub: Roberts

---

Leroy Rosenior grew up in Balham, South London. His father, Bill, was an electrician and his mother, Gladys, was a nurse: *"My dad played football and also tried his hand at high jumping whilst in the army."*

Rosenior was signed from Fulham for £275,000 and is largely remembered by West Ham fans for heading the winning goal against Arsenal at Highbury in a 1989 FA Cup third round replay. He is also a member of the scoring debutants club, having bagged the only goal of the game against Watford in March 1988. Another notable statistic on his West Ham CV is that he scored the last ever goal of the John Lyall era. It came against Liverpool, up at Anfield, at the end of the 1988-89 season, but wasn't enough to prevent the Hammers from being relegated.

Leroy attended the final match at Upton Park in May 2016, where he caught up with former teammates such as Alan Dickens. He had made the journey from his home in the West Country which was typical of so many from the Greenwood and Lyall era in attendance on that memorable evening.

"I live just outside Bristol and do a lot of work for the Premier League. I'm also involved with a Charity called 'Show Racism the Red Card'. I do a lot of broadcast work and brought out a book recently called "It's only banter."

Leroy played under John for 14 months but the memory has lasted a lifetime:

The earliest memory I have of John Lyall is of him coming to Fulham to sign me. Ernie Gregory was with him and I remember John being a really polite, straightforward, well-spoken man. After talking with him for a while I just felt that I'd like to play for him. I didn't even negotiate the contract, I just said: "I'm coming." I went straight in to the team to face Watford that Saturday.

My first impression of John was spot on. He was a father figure and had a gentle way about him. Like all the players at West Ham, I didn't want to disappoint him. That was a very strong feeling in me.

West Ham were going through a tough time while I was there, but he never changed his attitude or his manner, which was the mark of the man. He was always very calm and considered and explained his viewpoint rationally and in detail. He knew what he believed in, he knew what was best for the West Ham and he knew how to engage with his players. He never wavered from those beliefs.

I saw it many times with other managers. When things started going wrong, all their so called firmly held beliefs just flew out of the window. Not so with John. He knew his approach worked, he knew it would bring entertaining football and success. He loved West Ham, knew how it ticked and never lost sight of what was best for the club and how to move it forward.

He instilled so much belief in myself, both as a person and as a player. He made me feel better than I probably was but

Scoring against Watford on his debut, March 1988

that approach got the best out of me. His word was his bond and he was a very special guy. He was the best coach I played for because he improved me as a player. His coaching staff were excellent as well. Ronnie Boyce, Mick McGiven and Tony Carr all gave me little pointers which helped to add something extra to my game. Together, they created an environment where a player couldn't help but improve his game.

To me, John was a football genius. There are plenty of people who know the game inside out, but John knew how to communicate it. My technical ability and understanding of the game, both benefitted from John's expertise. Because he was so ahead of his time it felt special to be a part of it, exciting to be in the middle of it. You wanted to be there and you were happy to work long hours. He cultivated an environment at West Ham which improved every player lucky enough to be part of it.

I had a debut at West Ham. John signed me on a Friday and I scored the winner against Watford on Saturday. John took me off after 65 minutes. I'd never been so exhausted in all my life!

It's hard to compare John with any modern day coach because I don't have first-hand familiarity with how clubs are set up nowadays. But, on the surface, Jürgen Klopp seems to be creating a good culture at Liverpool. John wasn't as touchy-feely as Klopp, but he won the love and respect of his players. Klopp appears to be doing something similar.

When I joined West Ham the club was in a relegation battle. Before one game, the players were having lunch together and John was at the head of a long dining table. He delivered this Churchillian speech and in it, he compared our plight to that of a plane going down. If we didn't get a grip on the controls we were going to crash. He was a very good speech maker and made excellent analogies which were thought provoking and inspiring.

When John came in for me I think he'd just been let down by Chelsea's Kerry Dixon. John needed a goalscorer. It was a bit of a gamble signing me because although I'd played in the top flight with QPR, I had dropped a couple of divisions to play for Fulham. I think he liked my power, my strength, my goals, but more than anything, he saw that I had a good attitude and a hard work ethic. I was just under six feet and was strong in the air. Unfortunately, I suffered a knee injury which affected my pace and had a negative impact on my time at West Ham.

John had his players working on their strengths and weaknesses every day. Julian Dicks was usually in the gym, smashing a ball up against the wall, to improve his shot velocity. Alvin Martin was always heading the ball while Ray Stewart was working on pin point accuracy. They took all these well-honed skills into every game. It didn't matter how old a player was, John was still improving them in small or large measure.

I had some good times at West Ham and most people remember my goal at Arsenal in the FA Cup replay in 1989. We were bottom of the league at the time and rank outsiders

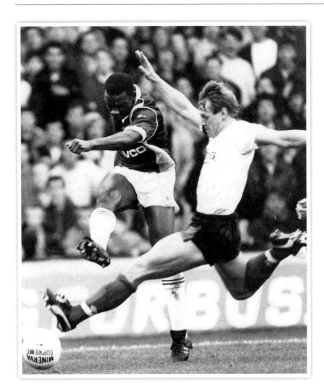

Being challenged by Stuart Pearce of Nottingham Forest, November 1988

the early 1960s so the omens were not good. I was carrying a bad injury but they kept wheeling me out and thankfully my form hadn't deserted me. We really believed we could do it and when I equalised on 30 minutes, we all sprinted back to the half way line to get the game going again so we could chase a winning goal.

It was a difficult time for me. My knee needed serious attention and time to mend, but they just kept draining it before every game. People said to me at the time that I was jeopardising my career and while I believe it did cost me some time in my career, I am unequivocal in my view: I'd only do that for someone like John Lyall. It is as simple as that. I had no doubt in my mind that the club was more important than myself. It's not the advice I'd give to my son, Liam, but I certainly have no regrets doing that for John. He was looking to me to score the goals to help the club survive. It was just a shame that we fell short. I didn't know it at the time but that was the last occasion I saw John. I went straight into hospital after the Liverpool match and then John was sacked in the summer. However, he's integrity and honesty would still save my life.

After various tests and operations, I was told that it was unlikely that I'd ever play again. I had a hole in my knee the size of a fifty pence piece. To add insult to injury, the club told me that I wasn't insured properly, and that there would be no payout should I be forced to retire. Thankfully, John had given me his word on a three year contract which meant I had an income and the time to try and get back to full fitness. It was a contract he didn't need to give me but it ended up being my saviour so I owe John a great deal. I like to think that we both put our necks on the line for each other and I'll always remember him for that and be grateful to him.

John instilled a love of West Ham United into all his players. He fostered an unbelievable commitment to the club and the vast majority of players coached by John will still have a great feeling for West Ham. He was such a strong family man and made sure all the players' families were part of the club, too. When we warmed up in the gym before a game, our kids would be there warming up with us. I can't imagine that would be allowed today, but it was typical of the culture John cultivated at West Ham. To John, family and fans were a big part of everything he did at West Ham. It was a wonderful place to be. Both Ron Greenwood and John Lyall had made it a very unique place to be and we were lucky and blessed to play for West Ham. Furthermore, I don't care whatever anyone says, there are no supporters quite like West Ham supporters.

John knew that the history of West Ham was very, very important, but he always had an eye on the future, always looking for the next best thing and anything that would improve the football club. He strengthened the incredible foundation which had been laid by Ron Greenwood.

I was at home when I heard the news of John's death.

to win that game, having blown a 2-0 lead at home in the first match. To score the only goal was a very special moment. Other highlights include the four goals I scored against West Bromwich Albion in the Full Members Cup. I'd also have to mention the two goals I scored against Chelsea at the end of the 1987-88 season, because they helped us stay up.

It was a very poignant occasion when West Ham played in the first match at Hillsborough after the terrible tragedy in 1989, which sadly took 96 lives. The Leppings Lane end was closed off and I remember looking at the size of that stand with all those fences and thinking, how can you put human beings behind something like that? It was horrific and just beggars belief that people could be treated like that. I'd never played in such an eerie atmosphere and all the players were affected by it. We were in a relegation battle at the time and were desperate for the points and the game was played in a very respectful manner which was absolutely right. We won 2-0 and I scored one.

Towards the end of the 1988-89 season, we got a bit of momentum going and won three out of four games to give ourselves an outside chance of staying up. I'd scored two at Brian Clough's Nottingham Forest which meant we had to win at Anfield to stay up. West Ham hadn't won there since

Enjoying a golf day with this teammates, 1988

It was like losing someone from my family. Even now John pops into my head from time to time, especially at Christmas, because John made that a special time at West Ham. One of the recurring images I have, is of him puffing away on a fag which he always held in his right hand.

John still has an effect on me now and I think he'll continue to do so until my dying day. He left a legacy, not just at West Ham, but with all his players, too. He was just a very special person.

There are a few people in my life that have helped shape it and make me the person I am today. There was my dad, Bill, who was an incredible influence on me. There was Jimmy Hill who taught me so much about how to conduct myself. There was a scout at Fulham called Derek Quigley, who signed me from school and looked after me until the day he died. John Lyall is firmly rooted amongst these very important people. Whenever I've had big decisions to make in my life, I often ask myself what these people would do. What advice would they give? John's voice is included amongst theirs, because he was one of the special men I've known. I can't think of any better way to give him higher praise.
Leroy Rosenior

Leroy did well at West Ham. He was only there a short time but he will always be remembered. That says it all really.
Alan Dickens

He had bad knees but always put in a good shift. I work down in Brighton so I see his son, Liam, quite a bit.
George Parris

Leroy

75 – JULIAN DICKS

"Everyone was looked after at West Ham, from the security guards and tea ladies to the players and fans. John treated everyone equally and was loved because of it. Not to give him that moment to say farewell to the fans was simply wrong."

Born: Bristol, August 8, 1968 • **Position:** Left-back • **Games played for John Lyall:** 56 (1988-89)

Games played for West Ham United: 326 (1988-1999) • **Goals:** 65 (19th on the all-time list) • **Honours:** Hammer of the Year: 1990, 1992, 1996, 1997 • **Testimonial:** August 13, 2000 v Athletico Bilbao

Debut: April 2, 1988 v Sheffield Wednesday (a) L 1-2 (Rosenior – Hirst, Chamberlain) Att: 18,435

Sheffield Wednesday: Pressman, Sterland, Worthington, Madden, Cranson, Proctor, Chamberlain*, Megson, Chapman, Hirst*, Jonsson. Subs: Bradshaw*/Fee.*

West Ham United: McAlister, Stewart, **Dicks,** Bonds,* Strodder*, Gale, Ward, Parris, Rosenior, Cottee, Robson. Subs: Dickens/Potts.

Julian Andrew Dicks was born to parents Ron and Carol and grew up in Kenmare Road, Bristol. "My dad was a forklift driver for Courage Brewery and my mum was a dinner lady and then a postwoman."

John Lyall paid Birmingham City £300,000 for his services. *"I played for two great managers in Ron Saunders and John Bond at Birmingham but it was a club which had to sell players to stay afloat."*

Dicks made 56 appearances for John Lyall. Interestingly, he didn't receive one yellow card during that time. The nickname 'Terminator' was a long way off. *"I didn't smoke or drink the whole time I played for John. I was only 19-years-old and was a little bit in awe of everything. I started drinking and smoking when I was 22-years-old. In that respect John had the clean years! I hope he looks down on me and thinks that I had a good career at West Ham."*

Julian went on to establish himself as one of the most popular players to pull on the claret and blue shirt. His penalty prowess was formidable and his 65 goals for the club will keep him inside the top 20 on the all-time list for some considerable time to come.

I am very appreciative of the time Julian gave for this interview. He had just lost his job at West Ham following

the sacking of Slaven Bilic, but, as usual, gave 100% to the matter in hand. *"I would love to work with Slaven Bilic and Nikola Jurcevic again. Slav stuck his neck out for me when I first got the job and I'm very grateful to him. Slav will be fine. He's treated like a god in Croatia and speaks five languages, so he's got a much better chance of getting a job than a lot of other managers. Unfortunately, we weren't getting results and patience is a rare commodity in the modern game. We were too close to the bottom. I fear that if West Ham are relegated to the Championship they'll struggle to survive."*

Julian had the following reminiscences about John Lyall:

When I hear the name John Lyall, I think of words like 'Gentleman', 'Honesty' and 'Smoker!' Sadly, I wasn't with John for very long but he was fantastic for me. He signed me from Birmingham City. I was training there one day and the manager, Gary Pendrey, called me in and told me I'd been sold to West Ham and that John Lyall was on his way up to see me. The next thing I knew I was sitting in the Chairman's office at St Andrews with John Lyall and Eddie Baily: "We'll pay you £650 per week and £50 appearance money," he said. "You've got five minutes to think about it." I left the

Taking on Liverpool, October 1988

room and came back after five minutes and said: "I'd love to sign for West Ham." Steve Whitton had instigated the move. He tipped off John about me so I owe him a big thank you.

I travelled down to West Ham and John put me up in The Bell hotel in Epping. West Ham were due to play Manchester United on Saturday. He called me into his office and asked me if I knew that I was suspended for the match? I told him that I did know but I could see he wasn't happy: "Well, I effing didn't!" he replied: "If I had known I wouldn't have bought you!"

John liked my ability and he told me I'd improve at West Ham because I was around better players. He didn't have to teach me how to play football or how to defend. He wanted me to enjoy playing football. He was very straightforward with his approach. In the changing room before a match, he'd say: "Julian, pick up their Number 5 at corners and free-kicks." He kept it simple. He never weighed his players down with too much instruction.

Ray Stewart was the penalty taker at the time, and rightly so. Tony Gale took the free-kicks but god only knows why!

It was only when Lou Macari arrived that I was given the responsibility of taking free-kicks, penalties and going up for corners. That's when I started scoring.

Lou was much more direct in his football than John and liked to get it to the strikers as quickly as possible. John loved flowing football, building from the back and keeping possession. He had the players to do that - Alan Devonshire, Alan Dickens, Alvin Martin, Ray Stewart, Tony Gale and Billy Bonds. All very stylish and composed players.

I played under quite a few different managers and John is right up there as a top coach and manager. I don't have a favourite manager but John always springs to mind. Ron Saunders game me my start in football and I also have a lot of respect for Graeme Souness, who I played for at Liverpool. John Bond was another who taught me a lot up at Birmingham.

Harry Redknapp was a bit like John. He'd put his arm around a player when they needed it, or a rocket up their arse if they weren't trying! He always got the best out of his players and John was a master at that.

Soon after I arrived at West Ham, John drove me to a Ford car dealership and arranged for me to buy a discounted car. Prior to that he always drove me to my hotel after a match. He was a chain smoker so my clothes reeked of smoke by the time he'd dropped me off!

Playing at Upton Park was an incredible experience. When the fans loved you, it was the best ground in the world. Big teams came down and you could see in their eyes that they didn't want to be there. It was such a tight, atmospheric ground, that some players didn't even want to take a throw-in. I played for Birmingham City against West Ham and it really wasn't a nice experience. The crowd could be viciously intimidating. West Ham always had a chance in any game at Upton Park. We beat Liverpool 4-1 in the League Cup which was a very special night.

I've always had a good rapport with the fans. Their expectations have never changed. All they want is for a player to give 100% for that claret and blue shirt they are wearing. They can put up with losing because they know that happens a lot. They just want their players to try, try and keep on trying. If they can see you are giving everything they can forgive all manner of sins – conceding goals, giving away penalties or, as in my case, getting sent off. I can't remember ever being slagged off by a West Ham fan. They love to see West Ham players wearing the shirt with pride.

John's training sessions were very similar to what clubs are doing now – Keep-ball, five-a-side, and passing drills. John loved to change things around. Once we played keep ball without a ball! It was ridiculous but that was the point. It got everyone laughing and relaxed and we all bonded as a team. We were struggling in the league at the time and there was a lot of pressure around the club and from the fans so it helped to lighten the mood. There was always a method in everything he did.

We made it to the semi-final of the League Cup in 1989 but got well beaten by Luton Town. I fouled Roy Wegerle and gave a penalty away and afterwards John asked me if I'd touched him. I looked him in the eye and explained that I hadn't. Afterwards, when I looked at the footage it was so obvious that I'd actually throttled the bloke! John would never lose his rag over anything like that anyway. He knew that player's made mistakes and did silly things, they were all part of football. It was only when he thought someone wasn't trying, that he'd get annoyed.

The sacking of John was handled really badly. I understand that managers lose their jobs but it needs to be handled in the right way. That wasn't the case with John. He had done so much for West Ham and was a big reason for it being such a great club. Everyone was looked after at West Ham, from the security guards and tea ladies to the players and fans. John treated everyone equally and was loved because of it. Not to give him that moment to say farewell to the fans was simply wrong. He should have been kept at the club in some capacity. It could have been worked through so much better. To treat such a man in such a manner was disgraceful. If he could see how the game is nowadays he'd realise that he coached during the best time. I've got my memories of John and they'll always be there. It was an absolute privilege to play for him.

Julian Dicks

There is never any shortage of comments about Julian:

Love him or loathe him, you just can't ignore him. I love him.
Tony Gale

A great player, a thunderous shot, a leader and as hard as nails.
Kevin Keen

I nicknamed him 'Mongo' after the character out of Blazing Saddles because he would run through brick walls. A class player.
George Parris

He was the size of a matchstick when I first saw him. We could have signed him as a youngster but let him go to Birmingham City instead. We ended paying a fee to get him back. Tigerish in the tackle with an absolutely outstanding left foot and all round ability. But he could not control himself and if you are getting wound up by opponents every week and getting sent off then you are no good to the team.
Mick McGiven

On the ball against Chris Waddle and Paul Gascoigne of Tottenham Hotspur, December 1988

After the Lyall era - Julian defending David Kelly in a free for all at Hull City, September 1989

We played against each other in a Merseyside derby once and there was only one winner. Everton won 2-0 and I scored. We battered them!
Mark Ward

I signed on the same day as Julian. Easily one of the best left-backs that I ever played with. There is no doubt that he should have played for England. Great left foot, great ability and a great attitude. Sure, he went over the top sometimes, but I like that in my defenders.
Leroy Rosenior

I spent many games walking alongside Julian when he'd been sent off! I would walk crowd side so he didn't get too much stick. I'd sit with him and have a chat while he calmed down. We had a good relationship.
Eddie Gillam (kit man)

I got on great with Dicksy and we had so many good laughs together. We were on the coach going to a game and he was drinking a litre of Coca Cola and a family-sized bag of crisps. When Macari asked him what he was doing: "It's my pre-match meal gaffer!" Fantastic left foot.
David Kelly

Dicksy

Back row: Dicks, Dickens, Stodder, McAlister, Parkes, McKnight, Martin, Gale, Walford

Middle row: Hilton, Harwood, Ince, Stewart, Devonshire, Parris, Livett, Kelly, Rosenior, Pearson, King.

Front row: Keen, Strain, Potts, McQueen, Ward, Brady, Slater, Robson, Dolan.

CHAPTER FIFTEEN
1988-89

❝ "It's a very sad day for me after so many happy years at the club. In saying that, it is only right and proper for me to thank all the staff and players and, especially the fans, for their great loyalty to me during my time at West Ham." **John Lyall**

John Lyall was sacked by West Ham United in the summer of 1989. A gathering of key board members, Len Cearns, Will Cearns, Martin Cearns, Jack Petchey and Charles Warner, took place and it was concluded that the 34-year association John had with the club would be terminated. Lou Macari was appointed as his successor.

West Ham had been relegated following a 1-5 defeat at Anfield in the final match of the season.

Start striker, Tony Cottee, had left the club in a £2m move to Everton during the pre-season. He was replaced by David Kelly from 3rd division Walsall for £600,000. Celtic's Allen McKnight became John Lyall's 77th and final first team player during his 15-years as manager of West Ham United. McKnight was brought in as a replacement for the ageing Phil Parkes. Frank McAvennie returned for a second spell with the club, but the old magic had disappeared and he failed to score in nine outings during the fight against relegation. West Ham United also lost to Luton Town in a two-legged League Cup semi-final.

To compound the sense of loss around the club, former chief scout Wally St Pier passed away, aged 84. His daughter, Shirley Peters, commented that the happiest days of his life were at West Ham. His ashes were scattered on the Upton Park pitch.

John Lyall's record in the hot seat reads as follows: P 621 W 238 D 155 L 228 F 853 A 834. He is the last West Ham United manager to win the FA Cup, reach a League Cup final and to come so very close to winning a major European trophy. The overwhelming majority of the 77 Hammers who played in his first team claim that he improved them as a player.

John gave two final debuts during his final season – David Kelly and Allen McKnight.

Here is their story...

John celebrating with Wally St Pier before the Chief Scout's testimonial in 1975. Wally passed away in 1989

76 – DAVID KELLY

"A gentleman of football and an extremely good manager. Even though it didn't work out for me at West Ham I definitely learned more there than at any of the other 10 clubs I played for."

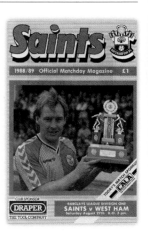

Born: Birmingham, November 25, 1965 • **Position:** Striker • **Games played for John Lyall:** 39 (1988-89)
Games played for West Ham United: 64 (1988-90) • **Goals:** 14
Debut: August 27, 1988 v Southampton (a) L 0-4 (Rideout 2, Cockerill, Le Tissier) Att: 18,407
Southampton: Burridge, Forrest, Statham, Case, Moore, Osman, R. Wallace, Cockerill, Clarke, Rideout, D. Wallace.* Sub: Le Tissier*
West Ham United: McAlister, Potts, Dicks, Gale,* Martin, Keen, Ward, Parris, Slater*, **Kelly,** S Robson. Subs: Hilton*/Dickens*

David Thomas Kelly was signed by West Ham United from Walsall in August, 1988 for £600,000. Having gained promotion with the West Midlands club, Kelly was attracting considerable interest from several top clubs: *"I spoke with Tottenham Hotspur, Bayern Munich, Derby County and Norwich City."*

Affectionately known as 'Ned,' after the nineteenth century Australian outlaw, the Birmingham-born striker failed to make his mark at West Ham, but did go on to score 250 goals from 744 career appearances, a goals-to-games ratio to be proud of: *"If I had to analyse myself as a player I would say I gave 100% and could score goals – except at West Ham!"*

It is a wonder that Kelly succeeded in football at any level given that, as a young boy, he suffered from Legg-Calve-Perthes disease, a condition which left him with one leg four inches shorter than the other until the age of 10.

Despite scoring only six league goals from 25 games under John Lyall, David has some great memories from his time at the club and forged many lasting friendships.

"After my playing days were over, I pursued a coaching career and have been at Tranmere Rovers, Sheffield United, Preston North End, Derby County, Nottingham Forest and Scunthorpe United.

David still lives in Sutton Coldfield, his home for the past 25 years and currently coaches at Port Vale. He continues to enjoy his involvement in the sport he loves: "I've been involved in football since 1983 so I am very, very fortunate."

I probably triggered John's radar after I'd scored 30 goals for Walsall and a hat-trick for the Republic of Ireland.

When I first came down to meet John Lyall, I thought he was a top-class guy. We met in a hotel in Epping and I found him to be really sociable, with tremendous knowledge of the game.

I know I didn't perform well at West Ham, but I'm pleased I went there because the experience taught me a lot about myself and football. That knowledge has served me well in my own coaching career. I have taken a little bit from all the coaches I worked for – John Lyall, Jackie Charlton, Kevin Keegan, Ossie Ardiles and David Pleat.

West Ham were a club in transition when I joined. A lot of the old guard had been at the club since the 1970s. There were quite a few young lads coming through, too, like Paul Ince, Kevin Keen and Steve Potts. There wasn't any middle ground to bridge the two extremes, which didn't help the balance of the team.

I don't blame anyone else for my poor form at West Ham. It was all down to me. It just wouldn't click. Throughout the history of football there have always been cases of footballers playing well for one club and badly at other clubs. Sadly, I was one of those players.

Battling with Paul Miller of Charlton Athletic during his home league debut, September 1988

I played in a pre-season friendly at Upton Park and the ball went into the Chicken Run. I went to collect it and was amazed by how intimidating that stand was. There were so many blokes effing and jeffing it was quite scary. Little did I know that I'd become a target of their anger and frustration.

My debut was a thumping 0-4 defeat at Southampton. When I got on the coach after the game, John said to me: "Don't worry, David. It will get better." I was so impressed by his humility because, as manager, he was going to be heavily criticised, but he took the time to make me feel better.

The 0-6 defeat up at Oldham Athletic in the League Cup semi-final was my worst experience at the club. John had left by then and we might have approached the game differently if he had still been in charge. We were all wearing the wrong footwear and couldn't play on their plastic pitch. It was all over by half-time. Even though I scored in the second-leg, we had already blown it up there. I felt it was a big opportunity lost. Who knows, if we'd made it to the final and I scored it would have been the making of me. Instead, I was jeered every time I played – mainly by those scary guys in the Chicken Run!

My confidence was low and on one occasion, when I was through on goal, I passed it inside to Kevin Keen. Afterwards, John said to me: "If you do that again, I'm going to run on the pitch and kick you up the arse! You're a striker – shoot!"

I was still being selected by Jack Charlton to play for the Republic of Ireland. Jack was the polar opposite to John. He wanted to play the ball in the air while John liked pretty little triangles on the ground. Jack was very loud and vociferous. John was calm and considered.

Before I arrived, John loved the fact that I scored goals. When I was there he probably thought I didn't score enough.

I was more disappointed than shocked when they sacked John. I was even more disappointed when Lou Macari walked through the door.

I have no complaints and feel very fortunate to have known John and had the chance to benefit from his enormous bank of knowledge.

David Kelly

Some comments about 'Ned' from his former playing colleagues at West Ham United:

He had to cope with the awful stigma of having to follow in Tony Cottee's boots but proved, when he moved on, that he was a decent player.

Tony Gale

Scoring his first goal for West Ham United, against Aston Villa, September, 1988

I played with David at Wolves after our time at West Ham. He had a shocking time with the Hammers, in a team which was going through a developmental phase. David went on to prove his worth at Wolves, Newcastle United and Leicester City. He is also a top, top lad.
Kevin Keen

He was used to a bit more space and time at Walsall. It took him longer to adjust to the pace in the top-flight. He's got a good football brain and has had quite a few successful coaching positions.
Mick McGiven

It was tough for David coming from Walsall, and trying to fill Tony Cottee's boots who had been averaging twenty goals every season for the past five years.
Alan Dickens

In my book he was an underrated player.
Paul Hilton

'Ned' was a great lad and really good in the dressing room. Sadly, he didn't hit the ground running and it was a tough time for him at West Ham. The fans weren't long on patience which was a shame because he was a really great lad and a good striker.
Leroy Rosenior

I really liked David. I know the fans didn't take to him but he just needed better supply. Then he would have made it at West Ham. He was really tough as well. He had a fight with Paul Ince once and I had to patch up Incey before he went out to play.
Rob Jenkins

Getting the better of Mike Duxbury at Old Trafford, September 1988

77 – ALLEN McKNIGHT

"John called me in before the Luton Town semi-final and told me that the fans and media had it in for me: "They want your head on a chopping block," he said. He told me he could play Parkesy if I preferred but I was adamant that I wanted to play."

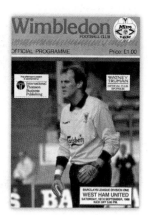

Born: Antrim, January 27, 1964 • **Position:** Goalkeeper • **Games played for John Lyall:** 35 (1988-89)

Games played for West Ham United: 36 (1988-92) • **Debut:** September 10, 1988 v Wimbledon (a) W 1-0 (Ward)

Wimbledon: Green, Joseph, Phelan, Ryan*, Young, Scales, Gibson, Fairweather, Fashanu, Cork, Wise. Sub: Brooke.*

West Ham United: McKnight, Parris, Dicks, Hilton, Martin, Ince, Ward, Kelly*, Rosenior, Dickens, Robson. Sub: Devonshire.*

Allen Darrell McKnight was born to parents Darrell and Margaret and grew up in Antrim, Northern Ireland. *"My dad ran a haulage company and actually helped to build part of the M25. He had 40 Lorries working on the stretch between Pinewood Studios and Iver Heath. Between the ages of 17-19 I lived in nearby Denham Village and worked for my dad. He was sub-contracted by Wimpey, the construction and civil engineering firm. It's known as Taylor Wimpey these days."*

At age 19, McKnight went back to Northern Ireland and played for Distillery and then onto Celtic, before West Ham United paid £250,000 for his services in the summer of 1988. He gained 10 caps for Northern Ireland, four of those as a Hammer. Mcknight was known as 'Bomber,' by his teammates: "Tony Gale gave me that nickname because I come from Ireland – the land of bombs!

Today, Allen works just a goal kick away from a well-known West Ham landmark.

"I run a timber merchants which is quite close to Little Heath training ground, where West Ham's Under 16s and Under 18s play. Sometimes, when I work on Saturday's I see the young lads arriving and wearing the West Ham shirt for the first time, with the ambition of being a West Ham player. They'd certainly have more chance to play in the first team under John Lyall. John was a great believer in bringing in local lads, usually friends, to play football together and develop

them into first team professionals."

"I've never drifted too far from the club so it proves there are no hard feelings! I try to get to watch all the first team matches and occasionally do a bit of matchday hospitality, which I really enjoy."

Allen took time-out, on the eve of a trip to New York with his family, to share the following memories:

My first impression of John Lyall was that he wasn't like a manager. He was more like a family member. He wanted to know about me and what my interests were. It was like talking to a friend. He asked me about my dad and what he did for a living. I moved to West Ham partly for football reasons, because I had a burning ambition to play in the big leagues. But a lot of it was also a feeling of wanting to be part of John Lyall's gang. I think Ray Stewart and maybe Frank McAvennie let John know that I was looking to leave Celtic. Frank and I used the same agent – Bill McMurdo.

I flew down to Heathrow and met John and Eddie Baily in a hotel. We had a soup and a roll and a chat. Once I'd met John there was absolutely no reason not to join West Ham. I stayed in the Bell hotel in Epping initially, but eventually bought a house in the Hornchurch/Emerson Park area. In between the hotel and moving into the house, I stayed with Ray Stewart in Gidea Park.

I was one of three new guys to join West Ham. David

Kelly and Julian Dicks were the other two. We were the new kids on the block and it was noticeable that John's team had been together for a long time. There was a whole spate of testimonials. Ray Stewart had one, Alvin Martin, Geoff Pike, Georgie Parris, Steve Potts, the list just seem to go on and on. It made it a bit daunting for us. It felt like John had a really tight ship and that we were coming in to rock the boat.

John brought me in to make my debut against Wimbledon at Plough Lane in September 1988. Tom McAlister had kept goal in the previous two matches which had ended in heavy defeats. Then, out of the blue, he arrived at the club with his arm in plaster. To this day I'm not sure if it was legitimate! Even the club doctor wasn't aware of it. John turned to me and gave me my first start for the club. It couldn't have gone any better. I kept a clean sheet and we beat the FA Cup holders 1-0, thanks to a goal by Mark Ward.

It was a weird situation because we were playing with so much freedom in the cups and were winning convincingly, but when it came to league matches, particularly at home, we played so negatively. The pressure started to build and we lost our focus. We thought we could play through it but our home form was shocking. We improved away from home and played well in the night matches but lost far too many of those bread and butter games at home. If we'd picked up more points in those matches we would have stayed up and probably kept John in a job, too.

I had played under Billy McNeil at Celtic and he would give his players the hairdryer treatment. He wanted to impose his authority over all his players. John wasn't like that at all. He

spoke to his players on their level, calmly and like a friend. He didn't play mind games, never demanded anything and certainly never made any threats towards anyone. It just wasn't his style. He wanted to make you a better player through hard work and application. John had the welfare of all his players central to everything he did.

Lou Macari was the opposite of John, too. He came in and tried to bully everyone into doing everything his way. He wanted to be controversial. He wasn't bothered about what was best for the player. The first thing he said to me was that I'd never play for West Ham again. I'd just signed a three year contract!

Every morning at Chadwell Heath, John would be there to greet the players as they arrived. First of all, he'd have a chat with Shirley, who'd worked in the canteen for a long time and, remarkably, is still there now. John always made sure that she was alright and that her family were alright. Only then would he catch up with everyone else. He worried about people first and then football after.

John took on the responsibility of so much charity work and public appearances at West Ham. At Celtic, Billy McNeil handed out a schedule of charity events to his players every week. After training on Friday afternoon, the players would receive this itinerary detailing where they needed to go. Sometimes it was a Hospital and other times it was a Community centre etc. A lot of my weekends were spent travelling across Scotland to appear at various Celtic Supporters' club dinners and presentations. At West Ham, John was doing all this largely on his own. He would travel here, there and everywhere. He carried so much responsibility for West Ham United football club. Of course, the players did a bit and Ray Stewart was particularly good on that side of things. I remember going to a Charity event with Frank Bruno to help raise money for an incubator for Old Church Hospital. But John dealt with the lion's share of public events. He was incredible.

I think my time at West Ham would have been a lot better if Phil Parkes had remained fit. It would have allowed me to have taken a rest from first team action and kept me out of the media limelight for a while. I could have returned to first team action once my confidence had returned and I didn't feel under so much pressure. Instead, I was playing every game and making more and more mistakes.

Another problem was that we weren't scoring goals. We'd sold Tony Cottee for a record fee, who was one of the best strikers in the league at the time. We replaced him with David Kelly - a striker from division three. He was supposed to score goals and he didn't. I was brought in to keep clean sheets. I didn't. Added to that, maybe John was waiting for the team to gel rather than making it gel.

The game most people remember is the Littlewoods Cup semi-final against Luton Town in 1989. It was televised live which didn't help. A couple of months earlier, I'd made an

Sharing a cuppa with John

Clearing from John Fashanu of Wimbledon on his debut, September 1988

error live on television at Norwich City, so I was nervous to say the least. I was under a lot of pressure and I think some of the players wanted a change. Little did I know that the media had its finger pointed at me, anyway.

Alvin Martin and Julian Dicks both made mistakes against Luton, but all the criticism was levelled squarely at me. Alvin made a bad tackle on the half way line and Kingsley Black went scooting down the wing. He put in a cross and I went out to challenge Mick Harford but he got to the ball first and headed it in. If Alvin hadn't made that bad tackle, then he would have been back in the box challenging Harford, leaving me on my line defending the goal. Of course, there were a handful of goals that I look back on and I'm not happy with my performance, but, in the end, the media and fans were hounding me for absolutely everything. I must say that John Lyall never once blamed me or criticised my performances.

My confidence was very low and the pressure was very high. I was going out almost waiting for my next mistake, because my head wasn't in the right place. It was a bit like what Joe Hart went through at West Ham. Goalkeeping is probably 25% ability and 75% confidence and mine was ruined by the press, a series of errors and the regular taunting from the fans.

It was a shame that John's last game ended the way it did. Not just the 1-5 defeat at Liverpool, but how it all unravelled afterwards. Not all the players came back on the coach. Many of us dispersed in different directions. I was on International duty with Northern Ireland that week, so we didn't really have a collective gathering as a team. Not many of the players and staff were around when John got the sack so that whole episode was very strange indeed. I wasn't a

big fan of picking up the tabloids as you can image – I'd read 'McKnightmare' quite enough by that stage. So, I heard the news second hand from a friend.

John was definitely ahead of his time and had so many good ideas. If I had to flag a shortcoming it would probably be that he stayed loyal to his players a bit too long. The comfort zone had maybe become a bit too wide and a bit too soft. Players were changing and becoming a lot more powerful. John needed to firm up a bit because football commanded it. Sadly, it wasn't in his nature to behave that way.

The last time I saw John was at a Gala Evening at the Britannia International Hotel, to celebrate John's FA Cup winning teams of 1975 and 1980. I had a table with a few friends and Frank McAvennie came over and sat with us for a while. The idea was for John to be introduced to the audience and be filmed making his way to the table with all those FA Cup heroes. As he walked in, he caught sight of Frank and me and came over and sat between us. We had a lovely chat and it was typical of John not to pass anyone he knew, in a room, or on the street. He liked Frank, who had done really well for John, but I hadn't done well for him, and he still afforded me the same amount of time. He was talking to me as a friend – just like the first time I met him.
Allen McKnight

He had a similar experience to me. He'd done so well at Celtic but had an unfortunate time at West Ham United.
David Kelly

I wish he'd had a better time at West Ham because you

In aerial combat with Mick Harford of Luton Town in the League Cup semi-final, February 1989

couldn't wish to meet a better person.
Tony Gale

We'd received good reports about Allen at Celtic and Northern Ireland and decided to take a punt on him, but it didn't work out. It was always going to be difficult for any goalkeeper to follow in the boots of Phil Parkes.
Mick McGiven

I think Ernie Gregory found 'Bomber' a bit frustrating because he was young and preferred to do things his own way. He didn't listen to me at the time but we've become great mates since and I've got a lot of time for Bomber. He always says: "Put the goalkeeping to one side and I had a great time at West Ham!"
Phil Parkes

I've got a lot of time for 'Bomber'. A really lovely bloke.
Alan Dickens

He was such a great lad that it was hard to see him have to endure what he did. We all tried to rally round and support him. I'll never forget the "McKnigthmare" head line in the Sun newspaper. We all supported him because that is what John would have wanted. Collective responsibility was how the club was run back then.
Leroy Rosenior
I love 'Bomber.' For someone who took so much stick he

handled it so well. Anyone coming in after Phil Parkes had no chance anyway. 'Bomber's' never too far away from a joke and a laugh.
Paul Hilton

Bomber

End of an era

JOHN LYALL's MEDAL COLLECTION
COURTESY OF YVONNE LYALL

A FEW MORE WORDS FOR JOHN...

My Dad and John shared a very good relationship. John had a pleasant manner and, of course, they both held a great affection for West Ham United. John was very much a family man, a caring man. I also had a great admiration for him. We know Yvonne, Murray, Samantha and their boys very well and you could not wish to meet lovelier people - we are very fond of them and always stay in touch.
Neil Greenwood (Son of Ron Greenwood)

He was a very loyal, honest and trustworthy fella. A big family man who loved his wife and their son, Murray. He was very proud of Murray. John had no airs or graces. Our friendship started in the 1950s and lasted a lifetime. He was a few years older than me and was very determined and strong willed. He appointed me as youth team manager in 1975 and we made it to the FA Youth Cup final during my first season. We were both heavy smokers and loved to talk about football and all manner of things. I think he liked me as part of his team because I'd kept things simple as a player and that is how he viewed football – a simple game that needed to be perfected through hard work.
Ron Boyce (FA Cup winner, European Cup Winners' Cup winner and coach)

When John finished playing football he worked for my husband Eddie in the office. We socialised a lot with John and Yvonne. My husband and Yvonne were always joking and laughing together. John and I tried to keep a straight face so as not to encourage them! The four of us got on so well and we had a lovely time. I met my husband when he was playing for West Ham before the War and he was the only man for me throughout my whole life. I'm 90 now.
Edith Chapman (Wife of club secretary, Eddie Chapman)

When Yvonne Lyall gave birth to their son, Murray, my father arranged for a bouquet of flowers to be sent to the hospital. It became something of a custom from that point on.
Hilary Tunbridge (Daughter of Chairman, Reg Pratt)

I knew John from when I joined West Ham in 1958. Not only as a rival player, we were both left-backs, but also as someone I used to socialise with. A group of use would take our partners out for a meal on Saturday evenings. We'd go out with Ronnie Boyce, Geoff Hurst, John Sissons, Martin Peters, Brian Dear, Joe Kirkup and their respective partners.

John was a determined person, whose playing career was unfortunately cut short due to injury. However, he made up for that with his time as Ron Greenwood's coach and then manager in his own right. I will always remember him for his dedication and willingness to help players improve themselves.
Jack Burkett (FA Cup winner and European Cup Winners' Cup winner)

It was well known that John was a tough man who didn't suffer fools gladly, although he had a caring nature. Over 50 years ago he invited me, and my girlfriend Jan, to his house for Sunday tea. Jan and I have now been married 51 years and John and Yvonne would be coming up to 57 years. God bless him. Sir Alex Ferguson confided in John. He was a very special man.
Brian Dear (1965 European Cup Winner's Cup winner)

A FEW MORE WORDS FOR JOHN...

If I close my eyes I can still picture John as a player. We used to play left and right-back in the reserves in the early 1960s. He was as hard as nails. When I got into management I took Dagenham to the 1980 FA Trophy final at Wembley. Our final was a week after West Ham were to play Arsenal in the FA Cup final. John gave me two tickets for the match and I went with Terry Dyson, the old Spurs' winger. When he gave me the tickets he joked: "It will give you a chance to see Wembley full." We only got 26,000 for our final. John was ever so good because he arranged for Dagenham to use the same coach that West Ham had travelled to Wembley in. He called up Bill Lacey and arranged it personally. John called me up one day and asked me to do a bit of scouting for him at Ipswich Town. That was the start of a new career for me and I ended up being chief scout at Tottenham. He was a terrific bloke.
Eddie Presland (West Ham United – 1965-66)

John Lyall was my youth team coach in 1964. I immediately felt that he was destined to become a leader at a higher level. He earned respect from us young players and we enjoyed his way of coaching, because he was fair and instilled in us the discipline we needed to play first team football.

John was a fierce competitor as a player and had a very good understanding of the game. Ron Greenwood recognised that in him and harnessed it to great effect. That is why he went on to become a successful manager. John also worked behind the scenes in the club office, learning the art of the other side of managing.
Trevor Hartley (West Ham United 1967-69)

While I did not play for John Lyall in his capacity as manager of West Ham United, I witnessed his managerial excellence on a tour to the United States in 1971. John stepped in for Ron Greenwood on that trip. It was evident that John was the heir apparent at that time.

I also had the privilege of working with John when we were appointed to conduct an FA Prelim Course for the professional players at West Ham circa 1970. John was the lead instructor.

His knowledge of the game and attention to detail were first class and while I was a fully qualified FA Full Badge coach at that time, this was an incredible learning experience for me.

It is rare that one person is a great teacher, an outstanding mentor and a first class manager of people. John had all those qualities
Bobby Howe (West Ham United 1966-71)

John was the first person to play me as a striker. I'd joined the club from school and had always been played at left-back or in midfield.

It was a Saturday morning at Chadwell Heath for a South East Counties league encounter against Bexley Health & Welling. One of our strikers, a lad called John Brookes, was unable to play and John said: 'Crossy, you play up front today, son'. I scored a hat-trick and another three which were disallowed! That really was the start of my career as a striker.

A FEW MORE WORDS FOR JOHN...

On the coach to South East Counties matches, John liked to talk about music and was interested in what we were all listening to. He thought Eric Burden of the Animals had a decent voice.

When I was transferred from West Ham to Brentford in 1970, John phoned me up and wished me good luck. "Sometimes you have to step down to step up again," he said. "Go and show us all at West Ham just how good you can be."
Roger Cross (West Ham United 1968-69)

When I joined West Ham John was very kind and helpful. He definitely helped to improve my game. A lovely man.
Dudley Tyler (West Ham United 1972-73)

John Lyall gave me my first proper coaching session. In different situations, he not only showed me what I needed to do, but also explained how that fitted in with what the rest of the team were doing. If you didn't have the technique to carry this out, he'd work with you until you mastered it. I was a 15-year-old kid at the time, so he had a tremendous impact on me and how I approached the game.
Joe Durrell (West Ham United 1971-72)

I loved John and John loved me. In 1969, on the eve of a youth tournament in Geneva, John took me to one side for a quiet word. He told me he thought I was one of the hardest and most physical defenders he had coached. "But, if you're going to be any good to anybody," he said, "You'd better start channelling your aggression in the right places and at the right times."

With that in mind he gave me the responsibility of youth team captain. I felt like my Welsh hero, John Charles, and my Hammers hero, Bobby Moore, all rolled into one!

We were only five minutes into our first game, against Etoile Carouge, when the red mist came over me again. Their player had spat in my face at a corner kick! He legged it back to his own half with me in hot pursuit and John screaming from the dug out to Tony Carr and Stevie Knowles to get to me, before I got to him! Nothing came of it and we ended up winning the game, the group and the tournament, beating Olympique Lyonnais in the final. I collected a lovely engraved plate which John said I could keep on account of the great skipper's job I had done. It still resides in my bar at home after nearly 50 years. Thank god it never ended up in the West Ham trophy cabinet because they sold everything off after the move to the London Stadium!

I suffered from a lot of headaches on that tour and suggested to John they were caused by all the balls I kept heading. He joked that it was more likely to be from all the centre-forwards I kept heading!
I left West Ham ten times the player I'd been before I'd joined. I'd arrived as a young kid from Swansea Schools and John offered me a lot of encouragement and improved my game before I moved on to Reading. I have a lot to be thankful to him for.
Stuart Morgan (Youth and reserve team player 1966-1969)

A FEW MORE WORDS FOR JOHN...

Sometimes in training John would join in, even though he had a bad knee. If he tackled you, it felt like being hit by Von Ryan's Express!
Barry Barnes (Youth team player 1968-1972)

Mr Lyall gave me an opportunity and I will always be grateful to him for that. Winning the FA Youth Cup in 1981 was a great experience and, almost 40 years on, I'm still mates with the whole team. John was very supportive when my brother Gerhard suffered a terrible injury. He spoke to me regularly and kept me positive during an awful situation. He gave 'Ger' a testimonial against Tottenham Hotspur and this was unheard of for a youngster who had never played in the first team. He was a great motivator. Inspiring and encouraging.
Chris Ampofo (FA Youth Cup winner, 1981)

I first met John when I was a schoolboy and he was taking the training at the ground on Tuesday and Thursday evenings. His sessions were all about technique - first touch, one-touch, body shape, visualisation and passing. All the basics. His approach was experimental rather than commanding. He'd always be saying: "What if we try this?" or "How do you feel about that?" He made his players think. He helped the creative players to express themselves and coached the everyday players to become better footballers. He was always striving to improve his players. I upset him once because I commented that I thought the players weren't good enough. He took me to task and said: "It's your job to make them better!"
Tony Carr (Youth team player and long serving youth team coach)

I got on really well with John and I am in no doubt that everyone you interview will have nothing but good things to say about him. So I am going to share a few stories that are a little bit different. Whenever I needed to order new supplies for my clinic I'd submit a list to Pauline Moss. One time I ordered a few boxes of condoms and Mrs Moss, as we called her, went straight to John Lyall and told him. I was called into his office and had to explain the thinking behind it. I told him there were a few single lads in the team and I wanted to make sure they were well covered, so to speak!

Another memory is from the 1976 European Cup Winners Cup final in Brussels. Gola offered me £250 to wear their tracksuit in the final. West Ham hadn't given me one of their tracksuits, so I said yes. I waited until everyone had left the dressing room before slipping into the tracksuit and going out onto the bench. John looked me up and down a few times, so on the way home I decided to tell him the story: "That money belongs to the club," he said. I just walked away.

Finally, after we won the FA Cup in 1980 I asked John if I could be in the team photo with the FA Cup. I have a photo of my dad with the 1964 team when they won the FA Cup, so I thought it would be a nice thing to do. John just turned me down flat. I laugh at all these stories and loved John dearly but I thought it would be good to share something different.
Rob Jenkins (Club physiotherapist, 1966-1989)

John liked to stay around a bit after a match. He'd invite a few journalists up to his office. Kevin Moseley, Michael Hart, Trevor Smith and Ken Montgomery, to name just a few. It was quite small and cramped so I liked to get up there first to guarantee a seat. John would pour the drinks for everyone. His favourite tipple

A FEW MORE WORDS FOR JOHN...

was Sherry so he would open up a bottle of Harvey's Bristol Cream. I was no great tactician or authority on the game but it was fascinating to hear John and those guys applying their great knowledge to those conversations. Sometimes one of the journalists wouldn't show because they'd written something that John wouldn't approve of. Vic Railton was one of the main culprits!
Steve Bacon (Club photographer)

John Lyall gave me the job of kit man. We had a little chat and he said to me: "You'll see a lot of things and you'll hear a lot of things but whatever you see or hear, stays within the club. He always looked after me. On away trips he'd give me a couple of tickets for the Directors' Box. It was funny, because sometimes I'd express an opinion on a football matter and he would tut and roll his eyes, in a friendly way. It was his friendly way of saying: "Leave the football stuff to me." He was never vindictive and just had a lovely way about him. You couldn't wish for a better manager. John and Yvonne and Ron Boyce and his wife, Dawn helped to arrange the kids' Christmas Party. I'd go out with Rob Jenkins to buy the presents and our wives would wrap them up. It was a proper family club.
Eddie Gillam (Club kit man)

John was a superb man. I still talk about him down at West Ham. He got me into coaching. I was a PE teacher and he put me on the right road and helped me to get a job at West Ham. Every day was an education with John. After the last ever match at Upton Park - against Manchester United - I went out onto the pitch. I stood in the centre-circle and had a few thoughts about John Lyall. There'll never be another one like him. Terrific times!
Jimmy Frith (Youth coach and unsung hero)

I never heard him swear or even raise his voice. He was genuine, fair, and lovely to work for. He always said it was a simple game, not a hard game. He kept it simple and emphasised the basics. I was something of a utility man at the time. I did a bit of coaching, driving the van and even picked up the sponge for the reserves when Rob Jenkins and Dave Gladstone couldn't make it. I brought a lot of young kids off the parks in the local area and into the West Ham Academy. They included Tony Cottee, Steve Potts, Paul Ince and Stuart Slater. A few got away like John Terry, Tony Adams and Jason Dozzell. I was in charge of youth games at Chadwell Heath and would set up matches for the Under-14s, 15s and 16s. To his credit, John would always try to watch those games.
Ronnie Gale (Scout and coach)

John was a gentleman and, with all due respect to other managers of West Ham United, the best manager the club has ever had. He was West Ham through and through and his sacking was one of the greatest travesties in the club's history.
John Helliar (Programme Master)

Now in 2017, it is impossible to think that Orient and West Ham were once in the same tier of English football, The Football League Division Two.

One very frosty afternoon on New Years' Day, 1980, the two teams met at Brisbane Road, both coming into the game fancying their chances.
The game was in doubt and the referee Colin Downey convened a meeting between John Lyall and

A FEW MORE WORDS FOR JOHN...

Jimmy Bloomfield, an ex-Hammer himself and Orient's manager. Both managers were keen for the game to go ahead and they jointly pledged that whatever the result they'd not whinge to the press afterwards about the decision for the game to be played.

Colin Downey subsequently used this example in his long career as a top-flight referee as to illustrate how managers and refs could work together and not be in opposite camps when an ON/OFF decision needed to be made.

Both managers were gentlemanly in their approach and Colin always made this point when he was telling this tale.

John need not have worried, many of his players had played in the USA and wore the then new-fangled 'astro-turf boots' and the Hammers romped home to a 4-0 victory by keeping their feet firmly on the ground, unlike the O's.

Now in 2017, with health and safety issue paramount, there is no-way the game would have gone ahead - whatever the managers might have wanted!
David Bloomfield (Son of Jimmy Bloomfield)

John never forgot his roots and treated people with dignity and respect. I knew Bobby Moore, Peter Brabrook, Budgie Byrne, and all that crowd, so was very close to the club. When John became manager, he'd always include me and invited me to sit with the players in the buffet coach on the train journey to a match. He was a very decent and honest man.
Terry Creasey (Friend to the stars)

I found John very accommodating and very straightforward. He took a shine to me. I don't know why, but he did. I saw a lot of him when I joined the Evening Standard. I wrote John's biography, Just Like My Dreams, and he was so very appreciative of everything he had learned from Ron Greenwood. John was the only football person at Ron's funeral. I can't recall seeing any other football people there, not even the FA. It was astonishing. John was one of the last old fashioned coaches, very principled and good fun. He was at his happiest when he had a glass of wine or a fishing rod in his hand.
Michael Hart (Journalist)

I learnt a great deal from John, not only about football but about how to treat people. After West Ham had won the FA Cup in 1980, John had done the formal press conference, when he spotted me. He asked me to follow him and we eventually finished up inside the dressing room. For an aspiring football reporter like I was then, that was a dream, but also proof that John would put his trust in you, as long as you didn't abuse it. I miss him still.
Ken Dyer (Journalist)

John was one of the nicest men I have ever met in my life. Two particular memories spring to mind. The first, at Noel Cantwell's funeral. We sat down with David Pleat at the wake and he and John struck up a conversation about football. It concluded with David saying: "I give up, John! You know too much for

A FEW MORE WORDS FOR JOHN...

me," and he left the table. The second, was at John Dick's funeral. The wake was at The Old King's Head, Chigwell, where we sat together having a pint and a chat. We talked about the 1957-58 promotion season, a happy memory on a sombre day.

Terry Connelly (Friend of the players and autograph collector)

Typically modest John found it much easier to eulogise about Ron Greenwood – his mentor and the man he believed was West Ham's greatest-ever manager – than he did his own achievements, as Terry Connelly and I quickly discovered when we interviewed him at length for EX Magazine at his beautiful farmhouse in Tattingstone, Suffolk one unforgettable day in August 2004.

He said: "Whenever I consulted Ron Greenwood or Eddie Chapman about a problem, they always had time for me. Time is the most important thing. We've got people today calling themselves 'time managers'. No chance! If you've got a problem that's big enough, you'd better give it enough time. If you don't, you'll get caught. It's a simple logic in life – if one of your people has a problem, you sit with them on it until you can work it out. You can't always control the problem, but you have to give it thought and time. That's what West Ham people did – they were always like that. I only returned what others did for me."
Lyall also learned from Greenwood how to conduct himself off the field. He explained: "I once gave an interview to the press and Ron pulled me aside afterwards. He told me: 'Always say "we" – not "I"– whilst talking in public about the club." He wanted me to talk in terms of the royal 'we', and it was more sound advice."

Watch games at the London Stadium, you will often see older fans shaking their heads in dismay at a misplaced pass or poor touch. 'He's not a West Ham-type of player,' you may hear them groan in the direction of a new signing. Lyall once defined the meaning of the phrase: "West Ham had no particular style but there were certain things that a player had to be able to do. And if you couldn't do them, you couldn't play for West Ham."

"In other words, you had to have a high degree of technique; you had to have mobility and movement; and you had to have knowledge of what other people were doing. Now how you did it was the bit that Ron and I got involved in. We'd say to the players, 'we'll give you all the options for a certain situation, and now you go and do them.' They call it flair but it's not. It's skill, and it's taught by dint of practice. You've got to work on it because it's not easy."

Tony McDonald (Author of Upton Park Memories and West Ham United: The Managers) www. footballworld.co.uk, www.ex-hammers.com

I went to John Lyall's testimonial in 1964. It took place on Monday night before the FA Cup final, the following Saturday. Ron Greenwood actually played the team which would be lining up at Wembley. John didn't play because of his knee injury. 18,000 turned up that night and I remember Bobby Moore going down during the match and lying still. There were gasps and groans everywhere because it seemed like a serious injury. There was real concern but, after a while, he jumped up and carried on. He'd been kidding the crowd all along!

Tony Hogg (Author of the Who's Who of West Ham United)

A FEW MORE WORDS FOR JOHN...

November 19, 1988. Kenilworth Road. Luton Town 4 West Ham United 1. Another defeat and another legendary Lyall lock-in for the hapless Hammers.

During John's reign, the worse the performance, the longer the dressing-room door remained bolted. And with relegation staring the East Enders starkly in the face, make no mistake, this was yet another unwelcome loss.

In the days before the warmth of purpose-built media mixed zones, the assembled press simply stood shivering outside the Visitors' dressing room waiting for yet another inquest to end. Boy was it cold. And with hats, gloves and scarves shielding the hacks from the inclement winter chill, John finally emerged into the November night to face his dozen or so inquisitors, including one rosy-cheeked, slightly-built scribe.

Magnanimous in defeat as ever, Lyall gave credit to Ray Harford's team before adding his trademark observation - as he always did after any away reverse - that "this is always a difficult place to come to." Certainly, the plastic pitch had not helped but there was no disguising John's anger at another poor display, which had undoubtedly confirmed that his sorry side were set for a long, claret and blue winter of discontent.

But, the experienced and wily Lyall knew how to head off red top hysteria in order to keep the tabloids on-side and, typically, he soon had them eating out of his hand as they hung on to every wise word. Post-mortem complete, an apologetic John then looked around the freezing press posse. "Sorry to have kept you all waiting gentlemen," he concluded, before casting a sympathetic eye towards that rosy-cheeked, slightly-built scribe, winking and adding: "And, of course, lady." At this point, a clearly agitated reporter unwrapped his scarf and tore off his hat to protest. "But I'm a bloke!" Any other manager would have wanted the Bedfordshire ground to swallow himself whole but, quick as a flash, the great John Lyall broke into a yet wider grin to rescue the situation with an unhesitating: "Just pulling your leg, son. Just pulling your leg!"
Steve Blowers (Author of Nearly Reached the Sky - West Ham United 1989-2005)

John Lyall was responsible for my obsession with collecting Hammers' autographs. It all started purely by chance. Back in 1975, West Ham played Darlington at home in the League Cup. I'd arrived early and as I walked through the main gates I saw a couple of youngsters kicking a football around. Suddenly they stopped and ran towards the players' car park. They'd spotted John Lyall's car pulling in. They were well prepared, carrying autograph books, magazine posters and stickers. John duly obliged with a neat scroll across their prized possessions. One of the youngsters offered me a piece of paper so I wasn't left out and I've been hooked ever since.
Steve Marsh (www.theyflysohigh.co.uk)

In 1987, I wanted to present John with a copy of my recently published book. We met in his office at Chadwell Heath and he immediately made me feel at ease. I was in awe of the great man but instead he made me feel important and asked me questions about the book. I spent a pleasant hour with John and came away thinking what a thoroughly nice man he was, giving up his valuable time for me. We were lucky to have a manager who treated the fans with respect and was grateful for their support.
John Northcutt (Historian and author of West Ham United - A Complete Record)

John -

    A few of us wanted to show, in some small way, our appreciation for your help and kindness this season, especially in Europe and during the League Cup run.

    Wishing you every success - on and off the field.God bless

       Ken Dyer
       Steve Bacon
       Mike Hart
       Kevin Moseley
       Bob Oxby
       John Davies
       Bob Driscoll
       Ken Montgomery
       Dennis Signy

P.S. We can change size if need be.

A card sent to John by the media at the end of West Ham United's 1980-81 season. They presented a gold ring with a West Ham crest

THE GREENWOOD AND LYALL FAMILY LIVES ON

Harry Hooper and Ken Brown

John Helliar

Keith Robson, Tony Cottee and Billy Jennings

Mervyn Day and Phil Parkes

Ken Brown, Martin Peters and Lawrie Leslie (seated)

Mick McGiven and Bobby Gould

Peter Brabrook, Ron Boyce and Martin Peters

Rob Jenkins and Frank Lampard

Roger Hugo

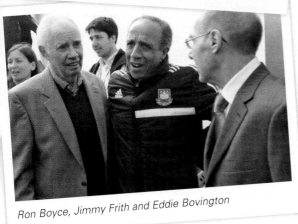

Ron Boyce, Jimmy Frith and Eddie Bovington

THE GREENWOOD AND LYALL FAMILY LIVES ON

Brian Dear, Alan Taylor, Keith Robson and Keith Coleman

Elaine Brown, Ken Brown, Janet Bond and Ron Boyce

Harry Redknapp and Frank Lampard

Jack Burkett

Trevor Brooking, Billy Bonds, Tony Gale, Julian Dicks, Steve Bacon

Martin Peters and Brian Dear

Rob Jenkins, Ron Boyce, Martin Peters, Ken Brown, Peter Brabrook, Eddie Bovington, Alan Dickie, Neil Greenwood and Harry Hooper (seated)

Eddie Bovington and Harry Redknapp

Harry Obeney and Tina Moore

Sir Geoff Hurst

THE GREENWOOD AND LYALL
FAMILY LIVES ON

Alan Dickens, Keith McPherson, Chris Ampofo, Mark Schiavi, Everald La Ronde and Steve Milton

Eddie Presland, Bill Lansdowne and Dennis Burnett

Peter Shearing and Peter Grotier

Trevor Brooking, Billy Bonds and Alan Devonshire

Peter Bennett and Harry Redknapp

Alan Stephenson, Andy Smillie and Trevor Dawkins

Harry Redknapp, Trevor Dawkins, John Dryden and Martin Britt

Kevin Lock, Billy Jennings and Keith Robson

Billy Lansdowne

Ronnie Gale, George Parris, Alan Dickens, Paul Allen, Tony Carr, Everald La Ronde, Brian Dear

READY FOR MORE WEST HAM NOSTALGIA?

89 HAMMERS PLAYED WITH BOBBY MOORE AND ALL THEIR PERSONAL RECOLLECTIONS AND PHOTOGRAPHS HAVE BEEN SHOWCASED IN THE FOLLOWING BOOK.

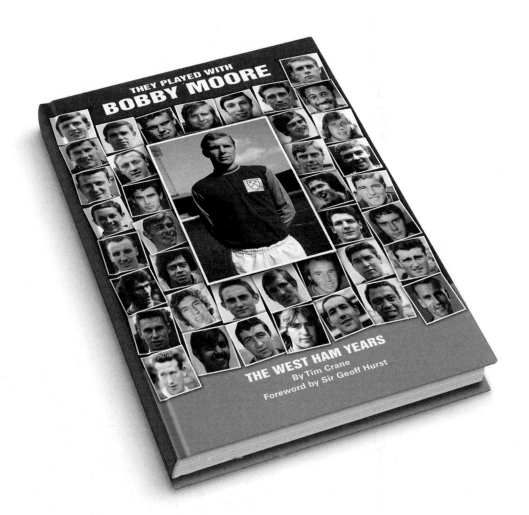

ORDER YOUR COPY ONLINE FROM AMAZON, EBAY, OR BY POST SENDING CHEQUE PAYMENT OF £25 (PLUS £2.85 P&P)

CHEQUE ORDERS MADE PAYABLE TO: TIM CRANE, 183 WESTCOMBE HILL, BLACKHEATH, LONDON, SE3 7DR.